Landscapes of Law

Landscapes of Law

Practicing Sovereignty in Transnational Terrain

Edited by

Carol J. Greenhouse

and

Christina L. Davis

PENN

UNIVERSITY OF PENNSYLVANIA PRESS

PHILADELPHIA

Published by
University of Pennsylvania Press
Philadelphia, Pennsylvania 19104-4112
www.upenn.edu/pennpress

Printed in the United States of America on acid-free paper
10 9 8 7 6 5 4 3 2 1

A Cataloging-in-Publication record is available from
the Library of Congress
ISBN 978-0-8122-5222-4

CONTENTS

Introduction. Mapping Culture onto Transnational Law
Carol J. Greenhouse and Christina L. Davis   1

Chapter 1. A Journey Through Law's Landscapes:
Close Encounters of the Scalar Kind   23
Tugba Basaran

Chapter 2. Intersecting Legal Spaces:
International Trade Law and Anticorruption Law   37
Rachel Brewster

Chapter 3. Changing Internally to Engage Externally:
China and the WTO Legal System   64
Gregory Shaffer and Henry Gao

Chapter 4. The "Africa Bar" of Paris: A Microcosm
of Interconnected Histories of Legal Globalization   97
Sara Dezalay

Chapter 5. Cultural Difference as Legal Resolution:
The Raising of the *Ehime Maru*   131
David Leheny

Chapter 6. Landscapes of Law in War-Torn Societies   157
Mark Fathi Massoud

Chapter 7. Uncertain Sovereignties:
Indigenous-State Relations in Colombia   192
Sandra Brunnegger

Chapter 8. Between Sovereignty and Transnationalism:
The European Union as an Incomplete "Transnational Legal Space"   216
Marie-Claire Foblets and Katayoun Alidadi

Chapter 9. The Emergence of Digital Communities:
Generating Trust, Managing Conflicts, and
Regulating Globality . . . Digitality   250
Teresa Rodríguez-de-las-Heras Ballell

Chapter 10. Landscapes of Actually Existing Liberalism:
Some Thoughts on the Historical Dialectic of Liberty
and Philanthropy   278
Mariana Valverde

List of Contributors   301

Index   303

Acknowledgments   315

Landscapes of Law

Mapping Culture onto Transnational Law

Carol J. Greenhouse and Christina L. Davis

The recent surge of right-wing populism in Europe and the United States is widely read as evidence of ongoing challenges to the policies and institutions of globalization (Korostelina 2017; Müller 2016: 1). Appeals to preserve a distinct national culture have become a mainstay of populist rhetoric and a refrain in scholarly and media accounts. But the appeal to *culture* as the basis for nationalism is not restricted to the ethnonationalisms of the developing world outside of industrial democracies, or insurgent groups within them. This volume reveals how national culture also emerges as a central idea in the pursuit of transnationalism. The premise that there is some inherent tension between nationalism and globalism is misleading. Nationalism—whether asserted explicitly as state sovereignty or implicitly as cultural community—is integral to the ways that interests, powers, and partnerships are mobilized in transnational law, and drawn into the contested zone between borderless capital and bordered states.

This Introduction begins with the observation that national culture is not derived only from localized processes of cultural identification that form an "imagined community" (Anderson 1991). Contributors illustrate ways in which claims of national difference are also produced within *transnational* institutions. In some of their case studies, such claims are worked into policy prescriptions or legal arrangements. In others, they provide ad hoc bargaining chips. In a variety of ways, contributors emphasize the formal and informal means by which the idea of a collective national subject is integral to the ways transnational institutions themselves work. They show that assertions of national culture outside of state boundaries consolidate states' representational efficacy. The stakes in such assertions, and the political risks associated with them, are potentially very high, both at home and abroad—recent populisms being a case in point.

Populist rhetoric often portrays transnational institutions as attacking national culture—a complex trope pitting national governments against alliances of homegrown and distant elites. Closer examination reveals circumstances in which transnational processes readily accommodate cultural claims—and even promote them—when these are formulated as expressions of national sovereignty. In such contexts, nationalism is not antithetical to the interests of global elites, but rather offers a discourse through which the very distinction between domestic and foreign interests may be expediently suspended or activated, depending on the circumstance. As each chapter reflects on the feedback processes between local and global assertions of *the nation* or *national culture*, contributors point to fresh paths for research about the relationships among transnationalism, law, and culture. The theoretical implications of this volume generate a fresh understanding of transnational law that challenges the conventional separation of the individual, community, society, nations, and international spaces into categories on a spectrum from private to public (see especially the chapters by Basaran; Valverde; and Rodríguez-de-las-Heras Ballell). *Landscapes of Law* shows the diverse ways in which the idea of national culture rearranges that spectrum, knotting it in unexpected ways—for example, placing the individual at the conjuncture of international and national spheres (see the chapters by Brewster; Dezalay; Foblets and Alidadi; Massoud; and Shaffer and Gao), or transforming private emotion into rights with transnational significance (see the chapters by Brunnegger; Leheny; and Rodríguez-de-las-Heras Ballell).

In standard accounts of transnationalism, *culture* is theorized as a channel continuously projecting local interests, meanings, and social patterns outward, to larger arenas. In our account, we suspend the primacy of localism in favor of examining the way cultural claims operate in transnational institutions and practices—and are sometimes generated by them. Again, we emphasize the dual character of *national culture* in such contexts—sometimes in a hard form as a bright line between international and domestic law (e.g., the chapters by Brewster and Shaffer and Gao), sometimes in a soft form as a generalized claim of national difference in cultural terms (e.g., the chapters by Brunnegger and Leheny). The writings here underscore the conceptual relevance of culture in both of these senses, in episodic contexts of relational uncertainty, for example, strategically clarifying distinct interests while avoiding an overt clash over principles or frameworks.

While contributors highlight the diverse relevance of nationalism within global contexts, they also demonstrate that the idea of national culture is neither limited to local origin nor erased in a transnational society. The interaction of states may support the emergence of larger identities as regions or collectives (see, e.g., Acharya 2012; Schimmelfennig 2001), but often this is alongside national expressions of authority and identity, rather than as their substitute. In Chapter 9, Rodríguez-de-las-Heras Ballell explores how even digital communities emerge from a "multi-national response to globality." The most advanced regional project in Europe faces an apparent impasse in which harmonization of law is conceived as entailing the creation of a transnational culture (see Chapter 8, Foblets and Alidadi).

This volume focuses on the practical workings of law in various settings. Contributors show how state-based transnationalism valorizes the idea of a national collective subject as a logical expression of state sovereignty, thus claiming (successfully or not) space to maneuver between countervailing global and domestic pressures. In this sense, discourses of national culture and global transnationalism are not automatically antithetical, as in those cases framed by an opposition between preservation of national culture and compliance with international law. Under other circumstances examined in this book, national and transnational discourses are mutually reinforcing, as states and international entrepreneurs within transnational agencies build complementary processes that either shape the law around cultural terms or provide exceptions that accommodate diversity. In the transnational arena, a claim of national culture can be an expedient proxy for state interests—a strategically placed cushion against breaks in the transnational order as borderless capital flows unevenly across sovereign terrains. As several chapters show, this insight also illuminates domestic situations in which cultural claims feature in a discourse of administration in contexts of legal and political ambiguity (see especially the chapters by Brunnegger and Massoud).

Recognizing that the idea of culture is integral to transnationalism opens fresh ethnographic questions with regard to transnational governance and legal mobilization, for example, in human rights, transitional justice, peacemaking, mediation and arbitration, rural and urban labor movements, and counterglobalization projects (Edelman 2005; Evans 2008; Hinton 2017; Santos 2008). At the same time, it rearranges other questions of long standing, particularly where these concern the relationship of local and global social orders (Hannerz 1989; Keohane 1995). *Landscapes of Law* presents several alternatives to well-established conventions of assuming a connective tissue of cultural and legal processes across diverse scales (a "justice façade" in Hinton's [2017] critical formulation) and a procedural congruence across local and international legal processes such that ethnonationalism is necessarily disruptive (see Goodale 2017: 186–193, esp. 187; Merry 2006a: 102). The contributors to this volume show that the effects of nationalism and transnationalism through law are not likely to be continuous in some causal, scalar, or temporal way—hence the value of examining them at close range, to see what they consist of from the standpoints of participants (Goodale 2007: 4–5; Goodale and Merry 2007). Moreover, they examine efforts by governments to insert national culture into transnational legal processes—not as legalities in themselves, but as symbolic operators in the politics of transnational negotiation and in the organization of legal activity. From these perspectives, claims of national culture are integral to transnationalism—expanding the bargaining room where national constituencies are involved and extending the cosmopolitanism of the international sphere. That said, for this same reason, we must stress that nationalist claims in the transnational context do not necessarily speak for majority or minority cultural communities within or among states. Nationalism is always ambiguous, its inclusivity or exclusivity undecidable in the abstract.

Contributors probe the relationship of transnationalism to claims of national culture from three main angles. The opening chapters (by Basaran; Brewster; Shaffer and Gao; Dezalay; and Leheny) show in detail how transnational law—in trade, investment, and diplomacy—relies on an explicit association of state sovereignty with national culture. The next two chapters (by Brunnegger and Massoud) retain those issues while also exploring transnational investments in law as integral to projects of economic development and democratization within states. The last chapters (by Foblets and Alidadi; Rodríguez-de-las-Heras Ballell; and Valverde) again retain the threads of earlier parts of the book while exploring transnational law projects outside the confines of state institutions—in relation to refugee law in the European Union, digitality, and liberal notions of liberty and philanthropy. In these latter chapters, jurisdiction becomes ambiguous in relation to the territoriality of states, inviting or demanding new forms of legal imagination. Overall, the book moves across a variety of transnational and national terrains, opening with situations defined explicitly as international, ultimately moving beyond sovereign territory to reveal a more diverse transnational legal landscape, especially in a chapter on the globalization of digital space.

Throughout, as the organization of the book implies, the internationalist model of transnationalism gives way to other paradigms—multiple sovereignties, contractual proliferation, and digital communities among them. From diverse perspectives, contributors examine those actors who struggle to sustain the law's relevance as a defense of their interests and values, and in the process cultivate the landscapes of law in the conceptual and practical spaces left open between varied constructions of state borders. This portrayal reveals the possibility for populism to coexist with and even reinforce globalization. For scholars and other observers, that possibility may not be evident in legal texts or institutional mandates, but it becomes visible to the extent that concrete circumstances of making and living with law are examined at close range—an approach that is axiomatic to ethnographers of law. The connecting theme of this book overall is thus the visible nexus of claims of national culture, state sovereignty, and transnational law.

In the contexts explored in these chapters, the idea of a collective national subject sometimes offers actors a degree of flexibility that allows them to avoid rigid compliance with treaties and institutional protocols under the rubric of national difference. The term *culture* often refers to a collective subject within its local context, and is ordinarily assumed to erode with the emergence of transnationalism. That understanding of culture has been advanced by anthropologists over the past century and more—an idea that now circulates widely within and well beyond academic disciplines as a rubric of (mainly) subnational identity, community, and attachment. It might seem to follow that transnationalism would mitigate claims to national culture, as states are drawn into myriad transnational arrangements. But transnationalism sustains its own characteristic reifications of culture. For example, actors negotiating global rules and markets may uphold cultural claims to insert their preferences within these transnational contexts. In this way, even as the essentialisms of culture as a concept are contested by scholars, the idea of culture represents forms of domestic interest that have been routinely used by individuals, firms, and governments in "two-level games" at the intersection of local and transnational (Putnam 1988). We see truth in the words of anthropologist William Mazzarella, who aptly refers to "the culture concept, half-abandoned in anthropological theory and celebrated everywhere else" (Mazzarella 2004: 345). The idea of cultural collectivity surfaces in a variety of ways in this volume, but always with a strategic element aimed at shaping the negotiation of global rules or the response to those rules, or to manage other sorts of transnational dilemmas at home or abroad.

Contributors to this volume examine how the idea of national culture functions as an assertion of state sovereignty in the settings of transnational law. Each chapter challenges the conventional wisdom that nationalism must assume an antagonistic relationship with transnationalism, as well as the underlying logic associating transnationalism with elite interests on which that assumption rests. For example, in Chapter 2, Rachel Brewster compares world trading rules and antibribery law, and observes that the separation of these two bodies of law purposely leaves room for what are presumed to be cultural differences with respect to customs of gifting and other transfers in the context of designing agreements. In Chapter 5, David Leheny details the deployment of an idea of cultural difference between the United States and Japan to defray tensions and recast questions of liability in the aftermath of an avoidable naval accident at sea. In Chapter 7, Sandra Brunnegger considers the investments of international NGOs in Colombia's legal pluralism to bolster indigenous legal authority—with unintended consequences. In Chapter 3, Gregory Shaffer and Henry Gao examine China's multifaceted effort to build capacity for using World Trade Organization (WTO) law by developing a WTO culture within China, involving a surprisingly wide range of legal and social institutions.

Landscapes of Law advances the claim that far from being inherently antithetical to transnationalism, key elements of nationalism that are now commonly associated with populism arise and circulate within transnational arenas—in spaces opened by the transnational arenas themselves. For example, demands for particular policies or parameters of diplomatic negotiations may seek domestic compromises rather than simply transactional bargains over discrete issues. Recognizing that cultural nationalism and globalism are mutually reinforcing should not be misread as assurance of some steady state equilibrium or promise of convergence. This volume's perspective emphasizes the synergistic relations of state sovereignty and transnationalism, illuminating both the "high politics" of transnationalism (see Krasner 1999: chap. 4, esp. p. 26) and the potential for alienation or fracture in the very situations where such politics take a cultural form (as in the chapters in this volume by Brunnegger; Dezalay; Leheny; and Valverde). We share Ruggie's view of the state as a mechanism of *social empowerment* under some circumstances, as state representatives seek to embed domestic demands within international institutions (Ruggie 1982, 1993: 160). As already suggested above, this observation seriously complicates the conventional explanations of recent political polarization in the United States and Europe, drawing attention to the inadequacy of an analysis of populism limited to the grievances of uneducated or un- or underemployed populations. Populism also expresses elite interests that form new coalitions among unlikely partners. While we do not examine populism directly, the book reveals the potential for conflict within and across populist movements and differences in how populist claims emerge within transnational venues.

When state and nonstate actors (including firms and activist groups) elevate the idea of a national culture, their advocacy does not automatically weaken the transnational arena. Under some circumstances, they strengthen it. Parties may use claims of national culture to shift between poles of cooperation and resistance to the global institutions that guide or govern trade, security, human rights, and other forms of transnationalism. The discourse of national culture pairs an idea of social substance with legal sovereignty that may help states position themselves amid an evolving set of transnational legal regimes. Such expressions of national culture within the process of regulating globalization potentially provide vital flexibility, similar to the escape clauses and loose enforcement rules that help sustain global regimes in practice (Davis 2012; Downs and Rocke 1995; Rosendorff 2005; Shaffer 2015; Simmons 1998). States are central in diverse and sometimes contradictory ways to the survival of global organizations (Niezen and Sapignoli 2017: 1). In short, the utility of culture as a tool for navigating international arenas serves a wide range of interests. Indeed, there is a new ambiguity with respect to standard accounts of divided interests between elites and the working class in that both advocate the need to preserve a collective state in a discourse of national culture, albeit with different goals.

In referring to national cultures, we do not mean that nations actually have characteristic cultures that could be objectively described and placed in juxtaposition to globalization. The history of anthropology's concept of *culture* points to nineteenth-century ideas of state nationalism, but questions of national culture and national character have long since dropped out of the discipline, having been settled (in the negative) by anthropologists and other scholars (see, e.g., Appadurai 1996; Mazzarella 2004; Simmons 1998). But the histories and "fantasies" (Navaro-Yashin 2002) that sustain the discourse of national culture within states do not end at the border; they may travel intact into the transnational space. Thus, this book's contributors pursue in various ways the political and legal implications of claiming an association between state sovereignty and a national culture in transnational spaces. As already suggested, such claims can be a strategic asset to signal areas of resistance or openness to international commitments (on states' motivations in international agreements, see Brewster 2003). Through acknowledging the cultural differences that are implied by sovereignty, states retain a strategic ambiguity about their willingness to cooperate. Leaving the parameters of national culture undefined better serves this strategy than could any definitive understanding of what constitutes a national culture in theory or practice.

Populism, Nationalism, Internationalism, and Transnationalism

When states embed national culture within their claims of sovereignty, they generate what has been referred to as *political nationalism* (Hurrell 2007: 122). Doing so asserts the legitimate authority of a state to act within the international community *by virtue of its role as a government that represents a national public*. Nationalism occupied a major research agenda in the social sciences in the late 1980s and 1990s, as socialism gave way to capitalism in many parts of the world, and as the retreat, and then the breakup, of the Soviet Union unleashed a wave of ethnonationalist movements in Europe and the Middle East. Those ethnic nationalisms involved strong claims to rights, recognition, and sovereignty—ultimately revising the map of Europe, the Caucasus, and the Middle East. The legal connection between culture, territory, and the legitimacy of sovereignty claims has been further tested by indigenous peoples before national and international law tribunals, as well as by ethnonationalist movements (Comaroff and Comaroff 2009). These are ongoing developments that yield horizons of conflict along which *culture* is widely taken to be external (if not an impediment) to international law (Goodale 2017: chap. 8). Such a framing rests on an assumption that culture is inherently exclusive—out of place in a cosmopolitan legal order (Goodale 2017: 190). As explained already, our starting assumptions resist any structural generality of culture in this sense.

Accordingly, what is different in the scenarios examined in this book is the association of culture/territory/sovereignty *by states* in their active management of relations within *trans*national legal regimes. It is in this context that we observe the surprising efficacy of nationalist (and even populist) discourse within the very legal arenas and instruments of transnationalism (negotiations, agreements, dispute settlement, etc.). In these circumstances, culture is not outside international law, but integral to its discourses, practices, and, as Annelise Riles has observed, its instrumentalities (2006: 61). In this sense, counterintuitively, perhaps, the notion of a global citizenry is antithetical to the forms of cosmopolitanism analyzed in this volume, as they circulate across transnational spaces. For some, if not most, actors discussed in these chapters, entry into the transnational arena is necessarily connected to national citizenship understood in cultural terms, such that a "global citizen" would have no place. Even the "civilization of modernity" described by Peter Katzenstein (2010: 1) as involving a pluralist order of states loosely bound by a shared sense of individualism and diversity entails parameters set by states when they insert exceptions based on claims of national culture into international law. Law privileges the credentials of a state represented by its government and individuals empowered by their status as citizens.

From this perspective, contemporary transnationalism can be understood as projecting the history of the modern state onward—a history that involved the appropriation of the moral discourses of diverse constituent communities into the self-legitimating discourse of states (as influentially remarked by Corrigan and Sayer 1985). The territorial state organized and consolidated formerly self-governing or semi-autonomous groups into a spatialized unit that asserted an over-arching autonomy to develop its own institutions for governance (Corrigan and Sayer 1985; Ruggie 1993)—leaving open the form of rule and the ideological content of political nationalism. In the same way, in the different contexts examined in this book, the discourse of political nationalism is viewed as inherently relational, diverse, and flexible. Indeed, political nationalism "has been the most persistent and pervasive ideology of the modern state system" due in part to "its capacity to meld and mesh with other ideological systems" (Hurrell 2007: 122). The systems at issue in this book include liberalism and communism, U.S. federalism and the European Union, indigenous and postcolonial communities within multicultural states, and digital and other social networks—among other relations and commitments.

These observations help account for the fact that the Brexit referendum and the Trump candidacy succeeded through an unexpected alliance between workers and capitalists. The populist antiglobalization movements that swept the UK and US in recent election cycles did not promote a redistributive program that would directly benefit their own local communities or a broad social movement. Rather, they focused on the distribution of globalization's benefits across participating *states*, dividing workers at the territorial borders. The decision process itself was a point of contention, as transnational government formed the bogeyman—a target that, in the political aftermath, has proven to be elusive given the mutual embeddedness of domestic and foreign interests.

These populist movements create a common cause between workers and employers within the state by blaming economic volatility on global markets for trade, immigration, and putative global elites who (by definition) fail to represent the national interest. They assert that only through rejecting the rules of the Trans-Pacific Partnership and the European Union could national governments set a future course on these critical policies. Encroachment of international rules on the autonomy of the state to shape policies about immigration and trade was framed as a threat to national culture and not simply a challenge to the interests of specific constituencies. As noted by Chantal Mouffe, "Populism is not an ideology or a political regime, and cannot be attributed to a specific programmatic content. It is compatible with different forms of government. It is a way of doing politics . . . [and] reconfiguring a social order" (Mouffe 2016; see also Green 2017; Mouffe [2000] 2005). Both elites and workers acting on both the right and left spectrums of the political arena could mobilize support by claiming to protect the state role as guardian of national culture. Those in the UK who called for leaving the EU also spoke of supporting trade liberalization but said the terms of engagement with the global economy should be set by the British government. Similarly, President Trump rejected multilateralism in favor of bilateral deals, without suggesting that the US should withdraw from the global economy. This volume does not engage directly with populism per se, but the contributions are evidence that populist challenges motivate a scholarly reexamination of the local and global as concepts that do heavy work within transnationalism.

In sum, to the extent that transnationalism leads governments to deploy their own powers in the global arena, it potentially exaggerates the importance of sovereign states as the nations they claim to represent. At the same time, to the extent that transnationalism requires that governments accept constraints imposed by international law, they can underestimate the importance of the nation in the lives of their own citizens. Accordingly, the idea of *culture* gains strategic value in the flexibility it affords key actors in accepting the benefits of participation in transnational governance while resisting the prospect of the dissolution of national publics and their interests within the transnational space. Under such circumstances it is pointless to ask whose culture it is; it belongs to no one, though it can involve strong attachments and exclusions—and it can be fueled by political demands based on group identity. This means that the spaces where transnationalism is actually made—at once social, legal, conceptual, and corporeal—merit close study.

Transnationalism and Law

Landscapes of Law addresses transnational law as it is applied in specific circumstances. The broad range of applications examined in these chapters serves two purposes. First, it allows each author to engage the substantive themes of the volume with theories and methods from their own disciplinary perspective. Second, the variety of cases reinforces the point that transnationalism eludes generality, given the proliferation of global institutions and their contradictory mandates and practices (Niezen and Sapignoli 2017: 1–2). The authority of law varies by context (Alter, Helfer, and Madsen 2016). The focus here is therefore selective: Legal doctrine or legal institutions are considered to be passages where transnationalism is visibly fashioned and refashioned by actors who may seek to deepen or create distance in their relationships with each other. Law is not a passive text but an active part of negotiation to be contested or celebrated and implemented or ignored as it changes over time in both words and interpreted meaning. Contributors avoid an a priori commitment to any fixed relation between law and society so as to more fully specify the associations they observe in each case that is examined; this effort forms the ethnographic core of the volume.

The authors examine the social relations of a transnational legal space that might seem to be located everywhere and nowhere (see, e.g., Goldstein et al. 2000; Latour 2010; for exceptions, see, e.g., Dezalay 2017; Riles 2006, 2011, 2017). This perspective complements those who explore the evolution of law as a matter of past trials shaping future behavior by forming new perceptions of the law (Johns 2015; Sikkink 2011) and models of institutional design (Alter 2014). The relationship between law and social life remains an elusive theoretical problem for legal anthropology (Kesselring et al. 2017; Sapignoli 2017), in part because *law* and *society* are conventionally portrayed as distinct jurisdictions and scales—placing law "above" or "outside of" social fields and beliefs.

By contrast, in these chapters, nationalism and transnationalism are considered to be made of the same cloth; they are not distinct *levels* or *scales* (see Valverde 2009). The contributors find novel ethnographic sites at the locations where the meanings of culture, territoriality, and sovereignty are implicated as open questions in the very ways transnational law is made and made to work. For example, in some contexts, transnational relations among firms or governments are also interpersonal relations among lawyers, subject to inequalities and exclusions that tether transnational law in practice to what may be highly personal repertoires of judgment, with significant material effects (see Dezalay and Massoud, this volume). The ethnographic implications explored here align with anthropological and sociolegal studies of law. *Landscapes of Law* is also indebted to international relations scholarship. Widespread attention to how domestic politics shape engagement with international law in the field of political science has divided into studies of interest groups and representation (e.g., Davis 2012; Moravcsik 1998; Simmons 2009) versus norms and transnational networks of nonstate actors (e.g., Sikkink 2011; Slaughter 2004). More complex interactions between interests, norms, and the state emerge in the chapters of this volume.

"Transnational legal ordering" (Shaffer 2016) is the subject of vast literatures in the areas of public and private international law, as well as law involving nonstate actors (see Halliday and Shaffer 2015). The legal aspects of transnationalism—together with the significant role they preserve for national states—have been less studied by anthropologists and international relations scholars. The reasons for this are complex, for the most part beyond the scope of this volume. But to the extent that one major reason is the conventional separation of the disciplines, we hope this volume will encourage others to paint doors on their disciplines' walls, and walk through them.

With regard to its legal focus, *Landscapes of Law* counters the view that transnationalism is primarily a natural consequence of global capitalism. The putatively borderless world of global trade is at the root of the now-classic metaphor that formulates transnationalism as "flows of people, ideas, laws and institutions across national boundaries" (Merry 2006b; Appadurai 1990). The idea of transnationalism as "flow" is now widely accepted across disciplines (see Darian-Smith 2013), but it imposes an unnecessary distinction between mobility *across places* and the recursive effects of transnationalism on domestic social and legal relations *in places* (see Aman and Greenhouse 2017: esp. pt. 3; see also Alter 2014; Putnam 2016).

Boaventura de Sousa Santos (1987) formulates the term *interlegality* as an alternative to the more jurisdictionally framed *legal pluralism*, to refer to the dynamic crosscurrents of legal institutions running concurrently. Valverde

(2009) subsequently develops the concept of *interlegality* to contest the dominance of jurisdiction in the conventions of scale. Landscaping is messy—proliferating norms yield their own characteristic excesses and omissions (de Herdt and de Sardan 2015: 2). The number and variety of courts and the rulings they issue continue to grow and populate an ever more dense terrain of law (Alter 2014). Areas with overlapping institutions such as trade may experience both positive competition that spurs growth and fragmentation that undermines effectiveness (Davis 2017). Some of the chapters included here address dilemmas involving territorial jurisdiction between or across states (in particular, Basaran; Dezalay; Foblets and Alidadi; and Leheny); others deal with the social production of interlegalities only partially involving national states (Brewster; Brunnegger; Massoud; Rodríguez-de-las-Heras Ballell; Shaffer and Gao; and Valverde). One implication of this volume, overall, is that territoriality and jurisdiction, and the relations between them, are never neutral. The image of landscape in the book's title is a reference not just to land, but to its cultivation in relation to law as a living institution that ideally grows and adapts within its environmental constraints.

A second theme in the volume is the authors' attention to the diverse complexities of what Saskia Sassen ([2006] 2008: 2) has called the *charged processes* of nationalization and denationalization in the context of globalization. Agreements to eliminate tariffs, trade, and other international or multinational arrangements originate as legal activity involving states (intergovernmental agreements, legislation, treaties, contracts, and so forth). States are key actors in all such arrangements, whether directly as drafters or signatories, or indirectly as agents of enforcement and protection of citizens' rights. Some institutions, such as the WTO, invoke the phrase "member-driven organization" and leave states in the role of gate-keepers for enforcement actions, while relying on information from societal groups (Davis 2012). Yet even for institutions such as the International Criminal Court that empower supranational actors and rights of the individual, the approach to legal norms within a state influences the prior decision of governments to accept the jurisdiction of the court, and state cooperation is necessary for the extradition and prosecution of criminals (Kelley 2007). Rather than focus on clearly delimited roles for the state and society, contributors to this volume highlight uncertain stakes and changing opportunities for actors to shape the form of transnational regulation and their own positions within the process.

In detailed qualitative accounts of trade, diplomacy, migration, and community building (key areas of modern transnationalism) this volume's authors show how nationalism can be integral to transnationalism. Their work casts a new light on current controversies to reveal ways in which globalization is held to account—whether in legal or administrative terms (Brewster; Foblets and Alidadi; Leheny; Massoud) or in terms of identifying its beneficiaries (Brunnegger; Dezalay; Rodríguez-de-las-Heras Ballell; Shaffer and Gao). The moral judgments implicit in populism are also relevant in this context. In Chapter 10, Valverde argues that contemporary notions of liberalism (in effect, conflating liberal subjectivity with individualism) are incomplete—neglecting the intellectual history that twinned the individual expression of liberalism to its collective form as philanthropy. Her reading of nationalist populist claims in the United States and Britain revisits that history, drawing its particular dialectic of imperialism and projects of moral improvement into the present.

Our objective in initiating the conference that inspired most of these chapters was to identify researchable problems in the interstices where legal and political anthropology, international political sociology, and international relations seemed due for productive exchange. This does not guarantee comprehensive coverage—on the contrary, we selectively sampled topics that arise in areas of overlap rather than those that may appear more central within a single discipline. Each of these fields offers abundant scholarship on issues directly related to those discussed in the separate chapters; however, as noted by Tugba Basaran and colleagues (2017), disciplinary silos remain strong, usually held apart by their conventions of scale (political science and sociology tending toward the large scale, anthropology and ethnographic sociology tending toward the small scale). We hope readers find the same intrigue we did in remixing these fields at the junctures where states, international institutions, communities, and individuals interrelate *on the same scale*. A common emphasis on ethnography (whether as research method or conceptual resource) creates unity across the studies and sustains the primary contribution of the volume, since ethnography—whatever its disciplinary home—insists that institutions and processes be seen first and foremost as human relations.

It was precisely to explore such possibilities that we gathered anthropologists, political scientists, sociologists, and lawyers for an exploratory conference about transnational law as a research topic and—equally important—as a source of ethnographic innovation. The conference set no constraints on what *ethnography* might be taken to mean, and, indeed, participants brought their own eclectic understandings and expectations to the discussion. In forming the present volume after the conference, we did not seek to adopt a unified theoretical or methodological approach; rather, we considered the diversity of perspectives valuable in itself as a basis for new insights into transnational law. "Thinking processually and relationally" (Basaran et al. 2017: 24) emerged from those conversations as an interconnecting thread across them. Most chapters in the present collection were first presented at the conference.

In addition to contributing insights with regard to transnational law and its social effects, our purpose is also to affirm the ethnography of transnational law as a fruitful inquiry (see, e.g., Alter and Meunier 2009: 18; Bearce and Hart 2017: 65, 67). We turn to ethnography—in the broadest possible sense of that term—for its particular suitability to the analysis of complex, overlapping, informal, and nonreplicable organizations and social situations. As Kim Scheppele (2004: 390) notes in a different context (discussing constitutional ethnography), ethnography "does not ask about the big correlations between the specifics of . . . design and the effectiveness of specific institutions but instead looks to the logics of particular contexts as a way of illuminating complex interrelationships among political, legal, historical, social, economic, and cultural elements" (see also Scheppele 2009). By opening the methodological doors widely, we improve our chances of discovering what ethnography may or must be to meet the analytical challenges of dynamic transnational landscapes of law such as those discussed here. Each author addresses methodological issues as an integral part of their discussion.

Transnational Landscaping

The chapters in this volume offer several paths for cross-reading in addition to the themes indicated above. Several key points emerge distinctly as a result of the multidisciplinary conversation that forms this volume, as well as from the diversity of the authors' efforts to identify fresh ethnographic openings in relation to transnational law.

The study of law helps locate and interpret the intersection of beliefs and strategies within transnational arenas of policy-making. As noted above, transnational (or global) institutions have assumed an increasingly large role as the subject of the ethnography of law. But less attention has been given to the "intersubjective frameworks of meaning" (Finnemore and Sikkink 1998: 887) involved in the weaving of transnational legal fabrics. Furthermore, these meanings are themselves up for challenge as the institutions evolve—in drafting the laws of world trade, the making and unmaking of the European Union in the context of the refugee crisis, and in the uneasy legacy of nineteenth-century philanthropy in the UK and the US, conceived as a modernist project aimed at the moral improvement of the Other (see, in this volume, respectively, Brewster; Brunnegger; Foblets and Alidadi; Leheny; Massoud; and Valverde).

The importance of culture has been widely noted in relation to issues of state and transnational legitimacy as "cultural infrastructures" that shape international cooperation (McNamara 2010: 154). This volume takes this as a departure point; it is not considered a given that culture in the transnational context will have some organic connection to actual localized practices (as would likely be inferred from the anthropological usage of the term). The expressions of national culture in the transnational scenarios discussed in this book are deliberate constructions, strategically built to meet the demands of particular situations—ranging from the politicization of territoriality to new institutions of dispute settlement and the "rule of law" in Colombia and the South Sudan and the investment in academic and industry-level organizational structures intended to support national and regional engagements in world trade (see the chapters by Basaran; Brunnegger; Dezalay; Massoud; and Shaffer and Gao). State actors may appropriate culture to serve their purposes in transnational law irrespective of whether its content has a basis in local legitimacy.

Scholars of transnationalism often use the metaphors of verticality and horizontality to refer to different combinations of state, substate, suprastate, and nonstate legal systems. Verticality presumes that the global is "above" the national; horizontality assumes parity, more or less, across such levels. The two-dimensional grid is inadequate to capture what Scheppele has called "the layering of governmental forms" (personal communication, August 30, 2016) and the myriad resources and engagements that distill such forms into recognition, and hold them together or apart. Brunnegger, Foblets and Alidadi, Rodríguez-de-las-Heras Ballell, and Shaffer and Gao focus on such processes in their analyses of how transnational law is unbundled and mixed with other technologies in the making or remaking of communities—in the creation of a customary court, Europe's failing asylum regime, the promise of Internet communities, and the mediatization of China's new WTO culture. These developments may then reverberate back on the state. As the use of courts for transnational activity is normalized, it changes how they are viewed as a mechanism of dispute resolution. In China, the use of litigation that was once outside of their cultural frame of reference has been elevated by the state as an important national assertion of influence on the international stage, which adds legitimacy to the process itself.

This volume also addresses the relationship between regime complexity and informality—a relationship well established in the scholarship on the structural dynamics of international organizations (see Alter and Meunier 2009: 13; Finnemore and Sikkink 1998; Helmke and Levitsky 2004: 725, 727). Several chapters highlight experiential dimensions of such dilemmas through illuminating both the critical junctures and the paths not taken. Each institution evolves through a complex interaction with other actors and resources that form an organizational ecology (see Abbott, Green, and Keohane 2016). As one institution emerges, it impinges on other institutions. The chapters by Brewster, Foblets and Alidadi, Rodríguez-de-las- Heras Ballell, and Shaffer and Gao address law-making in the WTO context, the instability of the European Union, current experiments in the development of digital communities, and projects of capacity-building in Chinese trade law.

A further aspect of the scholarship on transnationalism that this book addresses is the prominence of the logics of liberalism in the ways governance institutions are set up and scripted to operate (Acharya 2016: 453). Liberalism and the ironies of its contradictions in practice have been the foci of important studies in the anthropology of states and in theories about the emergence of order among states (see Gupta and Sharma 2006; Holsti 2004; Ikenberry 2001). In various ways, this book's contributors are writing from within the scholarship on transnationalism, even as they find critical distance in their own ways. The theoretical chapters by Basaran (on territory) and Valverde (on liberal subjectivity)—bookends to the volume—take up these elements of liberal logics explicitly, drawing into the same frame personal and political dilemmas of interpretive uncertainty.

Landscapes of Law opens multiple research agendas in relation to transnational law, and its main contribution is in the ways authors situate their purposes in relation to the human activity that constitutes transnational law—therefore, inevitably, resulting overall in a productive intersection of disciplines. The book responds to events, but much remains uncertain, and in any case, in rapidly changing circumstances, relevance requires imaginative work (Greenhouse 2011). The era of optimism for liberal government and global cooperation to uphold international law and free markets that began after the end of the Cold War arguably has come to an end. Yet, the new lines of conflict and alternative visions of order have also failed to coalesce into a clear set of norms and power relationships. Far from an end to globalization, we continue to see actors engaging in transnational space with new purposes. The chapters by Foblets and Alidadi, on the impact of the humanitarian crisis in Syria on Europe, and by Rodríguez-de-las-Heras Ballell, on the hopefulness of networked digital communities, point to two versions of transnationalism today: the uncontainable tragedy of war on the one hand, and the bright light of unexpected partnership on the other. Technology and identity politics play out in both experiences. These versions cascade in and out of each other, over-spilling law's purposes, changing the terrain as they run. Ultimately, such experiences will register as having formed something new, even if the values and structures of that terrain cannot be predicted or settled as something other than possibilities.

In these chapters, we find persistent patterns of states asserting their own position within global regulatory processes in their association of state sovereignty with national culture, as if this were its natural expression. Transnationalism can operate as a sphere above the state, or as one that lies between states, but this volume also reveals how it works *through* states when transnational law connects claims of national culture with demands for specific outcomes. Exploring transnational law's landscapes reveals how the terrain is designed and worked by those who inhabit it or travel across it—in the process, reacting to its constraints and changing its form.

References

Abbott, Kenneth, Jessica Green, and Robert Keohane. 2016. "Organizational Ecology and Institutional Change in Global Governance." *International Organization* 70 (2): 247–277.

Acharya, Amitav. 2012. *The Making of Southeast Asia: International Relations of a Region.* Ithaca, NY: Cornell University Press.

Acharya, Amitav. 2016. "The Global Forum—The Future of Global Governance: Fragmentation May Be Inevitable and Creative." *Global Governance* 22 (4): 453–460.

Alter, Karen. 2014. *New Terrain of International Law: Courts, Politics, Rights.* Princeton, NJ: Princeton University Press.

Alter, Karen J., Laurence R. Helfer, and Mikael Rask Madsen. 2016. "How Context Shapes the Authority of International Courts." *Law and Contemporary Problems* 78 (4): 1–38.

Alter, Karen J., and Sophie Meunier. 2009. "Introduction." In *Symposium—The Politics of International Regime Complexity,* eds. Karen J. Alter and Sophie Meunier. *Perspectives on Politics* 7 (1): 13–24.

Aman, Alfred C., and Carol J. Greenhouse. 2017. *Transnational Law: Cases and Problems in an Interconnected World.* Durham, NC: Carolina Academic Press.

Anderson, Benedict. 1991. *Imagined Communities: Reflections on the Origin and Spread of Nationalism* (revised edition). London: Verso.

Appadurai, Arjun. 1990. "Disjuncture and Difference in the Global Cultural Economy." *Theory, Culture and Society* 7 (2–3): 295–310.

Appadurai, Arjun. 1996. *Modernity at Large: Cultural Dimensions of Globalization*. Minneapolis: University of Minnesota Press.

Basaran, Tugba, Didier Bigo, Emmanuel-Pierre Guittet, and R. B. J. Walker. 2017. "Transversal Lines: Introduction." In *International Political Sociology—Transversal Lines*, eds. Tugba Basaran, Didier Bigo, Emmanuel-Pierre Guittet, and R. B. J. Walker, 19–31. New York: Routledge.

Bearce, David H., and Andrew F. Hart. 2017. "International Labor Mobility and the Variety of Democratic Political Institutions." *International Organization* 71:65–95.

Brewster, Rachel. 2003. "The Domestic Origins of International Agreements." *Virginia Journal of International Law* 44 (2): 501–544.

Comaroff, John L., and Jean Comaroff. 2009. *Ethnicity, Inc.* Chicago: University of Chicago Press.

Corrigan, Philip, and Derek Sayer. 1985. *The Great Arch: English State Formation as Cultural Revolution*. Oxford: Blackwell.

Darian-Smith, Eve. 2013. *Laws and Societies in Global Contexts: Contemporary Approaches*. Cambridge: Cambridge University Press.

Davis, Christina L. 2012. *Why Adjudicate? Enforcing Trade Rules in the WTO*. Princeton, NJ: Princeton University Press.

Davis, Christina L. 2017. "Overlapping Institutions in Trade Policy." *Perspectives on Politics* 7 (1): 25–31.

de Herdt, Tom, and Jean-Pierre Olivier de Sardan. 2015. "Introduction: The Game of Rules." In *Real Governance and Practical Norms in Sub-Saharan Africa: The Game of Rules*, eds. Tom de Herdt and Jean-Pierre Olivier de Sardan, 1–16. New York: Routledge.

Dezalay, Sara Résia. 2017. "African Extractive Economies and Connected Histories of Globalization: A Case Study of the 'Africa' Bar in Paris," 18 July 2017. https://ssrn.com/abstract =3004973.

Downs, George W., and David M. Rocke. 1995. *Optimal Imperfection? Domestic Uncertainty and Institutions in International Relations*. Princeton, NJ: Princeton University Press.

Edelman, Marc. 2005. "Bringing the Moral Economy Back In . . . To the Study of 21st Century Transnational Peasant Movements." *American Anthropologist* 107 (3): 331–345.

Evans, Peter. 2008. "Is an Alternative Globalization Possible?" *Politics and Society* 36 (2): 271–305.

Finnemore, Martha, and Kathryn Sikkink. 1998. "International Norm Dynamics and Political Change." *International Organization* 52 (4): 887–917.

Goldstein, Judith, Miles Kahler, Robert Keohane, and Anne-Marie Slaughter. 2000. "Introduction: Legalization and World Politics." *International Organization* 54 (3): 385–399.

Goodale, Mark. 2007. "Introduction: Locating Rights, Envisioning Law Between the Global and The Local." In *The Practice of Human Rights: Tracking Law Between the Global and the Local*, eds. Mark Goodale and Sally Engle Merry, 1–38. Cambridge: Cambridge University Press.

Goodale, Mark. 2017. *Anthropology and Law: A Critical Introduction*. New York: New York University Press.

Goodale, Mark, and Sally Engle Merry, eds. 2007. *The Practice of Human Rights: Tracking Law Between the Global and the Local*. Cambridge: Cambridge University Press.

Green, Sarah. 2017. "Relations and Separations." *American Anthropologist* 119 (3): 530–532.

Greenhouse, Carol J. 2011. *The Paradox of Relevance: Ethnography and Citizenship in the United States*. Philadelphia: University of Pennsylvania Press.

Gupta, Akhil, and Arudhana Sharma, eds. 2006. *The Anthropology of the State: A Reader*. Oxford: Blackwell.

Halliday, Terence, and Gregory Shaffer, eds. 2015. *Transnational Legal Orders*. Cambridge: Cambridge University Press.

Hannerz, Ulf. 1989. "Notes on the Global Ecumene." *Public Culture* 1 (2): 66–75.

Helmke, Gretchen, and Steven Levitsky. 2004. "Informal Institutions and Comparative Politics: A Research Agenda." *Perspectives on Politics* 2 (4): 725–740.

Hinton, Alexander Laban. 2017. *The Justice Façade: Trials of Transition in Cambodia*. Oxford: Oxford University Press.

Holsti, K. J. 2004. *Taming the Sovereigns: Institutional Change in International Politics*. Cambridge: Cambridge University Press.

Hurrell, Andrew. 2007. *On Global Order: Power, Values and the Constitution of International Society*. Oxford: Oxford University Press.

Ikenberry, John. 2001. *After Victory: Institutions, Strategic Restraint, and the Rebuilding of Order After Major Wars*. Princeton, NJ: Princeton University Press.

Johns, Leslie. 2015. *Strengthening International Courts: The Hidden Costs of Legalization*. Ann Arbor: University of Michigan Press.

Katzenstein, Peter J. 2010. *Civilizations in World Politics: Plural and Pluralist Perspectives*. New York: Routledge.

Kelley, Judith. 2007. "Who Keeps International Commitments and Why? The International Criminal Court and Bilateral Nonsurrender Agreements." *American Political Science Review* 101 (3): 573–589.

Keohane, Robert O., and Lisa Martin. 1995. "The Promise of Institutionalist Theory." *International Security* 20:39–51.

Kesselring, Rita, Elif Babul, Mark Goodale, Tobias Kelly, Ronald Niezen, Maria Sapignoli, and Richard Ashby Wilson. 2017. "The Future of the Anthropology of Law—Emergent Conversation." *PoLAR: Political and Legal Anthropology Review Online*, 10 February. https://polarjournal.org/2017/02/10/emergent-conversations-part-6/.

Korostelina, Karina V. 2017. *Trump Effect*. New York: Routledge.

Krasner, Stephen D. 1999. *Sovereignty: Organized Hypocrisy*. Princeton, NJ: Princeton University Press.

Latour, Bruno. 2010. *The Making of Law: An Ethnography of the* Conseil d'État. Cambridge: Polity.

Mazzarella, William. 2004. "Culture, Globalization, Mediation." *Annual Review of Anthropology* 33:345–367.

McNamara, Kathleen R. 2010. "Constructing Authority in the European Union." In *Who Governs the Globe?*, eds. Deborah D. Avant, Martha Finnemore, and Susan K. Sell, 153–179. Cambridge: Cambridge University Press.

Merry, Sally Engle. 2006a. "Anthropology and International Law." *Annual Review of Anthropology* 35:99–116.

Merry, Sally Engle. 2006b. "New Legal Realism and the Ethnography of Transnational Law." *Law and Social Inquiry* 31:975–995.

Moravcsik, Andrew. 1998. *The Choice for Europe: Social Purpose and State Power from Messina to Maastricht*. Ithaca, NY: Cornell University Press.

Mouffe, Chantal. (2000) 2005. *The Democratic Paradox*. London: Verso.

Mouffe, Chantal. 2016. *The Populist Moment*. Trans. Teresa Sastre. OpenDemocracy (Democracia Abierta), 21 November. Accessed 18 April 2017.https://www.opendemocracy.net /democraciaabierta/chantal-mouffe/populist-moment.

Müller, Jan-Werner. 2016. *What Is Populism?* Philadelphia: University of Pennsylvania Press.

Navaro-Yashin, Yael. 2002. *The Faces of the State: Secularism and Public Life in Turkey*. Princeton, NJ: Princeton University Press.

Niezen, Ronald, and Maria Sapignoli. 2017. "Introduction." In *Palaces of Hope: The Anthropology of Global Organization*, eds. Ronald Niezen and Maria Sapignoli, 1–30. Cambridge: Cambridge University Press.

Putnam, Robert. 1988. "Diplomacy and Domestic Politics: The Logic of Two-Level Games." *International Organization* 42 (3): 427–460.

Putnam, Tonya. 2016. *Courts Without Borders: Law, Politics, and U.S. Extraterritoriality*. Cambridge: Cambridge University Press.

Riles, Annelise. 2006. "Anthropology, Human Rights, and Legal Knowledge: Culture in the Iron Cage." *American Anthropologist* 108 (1): 52–65.

Riles, Annelise. 2011. *Collateral Knowledge: Legal Reasoning in the Global Financial Markets*. Chicago: University of Chicago Press.

Riles, Annelise. 2017. "Outputs: The Promises and Perils of Ethnographic Engagement After the Loss of Faith in Transnational Dialogue." *Journal of the Royal Anthropological Institute* 23 (S1): 182–197.

Rodrik, Dani. 2011. *The Globalization Paradox: Democracy and the Future of the World Economy*. New York: Norton.

Rosendorff, Peter B. 2005. "Stability and Rigidity: Politics and Design of the WTO's Dispute Settlement Procedures." *American Political Science Review* 99 (3): 389–400.

Ruggie, John G. 1982. "International Regimes, Transactions, and Change: Embedded Liberalism in the Postwar Economic Order." *International Organization* 36 (2): 379–415.

Ruggie, John G.. 1993. "Territoriality and Beyond: Problematizing Modernity in International Organizations." *International Organization* 47 (1): 139–174.

Santos, Boaventura de Sousa. 1987. "Law: A Map of Misreading—Toward a Postmodern Conception of Law." *Journal of Law and Society* 14:279–302.

Sapignoli, Maria. 2017. Untitled comment. In "The Future of the Anthropology of Law—Emergent Conversation," Rita Kesselring, Elif Babul, Mark Goodale, Tobias Kelly, Ronald

Niezen, Maria Sapignoli, and Richard Ashby Wilson. *PoLAR: Political and Legal Anthropology Review Online*, 10 February. https://polarjournal.org/2017/02/10/emergent-conversations-part-6/.

Sassen, Saskia. (2006) 2008. *Territory, Authority, Rights: From Medieval to Global Assemblages*. Princeton, NJ: Princeton University Press.

Scheppele, Kim Lane. 2004. "Constitutional Ethnography: An Introduction." *Law & Society Review* 38 (3): 389–406.

Scheppele, Kim Lane. 2009. "Liberalism Against Neoliberalism: Resistance to Structural Adjustment and the Fragmentation of the State in Russia and Hungary." In *Ethnographies of Neoliberalism*, ed. Carol J. Greenhouse, 44–59. Philadelphia: University of Pennsylvania Press.

Schimmelfennig, Frank. 2001. "The Community Trap: Liberal Norms, Rhetorical Action, and the Eastern Enlargement of the European Union." *International Organization* 55 (1): 47–80.

Shaffer, Gregory. 2015. "How the World Trade Organization Shapes Regulatory Governance." *Regulation and Governance* 9:1–15.

Shaffer, Gregory. 2016. "Theorizing Transnational Legal Ordering." *Annual Review of Law and Social Science* 12:231–253.

Sikkink, Kathryn. 2011. *The Justice Cascade: How Human Rights Prosecutions Are Changing World Politics*. New York: W. W. Norton.

Simmons, Beth. 1998. "Compliance with International Agreements." *Annual Review of Political Science* 1:75–93.

Simmons, Beth. 2009. *Mobilizing for Human Rights: International Law in Domestic Politics*. Cambridge: Cambridge University Press.

Slaughter, Anne-Marie. 2004. *A New World Order*. Princeton, NJ: Princeton University Press.

Valverde, Mariana. 2009. "Jurisdiction and Scale: Legal 'Technicalities' as Resources for Theory." *Social and Legal Studies* 18 (2): 139–157.

CHAPTER 1

A Journey Through Law's Landscapes

Close Encounters of the Scalar Kind

Tugba Basaran

Trapped in the International

The journey of the Amuur siblings started in Somalia and led over Kenya and Syria to the Paris-Orly Airport in France. Mahad, Lahima, Abdelkader, and Mohammed Amuur, all Somali nationals in their late teens and early twenties, arrived at the Paris-Orly Airport on 9 March 1992 and sought to apply for refugee status. The airport and border police, however, refused to admit the Amuur siblings (to the French territory). They fell under a special procedure, requiring them to apply for a "leave to enter the territory on asylum grounds." They also petitioned the French Office for the Protection of Refugees and Stateless Persons (OFPRA) to grant them refugee status, pursuant to the Geneva Convention of 1951, but the OFPRA ruled that it lacked jurisdiction, as they had not yet entered the territory. On 29 March, after the Minister of the Interior had refused their entry to the French territory, they were sent back to Syria. According to France, from 9 March until 29 March, the Amuurs were legally not in France (based on *Amuur v. France*, ECtHR, 19776/92, 25 June 1996). But, where were they then?

How does this case help us capture legal landscapes? How does it illustrate scalar politics as a modern form of governing? This chapter engages with visions and practices of law. First, I engage with scalar visions, which provide for a neat separation and hierarchy of scales (i.e., divisions into national, international, and transnational), counterpose these to the complex and messy practices of governing, and demonstrate how legal landscapes are too messy to be confined to scalar classifications. Second, I elucidate how scalar classifications authorize a particular form of politics, divisions, and discriminations. Third, I demonstrate how the messiness of practices combined with the orderly scalar visions is a precondition for powerful, as well as questionable, modern forms of governing.

Searching for France

A decree from 1982, known as "asylum at the border," mandated a permit, issued at the border, to (legally) enter French territory, pass by the border controls, and then apply for refugee status. Waiting for the permit to be issued or being denied the permit meant being restrained to the international zone. This led to a number of people waiting in the international zone of airports (in many aspects visually similar to Tom Hanks in the movie *The Terminal*). While French NGOs denounced this situation on humanitarian grounds, the French government insisted that the international zone is outside French territory and hence responsibility. It was only following lengthy struggles over almost fifteen years through national and regional courts that the French government had to acknowledge with *Amuur v. France* (1996) that the international zone (and its expansion through the waiting zone) is indeed within its territory and responsibility.

This prelude of the Amuurs illustrates how law's territory is distinct from physical territory, how inside and outside are susceptible to changes, and how borders shift through law. We could put the Amuurs and the international zone aside, if this was a singular case, an outlier, so to speak. The distinction between physical and legal presence is paramount, however, when applied at various ports of entry, including international airports, seaports, train stations, and even occasionally in territorial waters and land territories (under various names as reception, transit, or detention centers, see Basaran 2010). Here, mere physical presence on the territory is insufficient and only lawful entry amounts to entry, and by implication, access to constitutional protection (Hathaway 2005). We could even contend that scalar distinctions to some extent do not do their work, but paradoxically at the same time do more than their work through messy legal practices. Entering the spheres of the national, international, and transnational becomes dependent on a legal matrix of status and location. In some sense, this is new, and in other senses, not so. It goes against our *vision* of politics, scales, and divisions, but affirms what we have long known about their *practices*.

Statist and Scalar Visions

The political map has become our mental image of the state. The political map reflects states as neat formations of territorial pieces separated through flawless lines. Here landscapes of the state are arrested into particular spatio-temporal configurations, into static, stagnant, and lucent borders and boundaries. Law, sovereignty, and state are rendered visible through territory and geography, and these simplifications are generalized, popularized, vulgarized. This map also provides us also with rehearsed, trodden narratives and simplified visualizations of the boundaries, jurisdictions, and formations of law. Here, the image of territorial jurisdiction solidifies landscapes of law, makes them appear to be visible and enduring, contained and exclusive. Therefore, the map visually employs, first, the *politics of congruence*, where state, territory, law, and politics appear to be congruent and inseparable one from the other, identical in their scope, contained in a visible geographical materiality (Agnew 1994). The politics of congruence invokes and relies on, second, the *politics of limits* (Walker 2010), that is, strong legal and political delimitations. Creating the legible state requires that we pretend as if state power, politics, and law end at the state's territorial border. This vision is integral to international law and crucial to the principle of sovereign equality (UN Charter, Art. 2.1): Every sovereign state has their own part of the territorial puzzle of the world and may not overstep their borders.

Hereby, territory takes an important role. Territory renders power visible and legible. It simplifies, materializes, and geographically traces the borders of uncontested supreme rule, inviolable spaces of authority, or, in other words, state sovereignty. In modern political thought, the state is inherently a product of its material geography, its territory (Bodin and Franklin 1992; Hobbes [1651] 2006). The very definition of sovereignty as "supreme authority within a territory" reveals the search for a congruence of natural, legal, and political landscapes, an effort to make politics and law derivative of territory. Territory is also a fundamental attribute of statehood under public international law (Montevideo Convention 1933, Art. 1). We may even claim that the territorial principle is the ultimate principle of (inter)national law, in relation to which all jurisdictional questions arise. The absolute nature of territorial jurisdiction, inscribed into international law, is so much taken for granted that exemptions hereof, immunities and extraterritorial jurisdiction, ultimately serve to confirm its very significance. Territorial jurisdiction is a foundational authority of the state, providing the state with the highest form of political and legal authority within a particular territory and confirming it as the locus of politics (Walker 2010). In return, the definition of sovereignty as supreme authority is dependent on the very existence of territory.

This vision prescribes a particular mode of seeing. It provides us with the *statist vision* that emphasizes the state as the locus of politics and along with that the significance of *sovereignty* as the starting point for conceptualizing the world. This vision fulfills an ideological function by inscribing (not describing) states on the map, and through that very act legitimating state sovereignty and the sovereign's law, making things legible, orderly, simplified through geometrical design (Scott 1998). Here, the state becomes the predominant political unit, the sovereign. The politics of congruence, visibility, and legibility based on territory allow states to be arrested into particular spatio-temporal configurations, appear static, inert, and permanent. Landscapes of law are here, just like other modern accounts, "predicated on a specific topology of point, line and plane" (Walker 2010: 18) that enable and authorize modern techniques of governing. In its search for visibility, law is also simplified and rendered legible; materialized and geographically traced through lines, boundaries, and borders; contained by territory; molded into territorial jurisdiction. Nothing is more indicative of this than the political map, and nothing is more inadequate to portray political and legal landscapes.

This vision of the state has important implications for scalar orders. It results in a scalar vision of the world, the division into local, national, and international (and by extension also transnational). It is important to point out that the starting point for the scalar vision is the state, which then opens up possibilities of moving either down to the local or up to the international. Scalar conceptions of the world that separate the national from transnational and international are often perceived as the natural order of things and common to academic as well as everyday understandings of the world. Even disciplines such as international relations and international law reaffirm scales through a distinction between the national and international. A world without these scales is now unthinkable. Who can avoid writing about the national, even if only in contraposition to the international or transnational? Even the most vehement critics of scalar conceptions are struggling to find words and worlds beyond them. Certainly, this is not the first critique of this vision, nor the first effort to deconstruct scales through practices of law, sociology, or power (Basaran et al. 2017; Basaran and Olsson 2018).

Counter-Scalar Practices

If the scalar vision is misleading, however, what do we see when we investigate global landscapes? Practices of governing are complex and messy. The dispersion of power in practice is subsumable neither geographically nor institutionally in the form of the state. Many are "painfully aware of the tension that exists between the traditional view of sovereignty as an indivisible and discrete condition of possible statehood, and the actual dispersion of political power and legal authority" (Bartelson 2006). In an effort to deconstruct the conventional edifice of sovereignty, a variety of disciplines have targeted its symbolic conjunctures: They have fragmented the (symbolic) territory and state and explored multiple deterritorialized and dehomogenized formations of governing and sovereignties. In seeking to rethink statist visions, they have cultivated a grammar of global pluralities and fragmentations, along with innumerable analyses of transnational and global relations. Many have pointed to pluralities of governing and governance and the variety of dynamic landscapes that are produced as a result thereof. They have paid attention to movements, shifting boundaries, and historical roots of a great diversity of social configurations and formations. In particular, three approaches advanced by scholars focusing on (1) globalization, (2) geography and borders, and (3) law are of relevance here for deconstructing a scalar vision through practice.

First, in an effort to move beyond conventional accounts of the state, sociologies, geographies, and anthropologies of globalization and governance have emphasized complex political geographies, transnational geographies, heterogeneous landscapes, and how state practices, conceived of as domestic, take place beyond states' territorial limits. The emphasis on new forms of governance has also led to contemporary representations of the state and forms of governance: visions of hyperstates, fragmented states, and neoliberal states (Harvey 2005); sites of "effective sovereignty" (Agnew 2009); and globalizing "scapes" (Appadurai 1990). Along with a renewed interested in fragmented forms of analyzing and mapping sovereignties, these different approaches to deterritorializing governing and government have contributed to an understanding that territory and political authority are not congruent, that the state's jurisdiction is not limited to its territory and requires new forms of analysis to overcome outdated ways of seeing.

Second, the grammar of pluralities and fragmentation has also been significant in questioning geographies and borders, especially the understanding of borders as territorial borders, that they must somehow be located at the outer limit of the territory. Just like territory, borders are not presocial or prepolitical, but historically and spatially contingent, reflecting relations of power (Lefebvre 1991; Rumford 2006; Soja 1989). In fact, it was no longer the search for borders, but bordering as a process that has provided a complex view of state borders and their characteristics. With the detachment of borders from territorial borders, concepts of borders have multiplied to include a variety of geographical and nongeographical borders; borders have become mobile, temporal, and shifting; and selective, confirming distinction in mobility (Basaran 2010). Analyzing borders, not as boundary lines between sovereign states, but from the perspective of governing techniques, illustrates how borders and boundaries have been created through daily practices.

Third, in law, these developments have equally led to a questioning of conventional understandings of law. Counterposed to a statecentric notion of law along with an emphasis on formal law, legal pluralists have underlined the plurality of normative orders and contestations between legal regimes as well as legal scales. More specifically, a focus on global, transnational, and international practices of law, including their interaction with public and private legal orders, has emphasized the multiplicity and fragmentation of legal formations, within which the state, itself only one among multiple formations, exists (see, e.g., Koskenniemi 2009; Raustiala 2004). This has also led to the questioning of the concept of *the state*, its powers and scope of jurisdiction, the legal geographies of the state and the multiplicity of legal formations interacting with and within what we refer to as the state, and of statist visions of law and the spatiality of the state (Blomley, Delaney, and Ford 2001; Braverman et al. 2014).

A variety of approaches from different disciplines have profoundly contested scalar thinking. In order to rupture scalar visions, analytically they have often focused on practices, underlined interconnectivity, interactions and interconnections between different scalar levels, and interpenetrations of global and local (see, e.g., "glocalization" in Latour 1993; Swyngedouw 1997), moving from geometry to topology (Latour 1993: 117). Through the grammar of multiplicities and fragmentations, they have sought to break through scalar analysis (focused on a particular level, i.e., local, national, and international). Some have also sought to render social configurations (to a large extent) independent of scalar classification by emphasizing relations, fields, and flows to transgress scalar thinking and provide transversal lines (Basaran et al. 2017). With the intent of disrupting scales, these various approaches have often emphasized process, relations, singularities, and interconnectivities instead of structures, systems, and scales.

Even if we know that practices cannot be contained in scales, claims to scales prevail, and effectively so. This is because scales possess a useful authority. Like Hobbes's iconic image of the Leviathan, which symbolizes modern state authority, as well as its presumed foundations of consent and contract (Hobbes [1651] 2006: title page), statist visions produce perceptions of the political, the social, and legal. Territory and territorial borders become fundamental for producing territorial jurisdiction and the symbolic (b)order of law through "sharp distinctions" (Walker 2017: x) and divisions between here and there, inside and outside, order and chaos, just and unjust, liberal and illiberal, citizen and foreigner, national and international, within law and outside of law, the normal and the exception, the territorial and extraterritorial. These distinctions are crucial for our legal and political imagination. They inscribe statist visions of law, restrict and align our vision to the lenses of the Leviathan (see also Scott 1998). They shape our legal vision through statist imaginaries.

Scalar Authority, Divisions, and Governing

Scalar distinctions are not only of a technical and analytical nature, but these divisions carry authority and important normative functions, three of which I underline in the following.

First, a distinction between the inside and outside of law is drawn. Placing the Amuurs outside of constitutional law is a powerful act, only possible through the very distinction between the national and international, between inside and outside. The inside is equated with lawfulness, whereas the outside is equated to being outside of law, with a lack of law, as if such a condition could exist in modern life where subjectivities, materialities, and even physical landscapes have become products of law, deriving their identity, sense, and purpose largely from law. The Amuurs were under the policing power of France, under its jurisdiction, as underlined by the European Court of Human Rights (ECtHR), but the outside of law continues to be pervasive for locating refugees outside. Outside of law is a useful symbolic construction. Being outlawed, condemned to be symbolically outside of law, can even, as history reminds us, become the ultimate punishment, the ultimate dehumanization (Agamben 1998; Arendt 1973). When people die there, nobody is held responsible—whether refugees on the high seas or enemy combatants in Guantanamo or Afghanistan. What happens *there* (however *there* is defined), is considered to be no longer the responsibility of the state. The distinction between being inside and outside of law, however, as illustrated in the case of the Amuurs, is geographically indeterminate, but imagined as a geographical concept nonetheless.

Second, this distinction has significant implications for the liberal conception of human rights. The assumptions of territorial jurisdiction confer in liberal democracies a particular meaning that limits human rights and, by implication, the state's political project, to the state's (symbolic) territory. Here the sharp distinction at the territorial border appears to authorize differential treatment particularly regarding human rights for noncitizens. It is assumed that the state serves in the interest of its citizens, with the notion that liberty can best be safeguarded within a spatial order, territory, under the authority of the state. The state serves as the protector of its people against (outside) threats. Rule of law appears as the protector, the guarantor of rights and rules against the arbitrary power of the sovereign. Places of sovereign responsibility and rights are allocated to the inside, and charity at best to the outside. Like any other boundary, the boundary of politics, and its imaginary physical location on territory, serves and reinforces—whether intentionally or not—a particular political purpose. It justifies the political form of government and confines its scope of application, or, as some may say, the moral scope of the state. The refugee, until a lawful arrival, is located outside of it.

Third, a sharp demarcation is introduced between liberal and illiberal orders. With the liberal order contained inside, the illiberal must be outside. Hereby, *outside* is defined both in spatial and temporal terms as an exception to the liberal order (Basaran 2010). By implication, many debates, whether traditional or critical, appear to assume that ordinary law and democracy are safeguards against security practices. "It justifies the normative valuation of liberal democracies as a desirable form of government, a government of justice and the rule of law" (Basaran 2010: 19). The drawing of a boundary also hints at the constitutive nature of the terms *liberal* and *illiberal*, as one cannot be imagined without the other. With the monopolization of liberties as an area of liberal rule, the invention of *liberal rule* leads to the creation of its antithesis, *illiberal rule*. Liberal and illiberal rule appear to be mutually exclusive. The normative valuation of democracy has a stabilizing function, an ordering function, and, of course, a hegemonic function. It seeks to preserve the existing order.

It is when practices of constituting scalar boundaries and authority are combined that we find a particularly effective statist vision—one that is not constrained by particular scales but can practically make scalar claims from anywhere. This is what we will call *elastic scales*: How elastic scales function and how they are constituted are described in the last two parts of this chapter. It is these elastic practices of scales that make scalar conceptions effective and, as I argue, most powerful.

Elastic Scales and Authority

From 9 March until 29 March, the Amuurs were held in the international zone (and its expansion, the waiting zone) in accordance with a circular from the Minister of the Interior of 26 June 1990. According to this circular, "An alien who has been refused leave to enter and is waiting to be sent away has the right to freedom of movement inside the international zone, where such a zone exists and has facilities suitably adapted to the types of surveillance and accommodation required for the alien in question. If so, it will be necessary to provide accommodation and take the necessary measure to ensure that he does not enter French territory" (see *Amuur v. France* 1996). Hence, when border police refused to admit the Amuurs on French territory, the siblings were held at the "Hotel Arcade, part of which had been let to the Ministry of the Interior and converted for use as a waiting area for Orly Airport. . . . According to the applicants, police officers would drop them off at the airport's lounge very early in the morning and take them back to the Hotel Arcade in the evening" (ibid.). Here, the scales—national and international—are not fixed, but elastic, and it is through their elasticity that they can perform their authoritative function and make resistance to scalar divisions appear futile.

In fact, initially the international zone extended from the "points of embarkation and debarkation to the points where the control of people takes place" (Republic of France 2004: L221-2), that is, the conventional limits travelers encounter on arrival at airports until passport control. Incrementally, the waiting zone (and with it the international zone) was detached from this spatiolegal fixture. There was an established administrative practice that for accommodation purposes some people would be brought to a hotel on the grounds of the airport. The first floor of the hotel would then be declared an international zone, meaning that people in this area had not yet entered the territory of France. They remained outside of France. Based on the argument of necessity, the waiting zone thus became detached from the commonly accepted version of the international zone (as up to the passport controls). This practice was inscribed into law by including accommodation within the parameter of the port, airport, or train station (Republic of France 2004: L221-2). Later it was further extended to include the nearby neighborhood. What "nearby" meant was not further defined, providing for elastic spaces. The ultimate elasticity was added with the 2003 amendments to the law on the waiting zone: "The waiting zone extends, without the necessity to take a specific decision, to the places where the foreigner has to be, either in the framework of the procedure in process or in case of medical urgency" (Republic of France 2004: L221-2). The waiting zone now extended, based on administrative and humanitarian considerations, to all the places where the people caught in it needed to be. The legal status of the person came to determine the status of the place, or, alternatively, we could think of the waiting zone as attached to the person wherever he or she went. Some people were always (legally) outside of the French territory. This illustrates how legal landscapes prove to have an astonishing spatial and temporal elasticity. Equally, the scales—national, international, and transnational—are not fixed, but elastic. What is international space for the asylum seeker may well be national for the French citizen, as just illustrated. And when the international became contested, the waiting zone was opened up as an extension of international space to some extent, or as a space somewhere between the national and international.

Creating Scalar Authority

Nothing about scales is inherently stable, and there are many ways of creating law's landscapes and scalar authority, including local, national, transnational, and international instruments (to use and reauthorize scalar visions); administrative law and regulations; or even established practices. As in the example of the waiting zone, we can see that scales can be created through the simplest of tools: through administrative regulations, national law, and regional courts, such as the European Court of Human Rights. Bilateral approaches, including bilateral agreements, but also exchanges of diplomatic notes, memoranda of understanding, and even oral agreements; as well as cooperation with airlines, international organizations, and humanitarian organizations, is common (Basaran 2010). Paradoxically, the creation of scalar authority depends to some extent on the notions and visions of territory and authority and the significance attributed to extraterritorial issues in international public law.

Further, we have to keep in mind that "the state" is not a unitary actor. Legal landscapes are set through the legislative and executive, whether through unilateral, multilateral, or international law, as well as through adjudication, including national as well as regional and international courts. These account for differences in legal boundary settings, but also in scalar differentiations, depending on subject matter and actors involved. What may be transnational from a trade perspective may well be defined as extraterritorial from a human rights perspective. What may be national for one subject may be considered international for another. The notion of territorial jurisdiction, contested in private law, has remained of significance for human rights. Jurisprudence on jurisdiction has been conservative, limiting access to adjudication of rights, posing restrictions on the right to hear cases outside a particular geographic jurisdiction. This has been reinforced by legislative and executive claims that court jurisdiction should not apply in cases of human rights violations abroad or if delegated to third actors (e.g., Guantanamo, Australian offshore processing). Here, we can only hint at the complexity of questions of legal bordering and authorities involved in defining scales.

For analyzing legal landscapes, we have to keep in mind that there never was a unitary state, or a uniform scope of state jurisdiction. We have to analyze the practices of boundary and border settings. Multiple boundaries of jurisdiction and multiple boundaries of law coexist, and multiple scales, more often than not, coexist in conflict with each other. Analyzing legal borders helps identify some legal landscapes and allows us to reconsider scales; how inside and outside distinctions are created; and how we can re-envision the state, its legal geographies, its borders, its jurisdiction, and its responsibilities. Legal borders illustrate the fragmented legal infrastructure of the state. Legal borders are not lines in landscapes or fixtures; they cannot be pinned down geographically or temporally; they do not have visual permanence. Legal borders are plural, dynamic, and selective; temporally and spatially flexible; largely independent of physical territory; existent in a legal space. They allow for extensions of scope and multiplications.

Avoiding Symbolic Traps

The symbolic powers of scales indisputably shape our mind-set (Basaran and Olsson 2018). As with any other symbolic system, however, signifiers do not "represent" reality, in an empiricist understanding, but symbolic relations are arbitrary and conventional (Saussure, Baskin, and Meisel 2011). When analyzing scales, it is easy to fall into the trap of symbolic relations and landscapes, most commonly expressed through disciplinary distinctions, such as national and international law, but also through concepts such as within and outside of law, territoriality and extraterritoriality. The landscapes of law with apparently clear boundaries and borders are not where we assume them to be. The apparent visibility of law through its spatial imprint (territory) conceals the invisible operations of law. It confuses its symbolic form with its practices, and by implication preserves sovereignty as a symbolic form (Bartelson 2014; Beaulac 2004). It enforces an imaginary of the territorial state and territorial jurisdiction as the standard formation of modern past and present, taking words and symbols, rather than practices, at their face value. By implication, it provides us with a particular vision of the state, of scales, and of what lies beyond it, along with the clear boundaries of division that result.

Thereby, symbolic landscapes fulfill an important function, legitimizing a political order. They "conceal multiple phenomena in a claim to unity" (Walker 2017: 13). These visions allow us to see like a state; even more, these visions allow us to *make* the state. As James Scott correctly points out, "seeing like a state" is part of statecraft, authorizing and justifying the state (Scott 1998). Many concepts appear "almost natural," concealing the violent struggles and multiple claims to governing and state making (see also Tilly 1985). This has particularly important implications for human rights. Law provides a sophisticated tool for governing, visible in its restricted territorial version and invisible in its expansions and subjectifications (Basaran 2010). And even though scalar thinking constrains proper political, legal, and social analysis, many scholars, from political scientists to legal theorists, have taken this model at face value and, by importing its assumptions, have involuntarily restricted their capacity for analysis. Along with Rob Walker, we have to ask in frustration, "What would we do without them? What can we still do with them?" (Walker 2017: 13). It is impossible to separate our thinking from these concepts, but nonetheless we need to be aware of the boundaries and the limits they impose and the implications thereof. Ultimately, "while it may be that we still need these concepts, it is also probably the case that we are far less in control of them than they are of us" (Walker 2017: 13).

References

Agamben, Giorgio. 1998. *Homo Sacer: Sovereign Power and Bare Life*. Trans. Daniel Heller-Roazen. Palo Alto, CA: Stanford University Press.

Agnew, John. 2009. *Globalization and Sovereignty*. New York: Rowman & Littlefield.

Appadurai, Arjun. 1990. "Disjuncture and Difference in the Global Cultural Economy." *Theory, Culture & Society* 7 (2): 295–310.

Arendt, Hannah. 1973. *The Origins of Totalitarianism*. Boston, MA: Houghton Mifflin Harcourt.

Bartelson, Jens. 2006. "The Concept of Sovereignty Revisited." *European Journal of International Law* 17 (2): 463–474.

Bartelson, Jens. 2014. *Sovereignty as Symbolic Form*. London: Routledge.

Basaran, Tugba. 2010. *Security, Law and Borders: At the Limits of Liberties*. London: Routledge.

Basaran, Tugba, Didier Bigo, Emmanuel-Pierre Guittet, and R. B. J. Walker, eds. 2017. *International Political Sociology: Transversal Lines*. London: Routledge.

Basaran, Tugba, and Christian Olsson. 2018. "Becoming International: On Symbolic Capital, Conversion and Privilege." *Millennium* 46 (2): 96–118.

Beaulac, Stéphane. 2004. *The Power of Language in the Making of International Law: The Word Sovereignty in Bodin and Vattel and the Myth of Westphalia*. Leiden, The Netherlands: Martinus Nijhoff.

Blomley, Nicholas, David Delaney, and Richard T. Ford, eds. 2001. *The Legal Geographies Reader: Law, Power, and Space*. Oxford: Blackwell.

Bodin, Jean, and Julian H. Franklin. 1992. *Bodin: On Sovereignty*. Cambridge: Cambridge University Press.

Braverman, Irus, Nicholas Blomley, David Delaney, and Alexandre Kedar, eds. 2014. *The Expanding Spaces of Law: A Timely Legal Geography*. Palo Alto, CA: Stanford University Press.

Burbank, Jane, and Frederick Cooper. 2011. *Empires in World History: Power and the Politics of Difference*. Princeton, NJ: Princeton University Press.

Harvey, David. 2005. *A Brief History of Neoliberalism*. Oxford: Oxford University Press.

Hathaway, James C. 2005. *The Rights of Refugees Under International Law*. Cambridge: Cambridge University Press.

Hobbes, Thomas. (1651) 2006. *Leviathan*. London: A & C Black.

Koskenniemi, Martti. 2009. "International Law: Between Fragmentation and Constitutionalism." Accessed 5 March 2017. www.helsinki.fi/eci/Publications/MCanberra-06c.pdf.

Latour, Bruno. 1993. *We Have Never Been Modern*. Cambridge, MA: Harvard University Press.

Lefebvre, Henri. 1991. *The Production of Space*. Oxford: Blackwell.

Raustiala, Kal. 2004. "The Geography of Justice." *Fordham Law Review* 73: 2501–60.

Republic of France. 2004. Code de l'entrée et du sejour des étrangers et du droit d'asile (CESEDA), ordonnance no. 2004-1248 du 24 novembre 2004 [Code of entry for residence by foreigners and the right of asylum, ordinance 2004-1248 of 24 November 2004]. *Journal officiel de la République Française* (JORF) [Official Journal of the French Republic], no. 0274 (25 November 2004): 19924, text no. 12. Accessed 9 September 2019. https://www.legifrance.gouv.fr/eli/ordonnance/2004/11/24/2004-1248/jo/texte.

Rumford, Chris. 2006. "Theorizing Borders." *European Journal of Social Theory* 9 (2): 155–169.

Saussure, Ferdinand de, Wade Baskin, and Perry Meisel. 2011. *Course in General Linguistics.* New York: Columbia University Press.

Scott, James C. 1998 *Seeing Like a State: How Certain Schemes to Improve the Human Condition Have Failed.* New Haven, CT: Yale University Press.

Soja, Edward W. 1989. *Postmodern Geographies: The Reassertion of Space in Critical Social Theory.* London: Verso.

Swyngedouw, E. 1997. "Neither Global nor Local: 'Glocalization' and the Politics of Scale." In *Spaces of Globalization: Reasserting the Power of the Local*, ed. Kevin R. Cox, 137–166. New York: Guilford.

Tilly, Charles. 1985. "War Making and State Making as Organized Crime." *Violence: A Reader*, ed. Catherine Besteman, 35–60. New York: New York University Press.

Walker, R. B. J. 2010. *After the Globe, Before the World.* London: Routledge.

Walker, R. B. J. 2017. "Only Connect: International, Political, Sociology." In *International Political Sociology: Transversal Lines*, eds. Tugba Basaran, Didier Bigo, Emmanuel-Pierre Guittet, and R. B. J. Walker, 13–23. London: Routledge.

CHAPTER 2

Intersecting Legal Spaces

International Trade Law
and Anticorruption Law

Rachel Brewster

US efforts to create an international anticorruption regime began from the most domestic of concerns—national security—but the regime did not become effective until it was reframed as an economic trade, development, and competition concern. In the path that led from early security concerns to the present, the relationship between national and transnational law has been reciprocal and multidirectional. Domestic legislation, the American Foreign Corrupt Practices Act (FCPA), created a demand for international coordination, but was also dependent on it. National leaders found that the enforcement of a domestic statute was not politically viable until an international framework was in place. The creation of international coordination then, in turn, permitted the greater use of the most nationalist of measures—criminal prosecutions—to enforce international rules across multiple jurisdictions.

This chapter examines the transmission of national political demands to the international legal system, the subsequent incorporation and reformulation of these demands into transnational institutions, and the return of these norms to national politics. Far from being in opposition, national and transnational law creation and implementation have become mutually dependent and interwoven. National demands not only open up space in international discourse, but international agreements can then empower national-level actors by expanding their jurisdictional capacity and legitimacy. National goals can create the demand for transnational law, and transnational law can invigorate nationalist goals.

I focus here on the choice of a transnational forum for anticorruption principles within the global legal landscape. This transnational process of negotiation and contestation has consequences for the development of the international anticorruption regime, including its membership, legal character, jurisdiction, and reliance on domestic institutions. The paths not taken are, at once, the result of norms and power politics and constitutive of the diverse and fragmented international legal order.

This process is far from fluid. Legal norms fail to gain traction in some fora but later succeed in others. The process of state-to-state negotiations creates the topography of the international legal landscape. Decisions at one point set paths that shape the contours of international agreements and domestic economic policies going forward. As this study illustrates, the transnational legal system is a complex web of overlapping and conflicting elements. There is not a single legal and political system to engage but a dense set of complementary and competing legal arrangements that governments can strategically try to manipulate to reach nationalist ends. In elucidating that process, I examine the contested process of placing anticorruption rules within the transnational legal system.

This chapter has four main parts. The first explores the current relationship between national and international anticorruption rules and discusses their mutual dependence. The second part introduces the key domestic statutes, international organizations, and bodies of law that are the background for mapping the development of anticorruption rules in transnational legal systems. The third part delves into conceptions of fragmentation in the international legal order. It emphasizes that the international system lacks a centralized and coordinated system of rule creation, which effectively allows a broad range of complementary, competing, and conflicting legal obligations to emerge based on different treaty regimes. This part describes the process of negotiating a forum for anticorruption principles and the consequences of the forum on the form and substance of anticorruption law. The final section examines intersecting legal spaces. These bodies of law have now developed in separate fora (although they dive into each other's pools on occasion), but it was not a given that it would be this way. This part details how the reshaping of anticorruption as a criminal law issue, rather than a trade issue, has influenced its development and, in many ways, has allowed it to maintain its nationalistic character.

National and Transnational Anticorruption Law

The United States passed the Foreign Corrupt Practices Act (FCPA) in 1977 after the Watergate scandal revealed that American corporations had large slush funds that they used to bribe foreign governments (Koehler 2012). The FCPA prohibits American citizens, American corporations, or any corporation that lists on an American stock exchange from bribing or offering a bribe to a foreign government official for the purpose of obtaining or retaining business. The statute was originally framed as national security legislation, aimed at keeping corporations from interfering with international relations and preventing the fall of friendly foreign governments through corruption scandals. Yet for all the attention that the passage of the FCPA garnered, the federal government effectively did not enforce the statute for its first twenty years.

Only after the passage of the Organisation for Economic Co-operation and Development (OECD) Anti-Bribery Convention in 1995 did the United States ramp up both the number of prosecutions and the level of penalties for violations (Brewster and Buell 2017). The OECD Convention multilateralized the FCPA, requiring all members of the treaty to adopt similar national legislation criminalizing foreign bribery. As this section explores, this transnational framework allowed American prosecutors to make greater use of the broad jurisdiction rules established by national law. Today, the FCPA is considered to be one of the pillars of American corporate regulation and white-collar crime prosecutions, and the statute is described as being "at the nerve endings of corporate general counsels and executives" (Savage 2012).

The relationship between national law and transnational law is multidirectional in this case. After the passage of the FCPA, enforcement of the statute was unpopular as corporations argued that it would make them globally uncompetitive. The United States was the only country to adopt such legislation, and other countries continued to subsidy overseas bribery by making it tax-deductible (Abbott and Snidal 1998). Congress repeatedly demanded that the executive branch negotiate an international agreement that would make antibribery rules part of international trade law, but (as this chapter examines in depth) the executive branch had a difficult time convincing other nations to agree. Instead, the United States ended up negotiating an agreement in the OECD in the early 1990s: the creation of a forum that (at the time) contained most of the world's major exporters, and, thus, a second-best platform for regulating major multinational corporations. Here, the existence of the FCPA created a strong demand in American domestic politics for transnational law to regulate anticorrption efforts. That demand eventually led to the creation of the 1995 OECD Anti-Bribery Convention (Tarullo 2003).

The OECD Convention then, in turn, provided American prosecutors with the greater jurisdiction, legal cooperation, and legitimacy that they needed to dramatically increase their enforcement of the FCPA. The OECD Convention provided three elements that the American prosecutors needed to give the FCPA real bite (Brewster 2017). First, as a matter of social relations, the OECD treaty crystalized the idea that foreign corruption should not be tolerated (let alone subsidized) and legitimized American extraterritorial prosecutions to deter foreign bribery. Second, as a legal matter, the treaty created a binding legal principle for OECD members that each state had to criminalize foreign bribery to the same extent that it criminalized domestic bribery, and demanded that government officials collect and share evidence at the request of foreign prosecutors. Third, as a political matter, the treaty allowed all of the major exporting countries to act in concert (and thus avoid a collective action problem).

The formation of the OECD invigorated the enforcement of the FCPA. The treaty essentially gave American prosecutors the political and legal capacity to enforce the FCPA against American corporations and their foreign competitors.[1] Once American prosecutors had a means to prosecute foreign bribery in a competitively neutral manner (that is, against domestic and foreign exporting firms), the Department of Justice and the Securities and Exchange Commission dramatically increased the number of cases they brought, and the penalties for violations increased by several orders of magnitude.[2] The law went from being a legal backwater to one of the most feared corporate statutes inside and outside of the United States. Developments in transnational law had cleared away political hurdles to the robust domestic criminal enforcement of the law.

The case of the international anticorruption regime highlights the often underappreciated relationships between domestic and transnational law. There is little doubt that the OECD Anti-Bribery Convention would not exist without the FCPA. The existence of the law made the United States a consistent demander for transnational coordination of anticorruption efforts in international fora. Without a dogged and powerful country behind the international anticorruption push, the treaty would not have come into force. The treaty, in turn, allowed for a new era of vigorous enforcement of the FCPA. The modern incarnation of the FCPA as a powerful tool for the United States to prosecute domestic and foreign firms is due to the treaty's creation of a new competition-neutral extraterritorial enforcement strategy that is politically sustainable (both in the United States and in other OECD countries).Domestic law and transnational law here do not exist in separate spheres but are mutually dependent and supportive.

Two Bodies of Law: International Trade and Anticorruption

International trade law and anticorruption rules have developed as two very different systems of rules, although there were opportunities for the two to connect at various points. Corruption is often cast as an international trade, or at least an international economic law, issue (Pauwelyn 2013). At the most general level, a government official's demand for bribes for goods to enter a country or for businesses to operate effectively falls into the broad class of nontariff barriers to trade. Such nontariff barriers decrease the value of negotiated commitments to open markets made during trade rounds. Particularly in the service sector, where businesses open overseas offices, corruption can de facto close markets that governments have promised to open. In addition, empirical studies have repeatedly documented how corruption biases government spending toward large projects where opportunities for bribery are greater (Delavallade 2006; Mauro 1998a, 1998b). This generally results in more spending on projects such as military procurement or major construction projects, and less spending on small projects such as local health clinics and education. Corruption additionally decreases the quality of the public services that governments offer (Reinikka and Svensson 2004). As a result, the bundle of goods and services that the state purchases is influenced by corruption. One of the goals of anticorruption efforts is to reallocate government spending in a more socially beneficial manner.

On a more micro level, anticorruption law affects where corporations do business internationally. Firms that face strong anticorruption enforcement act more cautiously in countries with high levels of corruption. This influences where foreign direct-investment dollars flow as well as influences large government procurement sales (Cuervo-Cazurra 2008). Companies that do not face significant legal liability have greater leeway in offering illicit payments and are maybe more competitive in particular markets. So, much like a regional trade agreement, trade with firms from strong enforcement states is easier with low-corruption states. Firms from weak-enforcement states might find better opportunities in higher-corruption states.

Although foreign corruption concerns only seriously entered public debate in the last forty years, international trade law has existed in various forms through history. The modern multilateral trade system came into being in the post–World War II economic and political reconstruction of international institutions. The most important trade institution was the General Agreement on Tariffs and Trade (GATT), a set of barebones negotiating principles designed to structure countries' efforts to reduce trade barriers. Interestingly, the United States and other governments expected that the GATT would be an interim agreement. It was supposed to be replaced by the International Trade Organization (ITO), the trade institution that would stand alongside the other institutions of the postwar order, including the United Nations, the Bank for Reconstruction and Development (now the World Bank), and the International Monetary Fund. The ITO included a host of substantive agreements, as well as a robust organization staff and a dispute resolution system. However, the charter for the ITO failed to achieve a consensus among countries. When the US government announced that it would not support the ITO, the hopes for an advanced trade institution collapsed and the GATT became the default framework for trade agreement (Jackson 1998).

As a set of bargaining rules, the GATT emphasized two nondiscrimination principles as the basis for country-to-country negotiations: Most Favored Nation (MFN) and National Treatment. The MFN principle requires states to extend the lower tariff rates they offer one country to all GATT countries (so it is an "external" nondiscrimination principle between GATT members). This rule shaped bargaining because it eliminated certain deals. GATT countries could not make exclusively bilateral trades. Instead, any agreement had to be extended to other GATT states. This rule arguably broadened the benefits of trade concession to all GATT members, but it decreased the bargaining power of smaller countries. The GATT parties included an exception to this principle for preferential trading agreements, such as the then nascent European Communities and British Commonwealth preferences, so that

GATT countries could offer certain trading partners lower tariff rates than they offered other GATT countries.

The other major bargaining principle, National Treatment, requires countries to treat imported goods the same as domestic goods once the importer has paid the tariff. This is an "internal" nondiscrimination principle between domestic and imported goods—countries cannot subject imports to different regulatory requirements or tax systems. For instance, countries cannot require that imports be sold in "imports-only stores" or charge imports a higher sales tax.

International trade law under the GATT advanced by consecutive trade rounds. Countries would meet and hammer out lower tariff rates based on reciprocal concessions. The international trade system did not have an international organizational structure as other institutions did (such as the United Nations Secretary General, Security Council, and General Assembly). This changed in 1995, when the Uruguay Round of trade negotiations created the World Trade Organization (WTO), which incorporated the GATT, and other substantive agreements, and provided the trade system with a formal organization and an explicit dispute settlement system.

On the whole, international trade agreements do not directly regulate private actors. Trade agreements provide a framework to coordinate multiple states' tariff and regulatory policies in a manner that permits greater private (or public) international commerce. Trade scholars generally say that international trade promotes development by allowing all states to gain from trade, although there are some dissenting voices here (Rodrik 1997).

International anticorruption law also aims to promote development, primarily through discouraging government officials from making market interventions that promote the officials' personal interests rather than the country's interest. Unlike trade, corruption has traditionally been viewed as a domestic issue, not one that is a natural fit for international negotiations. As a result, interstate anticorruption agreements are a relatively new area for interstate cooperation that does not have international trade's history as a core area of international law or a formal organization. This body of law takes the form of state-to-state agreements to adopt certain foreign antibribery policies. Like international trade, the obligation is on states to coordinate their own laws, and these laws form a framework that structures how private actors engage with international markets.

There are two main interstate bribery situations (although the list of possible bribes is much longer). The first is where a private firm is bidding for a government contract (e.g., building a power plant) or government license (e.g., to offer broadband access). The government is going to award the contract or license to only a limited number of firms. Companies may pay a bribe to make sure that their bid for the contract or license is accepted. The second situation is tax or regulatory avoidance. Imagine that a firm is importing rice into Haiti and owes $100,000 in customs duties on that rice. The firm might try to bribe customs officials $10,000 to underreport the amount of rice imported and decrease the tax bill to $50,000—"saving" it $40,000 in the process (but depriving the local government of $50,000 in tax revenue). The FCPA makes both of these types of payments illegal, even if this is the way business is done in the country. There is not an "everyone does it" defense, although a payment may be legally permitted under the written laws of the host state.[3] Similarly, the FCPA does not excuse bribes if the government official demanded one as the price of doing business in the state. In short, the statute imposes civil and criminal liability on private actors operating in foreign markets if they offer bribes, even if the host government is highly unlikely to punish them.

The prohibition against offering a bribe is robust. First, the definition of a government official is broad. It includes high-level and low-level officials and can include employees of state-owned enterprises, political parties, and candidates for office. Private actors cannot simply funnel money to the official's family or favorite organizations. In a well-publicized case, J. P. Morgan entered into a settlement with US authorities regarding the bank's practice of hiring the children of high-ranking Chinese government officials who could steer business to the bank. J. P. Morgan paid a $264 million settlement and ended its so-called princeling initiative (Lynch, Hughes, and Arnold 2016).

The definition of a bribe is also very broad. The FCPA language covers offering "anything of value" as a bribe if it is offered with corrupt intent. Thus the definition is not limited to cash payments, and can include a wide array of benefits, such as luxury travel, aid in getting a government official's child into college, or paying for the wedding of a government official's children. The breadth of the "anything of value" definition is often criticized by businesses that claim that it creates potential liability for normal gift giving and hospitality (Salbu 2001). American government officials emphasize the corrupt-intent element and have issued statutory guidance that explicitly allows moderate tokens of esteem, such as giving a crystal vase at the wedding of a client's child (US DOJ and US SEC 2012).

Governments have entered into international agreements to mutually enact these types of laws. The most famous anticorruption agreement is the

OECD Anti-Bribery Convention, in which all of the members of the OECD (and several additional states) have outlined the minimum requirements for their own antibribery laws. These laws generally include imposing deterrence-level civil and criminal penalties on private actors who bribe in foreign states. There is also the United Nations Convention Against Corruption (UNCAC), which is broader in scope but has weaker language in terms of legal obligations (Rose 2015).

Like international trade law, international anticorruption law seeks to open markets by creating conditions where private actors compete on a "market-basis" (meaning price and quality) rather than by bribing government officials. Its goal is also to promote international development by drying up the source of bribes that hampers international economic development, diverts state revenues, and hurts government accountability.

Intersecting Legal Spaces

This section explores the transmission of the American FCPA to the international system. The international legal system does not have an exclusive, centralized means of creating legal obligations, instead allowing a diversity of legal institutions to gestate without obvious coordination. I first describe this so-called fragmentation of international law (often identified as an element in international complexity [Alter and Meunier 2009]) and examine how it can create overlapping but different rules and processes. Next, I turn to the United States' attempt to incorporate anticorruption rules in international trade law and its turn to an alternative forum after that failure.

Fragmentation in International Law

The international legal system hosts a wide range of intersecting and overlapping legal spaces. As a general matter, there is a not a hierarchy in international legal obligations. States form thousands of treaties with one another, and each one is equally legally binding on the ratifying states. The vast majority of these treaties do not have provisions to address "conflicts" with other treaties. As such, the treaties coexist on equally legally binding terms without clear mechanisms for reconciling varying obligations (Michaels and Pauwelyn 2011).

The term *conflict* here refers to the idea that treaties may address the same issue and have different substantive provisions (Born and Rutledge 2007). The difference in substance does not necessarily mean that the treaties are in opposition. Rather, the treaties' substantive terms overlap in an issue area and provide the ratifying states with more or fewer legal obligations. For instance, an environmental treaty may give states the possibility of choosing policies A, B, or C and require that they consult with other ratifying states, and a trade treaty may give the states an option of policies A, B, or D and obligate states to resolve differences through binding arbitration. Here, there is a conflict of law—the legal regimes regulate intersecting legal spaces with varying rules. States can comply with both treaties—so long as the states select policies A or B, consult with other states, and resolve their disputes through arbitration, then both treaties' legal obligations are met. Yet each treaty hems in the other—eliminating C and D as policy options—and thereby creating "conflict." The international legal system is further complicated by the fact that different states will be party to varying treaty regimes. As a result, the set of legal obligations a state has will vary between treaty parties.

In most situations, treaties will not be in direct opposition, but conflicts can arise where the state faces legal obligations that cannot be reconciled. The environmental treaty can demand that states ban the import of certain pesticides, and the trade treaty can demand that states not ban the pesticide unless there is sufficient scientific evidence that the pesticide is harmful. If the trade dispute resolution system determines that sufficient scientific evidence does not currently exist to justify a ban, then a state that is party to both treaties can face a nonreconcilable legal conflict. States still have legal options here: They can seek to amend or exit from one of the treaties. Alternatively, they can obey one agreement and offer compensation as a remedy to the breach of the other treaty (if that is permissible under the remedy rules of one of the agreements).

The uncoordinated manner in which international legal obligations can come into existence and create intersecting legal spaces is referred to in legal parlance as *fragmentation*. In effect, treaties are bilateral or multilateral contracts between states. Any two states can create new legal obligations between themselves regardless of the existing legal regimes already filling that space and without the consent of any other states that might be affected by their agreement. This system is described as fragmented because there is no coordinated (let alone hierarchical) manner in which new legal obligations are integrated into a coherent and consistent set of legal rules. The system does not have mechanisms for prioritizing competing goals, either through the lawmaking process (state centered) or through a quasi-judicial process (court centered).

Fragmentation is in some part accidental. States create legal obligations in specific issue areas and do not anticipate the conflicts that will arise between different regimes. By the time that the conflict becomes apparent, the treaties are difficult to renegotiate. The two treaty regimes both remain in place, and the parties informally attempt to manage the varying legal obligations.

Fragmentation, however, is also in no small part a contest between states to push for the dominance of their preferred legal rules (Benvenisti and Downs 2007). New treaty regimes—or new iterations of existing treaty regimes—often purposefully include the topics covered by other treaties as a means to drive legal developments in particular directions (Keohane and Victor 2011). This type of fragmentation is often referred to as "forum shopping" because states attempt to move issues to various fora to achieve their preferred mix of substantive law, legal coverage (the states governed by the treaty), and procedural protections.

The most well-documented fight over legal fragmentation has occurred in the area of intellectual property (Helfer 2004; Sell 2003). This episode is worth recounting briefly because it provides such a clear example of how fragmentation occurs and the policy impact that it can have (Sell and May 2001). It also offers a contrast to American efforts to incorporate anticorruption law in the GATT. Before 1995, intellectual property rules had been addressed at the international level through stand-alone treaties on individual issue areas. The Berne Convention of 1886 covered copyright, and the Paris Convention of 1883 covered patent, trademark, and other industrial designs. In 1967, the administration of these treaties (and other intellectual property treaties) was placed under the auspices of the World Intellectual Property Organization (WIPO), a United Nations–sponsored organization (May 2009).

From the point of view of developed countries, whose corporations were generally the holders of intellectual property rights, WIPO had considerable disadvantages as a host forum for intellectual property. First, the membership of WIPO was not particularly broad. Many developing countries did not join the agreement because they were simply not interested in adopting intellectual property laws. WIPO did not offer any non-intellectual-property benefits to countries, so there were few incentives to join. Second, WIPO functioned on a consensus basis. This made developed countries' efforts to increase standards for intellectual property protection difficult to achieve.

Developing countries, which generally preferred lower protections, could simply block efforts to raise protections. Third, WIPO did not have a robust enforcement mechanism. Disagreements between countries concerning their domestic enforcement of intellectual property laws were resolved through consultations (Dreyfuss and Lowenfeld 1997). Naturally, for developing countries, which generally preferred the status quo in intellectual property, WIPO was a good (if not ideal) organization because it allowed them to maintain their current levels of protection.

In the early 1990s, developed countries, particularly the United States and the European Community, made a concerted push to shift the forum for intellectual property from WIPO to the GATT/WTO regime.[4] During the Uruguay Round of GATT negotiations (which created the WTO), developed countries started to draft the Agreement on Trade-Related Aspects of Intellectual Property Rights (TRIPS). The TRIPS Agreement required that all members adopt a minimum level of protection of intellectual property, although states retained the discretion to provide more generous levels of protection. The minimum level, in fact, was quite high in the sense that it reflected American and European intellectual property standards (e.g., fifty years for copyright and twenty years for patent). Developing countries objected loudly and frequently to the content of the TRIPS Agreement (that is, the mandatory high level of intellectual property protection) and the form of the agreement (that a trade agreement should address intellectual property law). India and Brazil, in particular, vigorously rejected the agreement and announced that they would not join.

The United States and the European Community made two tactical decisions in the Uruguay Round negotiations that effectively left other countries with the decision to join the new WTO (with the TRIPS Agreement) or lose any preferential market access under the GATT regime (Steinberg 2002). The first tactical choice was to bind all of the new trade agreements negotiated in the Uruguay Round together into a "single undertaking." Countries could not choose which agreements they wanted to join, it was an all-or-nothing affair. Nonetheless, many developing countries looked as if they might vote no and simply retain their existing treaty commitments under the GATT regime. A no vote would allow developing countries to maintain their current level of access to other GATT country markets but forego any new obligations or benefits from the Uruguay Round's agreements.

The second tactical move was designed to raise the costs of voting no for developing states by decreasing their access to American and European markets. The United States and the European Community together withdrew from the existing GATT treaty (referred to as GATT 1947). In doing so, they ended their legal obligations to grant existing GATT members preferential access to their markets. The United States and the European Community joined the WTO's agreement covering goods (referred to as GATT 1995), which would reestablish the GATT's preferential access to their markets for all WTO members. However, only countries that joined the WTO—including all of the other agreements such as TRIPS—could join GATT 1995. In short, to keep existing GATT access to American and European markets, developing countries had to join the WTO and accept TRIPS. Brazil and India ended up joining the WTO, notwithstanding their resistance to TRIPS. China was not part of these negotiations. It acceded to the WTO (including the TRIPS Agreement) in 2001.

This shift in legal landscape had a notable impact on the substance and form of international intellectual property law. By fragmenting the intellectual property regime, the United States and the European Community were able to raise the floor for minimum national laws, increase the number of states that were required to adopt these laws, and increase the sanctions for violating intellectual property rules. This was arguably not a normatively positive development; a number of commentators have described it as a transfer of wealth from poor to rich countries (Bhagwati 2002; Gerhart 2007; Reichman and Dreyfuss 2007; Yu 2007). Yet, the ability of powerful states to select the institutional fora for various issues has had a notable effect on the content, development, and enforcement of the issue.[5]

Fragmentation in International Anticorruption Law

When first conceived, foreign anticorruption law did not fit neatly into international economic law. The US Congress was the first national body to pass a foreign anticorruption law, which it did in the aftermath of the Watergate scandal in 1977. Members of Congress understood foreign anticorruption efforts to be primarily a national security issue. In the midst of the Cold War, Congress viewed the behavior of American corporations in foreign markets through a security lens because it reflected on the desirability of the Western capitalist system. American foreign policy was in no small part based on promoting a free-market ideology that was heavily based on corporations as the primary economic actors. Reports of American corporations bribing foreign government officials undermined American foreign policy goals (Grimm 2010; Koehler 2012).

The framing of foreign anticorruption laws as an economic issue—that is, the regulation on American corporations' means of engaging in international commerce—became dominant only after the passage of the FCPA. By the early 1980s, many American corporations were complaining that the unilateral measure hampered their ability to compete in foreign markets, particularly in areas of government procurement (e.g., aerospace, construction, military arms). The newly elected Reagan administration commissioned a General Accounting Office report that highlighted that the competitive costs of the FCPA. This shift in emphasis from national security to economic disadvantage cast anticorruption measures in more of a trade light. American businesses focused their lobbying attention on either extending the reach of these prohibitions to other major exporting states or repealing the measure (Gutterman 2015).[6]

The Reagan administration made a concerted effort to integrate anticorruption principles into the GATT (Abbott and Snidal 2002). The US argument for the inclusion of anticorruption principles was straightforward. International trade rules existed to provide a framework for the opening of foreign markets and provide "equal" terms for competition in those markets. The toleration of private bribery of government officials fundamentally distorted the terms of competition and deprived states (and their nationals) of the bargained-for benefits of the trade agreement. Private actors did not have access to "equal" terms of competition if bribes (rather than price and quality) would determine who had access to a market or who would provide goods and services. To preserve the integrity of the benefits of the trade agreement, the United States argued that the GATT parties should include provisions that required governments to prohibit their corporations from engaging in foreign bribery, just as governments prohibited their corporations from engaging in domestic bribery.

Beyond the framing argument, the pragmatic case for inclusion of anticorruption measures into the GATT regime was an attempt to lessen the economic costs of the legislation for American firms. Much like the push to move intellectual property into the WTO, the effort to include anticorruption law in the GATT was aimed at extending the coverage of anticorruption laws to a broader set of economic actors. Incorporation into the GATT regime would have established a minimum level of national legislation for all GATT members, which included all developed states and most emerging markets. This would have decreased the costs of the FCPA to American firms as it would have bound their global competitors to similar rules. In addition, anticorruption policy would be part of the trade issues package. If a GATT government failed to enforce its own anticorruption policy, then this would be considered a breach of trade rules. At a minimum, GATT members would have a forum to discuss each other's enforcement of trade law as a commercial issue. If such discussions were not fruitful, then GATT members could use formal dispute resolution procedures to highlight each other's enforcement policies and potentially withdraw trade benefits.

The US push to include anticorruption rules in the GATT regime was met with significant resistance from other members. On one level, there was a norm within GATT negotiations of "trading" for progress on specific issues (Abbott 2001). If a government wanted to include a new issue in trade negotiations, then it would have to offer a concession in another area. This was most common in tariff negotiations. If a state wanted a partner to open its market to a category of goods (e.g., beef), then it would have to provide greater access to its own market in another category (e.g., rice). The United States was unwilling to make such a trade with regard to anticorruption principles: It viewed this not as a concession for others to open their markets but as a principle of market competition that was fundamental to global commerce.

On another level, opposition to the US push for the GATT was mercantilist. In the view of many European governments, the United States had adopted a naïve policy that happened to advantage European firms (Tarullo 2003). At the time, most of these governments not only permitted foreign bribery but also subsidized it by making bribe payments a tax-deductible business expense (Pieth 1997). Many European firms had started to rely on their ability to bribe foreign government officials as a means of countering American foreign policy power in aerospace and military arms markets. For instance, Frank Vogl (2012, 181) describes how many firms viewed bribery as a leveling device, recounting that:

> Swedish diplomats explained to me . . . that it was all very well and good for the United States to tell its arms manufacturers not to pay foreign bribes while at the same time deploying the huge power of the White House and U.S. embassies around the world to twist the arms of host governments to buy American goods. . . . Similar attitudes prevailed in many European governments. A senior French official told me that in the arms industry the French were forced to use bribes to

compete with the major American companies, which received huge subsidies from the Pentagon and the U.S. Export-Import Bank.

Against this backdrop, governments' resistance to incorporating anticorruption principles was simply a matter of retaining their competitive position in foreign markets. The lack of agreement between the major GATT powers—the United States, the European Community, and Japan—on anticorruption doomed corruption negotiations, where unity among these powers had led to success in the intellectual property area.

One of the characteristics of the international legal system is that failure in one forum does not necessarily indicate an inability to create binding international rules. Rather, multiple fora can create equally legitimate and binding rules, although each forum brings a different set of attributes, such as membership, issue linkage, and dispute settlement possibilities. Multiple agreements can create laws governing the same issue space. However, there is often variance in the membership of the agreements (the parties bound by the agreement), the content of the laws, and the remedies for breach. In addition, there are dynamic aspects to legal development. Embedding a rule in one regime over another can have a path-dependent influence, as the regimes develop in different directions. The ultimate failure to integrate anticorruption principles into the GATT regime did not thwart the project but created a need for the US government to seek an alternative forum to articulate these principles.

The lack of success in the GATT forum stalled the advancement of foreign anticorruption principles for over a decade.[7] By the mid-1990s, however, the United States made another push for extending the anticorruption rules to other major exporting states. Under the Clinton administration, the US government began negotiations at the OECD for a standalone foreign antibribery agreement. Instead of nesting anticorruption in broader trade issues, the United States determined that casting anticorruption as a good corporate governance issue would make the acceptance of these rules more palatable to partner states. Changes in the prevailing views about corruption had also changed in the period between the 1980s and mid-1990s, which made tolerance of foreign bribery less acceptable (Abbott and Snidal 2002). This aided American efforts (Tarullo 2003). The OECD had long produced nonbinding good governance guidelines for regulating international business, and anticorruption was initially framed in these terms. Eventually, the working draft took on a legally binding requirement, in part due to the US preference for a hard law agreement, in part as a credible commitment among member states, and in part due to changing views of the costs of corruption (Abbott and Snidal 2002; Tarullo 2003).

The consequences of addressing foreign anticorruption law in the OECD rather than in the GATT/WTO were both static and dynamic. In the immediate term, the number of states that became obligated to adopt foreign antibribery laws was far more limited in the OECD than the GATT/WTO. OECD states represent the major exporters of high-value goods and services and thus cover the highest capitalized multinational corporations doing business globally—Siemens, General Electric, Royal Dutch Shell, Boeing, and Airbus—but the OECD does not necessarily cover younger firms in emerging markets, particularly China and India. By contrast, the GATT/WTO has much broader membership, and thus embedding the rules in this forum would have broadened the number of governments adopting these laws.

The Topography of Anticorruption in Transnational Law

International trade rules and international anticorruption rules have very different geographic scopes. Trade agreements generally apply only to the states that join the agreements. By contrast, anticorruption rules apply wherever the private actors of the contracting countries do business. In addition, the enforcement of trade rules is robust and centralized, while the enforcement of anticorruption rules is much more diffuse. In this section, I explore the implications of these different structures.

The approach of international trade law is to treat "market access rights" as available only to members. Restated, the rules of the treaty apply only to countries that have joined the club. States outside of the agreement do not necessarily get any benefits.[8] Thus the WTO's nondiscrimination rules (MFN and National Treatment) demand nondiscrimination only between members, not between all states.

The WTO system is also highly centralized in terms of dispute resolution and enforcement. The WTO's formal quasi-judicial process, the Dispute Settlement Understanding, has compulsory jurisdiction for all WTO members on any issue of international trade law. WTO countries can (and do) sue one another for alleged violations of the WTO rules. The system has a permanent chamber of appellate judges ("Appellate Body members" in WTO terms) that provide authoritative interpretations of the WTO agreements and adjudicate disputes.

Enforcement of WTO judgments functions through the threat of exclusion from trade benefits. A country (or countries) can file a trade dispute against a respondent country for an alleged violation of trade law rules. If the WTO finds the respondent country to be in breach, then the respondent country has the opportunity to eliminate the breach without offering compensation to the complaining country for the injury that the breach may have caused. If the responding country fails to cure the breach, however, then the complaining country can withdraw access to its market from the respondent state. For instance, the Canadian government recently threated to impose close to a billion dollars in lost market access on the United States by banning the import of a range of American goods after the United States had failed to comply with a WTO judgment. All of the goods that the Canadian government selected were goods produced in the districts of power members of Congress—the retaliation was more about political pain than economic rebalancing (Bown and Brewster 2017).

Only governments can sue or be sued at the WTO. Private actors do not have standing to bring cases. If a private actor believes that a country is violating trade rules, that actor must convince its home government or another government to bring a case. The private actor cannot do so on his or her own. Trade obligations also only apply to government policy, and thus private actors cannot violate trade rules.

There are cases that push the edges of this hard delineation between private and public actors in international trade law. First, some regional agreements incorporate dispute settlement mechanisms that give private actors standing for some specific issue areas. The most notable area is international investment law, which provides foreign investors with the ability to sue governments for the expropriation of their property or other discriminatory treatment. This allows private actors standing for specific claims but not all trade rules (van Aaken 2008; Yackee 2009).

Second, the status of a corporation as a private entity, rather than a public body, is itself a slippery concept. Many of the largest corporations are state-owned (or state-controlled) enterprises, and their access to international trade institutions may be functionally the same as the state's. In addition, countries can be liable for actions of state-owned enterprises as government entities. For instance, the WTO's subsidies agreement explicitly considers the possibility that state-owned enterprises may be the source of prohibited or actionable subsidies that could be challenged by other member countries.

Nonetheless, international trade rules can still be classified as generally in the category of state-to-state rules. International trade rules are primarily aimed at governing state actions (such as regulations and tariff policy), and standing to raise trade disputes is generally restricted to the member countries' national governments.

International anticorruption law takes a much more decentralized, geographically broad, and unilateral legal approach. First, each state adopts laws aimed at private actors (individuals and corporations) that the state has jurisdiction over and then applies that jurisdiction everywhere in the world that the actor does business. In the United States, the claim of jurisdiction over natural and legal persons is very broad. It includes any American citizen, resident alien, or corporation that is incorporated or has its primary place of business in the United States, and any corporation that lists on an American stock exchange (including secondary listings) (Low, Sprange, and Barutciski 2010). Any employee or agent of an American corporation (or foreign corporation that lists on an American exchange) who offers a bribe to a government official anywhere in the world is liable under the FCPA. The unrestricted range of the statute makes it a geographically broader regime than international trade. Unlike trade, anticorruption law does not require treaty membership for the law's application.

Second, there is almost no formal state-to-state enforcement of treaty obligations. Unlike the WTO's well-developed legal system, neither the OECD Anti-Bribery Convention nor the UNCAC offer a judicial process where countries can challenge one another's compliance with the treaty's requirements. Rather, the systems rely on monitoring reports. In the OECD context, these reports have actually been influential. The OECD has been less than diplomatic in criticizing some members' lackluster efforts (Spahn 2012). In addition, the OECD reports highlight specific areas where national law is lacking and make fine-grained legal suggestions to improve performance.

Nonetheless, member governments do not face the threat of sanctions or other material harm if they fail to comply with the terms of the agreement. As a result, enforcement of the regime is quite decentralized. Almost all states have agreed—in principle—to adopt domestic anticorruption rules (from the UNCAC), and several states have a binding obligation to adopt these rules (from the OECD Anti-Bribery Convention), but rates of enforcement of these domestic laws vary tremendously across states.

The institutional structures are thus quite different. The trade regime resembles more of a tightly closed circle. The rules apply only in the territory of the member states, and only members may benefit from the regime. The robust enforcement mechanisms provide high levels of compliance with trade rules. By contrast, the anticorruption regime resembles overlapping fishing nets, woven at different strengths, emanating from national capitals. States need not be party to the treaty to be covered by the regime, and there is little connecting the national regimes.

These different institutional paths have shaped the current regime, both imposing limits on the nascent anticorruption regime but also freeing its development from some of the more restrictive aspects of the WTO regime.

The inclusion of anticorruption rules in the WTO might have provided for a more rigorous enforcement. The WTO has a strong third-party dispute resolution process where governments have committed to adjudicating almost all trade disputes. The WTO also has a remedy regime that allows complaining states to suspend trade concessions against states breaching their obligations. Certainly, national enforcement of domestic laws on anticorruption has been weak. Transparency International, which monitors states' compliance with antibribery laws, reports that only four OECD states are "robust" enforcers, and the majority of states have weak to no enforcement (Transparency International 2015). These numbers are somewhat misleading because the largest three exporters—the United States, Germany, and the United Kingdom—are all robust enforcers, so many of the largest exporting corporations are covered. In addition, American prosecutions are often extraterritorial and target non-American firms. As a result, many corporations in the OECD face liability for overseas bribery even if their own government is a weak enforcer (Choi and Davis 2014; Garrett 2011). However, the fact remains that weak enforcement continues to be a concern for the OECD treaty.

Nonetheless, the WTO dispute resolution mechanism probably would not have provided a powerful lever for monitoring and adjudicating other states' enforcement of their anticorruption laws. Having a third-party forum where neutral judges can review a state's compliance with international obligations encourages more states to bring complaints (where complaints are warranted) because there is a higher expectation that there will be some remediation of the policy. This expectation often does not exist in more diplomatic- and negotiation-based fora, and thus some good-faith complaints are simply never made. However, the WTO system has its own limits. Judges tend to review states' official policies for consistency with WTO rules and are reluctant to pass judgment on issues such as the level of effort and resources that a government should invest in a policy, which is perceived as more of a political decision. As a result, the WTO system might provide more leverage for ensuring that a state has the correct law on the books but little meaningful review of the implementation of these policies. Presently, most OECD states have adequate laws on the books, but are simply weak enforcers of these laws. Thus WTO review might have been less searching than necessary to ensure the meaningful domestic enforcement of anticorruption rules.

In a more dynamic sense, however, the OECD forum has provided some unique benefits. The first is that the OECD has isolated anticorruption as its own issue, not linked to other topics. Although "issue linkage" has traditionally been seen as an advantage of international organizations (Abbott and Snidal 1998; Keohane 1984), issue independence can allow policies to remain free from group negotiations. This has turned out to be a notable advantage of the OECD forum. The OECD Anti-Bribery Convention has not been revised, but the OECD has issued several important recommendations on the convention's interpretation and implementation, all of which require state agreement. By comparison, the WTO as a negotiating forum has been mired in gridlock for well over two decades now. The organization's large membership is an advantage for the coverage of existing agreements, but it makes forming new agreements quite difficult. The growing power of the emerging markets, particularly India, Brazil, and China, has diversified the range of trade philosophies in negotiations and made finding areas of agreement harder.

Possibly more importantly, the OECD treaty has allowed foreign anticorruption to maintain its character as a regulatory/criminal law issue rather than a trade issue. The OECD treaty has a working group made up of national prosecutors who specialize in bringing antibribery prosecutions in domestic courts. This keeps the focus on issues of criminal law, evidence gathering, and settlement negotiations. Prosecutors can share best practices and have the practical background to criticize or praise one another's enforcement efforts. This is clearly superior from an enforcement view to having a working group made up of trade negotiators, who have less experience in domestic prosecutions and may look to trade off anticorruption enforcement for other unrelated trade issues.

Finally, the framing of anticorruption as a criminal or regulatory issue permits greater extraterritorial enforcement. The United States currently prosecutes both domestic and foreign firms for corrupt practices in foreign markets. Extraterritorial prosecutions can be controversial as an overreach of a state's jurisdictional powers. However, the OECD Anti-Bribery Convention diffused any controversy in this area by explicitly encouraging states to adopt the broadest possible jurisdictional grounds for anticorruption prosecutions. This jurisdiction provision, along with provisions requiring mutual legal assistance, legitimated extraterritorial prosecutions, particularly where the bribing party's home state failed to take action. In fact, the United States did not seriously start enforcing the FCPA until 1998, after the signing of the OECD treaty. The treaty played a critical political role by allowing American prosecutors to pursue a wide range of domestic and foreign corporations and, thereby, make the enforcement of the statute competition-neutral for domestic firms (and thus more politically tolerable) (Brewster 2017).

Within the trade law realm, unilateral and extraterritorial actions are much less accepted. One of the fundamental principles of trade law is that states should abstain from unilateral action and instead seek multilateral consensus, particularly where a foreign firm or a foreign market is involved. The history of the United States adopting unilateral trade measures (particularly through the use of Section 301; see Bhagwati 1990) makes the extraterritorial enforcement of anticorruption law a particularly sensitive area and could lead to a strong backlash from trade partners. In short, American anticorruption enforcement through extraterritorial means may have been curtailed at the WTO because it might be understood as a unilateral measure. Thus the framing of anticorruption enforcement as a criminal law matter, rather than a trade measure, could be partly responsible for the US current robust enforcement of antibribery laws.

Conclusion

The selection of the OECD as a forum for anticorruption law rather than the GATT/WTO was not a decision initially preferred by American negotiators, but it has fundamentally shaped the character of the anticorruption regime. The GATT/WTO regime potentially offers a more robust international enforcement regime, including trade sanctions for failing to enact anticorruption rules. The OECD treaty, however, has allowed the anticorruption regime to maintain its character as a national criminal and regulatory law regime. National prosecutors run the OECD working group, and enforcement is still based on cases brought in domestic courts. The transnational regime supports national enforcement policies, and national cases remain the core source of enforcement and development of transnational law.

The relationship between the national and transnational in anticorruption law is mutually supporting and multidirectional. The US passage of the FCPA created a demand in American politics to extend the ban on individuals and corporations offering bribes in foreign countries to more states and, thereby, more competitors. Search for an international forum took decades. In the interim, American prosecutors faced political resistance to robustly enforcing the statute because of the disadvantage it would create in international commerce. When the OECD treaty entered into force in the late 1990s, the treaty not only represented a more general international consensus on the harms of engaging in foreign corruption but permitted American prosecutors to increase their own domestic and extraterritorial enforcement. The treaty legitimated a much more expansive jurisdiction for American prosecutors and provided national industry with some reassurance that a more aggressive enforcement policy would be neutral to international competition. Here, national politics created the demand that started a decades-long transnational legal process. The outcome of that legal process, in turn, resolved critical political concerns about international competition and created a path for domestic prosecutors to meaningfully enforce their own domestic statute.

Notes

1. The FCPA statute gives American prosecutors jurisdiction over any firm that lists on an American stock exchange or if any part of the bribery scheme occurs in the territory of the United States (Low, Sprange, and Barutciski 2010). The jurisdictional rules have the effect of permitting extraterritorial prosecutions, such as the United States' prosecution of Siemens (a German corporation) for their corrupt practices in Argentina, based on Siemens listing on American securities markets. This broad jurisdictional provision means that any corporation that wishes to access American capital markets is covered by the FCPA. Although this jurisdictional provision existed before the formation of the OECD Anti-Bribery Convention in 1995, American prosecutors could not effectively use it against foreign firms for several reasons, including (1) not being able to collect evidence abroad, (2) threats of political retaliation from other countries if the United States applied its law to foreign firms, and (3) social resistance in other countries to the idea that foreign corruption should be prevented, not encouraged.

2. The combined fines from the top ten FCPA cases before 1995 would not even rank in the top ten fines in the post-1995 FCPA cases (Brewster 2017).

3. There is a gray area for "facilitation payments," often called "grease payments," where a firm can pay for nondiscretionary government services that it is legally entitled to receive. For instance, a firm can pay a government official to get its mail delivered (if that is a government service that everyone is legally entitled to receive), but the firm cannot pay a bribe to avoid paying traffic tickets or for not complying with local regulations.

4. During most of these negotiations, the European Union did not exist yet (it came into existence in November 1993), and the contemporary iteration of the European supranational integration project was the European Economic Community, often called the "European Community." At the GATT (which the EU never formally joined), Europe was referred to as the European Communities; a term that included the European Economic Community, the European Coal and Steel Community, and the European Atomic Energy Community. The European Union only joined the WTO in 2009, and thus all references to the European Union in the WTO from 1995 to 2008 continued to be to the European Communities. For simplicity, I use the term European Community throughout this chapter.

5. Contestation concerning the correct institutional forum for intellectual property decision making continues. Particularly in the area of pharmaceuticals, there continues to be a push to move decision making to the World Health Organization under the rubric of the "Access to Medicines" campaign (Sell 2002).There has been a counterpush to put pharmaceuticals more firmly under trade rules in the "TRIPS Plus" provisions of regional trade agreements.

6. During this period, the U.S. government did not repeal the FCPA, but it simply failed to put significant efforts into enforcing the law. The government brought very few cases and settled those cases on very sympathetic terms.

7. The WTO still does not address corruption. It touches very lightly on it in two agreements—the Government Procurement Agreement (which is optional and only calls for transparency) and the Trade Facilitation Agreement (which is supposed to decrease bribery in collecting customs duties by streamlining the process)—but effectively excludes any discussion of corruption as a barrier to trade.

8. Individual WTO countries have the option to give nonmembers MFN status and thus provide these states with GATT member access to the country's market. This decision is within the discretion of each state.

References

Abbott, Kenneth W. 2001. "Rule-Making in the WTO: Lessons from the Case of Bribery and Corruption." *Journal of International Economic Law* 4:275–296.

Abbott, Kenneth W., and Duncan Snidal. 1998. "Why States Act Through Formal International Organizations." *Journal of Conflict Resolution* 42 (1): 3–32.

Abbott, Kenneth W., and Duncan Snidal. 2002. "Values and Interests: International Legalization in the Fight Against Corruption." *Journal of Legal Studies* 31:S141–S177.

Alter, Karen J., and Sophie Meunier. 2009. "Introduction." In *Symposium—The Politics of International Regime Complexity*, eds. Karen J. Alter and Sophie Meunier. *Perspectives on Politics* 7 (1): 13–24.

Benvenisti, Eyal, and George W. Downs. 2007. "The Empire's New Clothes: Political Economy and the Fragmentation of International Law." *Stanford Law Review* 60 (2): 595–631.

Bhagwati, Jagdish. 1990. "Departures from Multilateralism: Regionalism and Aggressive Unilateralism." *Economic Journal* 100:1304–1317.

Bhagwati, Jagdish. 2002. "Afterword: The Question of Linkage." *American Journal of International Law* 96:126–134.

Born, Gary, and Peter B. Rutledge. 2007. *International Civil Litigation in United States Courts*, 4th ed. New York: Aspen Publishers.

Bown, Chad P., and Rachel Brewster. 2017. "US–COOL Retaliation: The WTO's Article 22.6 Arbitration." *World Trade Review* 16 (2): 371–394.

Brewster, Rachel. 2017. "Enforcing the FCPA: Domestic Strategy and International Resonance." *Virginia Law Review* 103 (8): 1611–1682.

Brewster, Rachel, and Samuel B. Buell. 2017. "The Market for Anticorruption Enforcement." *Law and Contemporary Problems* 80 (193): 193–214.

Choi, Stephen J., and Kevin E. Davis. 2014. "Foreign Affairs and Enforcement of the Foreign Corrupt Practices Act." *Journal of Empirical Legal Studies* 11 (3): 409–445.

Cuervo-Cazurra, Alvaro. 2008. "The Effectiveness of Laws Against Bribery Abroad." *Journal of International Business Studies* 39 (4): 634–651.

Delavallade, Clara. 2006. "Corruption and Distribution of Public Spending in Developing Countries." *Journal of Economics and Finance* 30 (2): 222–239.

Dreyfuss, Rochelle Cooper, and Andreas F. Lowenfeld. 1997. "Two Achievements of the Uruguay Round: Putting TRIPS and Dispute Settlement Together." *Virginia Journal of International Law* 37 (2): 275–334.

Garrett, Brandon L. 2011. "Globalized Corporate Prosecutions." *Virginia Law Review* 97 (8): 1775–1875.

Gerhart, Peter M. 2007. "The Tragedy of TRIPS." *Michigan State Law Review* 143:167–169.

Grimm, Daniel J. 2010. "The Foreign Corrupt Practices Act in Merger and Acquisition Transactions: Successor Liability and its Consequences." *New York University Journal of Law & Business* 7:256–259.

Gutterman, Ellen. 2015. "Easier Done Than Said: Transnational Bribery, Norm Resonance, and the Origins of the US Foreign Corrupt Practices Act." *Foreign Policy Analysis* 11:109–128.

Helfer, Laurence R. 2004. "Regime Shifting: The TRIPs Agreement and New Dynamics of International Intellectual Property Lawmaking." *Yale Journal of International Law* 29:1–83.

Jackson, John Howard. 1998. *The World Trading System: Law and Policy of International Economic Relations.* 2nd ed. Cambridge, MA: MIT Press.

Keohane, Robert O. 1984. *After Hegemony: Cooperation and Discord in the World Political Economy.* Princeton, NJ: Princeton University Press.

Keohane, Robert O., and David G. Victor. 2011. "The Regime Complex for Climate Change." *Perspectives on Politics* 9 (1): 7–23.

Koehler, Mike. 2012. "The Story of the Foreign Corrupt Practices Act." *Ohio State Law Journal* 73 (5): 929–1013.

Low, Lucinda A., Thomas K. Sprange, and Milos Barutciski. 2010. "Global Anti-Corruption Standard and Enforcement: Implications for Energy Companies." *Journal of World Energy Law & Business* 3 (2): 166–213.

Lynch, David, Jennifer Hughes, and Martin Arnold. 2016. "JPMorgan to Pay $264m Penalty for Hiring 'Princelings'." *Financial Times*, 17 November 2016.

Mauro, Paolo. 1998a. "Corruption and the Composition of Government Expenditure." *Journal of Public Economics* 69 (2): 263–279.

Mauro, Paolo. 1998b. "Corruption: Causes, Consequences, and Agenda for Further Research." *Finance and Development* 35 (1): 11–14.

May, Christopher. 2009. "The Pre-History and Establishment of the WIPO." *WIPO Journal* 2009 (1): 16–26.

Michaels, Ralf, and Joost Pauwelyn. 2011. "Conflict of Norms or Conflict of Laws: Different Techniques in the Fragmentation of Public International Law." *Duke Journal of Comparative & International Law* 22 (3): 349–376.

Pauwelyn, Joost. 2013. "Different Means, Same End: The Contribution of Trade and Investment Treaties to Anti-Corruption Policy." In *Anti-Corruption Policy: Can International Actors Play a Constructive Role?*, eds. Susan Rose-Ackerman and Paul D. Carrington, 247–266. Durham, NC: Carolina Academic Press.

Pieth, Mark. 1997. "International Cooperation to Combat Corruption." In *Corruption in the Global Economy*, ed. Kimberly Ann Elliot, 119–131. Washington, DC: Institute for International Economics.

Reichman, Jerome H., and Rochelle Cooper Dreyfuss. 2007. "Harmonization Without Consensus: Critical Reflections on Drafting a Substantive Patent Law Treaty." *Duke Law Journal* 57:85–130.

Reinikka, Ritva, and Jakob Svensson. 2004. "Local Capture: Evidence from a Central Government Transfer Program in Uganda." *Quarterly Journal of Economics* 119 (2): 679–705.

Rodrik, Dani. 1997. *Has Globalization Gone Too Far?* Washington, DC: Institute for International Economics.

Rose, Cecily. 2015. *International Anti-Corruption Norms: Their Creation and Influence on Domestic Legal Systems.* Oxford: Oxford University Press.

Salbu, Steven R. 2001. "Transnational Bribery: The Big Questions." *Northwestern Journal of International Law & Business* 21 (2): 435–70.

Savage, Charlie. 2012. "With Wal-Mart Claims, Greater Attention on a Law." *New York Times,* 25 April 2012.

Sell, Susan K. 2002. "TRIPS and the Access to Medicines Campaign." *Wisconsin International Law Journal* 20 (3): 481–522.

Sell, Susan K. 2003. *Private Power, Public Law: The Globalization of Intellectual Property Rights.* Cambridge: Cambridge University Press.

Sell, Susan, and Christopher May. 2001. "Moments in Law: Contestation and Settlement in the History of Intellectual Property." *Review of International Political Economy* 8 (3): 467–500.

Spahn, Elizabeth K. 2012. "Multijurisdictional Bribery Law Enforcement: The OECD Anti-Bribery Convention." *Virginia Journal of International Law* 53 (1): 1–52.

Steinberg, Richard H. 2002. "In the Shadow of Law or Power? Consensus-Based Bargaining and Outcomes in the GATT/WTO." *International Organization* 56 (2): 339–374.

Tarullo, Daniel K. 2003. "The Limits of Institutional Design: Implementing the OECD Anti-Bribery Convention." *Virginia Journal of International Law* 44 (3): 665–710.

Transparency International. 2015. *Exporting Corruption, Progress Report 2015: Assessing Enforcement of the OECD Convention on Combatting Foreign Bribery.* Berlin: Transparency International.

United States Department of Justice [US DOJ] (Criminal Division) and United States Securities and Exchange Commission [US SEC] (Enforcement Division). 2012. *A Resource Guide to the Foreign Corrupt Practices Act.* Accessed 22 July 2019. www.justice.gov/sites/default/files/criminal-fraud/legacy/2015/01/16/guide.pdf.

Van Aaken, Anne. 2008. "Perils of Success? The Case of International Investment Protection." *European Business Organization Law Review* 9 (1): 1–27.

Vogl, Frank. 2012. *Waging a War on Corruption: Inside the Movement Fight the Abuse of Power.* Lanham, MD: Rowman & Littlefield.

Yackee, Jason Webb. 2009. "Pacta Sunt Servanda and State Promises to Foreign Investors Before Bilateral Investment Treaties: Myth and Reality." *Fordham International Law Journal* 32 (5): 1550–1613.

Yu, Peter K. 2007. "The International Enclosure Movement." *Indiana Law Journal* 82:827–907.

CHAPTER 3

Changing Internally to Engage Externally

China and the WTO Legal System

Gregory Shaffer and Henry Gao

From the perspective of transnational legal ordering, international trade law involves not just law at the international level, but dynamic interactions within states, between states, and with international organizations, implicating international, national, and local law and practice.[1] These interactions drive transnational legal settlement, unsettlement, and change. This chapter assesses the transformations China made in government, academia, law firms, and business to build capacity in trade law and defend its interests in the international legal system. Such investment embedded key parts of the Chinese government and Chinese stakeholders in transnational legal processes of international economic integration and cooperation. It rooted China in an international dispute settlement process through law and a third-party institution.

By transnational legal ordering, we refer to the recursive interaction and impacts of international law, national law, and local practice on each other (Halliday and Shaffer 2015; Shaffer 2013). These impacts involve law, institutions, professions, and professional practices conducted within particular normative frames (Shaffer 2015). The transnational processes encompass both strategic action and social interaction, since any strategic action takes place within existing institutional contexts, and socialization occurs within institutional frames shaped by, and reflecting the positions of, powerful actors. In this sense, transnational legal ordering entails a heightening, not a lessening, of relations of state and nonstate institutions through domestic law (for other scenarios involving domestic investments in transnational law, see Brunnegger; Massoud; and Rodríguez-de-las-Heras Ballell, this volume).

China joined the World Trade Organization (WTO) in December 2001, assuming major legal commitments that significantly affected its internal laws and institutions. WTO rules create an institutional context that plays into law and policy developments within countries like China. The aim of Western countries was to transform China and integrate it into the global economy. Such was the aim of China's leaders as well, although they wished to do so on their own terms, and they faced considerable opposition internally regarding these terms.

After China joined the WTO, the government invested massively in developing legal capacity to adjust to WTO requirements that the United States pressed upon it. In the process, it learned how to defend China's interests through the WTO to use the rules against the United States and European Union. This chapter tells the story of how China became enmeshed in transnational legal processes as it developed legal capacity to handle trade conflicts with the United States and Europe. Within China, actors use international legal norms as leverage to advance internal positions. China's response, in turn, affects American and European perceptions of the legal order, and their responses, in turn, further shape, or possibly erode, the international trade legal order.

Our project on China probes deeply the impact of the international trade law regime on institutions and professions within China, including within government, academia, law firms, business, and private trade associations. To implement its WTO obligations, China made sweeping changes in its legal system. The Chinese government took novel steps to spread understanding of WTO law and dispute settlement throughout society in ways that legitimated norms of litigation. Investment in teaching and research on WTO law brought new approaches such as the case law method for the study of law. Overall, by contributing to the opening up of the economy, and subjecting internal governance to external accountability norms and processes, the WTO increased the overall prominence of the legal profession within China. On the other hand, to preserve its unique political and economic system, China also introduced initiatives that violate WTO disciplines either in letter or in spirit.

This chapter builds on more than a decade of fieldwork and in-depth, semistructured interviews with Chinese officials, academics, and lawyers; foreign lawyers representing China, the United States, the EU, and companies implicated by Chinese practices; members of Chinese think tanks; and Chinese company and industry association representatives. We conducted forty formal interviews with more than sixty individuals in Beijing, Shanghai, Shenzhen, Brussels, Geneva, and Washington, DC. The vast majority of the interviews were with one interviewee, but some interviews included small groups of colleagues in government, law firms, academia, and think tanks. The interviews lasted from one to two hours. We arranged them most frequently in the interviewees' offices, but we also held them in neutral fora such as in restaurants and coffee shops. We conducted the vast majority of the interviews together.[2]

China's Challenges in Joining the WTO

The WTO is conventionally viewed as a creation of the United States and the EU, which harnessed the opportunities provided by greater ideological consensus at the end of the Cold War and the shift toward export-oriented development models to advance liberal trade norms (Barton et al. 2008: 56). While China was one of the founding members of the General Agreement on Tariffs and Trade (GATT) formed after World War II, it withdrew after the communist revolution in 1949 and did not play any role in the multilateral trading system until it sought to resume its membership in 1986.[3] At the time that the WTO agreements were signed in 1994, the United States and the EU collectively represented 56 percent of global GDP in real terms, and 45 percent in terms of purchasing power parity (*Economy Watch* 1994a, 1994b). Because of the importance of their markets, they exercised considerable economic power and leverage during the Uruguay Round negotiations that led to the WTO's creation. Commentators viewed the WTO as a victory of economic liberalism and described it in constitutional terms (Jackson 1998).

In order to join the organization, China agreed to a stringent accession protocol in November 2001 that granted greater rights to other WTO members against China, and reduced China's rights against them, compared to standard WTO rules. China agreed to open its markets, eliminate state monopolies on imports and exports, and significantly change its laws, regulations, and practices. Scores of Chinese officials, judges, and scholars came to the United States for training in WTO law, and scores of experts went to China to teach WTO law under technical assistance and capacity-building initiatives (Asian Development Bank 2001; Yang 2015). The United States and the EU hoped to use China's accession to the WTO to transform China into a market economy, and to encourage it to move toward a liberal democracy. It was a time of US triumphalism.

By 2009, however, following the global financial crisis, the continued rise of China as an economic power, and the significant strengthening of China's legal capacity to defend its interests in WTO dispute settlement and negotiations, the situation had dramatically changed.[4] China felt it had little to learn from the United States and the EU after their economic governance models lost credibility during the 2008 Great Recession. By 2010, China had become the world's second-largest economy, surpassing Japan (Barboza 2010; World Bank 2019). By 2013, it became the world's largest trader in goods, surpassing the United States.

The WTO's Significance for China

Managing its trade relations is crucial not only for China's economic development but also for its political stability. China has a strong state under an authoritarian (formally Marxist) government. The Chinese state invests significantly in industrial policies, ranging from direct state ownership to state subsidization of economic sectors, including (as alleged by the United States and the EU) through state bank financing at lower than market rates, state companies' selling manufacturing inputs at less than market value, and a state innovation policy that promotes indigenous research and development to upgrade China's economy (Wertime 2014). Law and lawyers play increasingly important roles in this mixed economy, whether one views it as "socialist with Chinese characteristics," or "capitalist with Chinese characteristics" (Huang 2008; Kennedy and Stiglitz 2015). Although many commentators maintain there has been a turn away from law in general (Minzner 2011; Peerenboom 2002), business, investment, and trade law flourish, creating new career opportunities for lawyers (Liu, Trubek, and Wilkins 2017).

The WTO system is arguably the most legalized and judicialized area of international relations at the multilateral level. The WTO's complex legal framework includes nineteen main agreements, the *acquis* developed under the GATT since 1948, and the decisions and understandings adopted by various WTO bodies since 1995. The WTO's compulsory dispute settlement system has given rise to more than fifty thousand pages of case reports (over ninety-five thousand when including annexes) developed by WTO dispute settlement panels and the Appellate Body in more than three hundred decisions (and more than four hundred when including compliance- and retaliation-related reports).[5] China had to develop significant legal capacity to engage effectively with the WTO system. It devoted significant resources to build that capacity within the government, academia, law firms, and business. With the use of litigation to solve civil and commercial disputes still developing within the domestic political context and strong deference to the government by the judiciary, building capacity to engage with the WTO represented a new emphasis on the rule of law, even though it was confined to a highly specialized area. It also formed the primary venue for China to engage with international law, as China has remained wary of the International Court of Justice and other international tribunals.

China's Challenges

On 10 November 2001, WTO members approved the terms of China's accession to the WTO at the WTO Ministerial Conference in Doha (WTO 2001). It was a momentous occasion for China. Although there was significant debate in government about the terms of China's accession, there was huge enthusiasm in China after the country joined the WTO (Yang 2015).[6] For the government, it presented an opportunity to showcase its success to engage with the global economic system. The government sponsored numerous WTO-related initiatives, such as the establishment of WTO centers around the country. Thousands of seminars were held and books published on WTO law, arguably constituting more publications on the WTO than the total published elsewhere in the world combined (Qin 2007). In 2003, the government even organized a national contest regarding knowledge of the WTO in which over five million people reportedly participated. The final session broadcast like a game show on China Central Television, and the winner was flown to Geneva to visit the WTO and meet with its director-general (Sun 2011a). Such popular participation in learning technical international law rules is unheard of and, we imagine, would be the envy of international law professors and international law enthusiasts around the world. The government trumpeted China's joining the WTO as leverage to carry out market-oriented reforms and further China's integration into the global economy and global institutions.

China, however, faced daunting challenges in joining the WTO. It agreed to open its economy to competition, and to overhaul its laws, regulations, procedures, and administrative and judicial institutions across all levels of government. It made deep tariff cuts for imports, and it agreed to significantly liberalize services. It agreed that all regulations affecting trade would be nondiscriminatory and that government standard setting would be transparent and based on international standards. It committed to stringent intellectual property protection (Wechsler 2012) and independent review by judicial or administrative tribunals of all trade-related administrative actions.

The country started the complicated process of revising its laws before it formally joined the WTO pursuant to a bilateral agreement with the United States on 15 November 1999. The United States, at the time, wielded significant leverage since it was essentially the gatekeeper to China's WTO accession. To implement the bilateral agreement and China's subsequent WTO commitments, the government established an "Office for the Clean-up of Laws and Regulations" on 1 December 1999, under the auspices of the Ministry of Commerce (then named MOFTEC, or Ministry of Foreign Trade and Economic Cooperation) (Zhang Yuqing Interview 2011). The "clean up" operation was immense, involving bureaucrats at all levels, from the central government to provincial and local administrations. The office first focused on the "clean up" of laws and regulations at the central level, starting with MOFTEC and expanding to other ministries. It then turned to provincial and local regulations. It classified laws and regulations into one of four categories: regulations "to be kept," "to be revised," "to be abolished," and "to be reenacted." Overall, the office reported that it oversaw the "cleaning up" of more than 3,000 laws and regulations, including around 1,150 at the central government level, in order for China to meet its WTO commitments. The office completed its work in around two years, constituting arguably the largest, most condensed exercise of lawmaking and law revision in China's (and perhaps the world's) history.

China's Participation in the WTO over Time

To participate effectively in the multilateral trading system, China invested in building legal capacity. Only then could it attempt to shape the interpretation of WTO law to better protect its access to foreign markets and defend its domestic trade-related policies. Most of its initial programs focused on building the capacity of government officials, but gradually the government turned toward enhancing the capacity of nongovernmental actors since it realized that private actors play important roles at the WTO, particularly in dispute settlement. By 2006, within five years of its accession, China emerged from being a reluctant participant that tried to avoid WTO litigation to being an active and formidable player that uses the system to defend its interests.

In WTO dispute settlement, China started passively. In the first few years, it tried to avoid WTO litigation by settling every WTO complaint brought against it (Gao 2006). As a Chinese official working on WTO matters confirmed in 2003, "China is uncertain about the DSU," "people in government do not like to bring cases," and "they also fear the US bringing cases against them." Thus, the official said that, in line with "Asian values," "you negotiate over disputes; you do not litigate."[7] In the meantime, however, the government invested in learning about the dispute settlement process through attending proceedings as a third party before almost every WTO panel. In the words of another official, China was learning from "the example of the United States and EU."[8] As a result, China has become the fourth-most active WTO participant as a third party after the United States, the EU, and Japan, despite its late accession.

After learning how the dispute settlement system operated, the government became more active as a litigant, first as a respondent and then as a complainant (Gao 2011). Starting with the *China–Auto Parts* case in 2006, China no longer favored settling claims over litigating them, but instead strove to raise strong defenses in almost every case through substantive and procedural arguments. In 2008, its litigation strategy became even more aggressive as it advanced creative interpretations of its accession protocol commitments in order to reduce asymmetries (Gao 2011). As an official told us, this change represented a "transformation for China from the perspective that litigation is not the goal" to one where "we now accept that multilateral dispute settlement process is an appropriate channel for resolving disputes. . . . Although many in government feel shocked that we are a defendant in an international court, and still think that litigation is not good, which is a reflection of our heritage, our culture, we now accept it."[9] The official thought "highly of the system" because it ultimately makes it "easier to settle" disputes thanks to the third-party ruling.

Without building strong capacity in WTO law, China's record would not have been possible. How did China, a country with an antilegalist, Confucian tradition not known for lawyering, a country also facing considerable language barriers in an organization where English is the de facto governing language, build its trade law capacity? What broader effects might those efforts have in embedding international trade law in China? In the following sections, we explain China's strategies, and their potential implications within China.

Building Trade Law Capacity in Government

Even before its accession to the WTO, the Chinese government realized that its lack of legal capacity could be a major challenge. For example, in early 2002, President Jiang Zemin stated that it was inevitable that China would suffer losses in WTO dispute settlements due to its unfamiliarity with WTO rules (Jiang 2006). To prepare China for its postaccession challenges, Jiang urged the government to prioritize the development of a team of professionals well versed in WTO rules, including experts on international trade policy, trade law, trade negotiations, and antidumping investigations. Pursuant to the high-level exhortations, central, provincial, and local government departments invested significantly in WTO-related capacity-building initiatives, expanding the role for lawyers.

In the central government, the State Council and the Central Committee of the Communist Party of China (CPC) issued a joint notice on China's WTO accession to all ministries and provincial governments on 20 November 2001, in which they called for party organs and government organizations at all levels to strengthen the study of WTO rules and the training of WTO experts (Zhonggong Zhongyang Bangongting 2001).[10] Many ministries restructured their internal organization in preparation for the upcoming accession. They worked with MOFTEC to "clean up" laws and regulations to meet China's new obligations and ensure that new laws and regulations would comply with WTO rules.

The government reorganized its lead ministry for international trade and renamed it the Ministry of Commerce (MOFCOM). MOFCOM has a Janus-faced role of looking both inward and outward. Internally, MOFCOM oversees China's compliance with its WTO obligations. Externally, MOFCOM protects China's trading interests abroad, including before the WTO. Following China's accession, MOFCOM (then named MOFTEC) established two new departments to address WTO matters that likewise have Janus-faced missions: the Fair Trade Bureau and the Department of WTO Affairs.

Internally, the Department of WTO Affairs reviews draft Chinese legislation and policy to ensure they are WTO consistent (Ministry of Commerce 2006). Externally, it represents China in WTO negotiations, WTO trade policy reviews, and before WTO committees, where it is responsible for reporting new and amended Chinese regulations as required under the WTO agreements (Li 2011). This dual role enhances its sensitivity to the importance of China's compliance with its WTO commitments since it needs credibility when pressing other countries to meet their commitments toward China.

MOFCOM's Fair Trade Bureau, in parallel, has internal and external responsibilities regarding antidumping, subsidy, and safeguards laws (collectively known as import relief law). Internally, it conducts import relief investigations of foreign products, administering these laws. Externally, it follows foreign import relief investigations of Chinese products (Ministry of Commerce 2006). In this way, it differs from the US Department of Commerce and the EU trade directorate that largely let companies fend for themselves in foreign antidumping and countervailing duty investigations. In contrast, MOFCOM's Fair Trade Bureau spends much of its time helping Chinese exporters in foreign proceedings, including through bilateral bargaining.[11] In particular, MOFCOM always pays the lawyers' fees in foreign countervailing duty investigations to defend Chinese interests.[12] Since most WTO disputes brought by China involve foreign import relief measures, the Fair Trade Bureau must keep abreast of WTO jurisprudence in this area. This dual internal-external role socializes the Fair Trade Bureau in its application of China's import relief laws.

MOFCOM has a separate Department of Treaty and Law (DTL) that is responsible for legal issues in China's international economic relations and handles cases before the WTO dispute settlement system. In 2001, MOFCOM created a division on WTO law within DTL to handle WTO disputes (Li 2011). It established a second DTL division on WTO law in 2009 when China faced a slew of new disputes. The total number of DTL officials dedicated to WTO litigation increased from five to nine (Li 2011). These officials work with China's diplomats responsible for WTO dispute settlement in China's WTO mission in Geneva, so that China has around a dozen officials specializing in WTO dispute settlement in total. China's WTO dispute settlement team enhances lawyers' roles in China's international trade relations.

The GATT requires WTO members to take "necessary measures" to ensure local compliance with GATT obligations (GATT, Article XXIV.12).

China's central government used this provision to try to assert greater control over local actors, which generally is a challenge (Potter 2008). The central government aimed to spur local government officials to become familiar with WTO rules. In February 2002, two months after China's formal WTO accession, the central government held a one-week training course for senior officials at the provincial and ministerial levels (Sun 2011b). The lecturers included President Jiang and Premier Zhu Rongji, as well as high-level officials from MOFCOM and other ministries, highlighting the political importance that the central government wished to convey. The training course explained the main rules in the WTO to senior officials and reminded them that all new laws and regulations needed to be consistent with WTO requirements.

After the training course, many provinces drafted Plans of Actions in response to China's WTO accession (Zhang 2003). A key component was to strengthen trade law capacity. To achieve this objective, local governments established what they called "WTO Centers." Funded by the local governments, these centers are semigovernmental institutions that conduct WTO-related training, research, and outreach activities. In the two to three years before and after China's WTO accession, the centers were the favorite pet projects of ambitious local officials who established them across the country. In 2014, the Shanghai center employed about forty professionals and the Shenzhen center about thirty.[13]

The centers have served important internal and external roles. Internally, when the local government passes a regulation, it is to consult with the local WTO center to confirm that the regulation is WTO consistent, and amend it as needed.[14] This process embeds the international rules within internal policy making. Externally, the centers are to provide information to companies to help them address trade barriers, such as antidumping and countervailing duty investigations, and seizures of goods on intellectual property grounds. As Chinese companies move up the value chain and produce technology-intensive goods, intellectual property issues have become more salient, such as under US Section 337 pursuant to which US customs seizes imported products that allegedly violate US intellectual property rights.[15] The centers also help MOFCOM prepare an annual trade barriers report regarding measures that Chinese exporters face. It is modeled after the annual US National Trade Estimates Report on Foreign Trade Barriers, once more illustrating the influence of US models in transnational legal ordering.[16]

When China first joined the WTO, WTO matters represented the cutting edge for policy, and the leadership spurred officials to exhibit WTO awareness.[17] The WTO "craze" has since faded, in part because of the turn away from multilateral trade negotiations to bilateral and regional ones, and in part because of disenchantment with the WTO given the widespread use of antidumping and other measures against Chinese products.[18] Most provincial and local governments quietly abandoned their WTO centers so that by 2014 only the WTO centers in Beijing, Shanghai, and Shenzhen remained active.[19] These centers broadened their mandates to encompass bilateral and plurilateral trade and investment agreements. For example, in 2012, the Shanghai center established an Institute of Global Trade and Investment under its auspices (Shanghai WTO 2016), and it played an important supporting role in the creation of the China (Shanghai) Pilot Free Trade Zone.[20] In addition, while in the early years, the majority of the Shanghai center's staff had a legal background and focused on WTO implementation, a growing proportion of the staff now has an economic background and provides economic analysis to support bilateral and plurilateral trade and investment negotiations.[21] Although the WTO has declined in relative importance in China, a member of the Shenzhen center told us that in the early years China likely "was overheated about the WTO; right now it is overcooling."[22] The role of international trade law disciplines remain in play.

The US election of President Trump and his trumpeting of economic nationalism and "America First" may deepen these trends. If the United States appears to ignore the multilateral rules, it lessens the pressure on China to conform. At the same time, the WTO rules represent a first recourse defense for China against US unilateralism. Cloaking its national interest within multilateral law and standing alongside other countries to oppose protectionism can strengthen China's international position legally and politically in the face of any new trade barriers that the Trump administration may raise.

WTO Law and Academia

In addition to boosting WTO-related capacity within central, provincial, and local governments, the central government took steps to build the capacities of other actors and incentivize them to invest in developing expertise in WTO law. Through these initiatives, WTO legal norms have diffused into many areas. The capacity-building initiatives spanned academia, law firms, private businesses, and industry associations. We will start by describing the impact on academia, which illustrates longer-term thinking about developing

WTO-related legal capacity and the implications for legal study, research, and practice in China in international economic law.

Teaching and Research

China is an authoritarian regime in which government exercises much influence in academia. With the government's promotion of the WTO's importance for China, WTO law became a popular subject and discipline in Chinese universities. In 2000, the year before China joined the WTO, the government made International Economic Law (which includes WTO law) a mandatory subject on the national bar exam (Ministry of Justice 2000). China's Ministry of Education included International Economic Law (and thus WTO law) as one of sixteen mandatory courses for all Chinese law schools (Ministry of Education 2012). As a result, in most of the more than six hundred law schools in China, there is at least one professor who claims to specialize in WTO law,[23] a much greater number and percentage than in the United States, where the study of WTO law has waned.

Because of the concentration of universities in major cities, the most reputable centers for WTO teaching and research are in cities such as Beijing, Shanghai, Guangzhou, Chongqing, and Xiamen. Many of these specialists teach in the traditional elite law schools, the so-called Five Institutes and Four Departments, which refers to the five independent law institutes and four law departments in comprehensive universities established when the government restructured higher education institutions in 1952. In addition, the government established two main foreign trade institutes in Beijing and Shanghai in 1951 and 1960, respectively, under the auspices of the trade ministry. These elite schools have multiple professors who teach international trade law, including specialized seminars on WTO law and specific topics such as WTO dispute settlement, trade in services, and TRIPS.

Most WTO scholars in China are graduates from these elite law schools, and the leading ones couple their degrees with overseas experience. The foreign study and experience of China's WTO scholars exemplifies the transnational nature of this legal field. Each of the eight Chinese academics on China's Indicative List of WTO Panelists have either studied overseas or been visiting scholars abroad.

Professors teaching WTO law in China have spearheaded use of the case study method in China. China is a civil law country where judges do not create jurisprudence, and it has thus been difficult to adopt the case law method in Chinese law schools. The WTO legal field, however, is completely different. WTO panels and the Appellate Body have decided more than three hundred cases and built an elaborate, evolving jurisprudence. To teach WTO law, Chinese professors thus include cases in the advanced curriculum.

In 2007, the Ministry of Education of China launched a comprehensive teaching reform plan to improve the teaching quality in Chinese universities. One important component of the plan was to develop "Bilingual Courses" that can "substantially improve the English levels of college students in their areas of studies and enhance their capacities to conduct research in English" (Ministry of Education and Ministry of Finance 2007). Among law school subjects, WTO law is considered one of the few that is most suitable for teaching in English. Many law schools thus began to offer courses on WTO law in English in order to build students' English language facility. In turn, this development helped professors and students become more familiar with foreign scholarship on WTO law.

The study of WTO case law could have broad implications on the formation of legal professionals in China, especially those who enter commercial practice, but also those who enter government or become judges. When graduates work in ministries outside of MOFCOM, not only does basic knowledge of WTO law diffuse through the government, but MOFCOM has interlocutors in other ministries acquainted with WTO legal rules and principles. Such diffusion of expertise facilitates compliance with China's WTO commitments and potentially deeper socialization processes regarding trade law principles and legal reasoning.

A senior MOFCOM official stressed to us how the judges of the Supreme People's Court know WTO law.[24] Although the Supreme People's Court rejected proposals that WTO law should be directly applicable before Chinese courts, their rules provide that Chinese law is to be interpreted where possible to comply with WTO requirements.[25] Chinese courts have referenced WTO law in a number of decisions (Cai 2016: 286–287).

China often includes Chinese law professors in its delegations to WTO hearings before panels and the Appellate Body, and they take these experiences back home with them. A law professor attending an Appellate Body hearing, for example, emphasized how quickly and repeatedly the legal issues arose, reflecting more of an "inquisitorial process" involving "common law" reasoning. From the experience of the hearing, he highlighted how "the training of our students should be harder, should be tougher."[26] Another law professor attending a WTO hearing noted that the experience gave him a completely new perspective on the WTO that he brings to his classroom. Now he gives factual scenarios to his students and lets them work through the facts while studying the WTO background rules on their own.[27]

The experiences of Chinese trade law professors abroad shape their teaching. As one law professor noted, "More and more professors in China are trained in the United States," many of whom take a course in international trade law, and these experiences could have significant effects over the next ten to twenty years for law teaching in China.[28] Many of these academics stress that much is at stake in the study of the WTO in China, both for the multilateral trading system and internally within China.[29] The mandatory study of WTO law in Chinese law schools has fostered transnational processes that affect legal training.

To promote research on WTO issues, the government supported the creation of several WTO research associations. The oldest is the Chinese Society of International Economic Law (CSIEL), which was established in 1984 by Professor Yao Meizhen from Wuhan University (C. Wang 2015) and later led by Professor Chen An from Xiamen University (Chinese Society of International Economic Law 2014). When China joined the WTO, the government established the WTO Law Research Society under the auspices of the China Law Society, and it appointed Sun Wanzhong, a former director-general of the Office for Legislative Affairs at the State Council, as its first president. Two years later, MOFCOM established the China Society for World Trade Organization Studies (China Society for World Trade Organization Studies 2013). China's first ambassador to the WTO, Sun Zhenyu, took the helm in 2011, and the society became quite active, organizing many training courses and research projects.

In addition to the formal research societies, entrepreneurial individuals have established informal networks to exchange views on WTO law. Yang Guohua, now a law professor at Tsinghua University, established an e-mail list entitled "Academic Circle on WTO" and a WeChat group named "Rule of Law Utopia" when he was deputy director-general in DTL. Most of China's leading WTO scholars are members of these groups, and they often engage in heated discussions on cutting-edge issues in WTO law.

In 2010, the WTO Secretariat launched the WTO Chairs Programme, which aims to enhance knowledge of the WTO and the international trading system among academics and policy makers in developing countries through curriculum development, research, and outreach by universities and research institutions. The secretariat announced a call for proposals in 2009 and selected the Shanghai Institute of Foreign Trade as one among fourteen centers worldwide. The Shanghai team (which has since changed its name to Shanghai University of International Business and Economics, SUIBE) includes three professors and around twenty researchers. The institute established initiatives on WTO dispute settlement and trade policy review, and it provides translation services for MOFCOM. It partners with the Geneva-based nongovernmental organization International Centre on Trade and Development (ICTSD) to publish a Chinese-language version of ICTSD's periodical on trade law developments, *Bridges*. These initiatives illustrate the broad transnational ties of WTO researchers in China, linking with the WTO Secretariat and other Geneva-based organizations.

Interactions with Government and Law Firms

Chinese law firms and MOFCOM occasionally seek advice from Chinese law professors on international trade matters. They initially did so on an ad hoc basis, such as when an individual official knew a law professor. This practice gradually became institutionalized after MOFCOM organized regular seminars on current WTO cases. The exchanges helped the government tap into academic expertise, and helped the academics keep abreast of legal developments.

In addition to its consultations with academics, MOFCOM runs a formal secondment program for law professors, which it started in 2011.[30] Under the program, MOFCOM selects young academics from elite law schools around the country and assigns them to the Department of Treaty and Law. During their one-year stay, the professors are treated as MOFCOM staff members and conduct research on legal issues and participate in all aspects of the WTO dispute settlement process. MOFCOM invites law professors to observe WTO hearings in Geneva as members of the Chinese delegation. It also invites them to hear presentations at MOFCOM by foreign lawyers who handle China's WTO cases.[31] These experiences help orient their research and pedagogy.

The government has nominated several Chinese academics to the Indicative List of Panelists maintained by the WTO Secretariat. MOFCOM nominated three individuals in 2004, followed by two in 2006, six in 2010, and eight in 2011. By 2012, the government had nominated a total of nineteen individuals, of which eight were full-time academics, eight were sitting officials at MOFCOM at the director or director-general level, and the remaining three were former government officials who practice as lawyers or teach part time as professors.[32] Since 2006, China has also nominated five candidates to the WTO Appellate Body. All but one of them are former MOFCOM officials. Among them, two were selected. Zhang Yuejiao, the first Appellate Body member from China, served as the director-general of the Department of Treaty and Law, while Zhao Hong, the second and current member, served in the same department as a deputy director-general.

Engaging Law Firms

Litigation in the WTO is a highly specialized activity that has spurred governments to hire and work with legal professionals, and in particular WTO law specialists in private law firms (Shaffer 2003). Given the stakes for China's development policy, the Chinese government developed a policy of hiring the world's best trade lawyers, who were in US and European law firms, to defend it. In parallel, it worked to foster the development of internal expertise within Chinese law firms. It did so by having a Chinese law firm work with a foreign law firm in all but one of the first twenty-eight cases that China faced before WTO panels.[33] As one US lawyer working for China stated, China has been "smart" in its dual use of foreign and domestic lawyers, which facilitates "technology transfer."[34] Over time, lawyers in Chinese private law firms developed significant WTO law-related expertise.

The government worked alone with Chinese law firms whenever China was a third party in a WTO case in order to help the government form its legal positions and, in the process, help train Chinese lawyers. For example, one Chinese lawyer now active in WTO cases worked with the government in about a dozen cases in which China was a third party between 2003 and 2008, including a number of subsidy cases involving the United States, the EU, Canada, and Korea, an area in which Chinese practices would subsequently be challenged before the WTO.[35] He stressed how "being a third party was important for capacity building. I saw and studied how others would write submissions, develop arguments; in some cases I could see how a party participated in oral hearings, such as before the Appellate Body."[36] As another attorney stated, "We copied, we learned, we pasted. As an entrepreneurial saying goes (in Chinese), 'creation starts from imitation.'"[37] The lawyer "loved" to see how "legal" the WTO work was. Through these processes of

public-private partnership in WTO litigation, the government helped build
expertise to defend Chinese interests, as well as to bring international trade
law home.

The Development of China's Trade Bar

The development of the international trade and business law fields in China
is a phenomenon that flourished after the WTO's creation. Between 1997 and
China's WTO accession in late 2001, the government launched a dozen antidumping cases (Q. Wang 2004). The trade bar, however, still remained un-
derdeveloped. As the *China Youth Daily*, a major national newspaper,
lamented in late 2001, "Chinese lawyers familiar with international law, international trade law, and WTO rules are extremely rare" (*Zhongguo Qingnian Bao* 2001). For China to effectively engage with WTO law, including for
the preparation and defense of its own regulations, it needed Chinese legal
professionals to enhance their competency in English and in trade law.

China's accession to the WTO was a catalyst for developing the Chinese
legal profession more generally, thereby facilitating transnational legal ordering in trade and business law. To promote such development, the Ministry
of Justice issued an opinion on "Accelerating the Reform and Development
of the Legal Profession after China's Accession to the WTO" in March 2001
(Ministry of Justice 2001).[38] The ministry noted, "Chinese lawyers are weak
in handling international legal business, and China lacks talents who can ex-
cellently handle foreign-involved legal services, and the lawyers' competitive capacity in the international legal service market are weak." It stressed:

> We should improve the continuing education of the practicing
> lawyers, strengthen the education and training of the lawyers in re-
> spect of newly arising economic and legal knowledge, scientific and
> technological knowledge, and foreign language ability. We should
> open various training avenues, select excellent talents to accept train-
> ings abroad, and meanwhile take corresponding measures to guar-
> antee those lawyers selected for overseas studies will come back to
> China to provide services. We should do our utmost to make the
> quantity and quality of China's foreign-involved lawyers reach a level
> in line with the demand of China's market economic construction and
> development by the year 2010.

In the area of trade law, MOFTEC and its Department of Treaty and Law took the lead in building the trade bar's capacity. In June 2000, the DTL organized a delegation to attend a training course in Washington, DC (Li 2011). The delegation included officials from the main ministries handling economic issues and legislative bodies, scholars from universities and research institutes, and practicing lawyers, all selected by DTL. The course was taught at Georgetown University Law Center by Professor John Jackson, widely referenced in China as the "father of the WTO" (Chen 2013: 248; Yang 2015). The course was a great success, and many participants became leading figures on WTO law issues in China, such as Yang Guohua, who would become lead counsel in many of China's WTO cases as deputy general-counsel at DTL.

Since no Chinese law firm had any experience in WTO dispute settlement, MOFCOM turned to foreign law firms for representation when China began to fully litigate disputes before the WTO rather than settle them. While the Chinese government is generally wary of involving foreign lawyers in other areas, and although there initially was some internal debate, the government continues to hire foreign law firms for WTO litigation.[39] Li Chengang, director-general of DTL, justifies the decision by noting that WTO litigation is a highly specialized activity that requires significant legal skills, and that this strategy has proven effective for long-time GATT/WTO members such as Japan, India, and Brazil (Li 2011). In response to concerns that foreign lawyers might be untrustworthy, his former colleague Yang Guohua noted, the "lawyers provide professional legal services. They will do their best no matter which country they work for. . . . As a client, all we care about is their capabilities to provide professional services" (Yang 2011). In the process, they also facilitate legal technology transfer.

Such transfer has particularly thrived in the area of import relief law. Although China had been the target of trade remedy cases abroad since the 1980s, it only launched its first trade remedy case in 1997 when Chinese lawyers on behalf of a group of Chinese newsprint manufacturers submitted a petition to MOFTEC to commence an antidumping investigation. The case heralded the legalization of the Chinese import relief administration and the development of China's import relief bar. The government official Wu Xiaochen later became a leading private trade lawyer at the Hylands Law Firm and wrote a book, *Antidumping Law and Practice of China* (UIBE 2016; Wu 2015a). The practice has since flourished in China, which has become one of the world's largest users of antidumping measures. China now uses antidumping law frequently against the United States and Europe, at times in a tit-for-tat fashion in response to US and EU investigations.[40]

Who Are the Government's Chinese Trade Lawyers?

Although the government hired foreign lawyers in order to be best represented in WTO cases, it also wished to build the capacity of Chinese law firms (Li 2011). From its very first case, the government deliberately hired domestic private law firms to work with the foreign firms. In the early years, the government selected ten Chinese law firms and tried to groom them for WTO work by having them provide support to the foreign law firms and work alone with the government on third-party submissions.[41] For example, in its first case, the *US–Steel Safeguard* case initiated in 2002, China hired the French law firm Gide Loyerette as its counsel, together with four domestic private law firms to assist in the background (Li 2011). Most of these Chinese firms were boutique law firms with trade remedies practices.

Over the past decade, however, all but one of the original ten discontinued their WTO litigation practices, although domestic trade remedies practices continued to grow. In 2016, only the megafirm King and Wood Mallesons (KWM), among the original firms, continued to handle WTO dispute settlement for the government, along with four other firms: Zhong Lun; Jincheng, Tongda and Neal (JTN); AllBright; and Gaopeng and Partners. When one compares these two groups of law firms, the new firms are much larger, including some of the largest law firms in China; are "full-service" firms; engage younger lawyers with experience abroad; and are based in Beijing.

These larger law firms have the resources to support a WTO legal practice, as their corporate practices generate sufficient surpluses.[42] Although WTO work remains much less lucrative than these firms' other practice areas, maintaining a WTO practice can greatly enhance the prestige of a firm since it involves representing the Chinese government, which every Chinese has been taught since their youth to be sacred and infallible. On the practical side, working on these cases helps the big law firms maintain *guanxi* (connections) with MOFCOM, which in addition to its jurisdiction on trade issues is entrusted with regulatory powers over commercially important areas such as the approval of foreign investment and the enforcement of China's competition laws. While different divisions within MOFCOM handle these issues, building *guanxi* with DTL officials through WTO cases makes it easier for the law firms to contact officials in other divisions. Navigating WTO law mixes with traditional Chinese ways of doing business.

These Chinese law firms have also generated work related to WTO law that has broader implications within China, as well as for the international trading system. As Yang Guohua writes, "Chinese lawyers have grown up to provide WTO legal services not only to MOFCOM in WTO disputes, but also to other government agencies and companies" (Yang 2015). The most clearly linked area is trade remedy practices, which reflect a legalization of Chinese import relief practices. Chinese law firms represent both the Chinese petitioner and the foreign companies in these cases. From 2003 to 2010, China implemented 122 antidumping measures and was the world's largest user of antidumping measures after India (Wu 2012). Since 2010, although the number of antidumping measures initiated by China dropped, the country still remained one of the main users along with India and Brazil (World Trade Organization 2019).

As Chinese law firms build expertise in this area, they increasingly represent Chinese companies and trade associations in foreign antidumping and other import relief investigations as well.[43] They often work closely with MOFCOM and industry associations to help overcome collective-action problems.[44] Often they work with foreign law firms, but sometimes they do the work alone, representing Chinese clients in foreign administrative processes. One of the leading practitioners, Pu Ling-chen of Zhong Lun law firm, returned to Beijing after more than twenty years in Brussels, where he had received a law degree at Free University of Brussels, interned for the European Commission, and practiced antidumping work with law firms from the United States and UK. He often defends Chinese clients in import relief investigations directly before EU administrative bodies.[45]

These law firms also have been able to expand into other areas, such as foreign investment law, international commercial arbitration, and bilateral and plurilateral trade agreements.[46] For example, the professionals in China that work on bilateral investment treaty (BIT) negotiations are the same who work on trade matters, and they build from their trade law experiences, exemplifying the interpenetration of these fields in China. Those in MOFCOM who work on the BIT negotiations come from the WTO department, and they work with outside Chinese law firms with significant experience on WTO disputes.[47] The government is harnessing their knowledge to form public-private partnerships in the negotiation of bilateral investment agreements with the United States, the EU, and others. If agreements are reached, these same private law firms hope to work on investor-state cases under the resulting rules. Once more, WTO legal knowledge practices diffuse.

Chinese Companies' and Trade Associations' Engagement with Trade Law

Thirty years ago, most Chinese companies were not only state owned; they were arms of Chinese ministries and local governments. Today, state-owned enterprises have become corporatized, and many have shares listed on stock exchanges (Milhaupt and Zheng 2015). Although private companies now represent around 54 percent of the country's GDP, the larger ones all have Communist Party representatives and committees within them, designed to exercise oversight (McGregor 2010: 72; Wu 2015b). Chinese companies are thus generally much more deferential to state officials than their US and European counterparts.[48] Many private Chinese companies find that government officials are difficult to approach. They thus have not developed a habit of hiring law firms to lobby and work with the government on trade disputes, and they have been further reluctant on account of the firms' fees (Kennedy 2005). In antidumping cases, many Chinese companies, in addition, face collective-action problems against which to organize and defend themselves.

The 2000s showed signs of change, as large Chinese companies and independent trade associations became more willing to hire trade lawyers and defend their interests as partners with the government. First, larger Chinese companies increasingly hired in-house counsel, and many hired trade lawyers. Second, some small- and medium-sized companies created industry associations independent of the Chinese state to work with private law firms on foreign and domestic antidumping investigations that eventually could (and did) lead to WTO cases. Both initiatives represent major changes in China and reflect a relative turn of Chinese companies to engage trade lawyers, thus supporting transnational legal ordering.

Chinese Companies and International Trade Law

Before China's accession to the WTO, Chinese companies also faced significant trade barriers abroad. Most of them chose to abandon the foreign market rather than fight a foreign legal procedure. As mentioned above, following

China's accession, in order to help Chinese companies understand and benefit from WTO rules, the government launched extensive education campaigns, which were conducted by WTO centers established around the country.

Larger Chinese companies independently saw the need to develop WTO knowledge from their experience with foreign antidumping and other measures, and they built in-house expertise. They have built internal legal expertise on many trade-related issues, including intellectual property, import relief, customs, trade facilitation, and investment law. For example, the Chinese technology giant Huawei has more than one hundred in-house counsel,[49] and its vice-president and head of Trade Facilitation and Market Access is an American who formerly was the chairman of the American Chamber of Commerce in Brussels.

Building in-house trade law expertise takes time and resources that most Chinese small- and medium-sized enterprises cannot afford. To encourage more Chinese companies to bring their problems to the government, MOF-COM introduced a Foreign Trade Barrier Investigation mechanism in 2002, which was modeled after US Section 301 legislation and the EU's Trade Barrier Regulation (Gao 2010). However, companies only formally invoked it in two cases in the first twelve years, the first involving a 2004 investigation regarding Japanese import quotas on laver (seaweed) that was successfully settled, and the second regarding US subsidies in the renewable-energy sector initiated in 2012.

Because the formal Foreign Trade Barrier Investigation mechanism was rarely used, MOFCOM introduced an informal alternative around 2005. This new approach—nicknamed the "Quadrilateral Coordination" mechanism—involves the cooperation of four parties: the central government, local government, industry association, and individual companies (Gao 2014). Under it, industry associations play a key role as the bridge between private companies and the government, thus resolving private companies' concerns about access. But to act effectively, industry associations had to enhance their trade law capacity and their independence.

Chinese Industry Associations and International Trade Law

Historically, industry associations have not been independent of the government in China. Rather, they were established by and affiliated with functional ministries in particular domains, which were separate from MOFTEC

(MOFCOM's predecessor). These associations, moreover, had no expertise on foreign trade issues. To address this problem, MOFTEC created in the late 1980s seven trade associations for importers and exporters of products, divided into broadly defined sectors.

Although these trade associations have closer links with MOFCOM, they still are ineffective in assisting most Chinese companies. Because they are established by the government, and not by the companies themselves, they are rather bureaucratic and irresponsive to the companies' needs and demands. Many companies rarely turn to them for help, since the companies view them as associations that govern them, rather than serve them. As one lawyer told us, "The trade association is a second government. . . . This is central planning" (Milhaupt and Zheng 2015).[50]

In the last decade, more independent industry associations have emerged, which represents a significant development in China resulting from its integration in the global economy. They do so to overcome collective-action problems and better address the information demands for defending (as well as avoiding) trade disputes. These private associations better respond to company interests because their scopes are very narrow and tend to cover just a single product or several closely related products. For example, there are trade associations for fasteners, for parasols, and for cigarette lighters. Such a high degree of product specialization facilitates their ability to identify specific trade measures affecting the industry, such as antidumping investigations. Moreover, these industry associations locate in the cities and counties where the industry operates, as in provinces such as Zhejiang and Guangdong. Most importantly, because these industry associations are formed on the companies' own initiatives, they are more responsive to the companies' needs and demands, and the companies are more comfortable approaching them when the companies encounter trade barriers. To help their members address trade barriers, the private industry associations hire personnel with trade law expertise, train existing staff, and work with government trade departments and private law firms in individual cases.

It remains a much greater challenge to form independent industry associations in China than in the United States or Europe. A Chinese lawyer who earlier worked for a law firm in the United States notes three particular challenges.[51] First, "the mentality in China" differs because the firms are so focused on competing against each other in foreign markets that they have trouble cooperating in foreign antidumping investigations. They generally have difficulty overcoming collective-action problems. Second, the firms lack faith that WTO law can help them gain real market access following a WTO case, given the drawn out legal procedures and weak remedies, including no retrospective remedies in WTO law, complemented by a protectionist turn in the United States and elsewhere. Third, creating ad hoc coalitions is much more difficult in China because they invite closer scrutiny by the Chinese government. There is thus less of a bottom-up push from Chinese industries to organize collectively, hire lawyers, bring matters to MOFCOM, and challenge foreign measures.[52] Nonetheless, the development of independent industry associations for trade matters represents a significant development in China, constituting both an offshoot of, and further conduit for, transnational legal ordering.

Conclusion

Bringing China into the WTO was about more than just opening China's markets and foreign markets to Chinese goods. It involved processes of transnational legal ordering that have broader implications for government institutions, the role of markets, the development of professions, and normative frames in which government accountability is assessed (Shaffer 2015). It involved internal Chinese contests over the direction of China's economic policy conducted within the context of an international legal regime. As Mark Wu writes, "Economic reformers, led by Premier Zhu, utilized the WTO accession process to push their agendas. WTO commitments served as a means to lock in desired reforms of China's economic structure" (2015b: 344–345).[53] Some even view the WTO in quasiconstitutional terms regarding its impact on Chinese public law. Tom Ginsburg writes, "The WTO became, in essence, an amendment to the Chinese constitution. Internal forces wished to 'lock in' commitments before they could be whittled away at the local level, and third-party monitoring, locked in by international agreements, provided the mechanism" (Ginsburg 2009).[54] The WTO, in other words, was more than just about international law and compliance with it; it was about transnational legal ordering.

The use and acceptance of WTO law and litigation has become somewhat normalized within China, as reflected in the 227 cases in which China has participated.[55] The former deputy director-general of MOFCOM's Treaty and Law Department underscores how this "was unprecedented in its [China's] legislative history in the sense of amending its laws according to international rules" following an international court ruling (Yang 2015: 11–12).[56] China, for example, complied with the *China–Raw Materials* and *China–Rare Earths* decisions because, in a Chinese official's words, "the Ministries see the WTO as a just process."[57] The official contended, "this is such an important progress," it helps one "envisage the rule of law in China."[58] Another MOFCOM official thus contends that the WTO has been a "pioneering area in China for the rule of law."[59] Similarly, one legal academic speculated that among the reasons MOFCOM created secondment programs for Chinese law professors to assist it on WTO matters is that the professors can become supporters of MOFCOM's efforts in China on WTO-related matters, thereby helping with China's compliance with its WTO commitments.[60]

Many of the Chinese practitioners we met said that they are trade liberals and believers in the WTO. They thus have clear predilections about the role of markets and law in society. Their hope is that WTO law can seep into the practices of local governments and firms. They stressed how far China has come in relation to its past. One told us that he "can't believe how much freer is China today, where one can be sarcastic, ironic, and criticize the government on trade law issues, at least privately."[61] China still has much to learn regarding the WTO, he said, but things are getting better.[62] As regards trade law and policy, he emphasized:

> I am a person who lived through the time of the Cultural Revolution. I was in China from the worst time and now, and I can say that it's not easy progress to become what China is today. . . . We went through lots of ups and downs, suffered a lot. . . . And now I see the people, news, criticism, comments, journalists. It's unbelievable. From your perspective it might be normal, but for me it's really unbelievable. . . . Now we can criticize the government, comment on the policies, talk about WTO law. It really changed a lot.[63]

Transnational legal processes involve conflicts within states as well as between states, and these different sets of conflicts interact. As time has passed, more Chinese officials and stakeholders have become skeptical and disillusioned about the WTO, which could deepen, given the rise of economic nationalism in the United States and its turn to unilateral trade sanctions. Some disenchantment also stems from China learning how to play the legal game and limit the impact of losses in WTO cases. As MOFCOM official Ji Wenhua noted after watching the tactics of others at the WTO, "We should try to employ some [such] strategies, including resorting to *sophistry* and *delay tactics*" (Gao 2011: 169). Yet, although WTO legal disputes are perceived as less important in China today because the dispute settlement system can be gamed, the WTO has served as a catalyst for reformers within China in the development of legal institutions and the disciplining of central, regional, and local decision makers to be more responsive to the WTO's legal constraints, including WTO requirements for transparency, judicial review, and nondiscrimination.

This article illustrates the enmeshment of international and national trade law in a major emerging economic power, China. The extensive changes to Chinese laws and the process of promoting consistency with WTO rules do not represent an abdication of sovereignty but rather a means for Chinese officials to achieve their own goals of economic and governmental reform within a broader transnational context. Building capacity in the legal profession and among firms to use the WTO rules served the dual purpose of transforming society and advancing the national interest within the transnational space of the global economy.

China's accession to the WTO serves to highlight how even a government that fiercely resists any external intervention into domestic affairs can embrace transnational law for its own transformative ends within the broader transnational context. Through these processes, the WTO helped advance the position of trade law norms in China's economic governance, increasing the role of law and lawyers. Compared to the baseline where China started, the country has opened its economy, integrated into the global economy, and invested in the diffusion of trade law norms. By investing in human capital to build legal capacity, China became a rival to the United States and Europe in WTO dispute settlement and other trade fora, in turn affecting that legal order itself. International trade law and Chinese law and policy mutually implicate each other in complex processes of transnational legal ordering and disordering. Developments in one cannot be understood without attending to the other.

Notes

1. This book chapter synthesizes and updates an earlier article. See Shaffer and Gao (2018).

2. For a fuller description of the methodology, see Shaffer and Gao (2018). Interviews were conducted on a confidential basis and are listed here by number.

3. China was an original member of the GATT in 1948, but the Kuomintang government in Taiwan, which occupied the Chinese seat at that time, withdrew from the GATT in May 1950 (Gao 2007: 41–48).

4. For differing assessments, see Jacques (2009) and Hung (2016).

5. Authors' calculations.

6. Stories of common people's interests in the WTO in China are legion. To give an example, *New Yorker* writer Peter Hessler's popular book *Oracle Bones* frequently refers to the excitement about China's joining the WTO among the people he meets. At one point, Hessler encounters a photographer on a bridge on the Yalu River in the town of Yabaolu across from North Korea who "kept bringing up the WTO. I asked him why he was so interested. 'The newspapers say that if we join the WTO, we'll have more foreign visitors coming to China,' he explained. 'And of course if China's economy improves, then there will be more Chinese tourists coming here, too. So it has an effect on me'" (Hessler 2006: 67).

7. Interview #20, 2003. As another official remarked in a July 2005 interview, it is "contrary to Chinese philosophy and culture" to litigate. If you litigate against a friend, then they "will no longer be a friend" (Interview #21, 2005).

8. Interview #21, 2005.

9. Interview #19, 2012.

10. Within the Chinese system, the State Council is the central government, headed by the premier.

11. Interview #3, 2014.

12. Interview #2, 2014.

13. Interviews #15–17, 2014.

14. Interview #17, 2014.

15. Ibid.

16. Interview #16, 2014.

17. Interview #7, 2014.

18. Interview #17, 2014.

19. Interview #16, 2014.

20. The China (Shanghai) Pilot Free Trade Zone (SPFTZ) was first established in the Pudong area in Shanghai in September 2013. It aims to become China's testing ground for new regulatory regimes on trade and investment. Initially covering only twenty-eight square kilometers, the SPFTZ quickly introduced many new regulatory reforms in a host of areas, ranging from investment and financial liberalization to the shift of government functions (Gao 2016).

21. Interview #16, 2014.

22. Interview #17, 2014.

23. Interview #28, 2016.

24. Interview #25, 2016. The TRIPs Agreement is also cited.

25. Article 9 of the Supreme People's Court's Regulations on Issues Concerning the Trial of Administrative Cases Relating to International Trade states, "If there are two or more reasonable interpretations for a provision of the law or administrative regulation applied by a peoples court in the hearing of an international trade administrative case, and among which one interpretation is consistent with the relevant provisions of the international treaty that the PRC concluded or entered into, such interpretation shall be chosen, unless China has made reservation to the provisions" (Cai 2016: 275–277).

26. Interview #11, 2014.

27. Interview #12, 2014.

28. Interview #11, 2014.

29. Interview #31, 2016.

30. Interview #12, 2014.

31. Interview #6, 2014.

32. Given the large number of cases in which China is a party, however, only one Chinese citizen has served on a panel, Zhang Yuqing, who was a member of an *EC-Bananas* compliance panel. (European Communities—Regime for the Importation, Sale and Distribution of Bananas, Recourse to Article 21.5 of the DSU by the United States, Constitution of the Panel, Note by the Secretariat, WT/DS27/84, 13 August 2007).

33. For example, in the 2014 *China–Rare Earths* case, the government worked with the U.S. law firm Sidley Austin, together with the Chinese law firm AllBright (Sidley Austin 2016). "We represented MOFCOM in a WTO dispute involving *China–Rare Earths*, in defense of export restraints responding to claims made by the U.S., the EU, and Japan" (AllBright Law 2014; describing the lawyer's role in the case).

34. Interview #6, 2014.

35. Interview #2, 2014.

36. Ibid.

37. Interview #5, 2014.

38. Translation by LawinfoChina, a legal database run by Peking University.

39. Interview #4, 2014.

40. Compare Freedman 2012 and Wu 2012.

41. Interview #22, 2013.

42. Other factors include Chinese patriotism ("it's good to help my country," noted one interviewee), and the career reputational opportunities for young ambitious lawyers with English proficiency and greater facility with common law reasoning (Interview #5, 2014).

43. One practitioner noted that the firm had represented Chinese firms in antidumping proceedings in the United States, the EU, Argentina, Brazil, Egypt, India, Mexico, South Africa, and Turkey (Interview #30, 2016).

44. Interview #7, 2014.

45. Similarly, another Chinese attorney told us he was about to go to India for an optical company to represent it in an antidumping case there (Interview #5, 2014).

46. Interview #2, 2014; Interview #35, 2016.

47. Interview #5, 2014; Interview #27, 2016; Interview #29, 2016.

48. Milhaupt and Zheng contend that "state capitalism as practiced in China today is largely synonymous with state capture. . . . Large firms in China—whether SOEs, privately owned enterprises (POEs), or ambiguous mixtures of state and private ownership—survive and prosper precisely *because* they have fostered connections to state power" (2015: 176).

49. Interview #9, 2014.

50. Interview #3, 2014.

51. Interview #7, 2014.

52. Ibid.

53. As President Jiang Zemin noted in the speech he gave at the WTO Seminar for Provincial-level Officials on 25 February 2002, "The accession to the WTO demands major

changes in the ways the economy is managed by our governments at all levels. We shall further adjust and improve our modus operandi and legal system to meet the demands of the socialist market economy in accordance with the general rules of the market economy" (Jiang 2006: 454).

54. One Chinese academic went so far as to affirm, "I was optimistic about China's joining the WTO . . . and the impact of legal reasoning [from engaging with the WTO]—that once the skill was mastered it would teach people to be rational, and once rational, they would manage their rights and obligations, . . . and this is the beginning of the rule of law" (Interview #28, 2016).

55. This figure is as of 19 January 2019.

56. The United States, however, lost on its key enforcement claims, which made it much easier for China to comply (Huang and Ji 2012).

57. Interview #1, 2014.

58. Interview #1, 2014. Other interviewees noted how the WTO has helped to discipline the government's application of antidumping law in China (Interview #5, 2014).

59. Interview #25, 2016.

60. Interview #12, 2014.

61. Interview #9, 2014.

62. Ibid.

63. Ibid.

References

AllBright Law. 2014. "AllBright Lawyer Participates in 2014 China Rare Earth Forum." Accessed 14 July 2019. http://www.allbrightlaw.com/EN/10482/2dd2370b90c2e048.aspx.

Asian Development Bank. 2001. *Technical Assistance to the People's Republic of China for WTO Membership and Foreign Trade Reform*. Manila: Asian Development Bank.

Barboza, David. 2010. "China Passes Japan as Second-Largest Economy." *New York Times*, 16 August 2010. http://www.nytimes.com/2010/08/16/business/global/16yuan.html?page wanted=all&_r=0.

Barton, John, Judith Goldstein, Timothy Josling, and Richard Steinberg. 2008. *The Evolution of the Trade Regime: Politics, Law, and Economics of the GATT and the WTO*. Princeton, NJ: Princeton University Press.

Cai, Congyan. 2016. "International Law in Chinese Courts." *American Journal of International Law* 110 (April): 269–288.

Chen, An. 2013. *The Voice from China: An Chen on International Economic Law*. New York: Springer Berlin Heidelberg.

China Society for World Trade Organization Studies. 2013. "Jianjie, zongzhi ji zhuyao Zhineng" [Introduction, objectives and main functions]. Accessed 14 July 2019. http://cwto.mofcom .gov.cn/article/about/201310/20131000353150.shtml.

Chinese Society of International Economic Law. 2014. "Xuehui jianjie" [About the society]. Accessed 14 July 2019. http://www.csiel.org/about.aspx?baseinfoCateID=72&baseinfo_Id =72&CateId=72&ViewCateID=72.

Economy Watch. 1994a. "GDP (Current Prices, US Dollars) Data for Year 1994, All Countries."
   Accessed 18 March 2019. http://www.economywatch.com/economic-statistics/economic
   -indicators/GDP_Current_Prices_US_Dollars/1994/.

Economy Watch. 1994b. "GDP (PPP), US Dollars Data for Year 1994, All Countries." Accessed
   18 March 2019. http://www.economywatch.com/economic-statistics/economic-indicators
   /GDP_PPP_US_Dollars/1994/.

Freedman, Jennifer. 2012. "China Floods the WTO with Tit-for-Tat." *Bloomberg,* 7 June 2012.
   https://www.bloomberg.com/news/articles/2012-06-07/china-floods-the-wto-with-tit
   -for-tat.

Gao, Henry. 2006. "Aggressive Legalism: The East Asian Experience and Lessons for China."
   In *China's Participation in the WTO,* eds. Henry Gao and Donald Lewis, 315–351. London: Cameron May.

Gao, Henry. 2007. "China's Participation in the WTO: A Lawyer's Perspective." *Singapore Yearbook of International Law* 11:41–48.

Gao, Henry. 2010. "Taking Justice into Your Own Hand: The Trade Barrier Investigation Mechanisms in China." *Journal of World Trade* 44:633–659.

Gao, Henry. 2011. "China's Ascent in Global Trade Governance: From Rule Taker to Rule
   Shaker, and Maybe Rule Maker?" In *Making Global Trade Governance Work for Development,* ed. Carolyn Deere-Birkbeck, 153–180. Cambridge: Cambridge University Press.

Gao, Henry. 2014. "Public-Private Partnership: The Chinese Dilemma." *Journal of World Trade*
   48 (October): 983–1006.

Gao, Henry. 2016. "TPP, Regulatory Coherence and China's Free Trade Strategy from A to Z."
   European Yearbook of International Economic Law 97:507–533.

Ginsburg, Tom. 2009. "The Judicialization of Administrative Governance: Causes, Consequences and Limits." In *Administrative Law and Governance in Asia,* eds. Tom Ginsburg
   and Albert H. Y. Chen, 1–20. Abingdon, UK: Routledge.

Halliday, Terence, and Gregory Shaffer. 2015. "Transnational Legal Orders." In *Transnational
   Legal Orders,* eds. Terence Halliday and Gregory Shaffer. Cambridge: Cambridge University Press.

Hessler, Peter. 2006. *Oracle Bones: A Journey Through Time in China.* New York: Harper
   Perennial.

Huang, Cui, and Wenhua Ji. 2012. "Understanding China's Recent Active Moves on WTO
   Litigation: Rising Legalism and/or Reluctant Response?" *Journal of World Trade* 46:1281–
   1308.

Huang, Yasheng. 2008. *Capitalism with Chinese Characteristics: Entrepreneurship and the State.*
   Cambridge: Cambridge University Press.

Hung, Ho-fung. 2016. *The China Boom: Why China Will Not Rule the World.* New York: Columbia University Press.

Jackson, John. 1998. *The World Trade Organization, Constitution and Jurisprudence.* London:
   Royal Institution of International Affairs.

Jacques, Martin. 2009. *When China Rules the World: The End of the Western World and the
   Birth of a New Global Order.* London: Penguin.

Jiang Zemin. 2006. "Zai jilie de guoji jingzheng zhong zhangwo zhudong" [Seize the initiative amid intense international competition]. In *Jiang Zemin wenxuan: Disan juan* [Selected works of Jiang Zemin: Vol. 3], 442–460. Beijing: People's Publishing House.

Kennedy, David, and Joseph Stiglitz, eds. 2015. *Law and Economics with Chinese Characteristics: Institutions for Promoting Developing in the Twenty-First Century.* Oxford: Oxford University Press.

Kennedy, Scott. 2005. *The Business of Lobbying in China.* Cambridge, MA: Harvard University Press.

Li Chengang. 2011. "Zhongguo canyu shimao zuzhi zhengduan jiejue shijian gaishu" [Overview of China's participation in WTO dispute settlement practices]. In *Shimao zuzhi guize boyi: Zhongguo canyu WTO zhengduan jiejue de shinian falu shijian* [Gaming with WTO rules: China's ten years' experience in WTO dispute settlement practices], ed. Li Chengang, 1–50. Beijing: Commercial Press.

Liu, Sida, David Trubek, and David Wilkins. 2017. "Mapping the Ecology of China's Corporate Legal Sector: Globalization and Its Impact on Lawyers and Society." *Asian Journal of Law and Society* 3 (2): 1–34.

McGregor, Richard. 2010. *The Party: The Secret World of China's Communist Leaders.* New York: Harper Perennial.

Milhaupt, Curtis, and Wentong Zheng. 2015. "Reforming China's State-Owned Enterprises: Institutions, Not Ownership." In *Regulating the Visible Hand?*, eds. Benjamin Liebman and Curtis Milhaupt, 175–201. Oxford: Oxford University Press.

Ministry of Commerce, Department of WTO Affairs. 2006. "Zhuyao zhineng" [Main functions]. Accessed 14 July 2019. http://sms.mofcom.gov.cn/article/gywm/200606/2006 0602467456.shtml.

Ministry of Education. 2012. "Putong gaodeng xuexiao benke zhuanye mulu he zhuanye jieshao" [Overview of the catalog of majors for institutions of higher education]. Accessed 14 July 2019. http://www.moe.edu.cn/s78/A08/A08_gggs/s8468/201212/t20121218_181006.html.

Ministry of Education and Ministry of Finance. 2007. "Guanyu shishi gaodeng xuexiao benke jiaoxue zhiliang yu jiaoxue gaige gongcheng de yijian" [Advice on the implementation of the project on quality of college teaching and teaching reform in higher education]. *Jiaogao,* January. Accessed 14 July 2019. http://www.moe.gov.cn/srcsite/A08/s7056/200701 /t20070122_79761.html.

Ministry of Justice. 2000. "Lushi zige kaoshi banfa" [Rules on lawyer's qualification exam]. Sifabuling no. 61, art. 16. Accessed 14 July 2019. http://china.findlaw.cn/info/lvshi/lsflfg /147454.html.

Ministry of Justice. 2001."Opinions of the Ministry of Justice on Accelerating the Reform and Development of the Legal Profession after China's Accession to the WTO." Sifatong no. 30. Accessed 14 July 2019. http://www.lawinfochina.com/display.aspx?lib=law&id =2970&CGid=.

Minzner, Carl F. 2011. "China's Turn Against Law." *American Journal of Comparative Law* 59:935–984.

Peerenboom, Randall. 2002. *China's Long March Toward Rule of Law.* Cambridge: Cambridge University Press.

Potter, Pittman. 2008. "China and the International Legal System: Challenges of Participation." In *China's Legal System: New Developments, New Challenges*, ed. Donald C. Clarke, 699–715. Cambridge: Cambridge University Press.

Qin, Julia. 2007. "Trade, Investment and Beyond: The Impact of the WTO Accession on China's Legal System." *China Quarterly* 191:720–741.

Shaffer, Gregory. 2003. *Defending Interests: Public-Private Partnerships in WTO Litigation*. Washington, DC: Brookings Institution Press.

Shaffer, Gregory. 2013. *Transnational Legal Ordering and State Change*. Cambridge: Cambridge University Press.

Shaffer, Gregory. 2015. "How the WTO Shapes Regulatory Governance." *Regulation and Governance* 9 (1): 1–15.

Shaffer, Gregory, and Henry Gao. 2018. "China's Rise: How It Took on the U.S. at the WTO." *University of Illinois Law Review* 2018 (1): 115–184.

Shanghai WTO Affairs Consultation Center. 2016. "About the Center." Accessed 20 March 2019. http://www.sccwto.org/introduce?locale=zh-CN.

Sidley Austin. 2016. "Relationships." Accessed 19 March 2019. http://www.sidley.com.cn/en/relationships/governmentagencies.

Sun Zhenyu. 2011a. "China's Experience of 10 Years in the WTO." In *A Decade in the WTO: Implications for China and Global Governance*, eds. Ricardo Meléndez-Ortiz, Christophe Bellmann, and Shuaihua Cheng, 11–16. Geneva: International Centre for Trade and Sustainable Development (ICTSD).

Sun Zhenyu. 2011b. "Renshi (Knowledge)". In *Rineiwa kongzong Suiye* [Busy years in Geneva], 28–75. Beijing: People's Publishing House.

UIBE. 2016. "93 jie xiaoyou, Sifeng lushi shiwusuo hehuoren Wu Xiaochen: Yi shisan nian, sishi qi fanqingxiao an" [Wu Xiaochen: Class of 93 alumni and partner at Sifeng Law Firm: Thirteen years, forty antidumping cases]." Accessed 19 March 2019. http://law.uibe.edu.cn/OutListContent/index.aspx?nodeid=109&page=ContentPage&contentid=2300.

Wang Chuanli. 2015. "Yao Meizhen yu Zhongguo Guoji Jingjifa" [Yao Meizhen and international economic law in China]. *Wuda Guojifa Pinglun* [Wuhan University international law journal], 18 (1): 1–15.

Wang Qinhua. 2004. "Zhongguo duiwai fanqingxiao de zhuangkuang ji anli" [China's antidumping experience and cases]. In *Fanqingxiao yingdui zhidao* [How to deal with antidumping], eds. Wang Qinhua and Zhang Hanlin, 27–46. Beijing: People's Press.

Wechsler, Andrea. 2012. "China's WTO Accession Revisited: Achievements and Challenges in Chinese Intellectual Property Law Reform." In *European Yearbook of International Economic Law*, eds. Christoph Herrmann, Markus Krajewski, and Jörg Philipp, 125–158. New York: Springer International.

Wertime, David. 2014. "It's Official: China Is Becoming a New Innovation Powerhouse." *Foreign Policy*, 7 February 2014. http://foreignpolicy.com/2014/02/07/its-official-china-is-becoming-a-new-innovation-powerhouse/.

World Bank. 2019. "China: Overview." Accessed 18 March 2019. http://www.worldbank.org/en/country/china/overview.

World Trade Organization. 2001. "WTO Ministerial Conference Approves China's Accession." November. Accessed 14 July 2019. https://www.wto.org/english/news_e/pres01_e/pr252 _e.htm.

World Trade Organization. 2019. "Anti-dumping Measures: By Reporting Member 01/01/1995-31/12/2018." https://www.wto.org/english/tratop_e/adp_e/AD_MeasuresByRepMem.pdf.

Wu, Mark. 2012. "Antidumping in Asia's Emerging Giants." *Harvard International Law Journal* 53 (1): 1–84.

Wu, Mark. 2015a. "Attacking with a Borrowed Sword: The Rise of Trade Remedies Law in China." *Harvard Globalization Lawyering and Emerging Economies China Series Working Paper*. Presented at the Chinese Legal Profession in the Age of Globalization Conference, Harvard Center Shanghai, 7–8 August 2015.

Wu, Mark. 2015b. "The WTO and China's Unique Economic Structure." In *Regulating the Visible Hand*, eds. Benjamin L. Liebman and Curtis J. Milhaupt, 313–350. Oxford: Oxford University Press.

Yang Guohua. 2011. "Zuihao de lushi" [The best lawyers]. In *Women zai WTO da guansi* [Litigating in the WTO], eds. Yang Guohua and Shi Xiaoli, 144–146. Beijing: Intellectual Property Publishing House.

Yang Guohua. 2015. "China in the WTO Dispute Settlement: A Memoir." *Journal of World Trade* 49:1–18.

Zhang Mao, ed. 2003. *Zhongguo jiaru shijie maoyi zuzhi guoduqi Beijing xingdong jihua* [Action plan for Beijing during China's transition period in the WTO]. Beijing: Social Sciences Academic Press.

"Zhang Yuqing Interview." 2011. In *Rushi shinian fazhi Zhongguo* [Ten years in the WTO, rule of law in China], eds. Lu Xiaojie, Han Liyu, Huang Dongli, Si Xiaoli, and Yang Guohua, 5–27. Beijing: People's Publishing House.

Zhonggong Zhongyang Bangongting. 2001. "Guowuyuan Bangongting Guanyu Woguo Jiaru Shijie Maoyi Zuzhi Youguan Qingkuang de Tongbao" [Announcement by the General Office of the Central Committee of the Communist Party of China and the General Office of the State Council on China's Accession to the WTO]. *Zhongbanfa*, no. 26. Accessed 14 July 2019. http://www.110.com/fagui/law_3491.html.

Zhongguo Qingnian Bao [China Youth Daily]. 2001. "Yang lushi qiangtan Zhongguo tiaozhan bentu lushi: Shuilai da WTO guansi" [Foreign lawyers entering China to compete with local lawyers: Who will litigate the WTO cases?]. 10 December 2001. http://news.sina.com .cn/c/2001-12-10/416084.html.

CHAPTER 4

The "Africa Bar" of Paris

A Microcosm of Interconnected Histories of Legal Globalization

Sara Dezalay

Over the past fifteen years, the African continent has gained renewed prominence as a "mining frontier" in the wake of the ascent of China as an economic superpower and acute global competition for critical raw materials and carbon energy.[1] In 2013, fuel and mineral exports from Africa reached $397 million, fifteen times more than development aid flows into the continent.[2] A 2010 McKinsey report estimated the potential benefits of consumer-facing industries, resources, agriculture, and infrastructure together across the continent at $2.6 trillion in revenue annually by 2020 (Roxburgh et al. 2010). This growth has been paired with what professional accounts describe as a new wave of corporate legal globalization into the continent (see Taylor 2016a). This is illustrated by the growing interest of multinational corporate law firms, including members of the "Magic Circle" in London and of Wall Street law firms, who are setting out to establish Africa offices in rising hubs on the continent—Casablanca, Johannesburg, or Abidjan—as well as in the usual global financial capitals and former *métropoles* of New York, London, or Paris.

Yet, this "Africa rising" picture contrasts sharply with the Afro-pessimist image of a continent invariably depicted as an indiscriminate geographical whole, doomed by the "resource curse" (Collier 2007) seen to be affecting resource-rich countries due to wealth capture by corrupt political elites, weak legal institutions, violent conflict, and political instability. It is also in these "new mining frontiers" like the eastern parts of the Democratic Republic of Congo, in which global capitalism "finds minimally regulated zones in which to vest its operations" (Comaroff and Comaroff 2012: 13), that the rush for extractive boons has been most pronounced since the 1990s.

The central role played by the African continent in the emergence and expansion of contemporary capitalism has long been established. The imagery of the "new frontier" is therefore not just historically inaccurate. Narratives that continue to portray Africa as a foil for arguments about European capitalist history (Cooper 2014) have important political effects—not least because they shape knowledge and scholarly hierarchies about legal, political, and social developments across the continent. This is especially true for legal and economic globalization dynamics in Africa.

"It's a White's business!" interjected a senior economic consultant asked about dealings between resource-rich African states and multinationals from the north.[3] The specter of neocolonialism in the ongoing rush for natural resources in Africa is intensified by the economy of appearances that shrouds the industry. Talks of mining "booms" or of the "perfect storm" are mired with rumors. Not only are extractive contracts between resource-rich states and multinationals for the most part sealed under a lid of secrecy, but accurate data on actual extractive potentials, projects, and economic returns are hard, if not impossible, to come by. The market for primary commodities itself is distorted by the entanglement of shadow and official trade routes and the multiplicity of intermediaries involved. It is also made more complex by the intense globalization and financialization of mineral value chains.

These barriers of entry are not only technical. There is certainly an acute knowledge gap about legal professions and, more generally, legal globalization dynamics on the African continent, compared to the important wealth of research on legal professions in Europe, North America, Latin America, and, more recently, Southeast Asia (with some exceptions, e.g., S. Dezalay 2015; Gobe 2013). Yet, the overwhelming script on law and legal institutions in Africa tends to reflect the ebb and flow of policy pulls. Lawyers, particularly, do not escape a protracted dependency lens. They are either hailed as missionaries of the rule of law in a continent marked by failed colonial legacies and transplants (e.g., Halliday, Karpik, and Feeley 2012; Massoud, this volume) or they are the new mercenaries of neocolonial corporate interests (e.g., Burgis 2015).

Further, the increasing globalization and financialization of mineral value chains raises an acute challenge for scholarship—and policy (see Cutler and Dietz 2017). The role played by extractive industries in European colonialism across Africa and in the expansion of modern global capitalism has long been studied (see Cooper 2014; Ellis 2012). Extractive infrastructures themselves are increasingly recognized as a driver shaping social and political change in the *longue durée* (see Acemoglu and Robinson 2014). Yet, the still predominant focus on the "resource curse" remains for the most part surprisingly ahistorical and state-centric.

These questions and difficulties challenge the common script of (legal, economic) globalization of the African continent. To escape these contradictory images, on what *scale* or *level*, indeed, should the analysis be focused? Taking a cue from the approach foregrounded in this volume, this chapter shifts the focus from globalization understood as flows between the "international" and the "national" toward "interconnectedness" (Subrahmanyam 2005) across time and scale, between dynamics of legal, political, economic, and social change across the African continent, and focuses on global transformations in capitalism. Embracing the recent global turn in historical studies, aimed at reglobalizing the African continent (Burbank and Cooper 2010; Cooper 2014), it builds on an ethnographic approach that emphasizes these interconnections as flows and "counterflows" (Ibhawoh 2013) between African settings, former *métropoles,* and global markets.

The case study that provides the empirical bulk of this chapter stems out of an apparently counterintuitive example. It focuses on the "Africa Bar" in Paris, a key site in which extractive deals between multinational corporations and resource-rich states in Western Africa are negotiated. Tracing the individual trajectories and professional strategies of the lawyers operating within this social microcosm underscores the dual characteristic of this space as *offshore,* yet connected. This reflects the enduring double position of Paris as a former colonial *métropole* and as a beachhead in the expansion of US- and UK-led corporate legal globalization into continental Europe starting in the 1980s, and more recently into Africa. The analysis of the social relations at play in this microcosm provides thereby an entry point to trace how the relationship between extractive economies, state transformations, and the unequal and uneven position of Africa in globalization have been negotiated in the *longue durée.* It is also a crucial site to map out law's entanglement with social networks, politics, and economics, across time and space. As such, the Africa Bar encapsulates the metaphor and materiality of "landscapes" as spaces in which tensions between the "Global North" and the "Global South," sovereignty and international law, borderless capitalism and bordered states, but also extraction and virtue are constantly (re)negotiated by and through law.

This chapter proceeds in three steps. The following section explains the ethnographic approach foregrounded in the analysis of the Africa Bar in Paris, which underscores the relevance of using lawyers' trajectories and professional strategies as an entry point to trace the interconnectedness between state transformations in Africa and global dynamics. Sections three and four detail the case study of the social microcosm of the Africa Bar in Paris. The last section offers concluding remarks opening up a wider research agenda.

From Lawyers as Intermediaries of the State and Globalization to Transnational Landscapes of Law

The first dimension of the research strategy suggested here follows the path opened by a political sociology of lawyers as power brokers in the formation of the state and globalization. This approach emphasizes the position of lawyers as "intermediary elites" or "double agents" due to their capacity to juggle contradictory social, political, and economic interests. This entry point contributes to explaining transformations of state power and patterns of globalization (Dezalay and Garth 2002; e.g., Vauchez 2012a and 2012b). This approach has proven particularly fruitful for the study of contemporary African contexts (see S. Dezalay 2015).

There is still an acute need to document the mediation roles played by lawyers in African contexts, and specifically extractive economies. It is a truism in media accounts that "an Africa office is no magic door to deals" (Taylor 2016b), especially if newcomers are not corporations with an imperial past (The Economist 2016). In Africa, social networks, trade routes, and political institutions have been shaped by these imperial flows and "counterflows" (Ibhawoh 2013). The positions, practices, and trajectories of lawyers provide a way to trace this interweaving between the local, the national, and the global, as well as the interplay between knowledge, law, economics, and politics.

Focusing on lawyers can also prove a fruitful avenue to trace the prominence of extractive economies on the African continent from the precolonial era to their impact on contemporary legal and political institutions and economic development (see Ellis 2012). Recent research on empires in world history has emphasized the role played by raw commodities in the consolidation of European empires in the long nineteenth century and the expansion of capitalism (Bertrand 2015; Burbank and Cooper 2010). This interest in the *longue durée* (Subrahmanyam 2005) not only recalls that the postcolonial "nation-state" is a modern political outcome of imperial legacies; it can also help us understand the role played by extractive economies in the uneven and unequal connections between Africa and the world, over time (Cooper 2014).

Indeed, the Africa Bar in Paris, just like other corporate bars, is a "crossroads" space where corporate power, politics, and social capital play a crucial role in the distribution of positions within it (Vauchez 2012a, 2012b; France and Vauchez 2017). The history of this bar and the specific context of the 1980s help explain the dominance of UK and US corporate law firms in this small professional market. Yet, this Africa Bar is not just a corporate bar; it is a space that is offshore, as it is located in Paris, yet it is deeply connected to power structures in African settings. Indeed, this bar is dominated by predominantly *French*, white, and male lawyers. It is deeply embedded in the corporate, political, and social networks that tie Paris to its former colonies.

This double geographical trope of Paris—as a beachhead of a US- and UK-led corporate legal globalization and as a former *métropole*—has defined the structure of this bar, that is, the resources that shape barriers of entry and privilege within it. The embeddedness of this bar in imperial legacies helps explain, in particular, the two apparently contradictory faces of legal globalization at play within it: corporate and human rights. This imperial legacy also accounts for the fact that this extremely restricted market of insiders has been defined, over time, by *charismatic* ties, that is, the social relations between a handful of multipositioned, predominantly French lawyers and political and economic elites in African contexts.

On the other hand, the smoothing out, polishing, and reconversion of this small network—under the impetus of global regulatory frameworks over minerals and the competition with increasingly powerful emerging economies like China (see Shaffer and Gao, this volume)—account for the prominence taken by US and UK multinational corporate law firms over this restricted professional market. Thus, though slightly enlarged, as it is now also defined by technical know-how, the restructuration of this professional market underlines the endurance of these imperial legacies.

Focusing on lawyers operating within this Africa Bar in Paris, I have relied on a qualitative methodology that can be described as "relational biog-
raphy."[4] Asking respondents *who* they are, that is exploring not only their
professional and educational background but also their social characteristics,
is a way to trace how successful their strategies could be in entering and positioning themselves within this small professional market. Beyond that, it
is a way to map out the configuration of this space across time and space. In
the following two sections, I build on exemplary trajectories of lawyers operating within this small professional market to trace, first, the structuration
of this bar out of imperial legacies, and second, its ongoing transformation
under the impetus of global regulatory pushes and financialization.

Mapping Out the "Africa Bar" in Paris: Between Deals of Law, Politics of Virtue, and Imperial Legacies

Far from anecdotal—examples could be multiplied in all African settings as
elsewhere—the two portraits below emphasize the continuous strategies of
double games played by lawyers. Lawyers, as Ernst Kantorowicz (2016) and
others in his wake have shown, while at the service of power holders and
thus playing a central role in the legitimation of state power, also needed to
distance themselves from politics, as a condition to protect the autonomy of
the law and with it their professional markets. These strategies are inscribed
in the very structure of the law. From Renaissance Italy (see Brundage 2008;
Martines 1968) until today, the law has been shown to be "a way to get access
to and draw strength from a sovereign administration (such as the city states);
to gain an academic and physical distance from state power; and to serve as
a go-between for different sovereign administrations and interests" (Dezalay
and Garth 2011: 53).

Between the state lawyer—for example, the *jurisconsulte* of a national
diplomacy—and the "merchant of law" at the service of corporations, there
is a community of situation, defined by the promotion, arguably multifaceted but in the end converging, of legal competency as a necessary condition
to negotiate conflicting social interests (see Vauchez 2010). This "fluidity of
the title" of lawyers qua lawyers (Willemez 1999) enables a capacity, varied
according to periods and spaces, to play a multiplicity of social and professional roles between different sectors at the national level—political,

economic, and administrative (Vauchez 2012b; France and Vauchez 2017)—as much as across the local, the national, and the global.

Further, the renewal of the debate on empires and their legacies has opened paths to reassess the roles of lawyers as intermediaries of the state and of globalization (see S. Dezalay 2015, building on Bourdieu 2014). Underscoring law as a central feature of European colonial empires (see Benton and Ross 2013; Ibhawoh 2013), this scholarship has paved the way for research exploring these multifaceted contributions of lawyers as brokers negotiating sovereignty as "shared out, layered, overlapping" (Burbank and Cooper 2010: 17): between corporate and state power, the colony and the *métropole*, interimperial confrontations, and across colonial and postcolonial time and scale. Imperial and postimperial legal realms indeed favored the positions of lawyers as both collaborators and rebels. "Politically mobilized and professionally effective, indigenous lawyers were a Frankenstein of colonial creation, doing much to dislodge the colonial establishment that gave them their profession life" (Oguamanam and Pue 2016: 480). In other words, lawyers are not just missionaries or mercenaries, they are both.

These imperial legacies also enabled the circulation of lawyers and their roles as go-betweens across time in the postcolonial trajectories of the state—between politics; society and the market; and local, national, and global scales.

William Bourdon: Juggling Between the Powerful and the Wretched of the Earth

The head of the nongovernmental organization (NGO) Sherpa, created in Paris in 2001 to "protect and defend victims of economic crimes,"[5] William Bourdon is an advocate for the criminalization of corporate crimes. This lawyer gained prominence after the amicable settlement he struck in 2005 on behalf of eight Burmese who had lodged a complaint against the French firm Total for forced labor. More recently, he endorsed the cause of whistle-blowers as the lawyer of Antoine Deltour—the alleged source of part of Lux-Leaks—as well as Edward Snowden, Hervé Falciani (ex-HSBC), and Stéphanie Gibaud (ex-UBS). While vice-secretary general (1994–1995) and secretary general (1995–2000) of the French human rights NGO International Federation for Human Rights (FIDH), he was one of the vocal proponents of the Rome Statute for the International Criminal Court throughout the 1990s, and the initiator, on behalf of the FIDH, of the complaint for crimes against humanity against Hissène Habré in Senegal in 2000 (see Seroussi 2008). He was also one of the drivers of diverse complaints against sitting and former African heads of state for their "ill-gotten wealth" in France on behalf of Sherpa and Transparency International and the defender of two French detainees at Guantanamo among other cases.

But Bourdon is also the counsel of private corporations—though his prominence as a "cause lawyer," as he explained, has driven some US and UK corporations away. "I think they are wrong, they are wrong in thinking that being a cause lawyer prevents me from having a cynical and manipulative side. I can be as cynical as they are."[6] What he described in his legal practice as "a constant juxtaposition, this medley between politicians, the powerful and the wretched of the Earth" is not simply a question of accommodating economic constraints by "playing on different fronts." It is a capacity of circulation that can be explained by Bourdon's background and trajectory, and his positioning at the intersection of multiple poles of power in France—political, economic, advocacy. This is a capacity in which his family capital played an instrumental role. He is the grandson of the engineer in chief at Michelin, and the great-grandson of one of the founders of Michelin, the rubber tire corporation, which has grown into a transnational and powerful corporation born out of rubber plants in Vietnam and other parts of the French colonial empire. Originally aiming for a diplomatic career, Bourdon ended up studying law and registering to the Paris Bar in 1980. He started his career with internships with two veterans of the Paris Bar: Philippe Lemaire, a criminal lawyer and one of the proponents of the abolition of the death penalty in the 1970s, and Marc Barbé, a founder of one of the first French corporate law firms, BCTG et Associés, set up in Paris in the early 1970s with a portfolio of powerful corporate clients (including Nike and Cadbury) built up by Barbé while at Stephenson Harwood in London.

Bourdon then set up his own law firms starting in the mid-1980s. He described his stint at the FIDH as a "parenthesis":

> I believe there is a pernicious cancer that constantly threatens NGOs, it's bureaucratization. . . . We strive to pave a way between the naivety of part of civil society that gets privatized through public subsidies, co-opted into public administrations—a dangerous partnership—and the near-systematic ideologization of the denunciation of corporate power. . . . If economic actors tell you that they are losing market

shares in Africa, you need to hear the argument. This is what enables me to circulate between spheres of power and conflicting interests.

Pascal Agboyibor: Not Just "the" African
of the Corporate Bar in Paris

Arms folded on a grey suit and blue shirt—the obligatory uniform of the corporate lawyer—Pascal Agboyibor hints with an imperceptible smile at the triumph that brought him to the cover of the monthly French issue of *Forbes Afrique* in February 2015 (Ngisi 2015). In his late forties, this Togolese lawyer is one of the very few—there are but a dozen—Africans working at multinational corporate law firms. What is more, he is a sitting member of the administrative council of the US firm Orrick Herrington & Sutcliffe LLP and the head of its Africa department in Paris. Agboyibor is hailed as a "shadow power broker" (ibid.) of transactions between states and foreign corporations in the African continent. With a sixty-person-strong department, Orrick, he claims, invests a huge proportion of its activities—20 percent—in Africa.

"I was taught very early on that I would become a lawyer."[7] The law, for Agboyibor, is an acute political and family matter. His father, Yawovi Agboyibo, a former president of the Lomé Bar, political opponent and prime minister in the transition between the Gnassingbé regimes (2006–2007), played a prominent role in the transition of Togo to multipartyism in 1991. Yawovi Agboyibo had also turned to corporate law in the early 1970s by integrating the country's very first law firm,[8] after studying law in France. During an era when the newly independent state of Togo was massively recruiting lawyers into the administration, this choice appeared like an anomaly. Yet, investing in corporate law had insured the conversion of the resources of the royal family, removed from local power since the 1930s by the French colonial administration,[9] to the political and economic networks tying the country to its former *métropole.*

One generation later, this proximity helped propel Pascal Agboyibor into the close-knit corporate Bar in Paris, first in 1993 at Jeantet et Associés, one of the French pioneers of corporate law, before he joined the Paris branch of the UK firm Watson, Farley and Williams in 2000, whose teams integrated with Orrick Herrington & Sutcliffe LLP in 2002. Agboyibor became a partner at Orrick in 2003. After studying law in Lille, Agboyibor built up his portfolio of African contacts during a secondment at the African Development

Bank in Abidjan in 1996 and through introductions from his father—notably to take on the latter's arbitration disputes between the Democratic Republic of Congo and "vulture funds."[10]

Agboyibor's trajectory thus unveils a "layered" habitus pointing to the multiple historical strata of legal globalization on the African continent as much as their connections with local struggles and political hierarchies. But it also points to the wider transformation of corporate legal markets since the 1990s and the prominent yet ambiguous position of Paris in these developments. When he started his career, Agboyibor strategically invested in securitization, positioning himself in the financialization of commodities markets. He reinvested fully his African portfolio in the wake of the 2008 financial crisis, which prompted the search of multinational corporate law firms for new markets in emerging economies, foremost Africa.

While only 10 percent of Agboyibor's practice involved business transactions on the African continent in 2008, such transactions now account for 99 percent of his time. When he entered Jeantet in the early 1990s, there were but a handful of Africans in corporate law firms in Paris—and elsewhere. His first "African" case involved the Chad-Cameroon pipeline. "It was the old argument at the time. They needed an African to sit at the table. There is a deep symbolic violence behind this. This is probably what made me leave Jeantet. There is a huge difference between French and Anglo-Saxon firms on this." The stormy creation of a branch of Orrick, orchestrated by Agboyibor, in Abidjan in 2014, triggering an outcry from the Bar in Abidjan (see Pierrepont 2014), also emphasizes the difficult, thorny dynamic of this new wave of legal globalization into Africa. "I am an anomaly," explained Agboyibor, "if it is only me, in Paris, it is not sufficient. You need lawyers who are concerned about the fate of Africa, not just mercenaries. . . . Training African lawyers by internationalizing them can amount to a form of parachuting."

Building Legal Know-How out of Imperial Legacies and Corporate Legal Globalization

The biographies of these two lawyers highlight connections—both spatial and temporal—that remain otherwise invisible in the contemporary period if attention is channeled to "national" boundaries or sectoral legal practice. Both trajectories underscore the resources, hierarchies, and social struggles that are embedded in their habitus that have been shaped by the transformations of the political and economic relations between Paris and its former colonies over time. Indeed, the trajectories and strategies of these two lawyers and their capacities to circulate across poles of power need also to be related to the position of this bar as a "crossroads" space that, structurally, is particularly amenable to these multiscalar double games.

The latter have been favored by recent and ongoing transformations in corporate dealings in Africa that are heavily mediated by lawyers: to negotiate extractive contracts; amend national mining codes and taxation regulations; advise foreign corporations against political, social, and economic risks, and, increasingly, local populations contesting the detrimental impact of extractive projects on social justice and development. Particularly in France, due to the sulfurous legacy of the *Françafrique*,[11] the reputations of lawyers involved in dealings with the African continent have been tainted with phantasms and denunciations. The "Club of Africans," hailed as the "white marabouts of the *Françafrique*" (Hugeux 2007), was described somewhat scathingly by a respondent as comprising the "incompetent," the "suitcase carriers," the "skilled ones who know how to carry suitcases," and the "skilled ones who carry portfolios."[12]

Major corruption cases have unveiled some of the shadow dealings of the *Françafrique*—like the Elf scandal, which erupted in 1994 and revealed major misappropriation of funds, while the French government, under the Mitterrand presidency, was involved in theaters of war in its enlarged *pré-carré* (zone of influence) in Central Africa (see Péan 2011). More recently, the operations of the French Bolloré group in Western Africa—aimed at rekindling the project left dormant since the French colonial era—of a railway linking Cotonou in Benin to Abidjan in the Côte d'Ivoire have been hurdled with a multifront legal war. Samuel Dossou-Aworet, *Monsieur Pétrole* (Mr. Oil) in Gabon, founder of the Petrolin Group and close advisor of President Bongo, successfully contested the concession rights of Vincent Bolloré over the Beninese stretch of the project before a Beninese court (see Maury and Vidjingninou 2015). Arbitration proceedings were lodged in parallel under the umbrella of the Permanent Court of Arbitration against Niger and Benin by the French engineering firm Geftairail—on behalf of the former French prime minister Michel Rocard—alleging to also have had a prior interest in the project (ibid.).

Lawyers as the discrete but all-the-more-powerful advisors of African heads of state also often occupy the front page of these political-economic scandals. These include the French-Lebanese lawyer Robert Bourgi, who accused former president Chirac among others—both to the right and the left sides of the French political spectrum—of having received bribes from African heads of states (see Hugeux and Thiolay 2011) and the late Jacques Vergès, the shadow advisor of Moussa Traoré in Mali, Abdoulaye Wade in Senegal, and François Bozizé in the Central African Republic.

Taming Global Markets for Extractive Commodities: Financialization and Regulation

Yet, the originally extremely select "Africa Club" of Paris has recently grown into an enlarged though still restricted market of about twenty lawyers, controlled by a dozen Paris offices of US and UK multinational corporate law firms. But this small market remains dominated by *French* male lawyers operating within these firms. The trajectory of a prominent member of this bar helps to explain what can thus be described as a symbolic revamping of legal deals between multinational corporations and resource-rich states on the African continent—but only through a slight displacement in the structure of positions within this small professional market.

"My specialty now is crisis management. Today, there is not one single country where there is not a risk of coup. But the risk is not only jurisdictional, it is also reputational."[13] This corporate lawyer has operated since 1998 at the Paris office of the UK corporate law firm Herbert Smith Freehills. Now a partner, he is the head of the firm's Africa practice, focusing predominantly on the energy and mining sectors. He is also the mentor of the bulk of the new generation of corporate lawyers operating in Africa from Paris offices and increasingly from offices based on the continent.

After studying law in France, "Antoine" left for Vanuatu, as a "conscientious objector,"[14] where he was appointed public prosecutor when the country achieved independence in 1980. Antoine then studied international law in Australia, which he described as "a rare vocation" at the time. After working at the Crédit du Nord for two years in finance, he moved to Gabon, as an associate at Fidafrica, the legal branch of PricewaterhouseCoopers (PwC), until 1998. In this capacity, he became the counsel of Samuel Dossou-Aworet—Gabon's "Mr. Oil."

> In Gabon I did everything: social security law, labor law. You needed to be able to deal with emergencies, relentlessly. . . . Twenty-five years ago, when I started, people were telling me: "He is doing tam-tam

fusions." . . . I became a project lawyer once back in France. But I had carved out this competency with the knife and the d*** [*la bite et le couteau*]. The new generation, they have not really ever been in Africa. They will never be "real" Africans. This does not mean they don't do good work. But I would like to see them in crisis situations. . . . Crisis management: It starts with me. In 95 percent of cases, the dispute is solved through settlement, especially in Africa. . . . These young lawyers, I would like to see them in a crisis situation. At some point, you need to stand straight, respectfully, and return to the law.

The conversion of this "White African" as a vocal proponent of the "social responsibility of corporations," notably as a member of the Corporate Social Responsibility Committee of the American Bar Association, can be explained by external shocks—politically and economically driven—that have contributed to transforming the social structure of this small niche of counsels for corporations and African heads of state. The growth of this legal market can be attributed in part to the increased financialization of commodities markets in the past fifteen years, and with it the growing technicality of dealings on the continent (see UNCTAD 2012). Because of these dynamics, multinational corporate law firms, with their collective know-how, from the negotiation of contracts to arbitration, could be better positioned. The 2008 financial crisis and, before that, the Enron scandal in 2002, which precipitated the demise of Andersen and shed light on the conflicts of interest of consulting firms like PwC, until then the most thoroughly and widely pre-positioned in the African continent, also opened new opportunities for corporate law firms in these new emerging economic markets (see *The Economist* 2015).

Other global drivers help explain the dynamics of this enlargement. On the one hand, incentives for the global regulation of dealings between foreign corporations and resource-rich states in Africa increasingly impact on the operations of multinational corporations on the continent. For the most part a set of soft laws—known as "corporate social responsibility" and nonbinding on corporations—these regulations carry heavy reputational costs. The growing reach of the 1977 US Foreign Corrupt Practices Act (FCPA) and the Extractive Industries Transparency Initiative (Rich and Moberg 2015) are also instrumental in these developments. But extractive deals in the African continent are most impacted by development policies and the role of invisible actors sitting at the negotiation table between multinationals and resource-rich African states—the World Bank and bilateral development agencies, a trilateral relation between development donors, corporations, and states that is specific to African continent. Most lawyers in the "Africa club" thus got their introduction to the developing continent by working on sovereign debt restructuring in the 1980s. The waves of privatization of extractive industries, spearheaded by the World Bank through the 1980s, opened up opportunities for corporate lawyers, and so did the promotion of "public-private partnerships" from the early 1990s, as they position the contract and the lawyer at the heart of the relation between the public sector and the private sector (see Vauchez 2012a: 79).

Driven foremost by the need to stabilize foreign investments against challenges to extractive contracts, like national fiscal policies of "upward adjustments" (so-called resource nationalism) and jurisdictional contests, a number of North-driven policy endeavors have aimed at "leveling the playing field" between foreign corporations and African states. For example, the "CONNEX Initiative" spearheaded by the German government during its presidency of the G7 in 2014 aimed at drafting a "code of conduct" to "strengthen advisory support to low-income country governments in their negotiation of complex commercial contracts—to make the support that is available more comprehensive and more responsive to government's needs and to contribute to fairer, more sustainable investment deals."[15] The African Legal Support Facility set up in 2010 in Abidjan under the umbrella of the African Development Bank—and the sponsorship of the NGO Transparency International—similarly endeavors to provide assistance to African countries to strengthen their legal expertise and negotiating capacity in debt management and litigation, natural resources and extractive industries management and contracting, investment agreements, and related commercial and business transactions.[16] For both initiatives, a core aim is therefore to restructure legal services to African states away from a charismatic market of shadow advisors and toward an enlarged and more transparent market of legal services to states.

From a Small Market of Insiders to Revamping the Terms of the Relationship Between Africa and the Global Economy?

To understand the ambiguous impact of these changes on the Africa Club in Paris it is necessary to relate them to two other connected dynamics: the structuration of the corporate bar in Paris over time and the threads of relations between France and its former colonies. Both define barriers of entry

and the distribution of positions in a space whose structure has been transformed under the impetus of the Wall Street law firm model, but whose
boundaries remain defined by the capacities to access and juggle the poles of
power (economic, political, social) shaped by the relations between Paris and
its former colonies.

The following series of trajectories illustrate the dynamics that have shaped
the structuration and transformation of the Africa Bar in Paris over time. These
portraits of four lawyers underscore a clear generational break between the veterans of the Africa Club and a younger generation that is both more technically
savvy and more attuned to the stakes involved in driving a sustained expansion of their firms on the continent, including the need to co-opt and train local, that is, African, interlocutors. All four trajectories, however, underscore
the endurance of the web of relations (political, economic, social) that connect
this professional market across French and African settings.

Tracing (Slight) Generational Breaks: From a Charismatic Market of Insiders to a Restricted Niche of Practitioners
TWO VETERANS OF THE AFRICA CLUB

"Julien" receives me in his spacious office—the first time during this fieldwork—a room with softened light, strewn with African masks, fabrics, and
a picture on the wall showing the basketball team of Zaïre in the 1970s, featuring a young Julien. A friend of Antoine, and the mentor of "Pierre" (see
portrait below), Julien is hailed as the "historical Godfather" of the Africa
Club by respondents and in media accounts. This amiable, White, French
lawyer, now well into his eighties, explained that he entered the field "by accident."[17] "My trajectory is unusual. I obtained a scholarship from the US
Officers' Wives Club after the Second World War to go study in the United
States." After obtaining a juris doctor degree, he entered the US corporate
law firm Duncan Allen & Mitchell, before being dispatched by the firm in
1974 to Kinshasa, the capital of then Zaïre. The firm wanted to set up a local
office: "The associate there was an American 'with big boots,' the son of an
infrastructure entrepreneur. He did not have the sensitivity to work for
Africans. At first, I was not interested, but I decided to stay. At the time (in
New York) there was hardly any international work, I never saw clients.
There I could combine the two."

The context was also that of the "white elephants" infrastructure projects in
Zaïre (see Verhaegen 1985). "Mobil, Texaco, First National Citibank: business

was booming." Julien returned to Paris at the end of the 1970s as an associate of the US corporate firm Coudert Brothers. "A month later, I was contacted by Air Zaïre, to be the advisor of the (Congolese) presidency." As counsel to the presidency, he was tasked with reforming the pharmaceutical sector, and was also in charge of military contracts and of course the negotiation of bank loans. "I came back to Paris. I was then inevitably branded with an 'African' label. Due to my Zaïran background, I have always done mining law. But I became a generalist 'African.'"

Julien developed Coudert's Africa practice—with, and that was exceptional at the time, a team of African lawyers. "At the time, Coudert was the only firm to do international law. If you came to Paris (to work at the Paris office of a US or UK corporate law firm), it was, as a Frenchman, automatically to do international law." After the disbanding of Coudert in 2006, Julien moved to the Paris branch of the US firm Dewey and Leboeuf and then that of the Canadian firm Fasken Martineau. Moving with the fast pace of the market for corporate law, he also brought with him his teams, striving to reconstitute the "Africa" teams he had developed at Coudert. He explained this strategy: "We do not do offshore law. But we do not need to work with local lawyers. Anyway, if clients contact us, we can do the work, we do not need to go through local lawyers."

In turn, "Pierre" was admitted to the Bar in Paris in 1991, and entered the French corporate law firm Jeantet et Associés in 1992. An associate and chair of the Energy, Mines and Infrastructure Department—focused predominantly on Africa—of the firm, Pierre is also an academic. He earned a research master of laws in international law and international trade law in 1981, a master's in international and comparative energy law in 1982 from the University of Paris 1-Sorbonne, a visiting scholarship at Berkeley in 1983–1985, and a juris doctor from the University of Paris 13 in contracts related to the exploitation of natural resources. He is now a law professor at the University or Paris 2, where he heads the diploma program in international economic law in Africa.

This academic profile is typical of the "alma mater" of French corporate law firms, Jeantet et Associés. The firm was founded in 1922 by Pierre Lepaulle, the first French man to obtain the Scientiae Juridicae Doctoris at Harvard, who was joined by Fernand-Charles Jeantet, a law professor at Harvard specializing in competition law, after World War II. In the framework of the Marshall Plan, the firm played an instrumental role in fostering the implantation of US corporate law firms in Europe—through Paris—and developing European Community law (see Vauchez 2012a).

Before joining Jeantet, Pierre had worked for five years at Coudert as well as at Total. He related: "The preparation of files (contracts, project finance), it has a snowball effect. Reputation is difficult to establish, but once it's there, it's there."[18] He said that once at Jeantet,

> I set up the energy structure in 1993. It was the only one, focused on energy and natural resources, to provide for the whole gamut of services—contract negotiation all the way through to arbitration. We have a single team that can deal with both. So if there are shifts in the market, one of the poles can compensate for the other. . . . When I started, I was derided. Everybody was criticizing the endeavor. . . . We were the only law firm with a local office in Africa, from the colonial era, then in Algiers, because Jeantet was from there. I innovated, I brought in an African to the office [it was Pascal Agboyibor].

Pierre is now orchestrating the setup of a local branch of the firm in Casablanca, Morocco, with the idea of "developing the practice of the firm" there.

TWO MEMBERS OF THE "NEW GUARD"

Hailed as one of the prominent corporate lawyers operating in dealings in Africa in the 2015 rating by *Jeune Afrique*, "Dominique," of counsel in the Paris office of the US corporate law firm Jones Day since 2010, predominantly advises corporations—recently for the negotiation of a concession for the airports of Antanarivo and Nosy Be in Madagascar on behalf of a consortium led by Bouygues and Aéroports de Paris—as well as states, as the counsel of Guinea in the Simandou project for the extraction of iron ore by the Australian mining corporation Rio Tinto (see *Jeune Afrique* 2015).

Upon obtaining a master's in public and administrative law in Paris, Dominique had a stint at the European Investment Bank before entering Herbert Smith Freehills—under the mentorship of "Antoine"—where he worked between 2001 and 2010. "I did not turn to Herbert Smith Freehills by accident. At the time, it was the only law firm that provided services to both states and corporations in Africa."[19] He explained:

> I have a background in public law. Administrative law is a supporting science in France. I did not want to be a "support" lawyer. I wanted to do business transactions. . . . Most of my experience is for the private sector. I am starting to work also for the public sector, but it is

less lucrative. . . . It is not an altruistic stance. Upstream (before projects are negotiated), there is an increased involvement of development
actors. Millions of pages have been written on public-private partnerships, but there is a tendency to ritualize these tools. It's the problem
of transplants. [However], relations with local lawyers [in Africa] are
extremely complicated. In Bangui, we simply had to "create" our local respondent. Because there were simply no corporate lawyers. . . .
In some countries, our local respondents do not want to take orders.
There is a locking up of the local legal market.

In turn, "Bruno," a partner at the UK corporate law firm Eversheds LLP,
where he heads the Africa Group of the firm's office in Paris, obtained a master's in common law and corporate law before joining Total in 1995 and
working for Landwell PwC (PwC's legal office in Paris) between 1995 and
2000, for a while under the aegis of Antoine. He reported, "I left in 2000
because I was looking for a smaller structure. I developed Eversheds' practice
in Africa between 2000 and 2007. I managed to convince colleagues of the relevance of working on Africa."[20] After launching the Africa Group of the firm
in 2007, Bruno contributed to developing its Africa Law Institute, a network
designed to enable members of its thirty-eight partner firms in Africa (in
both Francophone and Anglophone Africa) to access legal training. The firm
has now set up six local offices on the continent—in Casablanca, Johannesburg, Mauritius, Morocco, Tangier, and Tunis (see Gannagé-Stewart 2015). It
also played an instrumental role in the development of the Organisation
pour l'harmonisation en Afrique du droit des affaires (OHADA) system
in West Africa, including through an OHADA diploma delivered to
Francophone—French and African—students by the Universities Panthéon-
Assas and Paris 13 since 2014. He stated, "I think a lot of firms advertise an
opening toward Africa, but they are very far from having achieved it. We took
risks. Some individuals work predominantly on oil, minerals. I have had a much
wider portfolio of activities, from the start. As a firm, we provide a full service."

A (Slight) Reshuffling of the Cards in the Distribution of Positions Within the Africa Bar in Paris

As these portraits illustrate, the dominant position of US and UK multinational corporate law firms can be linked, firstly, to the transformation of the

corporate Bar in Paris. The demise of the "Republic of Lawyers" following World War II led to a gradual sidelining of lawyers as the main state elites in favor of an administrative-political elite. The relatively recent return of the profession to politics—illustrated by the move of former politicians to legal practice—has opened up a "contiguous" space of circulation between the legal field and the political field in France (Vauchez 2012a; France and Vauchez 2017).

This shift was fostered by changes in the regulation of the French legal profession, notably the widening up beginning in 1991 of the rules regulating access to the profession, and foremost its *aggiornamento* from the 1990s under the influence of US and UK corporate law firms (see Y. Dezalay 1992). The impact of this globalization of corporate law—notably the managerialization of the French legal field as a whole to adapt to the model of the Wall Street law firm—was all the more powerful given the long-standing shunning of business matters within a legal profession more willing to endorse "political" causes. In the 1950s there were only a handful of internationally oriented corporate law firms in France, and the growth of a corporate legal market, foremost in Paris, followed the drive of pioneers like Fernand-Charles Jeantet to convert to the Wall Street law firm model, based on their experiences in the United States and the UK in the context of the emergence of the European economic market (see Vauchez 2012b).

On the other hand, the strategic position of Paris in the political, legal, and economic world order of the post–World War II and Cold War eras played a decisive role in structuring the Africa Bar in Paris and the positions within it. The international and regional legal framework that was institutionalized beginning at the turn of the twentieth century, and grew in the wake of the World War II, specifically excluded colonies from the ambit of human rights and international law (see Madsen 2004). This also applied to the distribution of natural resources and conflicts over them (see Feichtner 2015). This meant that the conflicts that accompanied the waves of independence of the early 1960s were treated as "domestic" matters dealt with under the military clout of France as a former *métropole*.

The politics of the Cold War also reinforced the symbiotic and reciprocal relation between the field of state power in France and that of its former African colonies—economically, legally, politically, and relationally. In particular, the International Chamber of Commerce had been set up in the early 1920s in Paris out of a transatlantic alliance between a US legal elite with considerable economic and political clout and a small international legal community in Europe then relatively marginalized from diplomatic and doctrinal hierarchies. Building Paris as an "offshore" platform for the arbitration of disputes between multinational corporations and states was specifically an attempt to shield these conflicts from political and diplomatic interests.

However, until the boom of the market for international arbitration in the 1980s (Dezalay and Garth 1996) and throughout the bulk of the Cold War, conflicts of the 1960s and 1970s spurred by the nationalization of oil and other strategic resources in newly independent African states were managed through diplomacy, the threat of gunboats, and personal political relationships between political elites in France and its former colonies. This approach was favored by the French, who hailed themselves as the "policeman of Africa" (see S. Dezalay 2011).

The politics of the "cultural Cold War"—including the anti-US stance of Presidents De Gaulle and Mitterrand—were a key driver in the expansion of the human rights field in France (see Dezalay and Garth 2006). Decolonization struggles, foremost the Algerian war, were also instrumental in the reawakening of the French "old lady" of human rights organizations, the Ligue des droits de l'homme et du citoyen (LDH), through its international branch, the FIDH, and the aggressive anti-*Françafrique* stance adopted by the latter. These political struggles did not only contribute to the political and ideological spectrum of positions in France over its relations with its former colonies, they also built on a reciprocal web of relationships and socialization. While former colonial administrators were reinstated within the Ministry of Cooperation (see Meimon 2007), they also played a key role in inscribing cooperative relations and development with African states in the nascent European Commission (see Dimier 2003), including controlled access to raw commodities (including minerals) for European markets.

Emblematically, the Paris Office of the Secretariat International of Amnesty International was set up in 1978 precisely to benefit from the position of Paris and to access respondents from former French colonies in Africa. A great number of Francophone African political elites have studied there, and the French capital still constitutes a haven for exiles and political opponents. Effectively, Amnesty was de facto involved in dynamics of "reciprocal assimilations of elites" (to use Bayart's [(1989) 2009] concept) whereby political elites from Francophone African states would be, in turn, defended as opponents or denounced for their human rights violations by the organization (see S. Dezalay 2006).

From a legal point of view, decolonization of legal frameworks, institutions, education, and professions was a very slow process. While French magistrates continued to be seconded to former colonies throughout the 1970s—due to the relative if not total lack of trained lawyers available locally when they achieved independence—these webs of relations are still instrumental today. New legal elites are still trained in France; new law professors in Francophone Africa are still endorsed through the "agrégation" chaired by French professors;[21] and French mentor-pupil relations influence the selection of international arbitrators or counsels for the settlement of disputes between African states and multinational corporations over the distribution of natural resources (Dezalay and Dezalay 2017).

These developments have played an instrumental role in shaping the barriers of entry into the Africa Bar in Paris. New entrants come from either a corporate (e.g., Total), political platform or the nonprofit sector. The best positioned are endowed with all three types of resources at the same time, such as in the case of William Bourdon, who is better positioned to be a vocal proponent of the prosecution of corporate crimes, because he is well connected to the corporate milieu. The same applies on the other, nonprofit, end of the spectrum. The Comité Catholique contre la Faim (CCFD), one of the drivers of ongoing complaints about the "ill-gotten wealth" of African heads of state in France, often lodged by Bourdon, was founded by French missionary colonial networks on the African continent (see S. Dezalay 2011).

Part of the success of US and UK corporate law firms in dominating the commodities legal market in Paris also stems from the huge capacity of multinational law firms—as opposed to solo legal practices—to dodge the volatility of markets for commodities (and with them, legal markets), by waging multifront legal strategies, from the negotiation of contracts to arbitration or litigation. As underscored by a respondent: "The difference between Agboyibor and others is the structure of the firm: It is better than having solo practitioners doing all the work."[22] Yet, it is also no accident that predominantly French lawyers operate within this market. It enables these firms to build on a symbolic displacement, away from the stigmata of the *Françafrique*, while still also benefiting from the know-how of these lawyers. The US corporate law firm White & Case, for example, secured a foothold in Africa in the 1990s when it represented Algeria in the restructuring of its external debt. The selection of a US firm was then a decidedly anti-French and anticolonial stance on the side of the Algerian government—but the transaction was managed through a *French* lawyer operating within the firm.

The embeddedness of the Africa Bar in the fabric of French-African relations has also shaped the clientele—states and corporations—of corporate
law firms operating in Africa. "In the 1970s Elf had its own legal department. They would never even have had the idea of hiring corporate lawyers.
These inside advisors were from the Corps des Mines,"[23] explained a long-
term French associate within the Paris office of the US law firm Cleary
Gottlieb Steen & Hamilton.[24] Another lawyer stated, "Banks orient dealings
in Africa, mainly US and UK banks. The French have always done business in
Africa. Though they rarely invest. For Anglo-Saxon law firms (having
an Africa department) is certainly a marketing strategy" toward achieving
a corporate clientele of newcomers into the continent.[25]

Yet, a US partner at the Paris office of the UK firm Clifford Chance
Europe LLP explained:

> If you look at law firms' expansion, it is through project finance, and
> generally development and financing. At the moment, almost
> 100 percent of my time is on Africa. . . . We turned to Africa in the
> context of the crisis, in the late 2000s. I am not sure they will stay after
> the market picks up. Because it is certainly a lot easier to do business
> in New York. . . . The firm recognizes that its business in Africa is not
> the most lucrative. But we want to be a blue-chip firm that corpora-
> tions look to.[26]

A partner at the US corporate law firm Jones Day explained how this
"blue-chip" strategy worked, in terms of specialization within this small market: "When you look at the corporate side, you find a lot more firms. It is the
same for everything else: You do one transaction and then you become a specialist (in mining, oil, infrastructure), but when you look at the government
side it's completely different."[27]

It is perhaps on the side of services to states that the transformation of
the Africa Bar in Paris is the deepest—though the shift remains symbolic.
When Julien, the "Godfather of the Africa Club," started, "There was not
much regulation. We still work a lot for states, but it is mostly private practice. The practice of counseling for states has evolved. It is more transparent,
more open. Now it works a lot on the basis of tenders. Before, it was through
interpersonal relations; presidents and political advisors would meet their
counsels by chance encounters, in restaurants. Now, except for counsels to
presidents, where it is different, it is all on the basis of tenders."[28]

Initiatives such as CONNEX or the African Legal Facility mentioned above aim precisely at opening up this still extremely close-knit market defined by charismatic characteristics and interpersonal ties. They also endeavor to break the dual structure of legal services provided within this small market—between lawyers counseling states or corporations on the one hand, during the phase of contract negotiations, and, on the other hand, lawyers acting as counsel in disputes before international arbitration or jurisdictional fora.

As one interviewee stated, "African governments make a mistake when they do not have a counsel of a sufficient level" during the phase of negotiations.[29] Another added, "They look for the best bidder. It is only when there is a crisis, when the dispute goes to arbitration that they call in the big shots. The law then is dealt with at the highest levels. . . . CONNEX: it is an intelligent initiative. But the sticking point was that the Germans (just as other development partners) wanted services to states to be pro bono. Why ask law firms to do pro bono work? It's beautiful, but it's neocolonial. If you want to restructure the market, you need to do it right."[30]

At play in this battle is also, indeed, a question of gaining access to the continent. Opening the market of services to African governments—including through pro bono endeavors - has been a key strategy of US and UK corporate law firms. As explained by a partner at Jones Day who is based in the New York office of the firm and one of the promoters of the CONNEX initiative:

> You cannot make a career on Africa. Africa work is either for corporations or governments. For corporations it is primarily energy, project finance. You can do that full time. But you cannot do government work full time. It does not pay. There is no way you can make billable hours working for a government. It is a different way of doing business. If I have a corporate client, they will call me and ask me for the costs, then they will call back, and they will say: "let's move." As for governments, they never pay. There is always an international organization that pays. They always have a tender process that takes months, a technical proposal, a financial proposal that will take forty hours. And this, you cannot bill. My credentials are pretty well known. For instance, when GIZ (the German development agency) call, they know me, but still it takes months.[31]

As another interviewee stated, the difference indeed, lies in the *know-who*: "Then you have those people who have the know-how, like Pascal Agboyibor.

But those can also speak to heads of state. That is something else. It is also a question of positioning."[32] Pro bono initiatives thus tend to displace slightly the interpersonal relations between Paris-based lawyers and their political counterparts in African settings toward the framework of international development assistance. But this still reinforces the stronghold of agents with capacities of access built out of a portfolio of political, economic, social, and legal resources, such as Agboyibor. Yet, the position of the latter, and his difficulties in setting up a local branch of Orrick in Abidjan also highlight the thorny path of this new phase of legal globalization into the African continent.

As the Godfather of the Africa Bar explained: "International law firms are scared to be outpaced by local lawyers."[33] The offshore—yet connected—structure of the Africa Bar in Paris could thus be long term, depending on the pace of development and varied structure of national legal fields on the African continent.

Conclusion: The Africa Bar in Paris, a Landscape of International Law

In media and specialist accounts, talks of the end of the commodities' "super cycle," and with it, the fear of African states plunging into the debt crisis of the 1980s, have reignited the "resource curse" debate and the desirability of governing trade and financial flows globally (see Rich and Moberg 2015). In mainstream scripts about legal globalization in Africa, this weakness of African national economies has been linked to the failure of the legal systems inherited from colonization. The need to reform, if not reinvent, political, legal, and economic institutions continues to be heralded as a way to check the tendency toward personal, tyrannical, and antientrepreneurial governance.

Yet, the thriving of private foreign investments in the very countries hailed as "failures," like Angola or the Democratic Republic of Congo, opens a much more complex image than the mere economic dependency of the continent—notably with the expansion of a "Beijing consensus" freed from political conditionality, and outside the scope of US imperial politics (see Halper 2010). The renewed prominence of the African continent as a boon for extractive resources also comes in a context that contrasts markedly with the "new extraction" in Latin American contexts a decade earlier. The mining boom of the last two decades was most pronounced in Latin America, with a growth of the global share of Latin America in mining investment from 10 to 25 percent between 2003 and 2012 (see Deonandan and Dougherty 2016). But to a large extent the rush is yet to come in Africa, where mineral reserves remain for the most part untapped. In Latin American contexts, the new extraction has been accompanied by strong political and social movements that are fostering a radical agenda of postextractivism and asserting the Indigenous rights of local communities over extractive resources, notably through the increased exercise of the right to free, prior, and informed consent institutionalized in various international legal instruments since the 1980s.

By contrast, the rush for extractive minerals in African contexts, particularly in the conflict-rife Democratic Republic of Congo throughout the 1990s and elsewhere on the continent, came at the tail end of structural adjustment programs spearheaded by international financial institutions, which engineered the privatization of extractive economies to foster the regulatory strength of private actors and markets against political elites and weak governance. Not only did these policies do little to curb the rush into Africa, they also unleashed acute levels of violence. "It is precisely this dialectic that has pushed Africa . . . to the vanguard of the epoch, making [these old margins] at once contemporary frontiers and new centres of capitalism—which, to reiterate, in its latest, most energetically voracious phase, thrives in environments in which the protections of liberal democracy, of the rule of law, of the labor contract, and of the ethics of civil society are, at best, uneven" (Comaroff and Comaroff 2012: 19).

As this chapter has endeavored to highlight, the renewed—propounded or contested—prominence of the African continent in the global competition for extractive resources opens an opportunity, and needed inquiry, to assess the relationship between capital investment, politics, and law in these transformations.

The position of the Africa Bar in Paris underscores the relevance of looking at the past to understand these changes, and how Africa is being built into a new legal market for extractive resources. To account for this transformation, however, it is not sufficient to merely trace globalization as a flow driven by the North into the African South. Rather, channeling the attention toward the characteristics of the agents invested in the Africa Bar, their biographies, and their professional strategies underscores the specificities of this professional market as a "crossroads." Structured around combinations of resources—economic, social, political, and legal—this space is by definition transnational, shaped by imperial legacies and the 1980s wave of corporate legal globalization into continental Europe. It is also a symbolic space where the terms of the unequal and uneven relationship between Africa and the world economy can be (re)defined.

Paris, indeed, is a nexus of "connected histories": US-led corporate legal globalization, colonial, and postcolonial relations, and currently the global competition between the United States, Europe, and powerful new economic and political centers, like China, over raw commodities. These connected and layered developments help us understand historical change, including legal developments, in sequence, as a "revival" where "the colonial imprint of law provides the core that defines the revival" (Dezalay and Garth 2010: 2). Further, the rich and recent scholarship on empires (see Burbank and Cooper 2010) has traced paths to define a future research agenda amenable to connect state and legal developments, with economic models of extraction on the African continent and transformations in the structure of the global economy.

Arguably, the era of European colonial empires in Africa was exceptional, both in terms of scale and time, but there was a remarkable gap between the ambition of modern colonialism in terms of social and technological innovations and the limited spaces of deployment of colonial rule. Compared to other regions, such as Asia, the perhaps singular specificity of the colonial enterprise in the African continent was its extreme diversity, particularly between colonies of settlement and extraction. This uneven and patchy colonial enterprise left fragmented societies and great diversities of economic conditions in their wake. Legal pluralism, as the legal vehicle to accommodate diversity and meager colonial resources, became a constant and general fix of colonial rule. For their part, the legal institutions and professions that emerged out of the colonial era were vastly varied across regions, even sometimes in the same countries, according to the specificities of colonial legal, economic, and political strategies at the local level (see S. Dezalay 2015).

Thus, the boon of extractive economies from the slave trade through to the modern colonial era make this a paradigmatic site to trace the uneven and unequal connections between Africa and the world. This is the case not only because of the symbiotic relationship in the development of modern capitalist economies in the *métropoles* that were built out of their imperial synergies (see, generally, Etemad 2005) and the colonial roots of the contemporary legal and economic international system, but also because of the way the impetus for extraction shaped colonial and postcolonial fields of national state power in African settings.

Tracing this colonial imprint is instrumental to map out the postcolonial trajectories of African states, economically, politically, and legally. Frederick Cooper's image of the "gatekeeper state" (2002) is a useful entry point to look at this evolution both at the domestic level, in the legal, political, and social ramifications of extractive economies nationally, and in the relations between resource-rich states with global markets, former *métropoles* and the capitals of finance, international development institutions, and multinational corporations. For example, the logic of "ring-fencing" the oil industry in Angola, away from the wider economy of the state (see Ferguson 2006) contrasts with the economic path taken in South Africa from the turn of the twentieth century, which tightly articulated the exploitative dimension of the mining industry with a wider social (and racialized) development project (see Breckenridge 2011). These two contrasted economic models— replicated in varied modes across the continent—have impacted the "resource curse" of the dependency on primary commodities for the wider national economy. They have also contributed to shaping the routes, shadow and official, of capital flows, as much as the dynamic of capitalist expansion within the continent.

On the other hand, the structure of markets for extractives and these markets' evolution from the precolonial and colonial eras (from the slave trade onward) has continuously played into contests at the local, national, and international levels, which were also heavily mediated by lawyers, often from the *métropoles*, but also in some settings, like Ghana and Nigeria, by local lawyers, between merchants, colonial administrations, and local elites (see Luckham 1978). These layered connections and contests have shaped the subsequent waves of restructuring of extractive economies nationally, from the postindependence waves of nationalization to the "neoliberal" privatizations of the 1980s through to the current reinstatement of the state as a development partner in "public-private partnerships." They are also at the core of contests over the definition of *development* as a responsibility of private extractive corporations, development institutions, or NGOs, or as that of the state. Further, the highly fragmented structure of the global market for minerals, which gives the upper hand to private corporations (mostly Northern) in production, pricing, and investment decisions, while allowing for the multiplicity of intermediaries, from local chiefs to rogue business dealers to multinational extractive companies, plays into the relative breadth and scope of global regulatory frameworks, themselves shaped by intense economic and political struggles between the United States and Asia.

Law is at the core of these developments. Initiatives aimed at transforming the asymmetrical relationship between African states and private Northern corporations—like CONNEX or the African Legal Facility—stem from the desire to stabilize foreign investments away from the economic, political, and reputational costs of the renegotiation of extractive contracts and their contests in arbitrational and jurisdictional settings. The vindicated challenge, thus, of "leveling the playing field" is also to foster the emergence of trade-oriented national state elites as much as to control, rationalize, and open up the small markets of insiders—such as the multipositioned members of the Africa Club in Paris—away from the stigmata of *affairisme*. What makes the Africa Bar in Paris offshore, yet deeply connected, is precisely the tension between the need to rely on local structures of power to do business on the African continent, and the strategy of evading local legal institutions deemed inefficient and corrupted. But at stake is also the intense competition at play in this ongoing wave of legal globalization into the continent, with international corporate law firms vying to secure their turf in a volatile and fragile market against local competitors. The challenge now, in the next step of this research agenda, would be to zoom in precisely on these local legal markets to trace their transformation over time in relation to national fields of state power, regional dynamics, and their connections with former *métropoles* and emerging poles of global power.

Notes

1. This chapter builds on and extends from Dezalay (2018).

2. See Burgis (2015) and OECD (n.d.).

3. Interview with "Martin," Fair Links, Paris, 2 July 2015.

4. I have conducted about thirty interviews with lawyers from corporate law firms as well as other members of the Bar in Paris. All English translations of French-language interview responses are mine. Except for William Bourdon and Pascal Agboyibor, whose portraits are drawn below, and whose trajectories have been extensively documented in the media, I have used pseudonyms for all my other respondents. I built this fieldwork incrementally, based on my previous research (in the context of my PhD and postdoctoral work) on the transformation since the Cold War of militant fields of human rights, the institutionalization of international criminal law, as well as the social and professional structure of international dispute settlement mechanisms. Concerning the "corporate" lawyers from Paris who are operating in Africa, I used what could be described as a "swarming" technique to identify informants and key players within this small market: based on professional rankings of multinational corporate law firms, participant observation at professional conferences, and interviews.

Any English translations of quotes from other French sources cited here were also provided by me.

5. See the website of the organization: https://www.asso-sherpa.org/accueil, accessed 5 March 2019.

6. Interview with William Bourdon, Paris, 21 December 2012. Unless otherwise specified, subsequent quotes are derived from this interview.

7. Author's interview with Pascal Agboyibor, Paris, 22 May 2015. Unless otherwise specified, subsequent quotes are derived from this interview.

8. Founded in 1937 by the French lawyer Raymond Viale.

9. Through a continuous reinvention of tradition, the family was recently reinstated as chief of canton by presidential decree under its "royal" name, Tobgui Messan Agboyibo V, in May 2014.

10. See *Jeune Afrique* (2014). In particular, Agboyibor is one of the counsels of Gécamines, one of the jewels of the mining industry of the DRC, which won in 2012 a long-lasting legal battle against the U.S. investment management firm FG Hemisphere.

11. The term *Françafrique* refers to France's relations with its former colonies in Africa. It was coined in a positive sense by Côte d'Ivoire independence president Félix Houphouët-Boigny to allude to the country's economic growth and political stability under the umbrella of France. The term is now predominantly used to denounce the allegedly neocolonial relationship France has with its former colonies in Africa.

12. Interview with "Martin."

13. Interview with "Antoine," Herbert Smith Freehills, Paris, 4 July 2015. All subsequent quotes are derived from this interview.

14. The technical alternative to the military service.

15. See "Code of Conduct of the G7 CONNEX [Strengthening Assistance for Complex Contract Negotiations] Initiative," accessed 5 March 2019, http://www.bmz.de/g7/includes /Downloadarchiv/150505_CONNEX_Code_of_Conduct_final.pdf.

16. See the African Legal Support Facility (ALSF) website, accessed 18 July 2019, https:// www.aflsf.org.

17. Interview with "Julien," McDermott, Will and Emery, Paris, 5 May 2015. Unless specified, subsequent quotes are derived from this interview.

18. Interview with Pierre, Jeantet et Associés, Paris, 28 April 2015. Subsequent quotes are derived from this interview.

19. Interview with "Dominique," Jones Day, Paris, 9 April 2015. Subsequent quotes are derived from this interview.

20. Interview with "Bruno," Eversheds, Paris, 8 April 2015. Unless specified, subsequent quotes are derived from this interview.

21. The *agrégation* is a competitive examination for civil service in the French public education system.

22. Interview with Martin.

23. The Corps des Mines is the technical Grand Corps of the French state, which trains the state engineers of the mines.

24. Interview with "Claude," Cleary Gottlieb, Paris, 29 April 2015.

25. Interview with Julien.

26. Author's interview with "Fabrice," Clifford Chance, Paris, 5 May 2015.

27. Phone interview with "Louis," Jones Day, Paris, 1 April 2015.

28. Interview with Julien.

29. Interview with Fabrice.

30. Interview with Martin.

31. Interview with Louis.

32. Interview with Martin.

33. Interview with Julien.

References

Acemoglu, Daron, and James A. Robinson. 2014. *Why Nations Fail: The Origins of Power, Prosperity and Poverty*. New York: Crown.

Bayart, Jean-François. (1989) 2009. *The State in Africa: The Politics of the Belly*. 2nd ed. New York: Cambridge University Press.

Benton, Lauren, and Richard J. Ross, eds. 2013. *Legal Pluralism and Empires, 1500–1850*. New York: New York University Press.

Bertrand, Romain. 2015. "Dix mots pour un Empire" [Ten words for an Empire]. *Le Monde Hors-Série*, 18–29.

Bourdieu, Pierre. 2014. *On the State: Lectures at the Collège de France, 1989–1992*. Malden MA: Polity.

Breckenridge, Keith. 2011. "Special Rights in Property, Why Modern African Economies Are Dependent on Mineral Resources." In *History, Historians and Development Policy: A Necessary Dialogue*, eds. C. A. Bayly, Vijayendra Rao, Simon Szreter, and Michael Woolcock, 243–260. Manchester, UK: Manchester University Press.

Brundage, James. 2008. *The Medieval Origins of the Legal Profession*. Chicago: University of Chicago Press.

Burbank, Jane, and Frederick Cooper. 2010. *Empires in World History: Power and the Politics of Difference*. Princeton, NJ: Princeton University Press.

Burgis, Tom. 2015. *The Looting Machine. Warlords, Tycoons, Smugglers and the Systematic Theft of Africa's Wealth*. London: Harper Collins.

Collier, Paul. 2007. *The Bottom Billion: Why the Poorest Countries Are Falling and What Can Be Done About It*. Oxford: Oxford University Press.

Comaroff, Jean, and John Comaroff. 2012. *Theory from the South: Or, How Euro-America Is Evolving Toward Africa*. Boulder, CO: Paradigm.

Cooper, Frederick. 2002. *Africa Since 1940: The Past of the Present*. Cambridge: Cambridge University Press.

Cooper, Frederick. 2014. *Africa in the World: Capitalism, Empire, Nation-State*. Cambridge, MA: Harvard University Press.

Cutler, A. Claire, and Thomas Dietz, eds. 2017. *The Politics of Private Transnational Governance by Contract*. Abingdon, UK: Routledge.

Deonandan, Kalowatie, and Michael L. Dougherty, eds. 2016. *Mining in Latin America. Critical Approaches to the New Extraction.* Abingdon, UK: Routledge.

Dezalay, Sara. 2006. "Gérer un conflit armé comme une cause judiciaire: L'exemple d'Amnesty International en Côte d'Ivoire" [Managing an armed conflict like a court case : The example of Amnesty International in Côte d'Ivoire]. *Critique internationale* 36:55–70.

Dezalay, Sara. 2011. "Revamping Law by Circumventing the State: Non-Governmental Organizations in the International Management of Social Violence on the African Continent." PhD of Laws diss., European University Institute, Florence.

Dezalay, Sara. 2015. "Les juristes en Afrique: Entre trajectoires d'État, sillons d'empire et mondialisation" [Lawyers in Africa: Between state trajectories, imperial legacies, and globalization]. *Politique africaine* 138:5–23.

Dezalay, Sara. 2018. "Lawyers in Africa: Brokers of the State, Intermediaries of Globalization. A Case-Study of the 'Africa' Bar in Paris." *Indiana Journal of Global Legal Studies: 25th Anniversary Edition* 25 (2): 639–669.

Dezalay, Sara, and Yves Dezalay. 2017. "Professionals of International Justice: From the Shadow of State Diplomacy to the Pull of the Market of Arbitration." In *International Law as a Profession,* eds. Jean d'Aspremont, Tarcisio Gazzini, André Nollkaemper, and Wouter Werner, 287–310. Cambridge: Cambridge University Press.

Dezalay, Yves. 1992. *Marchands de droit: La restructuration de l'ordre juridique international par les multinationales du droit* [Merchants of law: The restructuration of the international legal order by multinational law firms]. Paris: Fayard.

Dezalay, Yves, and Bryant G. Garth. 1996. *Dealing in Virtue: International Commercial Arbitration and the Construction of a Transnational Legal Order.* Chicago: University of Chicago Press.

Dezalay, Yves, and Bryant G. Garth. 2002. *The Internationalization of Palace Wars: Lawyers, Economists and the Contest to Transform Latin American States.* Chicago: University of Chicago Press.

Dezalay, Yves, and Bryant G. Garth. 2006. "From the Cold War to Kosovo: The Rise and Renewal of the Field of International Human Rights." *Annual Review of Law and Social Science* 2:231–255.

Dezalay, Yves, and Bryant G. Garth. 2010. *Asian Legal Revivals: Lawyers in the Shadow of Empire.* Chicago: University of Chicago Press.

Dezalay, Yves, and Bryant G. Garth. 2011. "State Politics and Legal Markets." *Comparative Sociology* 10:38–66.

Dimier, Véronique. 2003. "Institutionalisation et bureaucratisation de la Commission européenne: L'exemple de la DG développement" [Institutionalization and bureaucratization of the European Commission: The example of the DG Development]. *Politique européenne* 11 (3): 99–121.

The Economist. 2015. "Attack of the Bean Counters." 21 March 2015.

The Economist. 2016. "Is It Worth It? For Outsiders in Particular, Investing in Africa Is Strewn with Hurdles." 16 April 2016.

Ellis, Stephen. 2012. *Season of Rains: Africa in the World.* Chicago: University of Chicago Press.

Etemad, Bouda. 2005. *De l'utilité des empires: Colonisation et prospérité de l'Europe* [On the profitability of empires: Colonisation and prosperity in Europe]. Paris: Armand Collin.

Feichtner, Isabel. 2015. "International (Investment) Law and Distribution Conflicts over Natural Resources." In *International Investment Law and Development: Bridging the Gap*, eds. Stephan W. Schill, Christian J. Tams, and Rainer Hoffmann, 256–284. Cheltenham, UK: Edward Elgar.

Ferguson, James. 2006. *Global Shadows: Africa in the Neoliberal World Order*. Durham NC: Duke University Press.

France, Pierre, and Antoine Vauchez. 2017. *Sphère publique, intérêts privés: Enquête sur un grand brouillage* [Public sphere, private interests: Investigating a major blurring of boundaries]. Paris: Presses de Sciences Po.

Gannagé-Stewart, Hannah. 2015. "Eversheds and Norton Rose Fullbright Ramp Up in Africa with Local Alliances." *The Lawyer*, 1 February 2015. https://www.thelawyer.com/issues /online-february-2015/eversheds-and-norton-rose-fulbright-ramp-up-in-africa-with -local-alliances/.

Gobe, Éric. 2013. *Les Avocats en Tunisie de la colonisation à la révolution (1883–2011): Socio-histoire d'une profession politique* [Lawyers in Tunisia from colonization to revolution (1883–2011): Socio-history of a politicized profession]. Paris: IRMC-Karthala.

Halliday, Terrence, Lucien Karpik, and Malcolm M. Feeley, eds. 2012. *Fates of Political Liberalism in the British Post-Colony: The Politics of the Legal Complex*. Cambridge: Cambridge University Press.

Halper, Stefan. 2010. *The Beijing Consensus: How China's Authoritarian Model Will Dominate the 21st Century*. New York: Basic Books.

Hugeux, Vincent. 2007. "La Françafrique fait de la résistance: Communicants, journalistes et juristes français à l'heure de la deuxième décolonisation" [The resilience of the *Françafrique*: French lobbyists, journalists and lawyers during the era of the second decolonization]. *Politique africaine* 105:126–139.

Hugeux, Vincent, and Boris Thiolay. 2011. "Les riches secrets de la Françafrique" [The rich secrets of the *Françafrique*]. *L'Express*, 14 October 2011. https://www.lexpress.fr/actualite /politique/les-riches-secrets-de-la-francafrique_1040383.html.

Ibhawoh, Bonny. 2013. *Imperial Justice: Africans in Empire's Court*. Oxford: Oxford University Press.

Jeune Afrique. 2014. "Pascal Agboyibor, le 'bélier noir' à forte tête" [Pascal Agboyiobor, the strong-headed "black ram"]. 7 March 2014. https://www.jeuneafrique.com/12058/economie /pascal-agboyibor-le-b-lier-noir-forte-t-te/.

Jeune Afrique. 2015. "Les avocats qui ont marqué 2015" [High-profile lawyers in 2015]. 20 December 2015. https://www.jeuneafrique.com/mag/284493/economie/avocats-ont-marque -2015/.

Kantorowicz, Ernst. 2016. *The King's Two Bodies: A Study in Medieval Political Theology*. With a new introduction by Conrad Leyser and a preface by William Chester Jordan. Princeton, NJ: Princeton University Press.

Luckham, Robin. 1978. "Imperialism, Law and Structural Dependence: The Ghana Legal Profession." *Development and Change* 9 (2): 201–243.

Madsen, Mikael. 2004. "'Make Law, Not War.' Les 'sociétés impériales' confrontées à l'institutionnalisation internationale des droits de l'homme" ["Make law, not war": "Imperial societies" and the international standardization of human rights]. *Actes de la recherche en sciences sociales* 151–152:96–106.

Martines, Lauro. 1968. *Lawyers and Statecraft in Renaissance Florence*. Princeton, NJ: Princeton University Press.

Maury, Frédéric, and Fiacre Vidjingninou. 2015. "Boucle ferroviaire: Samuel Dossou gagne en appel contre le Bénin et Bolloré" [Rail loop: Samuel Dossou wins on appeal against Benin and Bolloré]. *Jeune Afrique*, 20 November 2015. https://www.jeuneafrique.com/280166/economie/boucle-ferroviaire-samuel-dossou-gagne-en-appel-contre-le-benin-et-bollore/.

Meimon, Julien. 2007. "Que reste-t-il de la Coopération française?" [What remains of the French Cooperation?]. *Politique africaine* 105:27–50.

Ngisi, Mélina N. 2015. "Pascal Agboyibor, l'avocat qui murmure à l'oreille des grands" [Pascal Agboyibor, the lawyer who whispers in the ears of the powerful]. *Forbes Afrique* (February): 33–39.

Oguamanam, Chidi, and Wesley Pue. 2016. "Lawyers' Professionalism, Colonialism, State Formation and National Life in Nigeria, 1900–1960: 'The Fighting Brigade of the People.'" In *Legal Professions and Cultural Authority*, ed. Wesley Pue, 465–484. Vancouver: University of British Columbia Press.

Organisation for Economic Cooperation and Development (OECD). n.d. "GeoBook: Geographical Flows to Developing Countries." Statistical database. Accessed 4 March 2019. http://stats.oecd.org/Index.aspx?DataSetCode=DACGEO.

Péan, Pierre. 2011. *La République des mallettes: Enquête sur la principauté française du nondroit* [The Republic of suitcases: Investigation on the French principality of lawlessness]. Paris: Fayard.

Pierrepont, Nathalie. 2014. "Orrick's New Abidjan Office Sparks Harsh Words from Local Bar." *American Lawyer*, 3 November 2014. Accessed 5 March 2019. https://www.law.com/americanlawyer/almID/1202675395899/Orricks-New-Abidjan-Office-Sparks-Harsh-Words-From-Local-Bar-/.

Rich, Eddie, and Jonas Moberg. 2015. *Beyond Governments: Making Collective Governance Work: Lessons from the Extractive Industries Transparency Initiative*. Abingdon, UK: Routledge.

Roxburgh, Charles, Norbert Dörr, Acha Leke, Amine Tazi-Riffi, Arend van Wamelen, Susan Lund, Mutsa Chironga, Tarik Alatovik, Charles Atkins, Nadia Terfous, and Till Zieno-Mahmalat. 2010. *Lions on the Move: The Progress and Potential of African Economies*. McKinsey Global Institute. Accessed 5 March 2019. https://www.mckinsey.com/featured-insights/middle-east-and-africa/lions-on-the-move.

Seroussi, Julien. 2008. "La cause de la compétence universelle: Note de recherche sur l'implosion d'une mobilisation internationale" [The cause of universal jurisdiction: Research note on the implosion of an international mobilization]. *Actes de la recherche en sciences sociales* 173 (3): 98–109.

Subrahmanyam, Sanjay. 2005. *Explorations in Connected History: From the Tagus to the Ganges*. New Delhi: Oxford University Press.

Taylor, Margaret. 2016a. "Africa Elite 2016: Vinson & Elkins Leads Energy Deal Rankings." *The Lawyer*, 21 March 2016. https://www.thelawyer.com/issues/21-march-2016-africa-elite /africa-after-30-oil/.

Taylor, Margaret. 2016b. "An Africa Office Is No Magic Door to Deals." *The Lawyer*, 21 March 2016. https://www.thelawyer.com/issues/21-march-2016-africa-elite/an-africa -office-is-no-magic-door-to-deals/.

UNCTAD. 2012. "Don't Blame the Physical Markets: Financialization Is the Root Cause of Oil and Commodity Price Volatility." Policy Brief 25 (September).

Vauchez, Antoine. 2010. "The Transnational Politics of Judicialization, *Van Gend En Loos* and the Making of EU Polity." *European Law Journal* 16 (1): 1–28.

Vauchez, Antoine. 2012a. "Élite politico-administrative et barreau d'affaires: Sociologie d'un espace-frontière" [Politico-administrative elite and corporate bar: Sociology of a cross-roads space]. *Pouvoirs* 140 (1): 71–81.

Vauchez, Antoine. 2012b. "L'avocat d'affaires: Un professionnel de la classe dirigeante?" [The corporate lawyer: A professional of the ruling class?]. *Savoir/Agir* 19 (1): 39–47.

Verhaegen, Benoît. 1985. "Les Safaris technologiques au Zaïre" [Technological safaris in Zaïre]. *Politique africaine* 18:71–87.

Willemez, Laurent. 1999. "La République des avocats: Le mythe, le modèle et son endossement" [The Republic of lawyers: The myth, the model, and its endorsement]. In *Profession politique XIXè–XXè siècle*, ed. Michel Offerlé, 201–229. Paris: Belin.

CHAPTER 5

Cultural Difference as Legal Resolution

The Raising of the *Ehime Maru*

David Leheny

When US Navy Commander Scott Waddle ordered an emergency ballast blow on the USS *Greeneville* on 9 February 2001, he apparently meant it to be viscerally exciting. The Los Angeles–class nuclear submarine was, at the time, about an hour off the coast of Honolulu, entertaining a group of VIPs invited onboard as part of the US Navy's Distinguished Visitors Program, one of its foremost public relations initiatives. To give a sense to the energy company executives and journalists on board of what the five-year-old sub could do, Waddle led the boat through a series of evasive maneuvers, demonstrating how the *Greeneville* might try to escape from enemy vessels. As the final flourish, he ordered a blow of the main ballast tanks, flooding them with air rather than water, and propelling the submarine to the surface in a rapid ascent of only seconds. Presumably because of some chaos on board the bridge with the visitors sitting at many of the controls, Waddle and his crew failed to perform a full periscope check of the surface and were therefore unaware that the *Ehime Maru*, a Japanese fisheries training boat with dozens of students from a rural high school, was immediately in the *Greeneville*'s path. The resulting collision broke the *Ehime Maru* in half, sinking it in roughly five minutes, and taking the lives of nine onboard, including four of the students.[1]

This chapter examines the political and juridical aftermath of the accident, focusing particularly on the ways in which transnational legal space produced not just the opportunity but also the demand to inscribe national cultures as fundamentally distinctive and different. As Greenhouse and Davis note in their introduction to this volume, culture is often viewed in national terms, with international law operating as a node for negotiations between them. And yet in this case, "culture" emerged in part through the political wrangling over appropriate legal measures that could simultaneously compensate the accident's victims and their families, mollify angry Japanese public opinion, and yet preserve crucial priorities for the US Navy that might have been threatened by a criminal indictment of Commander Waddle. The United States and Japan pursued a political solution that lay outside of the thicket of criminal law, lighting upon a solution that emphasized national cultural difference through a focus on nationally unifying emotions. The *Ehime Maru* case has typically been described as an exemplar of the importance of mutual understanding in crisis resolution. But it more persuasively shows how the sidestepping of criminal justice institutions, almost certainly for clear political reasons, that might have represented a pattern of transnational commonality instead demanded the creation and consolidation of national cultural differences that could then be overcome politically through a gesture of transnational recognition and respect. These national cultural differences, ostensibly marked by the emotional investment among national communities in identifiable and distinctive forms of grief, remained powerful and widely accepted motifs despite clear evidence of their basic fictiveness.

Though largely now forgotten, at the time the *Ehime Maru* incident became arguably the second-worst crisis in US-Japan relations since the 1960 security treaty demonstrations that had forced the resignation of then–Prime Minister Kishi Nobusuke. The only greater crisis had also involved a child and was in the recent memory of both governments as they aimed to contain the damage from the sinking of the *Ehime Maru*: the 1995 schoolgirl rape case, when three American service members based in Okinawa had kidnapped and raped a twelve-year-old girl. And crucially, both cases hinged on law, or rather on how law was meant to be responsive to the needs of victims of the US-Japan alliance. In 1995, massive protests roiled Okinawa, where there have been periodic though peaceful outbursts against the extraordinary burden the prefecture carries in hosting so many of the US bases in Japan, but there was also widespread anger that the Status of Forces Agreement (SOFA) between the United States and Japan dictated that the suspects would be tried by US court martial rather than in Japanese criminal courts, despite the fact that the victim was Japanese and the crime took place outside of the base (Johnson 2003). The three suspects were turned over to

Japanese courts only a month after the attack and after nationwide condemnation and a precipitous fall in Japanese public support for the US-Japan alliance threatened bilateral relations (Kristof 2005). Indeed, a subsequent set of reinterpretations of the SOFA gave more leeway to Japanese prosecutors in the event of crimes by American military personnel, aiming to ensure that legal negotiations between the two alliance partners would be based on notional equality and sovereignty, and to acknowledge that Japan's justice system could be trusted to be as fair to defendants as the American military justice system ostensibly is.

This became, though partly in reverse, the crux of the *Ehime Maru* case. Because the accident took place in American waters, there was no question of Japanese jurisdiction, but a broad range of Japanese journalistic and political voices joined the victims' family members in the expectation that American military justice would find Waddle criminally responsible, at least for negligent homicide, and that the US system would treat him as sternly as they expected their country's courts would a Japanese military commander whose careless and unnecessary blunder resulted in the deaths of so many civilians. The subsequent decision of the US Navy's court to handle the accident with administrative punishment rather than a criminal trial thereby provoked widespread Japanese outrage and led to a remarkable initiative: an ambitious effort to raise the shattered *Ehime Maru* from its deep underwater grave, move it to shallower waters, and to search it to find the bodies of the victims so that their families might hold proper funerals and to cremate the bodies, in accordance with Japanese Buddhist conventions. The US Navy thus resolved the political crisis through a challenging and costly gesture that demonstrated respect for Japanese grief, however incomprehensible Japanese practices and religiosity would purportedly be to American observers. Where the revision of the SOFA after the 1995 rape crisis had emphasized commonality in criminal justice systems, this effort rested on and contributed to an understanding of ineffable and inherent cultural differences between the two countries.

Japanese Law as Japanese Culture

In a superb overview, Eric Feldman describes the remarkable influence on the field of Japanese legal studies of a single paper: Kawashima Takeyoshi's "Dispute Resolution in Contemporary Japan," a 1963 chapter in an English-language edited volume on Japanese law. Kawashima, a dominant figure in the University of Tokyo's Faculty of Law, argued that Japan's comparatively low rates of adjudication of disputes through formal legal mechanisms marked the country's interwar and postwar approaches to courts. Although Kawashima would make frequent reference to features of Japan's legal culture as well as, particularly in a subsequent Japanese-language book, the "legal consciousness of the Japanese,"[2] his work was not simple cultural essentialism. Rather than suggesting that Japan's legal values emerged from the timeless murk of tradition, he suggested both that a seeming Japanese preference for extrajudicial or informal settlement was likely a broader pattern common among people across the world, at least in earlier days, and that Japan's continued legal modernization would likely shift legal consciousness and practice toward the more litigious activities of citizens in other advanced industrial countries. Indeed, as Feldman notes, a variety of scholars studying Japanese law—from cultural determinists to historical institutionalists to law-and-economics rational choice theorists—have in many ways built upon and responded to Kawashima's work.

It has long been far easier to publish work on Japanese law that rejects simple cultural explanations for law-related practices than to subscribe to the notion of a holistic national culture that plays a clear causal role. But it is far more common to rely on institutional, political, or historical explanations that stipulate clear boundaries between Japanese legal practices and those on evidence elsewhere—particularly in the advanced industrial West. To the extent that Japanese law remains heavily centralized, with strong national control over legislation, licensing, authorization, and punishment, it is unsurprising that much of the scholarship treats Japanese law as a realm that bears at least as strong a connection to "Japanese Everything Else" as it does to "Law Everywhere Else." When Law Everywhere Else has mattered, it has largely been in the form of practices to which Japan ought to aspire or to which it would inevitably move through the irreversible pull of modernization (Leheny and Liu 2010). Indeed, even recent proposals for changes in Japanese legal institutions have been couched in the desirability of the country's continued modernization (*kindaika*), a term used unproblematically and unironically despite Japan's status, by whatever measure one might choose, as an "advanced," modern nation. If one were to make the case that Kawashima seems to have been prescient, it might not be because he accurately predicted that the country's legal system would inevitably modernize, but rather because modernization—particularly in the form of institutional isomorphism based on a teleology interpreted from contemporary practices in northwestern

Europe and North America—would remain a discursively powerful form for political actors and intellectual figures in early twentieth-century Japan.

In part for these reasons, transnational law, or the transnational practice of law, maintains a certain kind of representational force in Japan. At times it offers the chance for Japan to build legal norms at home that match practices in the advanced industrial West. At others, it offers Japan the chance to take advantage of tools and instruments it did not create to further national interests in an uncertain international environment. But it has long remained understood as a thing external to Japan, something to which Japan must acclimate and adjust, not something endemic to or emanating from Japan itself. The criminal legal standards in the US Status of Forces Agreements that largely dictate relations with countries hosting American bases have been premised on the concern that American soldiers would become political pawns if tried by foreign powers, or that, even with friendly countries like Japan, local legal systems would provide inadequate protections to the defendants. Concerns raised during the 1995 schoolgirl rape case about Japanese prosecutors' ability to question defendants for weeks without their attorneys present for more than token periods each day amplified the political tensions between the two countries during the crisis. Subsequent reinterpretation of the agreement to stipulate that suspects in criminal cases on Japanese soil would be handled by Japanese criminal justice authorities thereby reflected not just a recognition of Japanese sovereignty but also of Japanese legal practice—that whatever its differences or imperfections, it could be counted on to be just and impartial.

And so the decision, clearly marked by important political concerns, to punish Waddle and his senior crew in the *Ehime Maru* case through administrative tools rather than with military criminal justice seemed both a betrayal of this recognition of legal equality as well as a reaffirmation of America's dominant role in the alliance. After all, if criminal justice could not touch even a ship captain who split a civilian ship filled with high school students in half while engaging in an emergency maneuver to entertain nonmilitary VIPs sitting at the submarine's controls, what good was law itself? And was this really the kind of institutional model to which Japan was supposed to aspire? The US Navy's effort to quell Japanese anger while maintaining key policy priorities, especially protecting its prized Distinguished Visitors Program, could not rest on the notion that there was something fundamentally proper about US military justice, particularly when it yielded a result that seemed on its face so unjust to so many. But it could offer a different kind of settlement, one based in part on the claim that Japanese grief over the accident's victims demanded special cultural sensitivity and an ambitious plan to recover the victims' bodies from their watery grave.

A Golf Game and Other Things Worth Preserving

When the first word of the *Ehime Maru* accident reached Japan on the morning of 10 February, within an hour or so of the actual collision, Prime Minister Mori Yoshirō was in the middle of a game of golf. He took the call on the course—later explaining that there was no word on the severity of the accident and he was advised not to rush back to the prime minister's office—and completed his game. An effective campaigner but laughably tone-deaf as Japan's prime minister, Mori had already earned some of the lowest public approval ratings in Japan's postwar history with his gaffes, like his statement (which might have been less controversial in, say, 1938) that "Japan is a country of the gods with the emperor at its center. . . . We have been working for 30 years to have people firmly acknowledge that" (Watts 2000). His decision to remain on the links as the government collected information on the victims served as the coup de grâce to his lamentable, if mercifully brief, tenure as prime minister, with public anger pushing his approval ratings to the single digits and forcing Liberal Democratic Party leaders to urge his resignation.

But Mori was a sideshow to the real political battle,[3] one that focused on the US military and its new pattern of harming Japanese children. In the weeks after the accident, television news and print media covered the sad spectacle of parents from Uwajima, in rural Ehime prefecture, begging for news of what had happened to their children; the images of haunted survivors describing the struggle to pull themselves out of the oil-slicked wreckage before the ship sank beneath the waves; and the seemingly odd decision of the *Greeneville* to keep its distance rather than helping the survivors. While there is little dispute that this was likely the right decision, as further motion by the massive submarine threatened to cause waves that would capsize life rafts and floating debris, imperiling the survivors, frequent references to it only enhanced the sense that the US Navy's stance toward the victims was brutally callous. To many observers in Japan, despite the differences between a vicious sexual assault of a child on Japanese soil and a maritime accident in American waters, the *Ehime Maru* accident was a repeat of the 1995 schoolgirl rape case, with a US military that remained at best indifferent to innocent life in an ally that Americans too often took completely for granted. Two demands, one seemingly obvious as a legal matter and one less so, quickly rose to the surface in debates in Japan. First, many expected that Waddle—who by all accounts wanted to apologize to victims immediately but was prevented from doing so as the Navy determined what legal steps would take place—would be held criminally accountable. A Maritime Self-Defense Force submarine commander, Yamashita Keisuke, had received a sentence of thirty months behind bars for a 1988 collision in Tokyo Harbor that killed thirty civilians on a fishing boat. Second, the Japanese government asked the US Navy to recover the bodies of the victims so that their families might give them proper funerals. These would shape the controversies and responses that followed.

Recognizing the grave crisis that the accident had caused, American officials moved quickly to apologize, an act often described as deference to Japan's "apology culture" rather than part of the regular stuff of international diplomacy. The apologies came from myriad levels of American leadership, from Ambassador Thomas Foley to new Secretary of State Colin Powell and the new American president, George W. Bush. Indeed, the apologies were so thick in the air, and did so little to mollify most Japanese, that *Washington Post* columnist Richard Cohen famously and controversially wrote that "We've apologized enough to Japan," because it was a simple accident off the coast of Hawai'i "for crying out loud," and that Japan, with its rich history of amnesia surrounding Japanese atrocities during World War II, was hardly in a position to demand more (Cohen 2001). One conservative figure in Japan agreed with the thrust of Cohen's article, writing in *Shokun*, a strongly right-leaning monthly magazine, that his country resembled a foot-stamping child, petulantly repeating "No! No!" (*ee, iya da iya da*) in the face of repeated American apologies and entreaties to move beyond the crisis for the good of the alliance (Takashima 2001: 88).

But this was a tiny minority view in the midst of wide condemnation of American actions. In subsequent Diet debates, conservative government figures sought to contain public outrage so that it would not imperil the alliance with the United States, but did so largely by emphasizing that American officials acknowledged the outrage and were seeking in good faith to respond to it. The criticism from parliamentarians was broad and highly emotional, frequently describing the tension with the United States as a clash of cultures. At a hearing two weeks after the accident, Den Hideo, a Socialist MP who had long been an antiwar activist and a critic of Japan's security treaty with the United States, emphasized that Japanese viewed family relationships differently than did Americans:

> People my age were raised partly in an education system that emphasized that Americans and British were savages [*kichiku beiei*]. But now, I have very friendly feelings toward America as well as Americans themselves, and I have actual American friends. Despite that, it's important to recognize that this thing is really terrible.
>
> At the same time, it's been said that there are cultural differences in the ways in which the American side and the Japanese side are approaching this, and I feel the same way. Actually, for Japanese people, family-centeredness [*kazoku-shugi*] is, so to speak, extremely important. You could probably say the same about all of Asia. America is all about individualism, so even when family members die, it's sad and regrettable, but it's still seen from the perspective of individualism. And that's different from Japan.
>
> You'll remember when ten young Japanese who had gone skiing in Austria died in a cable car [fire in Kaprun, 1990]. At the time, the country with the largest number of victims was Austria itself, and then Germany was next, with Japan losing ten. But the telling part is that thirty Japanese relatives, the most of any country, then visited the spot. And this really shocked the people in Austria, but it really showed the feeling of Japanese about the importance of their families.
>
> It's the same with America this time, I think. And I actually think that in a sense, it's the perfect opportunity to give a piece of our mind to the Americans, to explain without restraining ourselves how Japanese feel and think. Americans are under the impression that they themselves are the world's "Number One" [*nambā wan*] in all matters. And isn't it about time for us to say, no, that American democracy, the culture of America, and of Americans, simply isn't the best in the world? ("Kokkai Gijiroku" 2001)[4]

Den's logic is elaborate, and marked by his socialist politics: referring to American imperialism, cultural commonalities among Asians, and the ways in which a putative American individualism might affect one's feelings toward the death of a loved one. But it also neatly sums up a set of broader concerns about the politics of the US-Japan relationship that go far beyond anger over the negligence of one submarine commander. Instead, Americans would need to understand and to respect the community of feeling that Japan represented, a community shaped here in large part by its difference from the ways in which Americans might approach grief.

This stipulation of national cultural difference between Japan and the United States had quickly became a central theme in much of the discussion of the disaster, and one that was broadly shared by observers across the political spectrum. Ambassador Foley, whose tenure was extended several months into the new Bush administration because of the crisis, agreed to it himself during a press conference with the Japanese press. One especially provocative question referred to different Japanese and American views of death at sea by noting that the United States had a memorial at the site of the sinking of the USS *Arizona* in the December 1941 Pearl Harbor attack, in which more than a thousand crew members died. Seemingly unfazed by the comparison, Foley took the opportunity to speak about cultural difference and the importance of mutual understanding and respect:

> Well, I think it is sometimes very difficult for people in each culture to fully appreciate and understand the attitudes in other cultures. When John F. Kennedy, Jr., and his wife were lost in an aircraft accident, they had a ceremony at sea, commending their bodies to the deep in effect. As in the case that you mention, the USS *Arizona*, we often regard the bodies of those lost at sea as a special matter for respect and that there is more attention and demand often; and it is an understandable but different part of the culture in Japan to recover the bodies at virtually every opportunity where it's possible (US Department of State 2001).

Given the context, it seems unlikely that Foley was being deliberately dishonest, but the answers here are at best misleading. The decision to commend the *Arizona's* crew to the deep was driven largely by the expected impossibility of identifying the remains of the victims in the ship's aft (National Park Service n.d.), and subsequent recovery and identification efforts have continued for victims in the Pearl Harbor attack even more than seventy years later (Associated Press 2015). And the decades-long efforts to recover the remains of American soldiers in Vietnam ought to have ensured at least some skepticism toward any claim of American nonchalance toward dead bodies.[5] Foley's reference to John F. Kennedy Jr.'s death two years earlier was even stranger. After all, while the remains of Kennedy, his wife, and his sister-in-law were indeed commended to the sea, this happened only after a remarkable endeavor by the US Navy and Coast Guard to locate the wreckage and recover the bodies, an expensive effort that was justified by the Coast Guard and President Bill Clinton because of the unusually public nature of the private citizens on board. And their cremation and subsequent commending to the sea was itself a source of controversy, as it appears that there were quarrels between the Kennedy and Bessette families about cremation and the proper location of the burial. None of this is to suggest that Foley deliberately lied in his response, but his depiction of an American approach to the bodies of those killed at sea dramatically overstates a national unity about grief and profoundly misrepresents the necessarily fraught nature of these concerns.

Foley's statement thus not only dovetailed with Japanese concerns but also pointed toward a kind of solution: an American effort to overcome cultural difference through the expression of cross-cultural understanding. Indeed, in the very Diet session in which Den Hideo lamented American individualism and chauvinism, and in which he essentially demanded American recognition of Japan's cultural position, Foreign Minister Kōno Yohei warily praised Foley's stance while conceding that the United States would need to do more to show its concern for Japanese mourning:

> Truly, in this incident—whether we call it an "incident" or an "accident"—the sense of how to deal with it afterwards is different in the United States and Japan. But, as I said to Mr. Koizumi as well, there are differences, in this case with the United States, I think it's definitely correct to make sure that the United States is thinking about how to deal with this problem while obviously taking care to consider the feelings of the Japanese people, or perhaps Japan's spiritual culture. In particular, Ambassador Foley has demonstrated a great deal of heart-felt consideration [kokoro zukai]. He's been ambassador here for an awfully long time and was supposed to return home, having finished his term at the end of this month, but he said that he would stay on a little longer because of this problem that occurred right before his departure. Of course, in America, there are people like this who really understand Japan, though I know that there's a part of America that can't understand. But I believe it's necessary to take efforts to make them understand ("Kokkai Gijroku" 2001).

During the hearing, parliamentarians referred to a request that Kōno had made in a letter to the US government: that the United States try to raise the

Ehime Maru from its deep-water resting place to search for bodies of the dead. Communist MP Koizumi Chikashi, who highlighted his own connections with the victims' families, explained the request fully in the context of accountability, not primarily in terms of any culturally specific concerns about death:

> [Having now had the opportunity to read the letter from the Foreign Minister to the US government], it's written that the US government is strongly requested, because of the most important request from the families, to raise the boat itself. But in terms of the problem of raising the boat, for the families themselves, the most important issue is, after all, that the navy that's responsible, the government that's responsible, make a clear promise to raise the boat. And that's what they've emphasized ("Kokkai Gijiroku" 2001).

This was not, however, the sentiment that would prevail in subsequent discussions between the American and Japanese governments about the nearly unprecedented recovery mission to follow. The focus would instead be on the kind of national cultural practices and emotional frames to which Foley had gestured and Den had emphasized. And the construction of cultural difference, and of a resolution that emphasized mutual understanding rather than the legal stipulation of criminal fault, allowed the two governments to sidestep a number of thornier issues in the relationship and in the US Navy's goals in managing the crisis.

What Criminal Responsibility Would Have Meant

While not especially decorated, Scott Waddle had built a reputable career in his twenty years in the Navy. He was known largely as a garrulous, engaging figure, exactly the sort who might represent the Navy well during a visit arranged by the Distinguished Visitors Program. Explained largely because of its ability to break down walls between the Navy and US civilians, the program has a clear public relations purpose; indeed, visitors (sometimes celebrities, often journalists, and frequently those with politically powerful connections) are typically selected because of their ability to convey the work of the Navy to large or desirable audiences. On the day of the *Greeneville-Ehime Maru* collision, the sixteen civilians on board included several connected to the new president, George W. Bush, including a set of energy company executives, two of whom were at the submarine's controls (under supervision) at the moment of the collision. Indeed, it was reported at the time that several had been named to that day's excursion because of their participation in or donations to a charity golf match with proceeds going to a memorial to the USS *Missouri*, the Navy battleship on which the representatives of the Japanese empire signed the formal instruments of surrender to end World War II (Moton 2001).

The day's events were planned to go well with the overall structure of the Distinguished Visitors Program. Given extensive time with the submarine's commanding officers, the civilians on board accompanied the crew in a launch just before 8 A.M., finally submerging after 10 A.M., when the submarine had reached nearly twenty nautical miles from the coast. Crew members collected, bottled, and labeled water samples from the ocean at different depths along the way to distribute to the visitors as souvenirs. Because of the large group size, lunch was divided into two seatings, beginning at 11 A.M. and scheduled to finish before 12:30. Waddle, whose flamboyance and adventurousness had made him popular among many of his crew, decided on a set of evasive maneuvers to show the visitors the capabilities of the submarine. While the US Navy's report would absolve the visitors themselves of responsibility for the collision, a subsequent report by the National Transportation Safety Board left little doubt that their presence on board had created an environment in which the commander and senior crew, expected to entertain them, would be more prone to making mistakes. With a substantial number of visitors at the ship's instruments during the evasive maneuvers, Waddle ordered the *Greeneville*'s ballast flow and rapid rise to the surface without a periscope check sufficient to identify nearby vessels that might have escaped immediate radar or sonar contact. When, at noon, the submarine rose rapidly and smashed into the hull of the large fisheries training vessel, the entire submarine shuddered from the impact, shocking the visitors and crew alike (National Transportation Safety Board 2005).

The *Ehime Maru*, of course, was in pandemonium. Having just wrapped up lunch after a maintenance stop in Honolulu earlier, the ship was headed back into international waters to continue its training run for the high school boys on board. Because of Japan's unusual position as a wealthy, advanced industrial country marked largely by extensive island coastlines, fisheries remain a sufficiently important industry to justify substantial government outlays for schools like Uwajima Fisheries High School, located on the far western side of Shikoku, the smallest of Japan's major islands. While not a purely vocational school, it does focus a substantial amount of its training and curriculum on marine science and fisheries techniques, and the long Pacific runs on the *Ehime Maru* were among its most distinctive features. Particularly in a town like Uwajima—which had thrived in early postwar economic growth and investment but had fallen prey to the depopulation and deindustrialization that have marked most of Japan's nonurban peripheries—a school like this offered important opportunities to families seeking to build or to maintain economic viability close to home. At the time of the collision, a number of the budding fishers were still in the mess, wrapping up lunch and preparing for more training and work. The sudden strike from the *Greeneville* nearly broke the ship in half, with power outages plunging the lower decks into darkness and oil from the severed lines spilling into the sea, making it nearly impossible for people to get a grip on the ladders and stairway rails that were necessary to allow them to pull themselves to safety.

In the subsequent investigations, Waddle was unsurprisingly deemed to be responsible, but the Navy stopped short of a court-martial that might have held him criminally liable. Even to a number of American observers, this seemed surprising, particularly given the Navy's emphasis on accountability as well as its own standards for findings of criminal fault. One PBS reporter asked then commander-in-chief of the Pacific Fleet, Admiral Thomas Fargo, why Waddle had been allowed to retire with a pension rather than tried in a court-martial:

> *Reporter:* From the manual for courts martial, all that's necessary to charge for negligent homicide is that someone died as a result of simple negligent behavior, not exhibiting a degree of care of safety, that an otherwise careful person would have exercised, and no intent is necessary. Why does this case not live up to charging for negligent homicide?
>
> *Admiral Thomas Fargo:* Well, obviously I charged Commander Waddle under two very serious counts of the Uniform Code of Military Justice. It was in my judgment that further charges were not necessary, and that we could achieve proper accountability without that (*PBS Newshour* 2001).

This might be viewed as admirable, a recognition that punishment need not be maximally cruel to be effective. But it also rang hollow, as it seemed to elevate the sense that Waddle himself had suffered enough—and there is little doubt that he was himself emotionally devastated by the accident—above the concerns of the accident's victims.

Indeed, as in critical American circles, the view within Japan was largely that Waddle had been spared to protect the Distinguished Visitors Program itself. That is, in a court-martial, any defense attorney worth his or her salt would have emphasized it for its exculpatory or mitigating value.[6] Waddle would have been unlikely that day to perform a ballast blow unless he were performing it for powerful people whom the Navy wanted him to entertain; he would have been equally unlikely to be cavalier in his safety checks had not the chaos on board the submarine's crowded bridge because of the inclusion of these visitors into the submarines' routine. Unlike with an administrative hearing largely handled outside of public debate, a court-martial would almost certainly have forced the Navy into the highly uncomfortable position of defending a valued public relations program because it would otherwise have been the linchpin to a defense case. While there is no doubt that Admiral Fargo was within his rights as commanding officer of the Pacific Fleet to pursue administrative rather than criminal punishment for Waddle, the decision is so closely aligned with the Navy's obvious hope to defend the Distinguished Visitors Program itself—which Fargo did during his PBS interview—that there is certainly room for deep suspicion of its motives.

And this left the victims, their families, and their often self-designated advocates in Japan and Hawai'i without any hope that law itself would designate responsibility in a fair, meaningful, and accountable way. Particularly just six years after US officials and journalists raised concerns about Japan's criminal justice system as a partial defense of the Status of Forces Agreement, the Navy's decision was represented as a profoundly and mercilessly unjust one.

How They Grieve, How We Grieve

Partly for this reason, the US and Japanese governments, both eager to overcome the crisis and get back to their normal military and diplomatic cooperation, chose to focus on the second kind of potential resolution: a display of American recognition of Japan's emotional needs. The Japanese government had already raised the possibility of an American effort to salvage the *Ehime Maru* and search its wreckage for bodies, an initiative greatly complicated by the ship's depth. Unlike, say, John F. Kennedy Jr.'s ill-fated airplane, which was only about 35 meters underwater, the *Ehime Maru* lay 610 meters, over a third of a mile, below the waves. The only precedent for a salvage of this sort was the 1974 CIA covert operation Project Azorian, funded and managed in part with the cooperation of Howard Hughes, to raise a Soviet ballistic missile submarine that had sunk to more than 4,000 meters in 1968. In the end, the operation retrieved only a portion of the submarine, but managed to bring up the remains of six sailors, who were then memorialized and given a burial at sea in a secret ceremony. Eerie footage of the memorial shows a chaplain, in front of flags of both the US and the Soviet Navy, solemnly reminding others present of the valor of the dead sailors:

> The fact that our nations have had disagreements does not lessen in any way our respect for them or the service they have rendered. And so, as we return their mortal remains to the deep, we do so in a way that we hope would have meaning to them. . . . We therefore commit these crew members of this ship to a proper resting place to join the Valhalla of sea heroes who have gone before them. We commit their remains to the deep, looking for the resurrection of the body when the sea shall give up her dead, and the life of the world to come. Amen.[7]

The video later was declassified and released, with the US government giving a copy directly to Russian president Boris Yeltsin in 1992, evidently in part to encourage the Russian government to provide any information it might have on missing US service members in Vietnam (Sontag and Drew with Drew 1998).

The episode, though hardly of much interest in Japan before 2001, became the linchpin of the Japanese request that the United States raise the *Ehime Maru*, which was in far shallower waters and could presumably benefit from technological advances in the intervening years. And surely the United States owed Japan that, particularly because the families desperately wished to give their loved ones proper funerals. George Tanabe, a Japanese American professor of religion at the University of Hawai'i, became an important source for both the US media and for the US Navy in explaining their concerns. As he noted, under Japanese Buddhist rituals, dead bodies would be cremated and protected, to prevent them from becoming wandering spirits:

> If the bodies of the missing *Ehime Maru* crew members are not retrieved, they cannot be purified by fire, preserved as ashes, placed in

safekeeping and prepared for postmortem care. They will remain in anguish, never resting in peace (Tanabe 2001).

Tanabe correctly described one explicit meaning of the funerals, though at least one Japanese specialist would articulate it differently. Nawa Kiyotaka, a young religion scholar writing after the November 2011 operation to raise the *Ehime Maru* and the recovery of eight of nine bodies, used local news reports from Ehime to describe how family members dealt with the recovery of their loved ones' bodies. The father of high school student Terata Yūsuke reportedly spoke late into the night directly to his son's ashes after the cremation, almost as if he were alive, saying, "You've arrived in a different form, but I'm so relieved that you've come back home, where you are loved."[8] Yūsuke's mother, Masumi (often identified as the leader of the victims' families), talked about the agony of his being underwater for more than half a year as if he had been alive to experience it:

> [His] training uniform and the underwear in which they'd found him had been covered with heavy oil that had hardened into clay. . . . The smell was so awful that it hurts the eyes, and I realized now that it must have been a terribly brutal experience for him to be lying in that oil for eight months. (Nawa 2005: 114–115)

Nawa suggests that this fit well with Sakurai Tokutarō's theory of souls of the dead in Japanese Buddhism: A proper funeral and continual prayers from the living allow the soul, immediately separated from the body after death but soon returning to it, to move comfortably and smoothly between this world and the next.

Judged from the perspective of these sympathetic expert voices, the ultimate raising of the *Ehime Maru*—completed with the use of the *Rockwater II*, an oil-drilling platform contracted by the US Navy, through a special Congress-approved budget, from the Halliburton Corporation—and subsequent recovery of eight of nine bodies would have to be considered a remarkable success. After all, the United States had made a "costly signal" (Martin 2004) to the Japanese that it took their concerns seriously, paying for an expensive recovery, moving the *Ehime Maru* to shallower waters in October–November 2011, and deploying some of the country's most skilled salvage diver personnel in the search. All of this despite the large-scale mobilization that the United States undertook in the aftermath of the September 11 attacks, including the war in Afghanistan and rumored plans to invade Iraq. The seriousness of the Navy's handling of the cultural dimensions of the recovery was widely covered in the Japanese press, as naval personnel—following advice from Tanabe and other experts on Japanese religious practice—placed the recovered bodies into body bags feet-first, to approximate Buddhist rituals, and brought them to the surface only after sundown to maintain some privacy from circling media helicopters (Apgar and Tolbert 2001).

While family members remained guarded in their praise of the efforts, as did critics of the United States in the media, representatives of the Japanese government emphasized the extraordinary care taken to allow people to be reunited with their loved ones. Maritime Self-Defense Force (MSDF) Commander Hayashi Hideki, who served as a liaison with the US Navy during the recovery effort, contributed the most extensive praise of the effort in an essay penned for the conservative monthly magazine *Seiron*. Hayashi, detailing the operation in remarkable detail, emphasized the extraordinarily close collaboration of the US Navy divers and a crew of six divers from the *Chihaya*, a Japanese MSDF ship sent to take part in the mission, and the almost obsessive concern for the families. When one Japanese diver was injured, he reportedly begged his commander not to send him back to Japan for treatment:

> It's okay with me even if I have to have another surgery here in Hawai'i, so please don't make me return home until we have fulfilled our duty [*saimu o mattō suru made*]. . . . I represent the Maritime Self-Defense Forces, and I was dispatched here for the families, as well as to maintain the friendly relations of the United States and Japan, so I cannot return home until we have completed the mission. (Hayashi 2003: 322)

But Hayashi also emphasized the emotional commitment of the Americans, describing a moment—one that was absent in virtually all of the extensive English-language coverage of the recovery—when the respective navies brought the victims' families to the shallow-water recovery area where they could throw flowers into the ocean to commemorate the search. As the Japanese families asked to send messages of thanks from the microphones on board the Japanese boat to the US Navy personnel on board their own ship, they began to break down in tears, followed by the US commanding officer and then all of the American crew. I have no reason to suspect that the episode itself was inaccurately reported, but its central place in Hayashi's story and absence in American descriptions of the recovery effort is telling, as is the tone of official American communiqués on the successful effort.

Indeed, in the aftermath of the recovery, American reports focused instead on Navy generosity as well as the same kind of technical skill, commitment, and courage that the Distinguished Visitor Program itself was designed to highlight to domestic audiences. They would rarely if ever touch on the issues of accountability that had been at the center of the original Japanese requests. In an official newsletter for Navy divers, Captain Bert Marsh, US Navy director of Ocean Engineering and Supervisor of Salvage and Diving at the Naval Sea Systems Command, wrote:

> I urge you to read and take pride in what your community has accomplished. As I mentioned to the MDSU ONE Divers, when assigned to determine if raising the EHIME MARU and recovering the remains was feasible, I knew I had an ace-in-the-hole with the MDSU located at Alpha docks on Hickam AF Base. My confidence was fully justified. They not only succeeded in recovering the remains and personal items, they became America's best Ambassadors to Japan. Through their meticulous awareness of cultural issues and the establishment of an exceptional working relationship with their Japanese counterparts, they restored trust between our two countries. (Marsh 2002: 2)

In the same issue, another US Navy Salvage specialist wrote:

> The full impact of the success of the operation will probably never be known. What is already clearly apparent is that eight families of those nine unfortunate crewmembers have been able to bring home their loved one and that the ninth family has been greatly assisted in their grieving process. Everyone who participated in the recovery has assisted in accomplishing an act of kindness that will be remembered for a long time. (Baumann 2002: 5)

In a statement made several years later and translated and published by the US-Japan Navy Friendship Association, retired rear admiral Robert Chaplin, who had served as the commander of US Naval Forces in Japan throughout the Ehime Maru crisis, emphasized the emotional benefits of the operation to the Japanese victims as well as their gratitude to the United States:

I received a letter from a family that had lost a son in the accident. The letter stated that the family watched the television reports of the horrible events happening in the United States. They knew they would have to wait for the recovery of their son because they were certain that the US Navy would focus on this war on terror. But to their surprise the Navy continued the recovery operations of *Ehime Maru*, and because of this, this family truly understood the meaning of freedom. (Chaplin 2009)

And if Japanese appreciation for American efforts revolved around the kinds of moral qualities valorized in US Navy rhetoric—honor (*meiyo*) for Hayashi, freedom for Chaplin—they also resulted from the keen cultural awareness put on display by Navy personnel. As Chaplin wrote:

This incident caused the USN [US Navy] to work through the cultural differences of our two countries. In the US, survival charts would be consulted and a timed search would be conducted, after that period of time the search would be concluded and those people not recovered would be declared lost at sea. In Japan one searches until the families of those lost feel it is time to stop. The Japanese culture also desires that the remains of loved ones return to their home country for appropriate services. (Chaplin 2009)

The Durable Fragility of Cultural Difference

Even if shorn of some of its uncomfortable language that not only consolidates a Japanese national culture but also assigns agency to it, Chaplin's claim—widely shared in the Japanese and American media—here would be empirically problematic. Unsurprisingly, given Japan's geographical status as an archipelago, roughly two hundred to three hundred Japanese are lost at sea each year, mostly in boating or fishing accidents. And while the Japanese Coast Guard, which keeps the relevant statistics, is an exceptionally capable force, it too observes limits that are functionally identical to those of the US Coast Guard in searching for bodies: depth charts, tidal patterns, ocean condition, time in the water, and so forth (Shimizu 2010: 120–121). While it became conventional wisdom that American search patterns are driven by the cold, clinical determinations of scientific rationality and Japanese ones by the depth of human bonds, the actual practices are far more complex. For the son of a martyred president, of course, the US Coast Guard and Navy would engage in expensive and tireless recovery efforts, though probably not for an average private pilot; and Japanese families, like their American counterparts, must resign themselves to losing the bodies of loved ones when officials determine that further search efforts are pointless.

One of the few US Navy personnel to frame the recovery effort and the care for the bodies in the language of accountability, Admiral William Klemm, told the *New York Times* in an interview, "'We not only killed some people, but we messed up their families, and we owed them something. It meant respecting their dignity, and that requires a lot more than just dredging up some scraps of metal and delivering some clothing" (French 2001). In the final Navy report on the recovery, however, he is quoted in the more widely used language of generosity afforded by the Navy's technical skill and courage:

> [The recovery personnel] have overcome significant technical difficulties in order to provide *closure* to the families of the missing crew members. The gratitude they showed us justified the operation. We are pleased that we were able to recover the remains of eight crew members, but our prayers continue to be with the Mizuguchis (the family of the ninth missing crew member) in their loss. (US Pacific Fleet Public Affairs 2001; emphasis added)

When I have delivered talks in Japanese about the *Ehime Maru* incident, I have struggled with translation of the word *closure*. It can, of course, be explained with a relatively lengthy phrase, but what this misses is the word's connection to American therapeutic language and the easy way it trips off the tongue. The American use of the word, of course, struggles with something almost fundamentally dishonest about it, at least in the context of grief over the loss of close loved ones. Writing of grief in his brilliant *Flaubert's Parrot*, the English novelist Julian Barnes lays waste to the idea that there is anything like real closure:

> And you do come out of it, that's true. After a year, after five. But you don't come out of it like a train coming out of a tunnel, bursting through the downs into sunshine and that swift, rattling descent to the Channel; you come out of it as a gull comes out of an oil-slick. You are tarred and feathered for life. (Barnes [1984] 1990: 161)

Unsurprisingly, the families of the victims, in accounts published later, seemed more like Barnes's wounded gulls than like people who had moved on neatly from the deaths of their children and other loved ones. Ikeda Naoki, an attorney who had represented several family members during the crisis, recognized that the financial settlements provided by the US Navy were beyond what the families would have been awarded in Japanese courts, but noted in a major legal journal that the accountability that they demanded most strongly, in the form of criminal punishment for Waddle, remained out of the question (Ikeda 2004). For a wider audience, he also described the fraught nature of the families' emotional states after the completion of the recovery mission, and in a way that fundamentally challenged the American reports of emotional closure.

The story's villain in the Japanese press had largely remained Waddle, reviled for not apologizing immediately (though he did so as soon as permitted by the Navy) and for seeming less than completely forthright in accepting responsibility. Waddle, however, seems to have been committed to the idea of apologizing directly to the families as part of his determination to do "the right thing."[9] More than a year after the disaster, Waddle (now a private citizen, paying his own way) made his way to Japan, traveling to Uwajima to lay flowers at a memorial to the accident's victims. His book—written entirely in the first person except for the brief epilogue describing his trip there—concludes with a short, third-person description of the trip:

> To the Japanese public, Scott's apology was not an admission of guilt, but a gesture of integrity, humility, and honor. They recognized the importance of having Commander Scott Waddle stand before the family members and bring as much closure as possible to the incident that took the lives of their loved ones and sparked a firestorm of international controversy. (Waddle with Abraham 2002: 242)

But many of the family members reportedly left town during his visit in order to avoid the media, and none were willing to attend his visit to the memorial. Indeed, only the Terata family explicitly announced their willingness to meet with Waddle, and, in the end, only Terata Masumi spoke with him, arranging the meeting at a hotel conference room in Tokyo. The Terata family makes several appearances in Waddle's book as especially vocal leaders of the angry families, though Waddle's confusion about their given names makes it difficult to know at times if he is writing about the mother or father.

Ms. Terata meets Waddle in Tokyo, and Waddle indicates in his book that they connected over her grief and through his explanation of the accident (Waddle with Abraham 2002: 232). But Ikeda, writing for a local magazine in Osaka after interviewing Ms. Terata, frames it differently. She tells him that they did in fact connect, as Waddle broke down in tears when she showed him photos of her son. And in doing so, he demonstrated a level of humanity and decency that she had not fully expected:

> As for my son whom I loved desperately, who was everything to me— the fact that he was taken away from me by the crew of the *Greeneville* with Captain Waddle in charge, it doesn't erase his life for me. I can't forgive them for the accident itself. But I think it's possible in a sense that Waddle himself is a victim of the Navy as an organization. (Ikeda 2003)

And the word she evidently uses to describe her tarred-and-feathered emotional state to Ikeda is about as far from closure, or whatever Japanese translation one might want to offer, as one can get: *jiseki*, or "self-reproach." Meeting Waddle had indicated to her that he was not a monster, and that the Navy itself was at fault, but she could still not bring herself to forgive him for taking her seventeen-year-old son away from her.

Ikeda notes that the family members were in no position to demand more. They had received apologies from the US Navy and other senior officials in the American government. They had received, by Japanese standards, large financial compensation packages from the Navy. Almost all had had their loved ones' remains returned to them, after extraordinarily careful searches and treatment by US Navy personnel, vouchsafed by representatives of Japan's own naval forces. Particularly as the US and Japanese governments were drawing their alliance together tightly during the "war on terror" and the rise of China, the families were, Ikeda implies, told by others in their tight-knit community in Uwajima that it was time to move on. How much more could the United States reasonably do to show that it cared how Japanese felt?

In Place of Law

None of this overstates what criminal prosecution of Waddle or his senior officers would have accomplished, at least as far as the victims' families are concerned. While victims' rights movements have made important gains in

Japanese politics in recent years, the evidence is, broadly speaking, inconclusive about the consequences of severe punishment for the lives of victims and their families.[10] Indeed, if anything, Ms. Terata's statement to her attorney indicates a complex and unresolved set of feelings that unsurprisingly go beyond a simple desire for vengeance even if, to her own shame, she cannot bring herself to forgive Waddle. The law, which had previously been coordinated politically by the US and Japanese governments to deal with contested transnational events, was deemed insufficient to provide an adequate solution that could simultaneously preserve valued institutional prerogatives of the US Navy and the grief of coastal families far from the seat of Japanese government power.

My point is that in place of the criminal remedies, the US and Japanese governments settled on a remarkable effort that allowed a performance of alliance unity, with the Japanese MSDF playing a small and final role in the search for bodies, as well as of cultural sensitivity, which was enabled by the construction and articulation of national cultural difference. As Greenhouse and Davis note in their introduction to this volume, culture does not simply emanate from local tradition but rather operates within and is even produced through transnational interactions, conflicts, and contestation. Primarily because the shared criminal legal remedy was largely unacceptable to the American side, Japanese and American "cultures" were both idealized as internally coherent, commonly shared, and nationally distinctive backgrounds that demanded a different kind of gesture of mutual respect. But, if anything, the inability of the mostly successful recovery mission to resolve the grief of the victims' families might have been, had it been acknowledged, the source of some genuine transnational recognition; after all, what American family, having lost a child, would have been unable to see how durable that grief and its effects would likely be?

But in the world of alliance diplomacy, the focus for both governments had to be on the maintenance of the relationship through an effort that could in the end be judged as providing a final outcome: the evidence of mutual respect and care that would allow the families to move on with their lives without rancor or justifiable bitterness. Criminal law lay at the heart of the initial disagreements over the *Ehime Maru* in part because of the expectation that its deployment would have allowed a mutually legible way to settle accounts, to show responsibility, to demonstrate commonality. That it too would likely have failed, at least in terms of the most intimate grief of the victims' families and friends, remained outside of the discussions of how the two countries could move forward together through shared sentiments of honor, courage, freedom, and sympathy. After all, the two governments needed closure as much as the victims' families ostensibly did, and theirs could be far more easily produced.

Notes

1. The most thorough English-language account of the accident was provided four years later by the National Transportation Safety Board (2005).

2. Feldman (2007) focuses primarily on Kawashima's chapter "Dispute Resolution in Contemporary Japan" (Kawashima 1963). Kawashima's subsequent expansion appeared in *Nihonjin no hōishiki* (Kawashima 1967).

3. One of Japan's most astute diplomatic observers, Tanaka Akihiko (2004: 35), has argued that Mori was more than a sideshow, in that his gaffe cost him the opportunity to be a credible representative of Japanese grief to the Americans at a time that the country needed steady alliance leadership.

4. All translations from the Japanese are mine unless otherwise noted.

5. For a thorough discussion, see Schwenkel (2009).

6. Curtis Martin (2004), one of the few scholars to have written specifically about this case, comes to this same conclusion.

7. Material related to Project Azorian declassified in 2010 can be seen in the Nuclear Vault in the National Security Archive at George Washington University. See http://www.gwu.edu /~nsarchiv/nukevault/ebb305/index.htm.

8. This is my best effort to translate the original Japanese, which is "Kawari hateta sugata datta ga, ito-oshiku, jibun no moto ni kaette kita to iu anshin ga atta."

9. Waddle used the term somewhat defiantly in explaining his decision to testify, against his lawyer's advice, at the hearing, despite the Navy's refusal to offer him testimonial immunity. It also became the title of his book about the accident and investigation.

10. This is a widely covered topic in the United States, particularly as it pertains to the death penalty. For brief overviews, see Bandes (1999) and Kanwar (2001).

References

Apgar, Sally, and Tolbert, Kathryn. 2001. "Navy Pays Respect in Recovery Effort." *Washington Post*, 21 October 2001. https://www.washingtonpost.com/archive/politics/2001/10/21 /navy-pays-respect-in-recovery-effort/dac7b696-da42-4d16-9bdb-73851d784b13.

Associated Press. 2015. "Remains of 7 Pearl Harbor 'Unknowns' Identified." 10 November. http://www.cbsnews.com/news/remains-seven-pearl-harbor-unknowns-identified/.

Bandes, Susan. 1999. "When Victims Seek Closure: Forgiveness, Vengeance, and the Role of Government." *Fordham Urban Law Journal* 27 (5): 1599–1606.

Barnes, Julian. (1984) 1990. *Flaubert's Parrot*. New York: Vintage.

Baumann, Greg. 2002. "*Ehime Maru* Recovery Successful." *Faceplate: The Official Newsletter for the Divers and Salvors of the United States Navy* 6 (1): 3–5.

Chaplin, Robert C. 2009. "Bonds of U.S. Navy and JMSDF That Experienced [*sic*] Through CNFJ Work." Accessed 10 January 2011. http://www.janafa.com/ronbun/2009-0901-1.pdf. On file with author.

Cohen, Richard J. 2001. "We've Apologized Enough to Japan." *Washington Post*, 28 February 2001, A23.

Feldman, Eric. 2007. "Law, Culture, and Conflict: Dispute Resolution in Postwar Japan." *Faculty Scholarship Paper* 148, University of Pennsylvania Law School. http://scholarship.law.upenn.edu/faculty_scholarship/148.

French, Howard W. 2001. "U.S. Makes Amends to Japan for Sinking of Ship." *New York Times*, 5 November 2001. http://www.nytimes.com/2001/11/05/world/us-makes-amends-to-japan-for-sinking-of-ship.html.

Hayashi Hideki. 2003. "'Meiyo' to wa nani ka: Ehime Maru jikō o tsūyaku to shite mitodoketa kaijōieikan no omoi" [What is "Honor"? What I saw as the JMSDF officer translating the *Ehime Maru* incident]. *Seiron*, February, 318–327.

Ikeda Naoki. 2003. "Ehime de nani ga okotta ka?" [What happened in Ehime?]. *Ōsaka no machi* 53. http://www.mmjp.or.jp/machi/53forWEB/page10.htm.

Ikeda Naoki. 2004. "*Ehime Maru* jiken ni okeru beikaijihō to shibō songai baishō no hōteki ronten" [Legal analysis of American maritime law and casualty damages compensation in the *Ehime Maru* incident]. *Hōritsu jihō* 76 (2): 113–117.

Johnson, Chalmers. 2003. "Three Rapes: The Status of Forces Agreement and Okinawa." *Asia-Pacific Japan Focus* 1 (4). Accessed 26 July 2019. https://apjjf.org/-Chalmers-Johnson/2021.

Kanwar, Vik. 2001. "Capital Punishment as 'Closure': The Limits of a Victim-Centered Jurisprudence." *New York University Review of Law & Social Change* 27:215–255.

Kawashima Takeyoshi. 1963. "Dispute Resolution in Contemporary Japan." In *Law in Japan: The Legal Order in a Changing Society,* ed. Arthur Taylor von Mehren, 41–72. Cambridge, MA: Harvard University Press.

Kawashima Takeyoshi. 1967. *Nihonjin no hōishiki* [The legal consciousness of the Japanese]. Tokyo: Iwanami Shinsho.

"Kokkai Gijiroku, Sangi-in Gaikō Bōei Iinkai" [Minutes from the House of Councilors Committee on Foreign Affairs and Defense]. 2001. 27 February.

Kristof, Nicholas D. 1995. "U.S. to Turn Over Troops Accused of Murder or Rape to Japan." *New York Times*, 26 October 1995.

Leheny, David, and Liu, Sida. 2010. "The Politics of Crime, Punishment, and Social Order in East Asia." *Annual Review of Law and Social Science* 6:239–258.

Marsh, Bert. 2002. "SUPSALV Sends." *Faceplate: The Official Newsletter for the Divers and Salvors of the United States Navy* 6 (1): 2.

Martin, Curtis H. 2004. "The Sinking of the Ehime Maru: The Interaction of Culture, Security Interests and Domestic Politics in an Alliance Crisis." *Japanese Journal of Political Science* 5 (2): 287–310.

Moton, Tony. 2001. "No Loose Lips." *The Pitch*, 8 March. http://www.pitch.com/news/article/20614959/no-loose-lips.

National Park Service. n.d. "USS *Arizona* Memorial Frequently Asked Questions." Accessed 26 July 2019. https://www.nps.gov/valr/faqs.htm.

National Transportation Safety Board. 2005. "Marine Accident Brief (No. DCA-01-MM-022)." Washington, DC: NTSB.

Nawa Kiyotaka. 2005. "Itai to reikon: Ehime Maru jiken yori miru" [Dead bodies and souls: Examining the *Ehime Maru* case]. *Taishō daigaku sōgō bukkyō kenkyūjo nenpō* [Annual of the Institute for Comprehensive Studies of Buddhism] 27 (March): 112–115.

PBS Newshour. 2001. "Commander Scott Waddle to Retire." 24 April. http://www.pbs.org /newshour/bb/military-jan-june01-sub_4-24/.

Schwenkel, Christina. 2009. *The American War in Contemporary Vietnam: Transnational Remembrance and Representation.* Bloomington: Indiana University Press.

Shimizu Kōichi. 2010. "Sentai hikiage ni yoru itai shūyō to hoken" [Insurance and the accommodation of dead bodies from raised ships." *Songai hoken kenkyū* [Indemnity Insurance Research] 72 (3): 117–139.

Sontag, Sherry, and Christopher Drew, with Annette Lawrence Drew. 1998. *Blind Man's Bluff: The Untold Story of American Submarine Espionage.* New York: Public Affairs.

Takashima Masayuki. 2001. "Nichibei 'hikaku shazai' kō" [Considering Japanese and American "comparative apologies"]. *Shokun,* May, 86–93.

Tanabe, George J., Jr. 2001. "Japanese Need Body Remains of Ehime Maru Victims." *Honolulu Advertiser,* 25 February 2001. http://the.honoluluadvertiser.com/2001/Feb/25 /225opinion17.html.

Tanaka Akihiko. 2004. "2001 Jihyō: 'Ehime Maru Jiken' to Mori Yoshirō" [2001 Comment: Mori Yoshirō and "The *Ehime Maru* Incident"]. *Chūō Kōron,* April, 34–37.

US Department of State. 2001. Washington File: "Transcript: Ambassador Foley's Farewell Speech to Japan Press Club." 23 February. Accessed 26 July 2019. https://japan2.usembassy .gov/e/p/2001/tp-20010223-65.html.

US Pacific Fleet Public Affairs. 2001. "Ehime Maru Successfully Moved to Final Relocation Site." Story Number: NNS021122-14. 25 November. http://www.navy.mil/submit/display .asp?story_id=4723.

Waddle, Scott, with Ken Abraham. 2002. *The Right Thing.* Nashville, TN: Integrity.

Watts, Jonathan. 2000. "Japan Divine, Claims PM." *The Guardian,* 17 May 2000.

CHAPTER 6

Landscapes of Law in War-Torn Societies

Mark Fathi Massoud

The purest type of exercise of legal authority is that
which employs a bureaucratic administrative staff.
—Max Weber, *Economy and Society*

I'm put in a cage [in civil society]. It's hard for me to
believe that working with the United Nations or an
international NGO will give me freedom.
—Interview with Dominic, youth activist and NGO
program manager, Juba, South Sudan

Drawing on sociolegal literature and fieldwork in South Sudan, this chapter argues that international aid groups operating in conflict and postconflict settings create and impose a transnational, rules-based, and regulatory culture on the local people they hire and on the domestic organizations they fund.[1] Civil society actors in these places experience law's *soft* power through their daily, tangible, and mundane contact with aid agencies. As employees they are subject to contracts and other rules of employment, work under management and finance teams, document routine activity, and abide by organizational constitutions. In analyzing how South Sudanese activists confront, understand, conform to, or resist these transnational regulatory cultures and workplace practices, this chapter decenters state institutions as sites for understanding law's power and exposes how aid organizations instead become arenas of significant legal and political struggle in war-torn societies. Ultimately, ethnographic inquiry into the micropolitical processes that exist within international aid groups reveals how workplace regulatory cultures transmit transnational legal categories and create new forms of sovereignty, generating daily tensions for survivors of civil war.

While conducting research in South Sudan in the years leading up to its 2011 secession from Sudan, I met with a justice of the Supreme Court. South Sudan had just emerged from one of Africa's longest and deadliest civil wars, and, aside from a single petition on his desk, there were no legal proceedings before the court. His computer was off (there may not have been electricity). His office was sparse. Down the road from the court, the legislative assembly was at the time still drafting and debating legislation to govern the country after the war's end. In a territory the size of France, the South Sudanese Bar—a dozen or so lawyers at the time—could easily be squeezed into a small sitting room.

What forms do law, sovereignty, and culture take in new or weak states like South Sudan? When a national government is emerging, legal doctrine and regulations are under development, and lawyers and federal judges are in short supply, where is the law? Citizens historically have experienced legal culture through interactions with local courts, chiefs, and military officials applying distinct conceptions of tradition, community, and authority (Leonardi 2013; Deng 2011). A parallel story can also be told of law's power in civil society. Juba, South Sudan's capital city, has teemed with activity from dozens of international aid groups and nongovernmental organizations (NGOs) that arrived after the war to build up state institutions and the rule of law. In addition to their laudable substantive goals of promoting human rights and democracy, these groups also brought with them shared internal management cultures, institutional practices, and human resources procedures rooted in bureaucratic rules and abstract legal logic. Junior South Sudanese staff members are required to assimilate to and abide by these foreign managerial rules, and South Sudanese NGOs are encouraged to replicate them. These transnational legal cultures rooted in standardization and formalization are controlled by expatriate elites and reside outside the "official" purview of domestic courts, legal officials, and lawyers. War-torn societies seeking to rebuild paradoxically become simultaneous transnational and domestic spaces in which national legal cultures and state sovereignty must contend with the foreign idioms, practices, and authorities transmitted by aid groups.

Among civil society organizations in war-ravaged South Sudan, an unexpected transnational regulatory and legal culture has flourished. It is a legal culture predicated not on domestic democratic authority, judicial power, or human rights but on plain knowledge of routine organizational practices, documentation procedures, strategic plans, and written files. While participating in these juridical practices advances local activists' legal consciousness and knowledge of international law, workplace directives, and spreadsheet menus, it paradoxically disables them from organizing effectively and making their own rights claims when job-related grievances arise against employers. Ultimately, the transnational migration of Western regulatory processes and workplace practices reveals how the politics of law exists beyond the state courtroom and in people's daily work lives.

When state regulations are under development or weakly enforced, Western aid groups have wide latitude to construct the terms of their relationships with local employees and organizations, drawing from regulations and procedures used in home offices and then exported to field offices abroad. Almost invariably, this dynamic subordinates local personnel to expatriate managers who arrive with preconceived notions of how traditional authority operates and then attempt to replace it with bureaucratic authority in the name of modern professionalism. To the South Sudanese employees, the policies enforced by managers generate a rules-based and technical culture of sovereignty. Sovereignty's mundane technologies—organizational constitutions, employment contracts, staff handbooks, reporting requirements, and accounting systems—become part of an everyday regulatory culture pervading the lives of civil society activists.

By describing this legal culture of workplace sovereignty and analyzing its impacts on the legal consciousness of civil society actors, this chapter illuminates the unlikely spaces that law inhabits in conflict and postconflict settings and a micropolitics of aid work that privileges technical skill over rights mobilization, that pressures local activists to accept foreign bureaucratic and regulatory forms, and that ultimately entrenches rather than topples historic inequalities between foreign aid workers and their local staff. In these ways, it is through law's *soft* power—its capacity to reframe political conflict and structure ongoing relationships—and not only its power to compel that law exercises its claims to authority and sovereignty in war-torn societies.

In this chapter I first situate my research investigating transnational legal culture and workplace practices in war-torn societies in the context of sociolegal literature on judicial politics, humanitarian intervention, and organizational behavior. Second, I describe the field research methods I used in this inquiry. Third, I detail how law operates in aid agencies, its impacts on South Sudanese employees, and sites of resistance to the new hierarchies that organizational rules introduce. Finally, I conclude by discussing the implications of the diffusion of transnational legal cultures for research on state legal cultures and for civil society development in fragile states.

Locating Legal Culture in Humanitarian Organizations

Legal scholars and social scientists have been preoccupied with finding law in the most likely places—in courts in settings where courts are strong, or in human rights and rule-of-law promotion efforts in settings where courts are weak. Studies of judicial power have shed light on the relative strength of courts across regions and regime types.[2] But socioeconomic constraints matter: Individuals and social-change groups with limited time and money are often unlikely to mount or prevail in lengthy and costly legal battles (Bumiller 1987; Felstiner, Abel, and Sarat 1980; Galanter 1974). In war-affected regions where poverty is compounded by the experience of state violence and political repression, lawyers are silenced, and judicial institutions are weak, the challenges are even more acute. Indeed, new high court justices appointed in the aftermath of a civil war typically find themselves spending much of their time in workshops sponsored by foreign aid groups or international legal consultants (Mason 2011). For this reason, development practitioners and scholars have begun to evaluate the impacts of these efforts designed to encourage government officials and community leaders to respect international law and constitutionalism (see Carothers 2006; Hagan, Ferrales, and Jasso 2008; Heckman, Nelson, and Cabatingan 2010; Heller and Jensen 2003; Massoud 2011).

But focusing on courts or other state and local institutions of justice means potentially missing the meaningful ways nonstate actors import transnational regulatory norms and practices into civil society in the most troubled corners of the world. Filling this gap has been a growing body of research on the diffusion of justice norms (Keith 2012; Meyer et al. 1997; Sikkink 2011; Zwingel 2012) and on the consequences of the *outward activities* of aid groups, particularly organizations seeking to build human rights in the Global South (Falk 2009; Goodale and Merry 2007; Keck and Sikkink 1998; Kennedy 2002; McClymont and Golub 2000; Merry 2006; Mutua 2008; Rajagopal 2003).

Comparatively little has been said about the *internal regulatory processes and structures* by which aid groups seek to accomplish their goals and the impacts of those mechanisms. In recent years, however, critical scholarship on the politics and consequences of humanitarian intervention has emerged, probing how the transnational bureaucratic structures and regulatory practices of international NGOs weaken domestic political organizing across the Global South. Cultural anthropologists have documented how the "NGO form" transforms and tempers social organizing, particularly around feminism (Bernal and Grewal 2014). Once-militant collectives in northeast Brazil, for instance, have exercised agency by "bureaucratizing" into NGOs in order to capture aid dollars (Thayer 2010). Similarly, the "regime-like" qualities associated with international NGO interventions lead these groups to reinforce hierarchies between donors and dependents, thus limiting activists' participation and autonomy, distancing donors from the groups they fund, and disassociating civil society activists from the local communities they purport to serve (Autesserre 2010; Englund 2006; Jalali 2013; Schuller 2012). While the subordinating process of professionalization enables international NGOs to strengthen the managerial and technical capacities of employees, it simultaneously depoliticizes employee behavior (Kamat 2004: 167–168). These processes of transnational bureaucratization demonstrate that legal practices are at work—from registering NGOs to maintaining documents and files. These legal practices saturate civil society, particularly in communities facing legacies of poverty, war, or authoritarian rule (Asad 2004; Poole 2004).

A parallel strand of literature, primarily in the fields of law and society and organizational sociology, has scrutinized organizational behavior, contending that managers paradoxically shape the very laws that are meant to restrict their behavior. They infuse "managerial interests" into policies and procedures otherwise intended to promote objective legal compliance (Edelman et al. 2011: 899). For instance, narrowly defined workplace sexual harassment policies can have negative effects on women by "altering the [legal] definition of sexual harassment . . . and construct[ing] a legality . . . that offers only limited" rights protections to claimants (Marshall 2005: 83). The employer acknowledges the law but defines legality in a way that suits the bottom line. In other words, law is endogenous to organizations (Edelman et al. 2011; Edelman, Uggen, and Erlanger 1999). Similarly, patterned interactions in the transmission of mundane rules of employment and staffing construct a collective experience of legal norms (see Knop 2011; Riles 2001). This research has been replicated in a variety of legal fields, including civil rights, consumer protection, and insurance law (Edelman 1992; Edelman and Suchman 1997; Marshall 2005; Suchman and Edelman 2007; Talesh 2009). While significant in revealing how organizations shape law, these studies have been largely confined to the United States and have rarely been applied to environments with weak regulatory frameworks. Indeed, Edelman and colleagues (2011: 934) have called for scholarship examining whether and how law's endogeneity operates outside the United States.

In settings marked by violence, weak state regulation, limited opportunities for employment, and a nascent legal profession, the structure of the legal order is unclear. Combining the literature on law and courts, humanitarianism, and organizations opens a new space for research on the internal practices of aid groups and reveals an unresolved research question: *To what extent do foreign aid organizations construct legal cultures in postconflict settings, and what are the impacts of these legal norms and processes on the civil society actors subjected to them?* South Sudan, a new state emerging from decades of war, offers a valuable site for legal scholars, anthropologists, and political scientists to interrogate how organizations create legal order and mediate the meaning of the law within civil society in conflict settings.

Methods

Because the literature has been remarkably silent on foreign aid organizations' internal policy practices, my work has been purposefully inductive and theory generating. The paucity of empirical data demanded a bottom-up, case-study approach (Massoud 2016). By privileging in-depth, richly contextualized, and fine-grained analysis, case studies can "reveal the . . . complexity" of social phenomena under investigation (Stake 1995: 126). Within-case qualitative research helps to illuminate social processes and develop theory in the social sciences (Massoud 2014: 8; see also George and Bennett 2005; Seawright and Gerring 2008).

For this chapter, I draw material from 41 interviews conducted primarily in Juba, South Sudan. (These interviews are a relevant sample from 205 interviews I conducted in Sudan and South Sudan between 2005 and 2011.) I chose Juba because it is the seat of government, headquarters of the South Sudanese judiciary, and nerve center of aid operations in the country. Interviews were conducted with South Sudanese employees of international aid organizations and United Nations (UN) and donor agencies; South Sudanese personnel working for or launching their own domestic civil society organizations (where it was rare to find expatriate workers); and expatriate (typically European or North American) staff of international aid or UN agencies. Interviewees came from seven international NGOs with operations in South Sudan, three UN and donor agencies, and eleven Sudanese ("national") NGOs.

To learn about the development and impacts of legal order in these organizations, I interviewed South Sudanese employees of national NGOs, and South Sudanese ("national") and expatriate ("international") employees of international aid groups. Best efforts were also made to obtain gender balance; twenty-three of the forty-one interviews were with women.[3] I began by meeting respondents I knew from my previous fieldwork in Khartoum, Sudan's capital city (Massoud 2013). I also observed NGO coordination meetings and followed up with attendees for interviews. To obtain additional interviews, I employed a snowball approach, asking interviewees to recommend others with whom I should speak. Using networks of trusted colleagues helped build confidence in the researcher and this inquiry. Particularly important to build trust in an environment in which NGOs are seen as gatekeepers to essential resources, I clarified my position as a university researcher conducting a study for educational purposes and that I was unaffiliated with any NGO or international aid agency.

Interviews were recorded and semistructured. They lasted from 45 minutes to 3 hours, with most about 1.5 hours. To understand the influences on their behavior, I asked interview subjects to give examples of successes and challenges they faced in their work. I asked them about daily professional life and their relationships (if any) to foreign aid agencies. South Sudanese staff spoke of employment-related grievances, how they managed those grievances, and how complaints at work were handled. Because of the sensitivity of these employment matters, and the risk they felt in potentially violating staff regulations, many interviewees declined to share with me the protocols, frameworks, and procedures enforced by their managers and only agreed to speak with me far away from their offices and out of view of expatriate managers—in an unused staff room or off-site under a tree and during lunch or nonworking hours. Interviews with South Sudanese employees were conducted in a combination of Arabic and English. I translated all interviews into English and coded the interview data and field notes using the TAMS Analyzer qualitative analysis software program. Coding categories separated perceptions from behaviors, classified organizational and employee types, and isolated the types of challenges faced by employees and managers to understand the impacts of the juridical order produced in these postwar workplaces.

Empirical Setting: A New Nation Emerging from War

Building South Sudan

Landlocked and bordering other fragile states (see Figure 1), South Sudan became the world's newest country in 2011 following a near-unanimous plebiscite in favor of partition from Sudan. The plebiscite shadowed a half-century of war (rather, two related civil wars fought in 1955–1972 and 1983–2005). Best estimates suggest that ten million people were killed or forcibly displaced during the decades of violence—nearly equivalent to South Sudan's total current population (World Bank 2019).

South Sudan's national legal infrastructure remains one of the world's youngest and weakest. As one senior UN official explained to me, "Law is starting from scratch [and] is moving slowly."[4] With assistance from the Ministry of Justice, Parliament has debated and passed new legislation, and officials have struggled to integrate diffuse customary laws with new federal and provincial judicial systems. While chiefs' courts are active throughout the country, private enterprise and regulation remain scarce and the legal profession miniscule, particularly in light of ongoing political violence since the 2011 independence. The number of registered lawyers in South Sudan grew from twelve in 2007 to thirty-six in 2010, and the country's first law school opened in 2012 (see IDLO 2011).

Colonial and authoritarian rule and decades of civil war mark South Sudan's pre-independence political history (Leonardi 2013). The near-constant fighting stemmed largely from opposition to governments in Khartoum that failed to represent Southern Sudanese interests (Deng 1995; Johnson 2003). During the civil war, South Sudanese contact with international aid groups was limited. The military regime in Khartoum controlled access both to the sprawling desert camps for displaced persons outside of Khartoum and to war-ravaged areas in what is now South Sudan. Some foreign charities provided emergency humanitarian relief under the auspices of Operation Lifeline

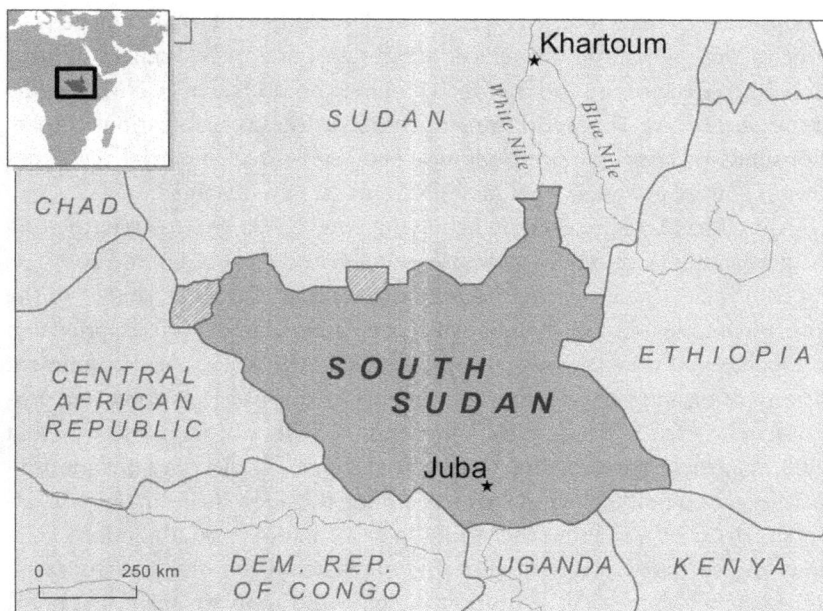

Figure 1. Contemporary Map of South Sudan (South Sudan's northern border with Sudan is contested, including in the shaded Kafia Kingi/Raga and Abyei regions). Source: Author, using ESRI and OpenStreetMap base data.

Sudan. By the time war ended in 2005, much of the South was decimated, interethnic rivalries were fierce, and infrastructure was all but collapsed.

The Arrival and Goals of Aid Groups

Operating from neighboring countries during Sudan's civil war, Western-based aid agencies converged upon Juba after the war's end in order to engage with once-unreachable communities. As they moved into South Sudan, the organizations also shifted focus from emergency relief (e.g., food, shelter, and medicine) to educational initiatives in peacebuilding and human rights.

Field offices in Juba brought opportunities for South Sudanese people to work for aid groups or to form groups of their own to implement aid projects designed by foreign agencies. The new government gave these foreign aid groups wide latitude to hire employees and to enforce internal management policies and regulations. Dozens of aid groups have opened offices in Juba, including UN agencies and the UN Mission in South Sudan (UNMISS), one of the world's largest peacekeeping operations.[5] These organizations employ thousands of largely South Sudanese staff and direct material resources toward South Sudanese ("national") NGOs that have emerged.

Aid efforts have focused on achieving two related goals: strengthening the government's capacity to impose political and legal order and supporting civil society's capacity to promote social order. Direct assistance to the government includes construction of courts, prisons, and libraries; provision of supplies and vehicles for government agencies and officials; development of accounting and payroll programs; support for drafting legislation; and provision of training and advice to all levels of staff. Since the civil war ended in 2005, aid groups have also supported efforts by civil society organizations to raise legal and political consciousness among the poor, including by educating survivors of war about their right to cast a ballot in South Sudan's elections and secession plebiscite. Echoing many activists I met, one Sudanese civil society leader said his substantive goal was simply to "train [the poor] to know their rights."[6]

South Sudanese activists I met shared a set of common aspirations: find and keep a stable job, hone skills, develop professionally, and undertake humanitarian-oriented work to benefit South Sudan's future. When international aid groups with substantial material resources first arrived, war survivors flocked to these organizations, looking for employment as janitors, drivers, program assistants, and managers. Among the varied ways that norms and institutional practices diffuse across political contexts, legal norms and practices are transmitted largely through these personnel in aid groups, which the following section details.

Constructing Legal Cultures in Conflict Settings

The combination of the end of war and the arrival of aid agencies, each with its own bureaucratic and legalistic structure, impacts local residents' daily existence, work lives, and perceptions of legal norms. The technical details of work and mundane employment regulations generated within aid groups have come to represent a new local legal order with which an emerging national legal culture must contend. My data from civil society actors in South

Sudan uncover a variety of overlapping mechanisms that together reveal how law exerts a soft power over their lives, infusing nonjudicial institutions with legalistic grammar (Kawar 2014). These include training and certification programs, employment regulations (e.g., Internet and sexual harassment policies), hierarchical reporting structures (e.g., management teams), grievance procedures and spaces for dispute resolution (e.g., staff meetings), and documentation protocols (e.g., maintaining spreadsheets and keeping receipts). This section explains the functions and limits of these mechanisms to lay the groundwork for the following section, which uncovers their impacts for war survivors who work in civil society. Each of these mechanisms allows aid agencies to construct the terms of their relationships with local staff and local NGOs and reveals the ways legal practices become a source of sovereignty, shaping the experience of law even in settings where state regulation remains weak.

The Examination Process Prior to Employment. The experience of a juridical and regulatory order governing workplace life begins when a survivor of war applies to work with an international NGO. The application process includes examinations not of the human rights principles guiding the organization's mission but of mundane technical and accountability practices. "I applied for a program officer job with [an international NGO]. I took a written exam [and] an oral exam," said one Sudanese activist. But his application to work with the international NGO was unsuccessful because he "did not know Excel [for the exam. I did not know] Microsoft. You need these skills to work at international NGOs."[7] To those I met, computer software and spreadsheets served to document activities to hold employees accountable to workplace policies.

Training Programs. International aid groups typically hold training programs and workshops for South Sudanese persons to enhance their job applications and the ability of local staff to follow the accounting and reporting practices of aid groups. When I asked one interviewee what she learned in the educational workshops, she did not mention human rights or her organization's substantive mission. She spoke instead of new formalized procedures and regulations for payment verification, supplies procurement, and logistics. "I learned about all the different codes for charging [expenses.] Like project codes," she concluded.[8]

South Sudanese activists I met often spoke of these standardized technical-skills training programs offered by aid organizations as providing important and transferrable benefits. Joining an international NGO is "a step forward" in one's career for this reason.[9] One interviewee said that an international NGO where he had worked was "good at" training new staff because "they had a lot of technocrats" do the teaching.[10] Once training is complete, an employee-participant typically receives a certificate demonstrating his or her successful completion of the standard program. In a region where universities are few and diplomas are costly, these certificates are prized possessions that bolster applications for future employment, particularly transnational employment, once a contract ends.

The content of these training programs is varied, but generally they focus on educating staff to follow the routinized daily practices of employment in a bureaucratic context. Workshop topics typically cover financial procedures, procurement systems, security (including emergency and fire), Internet and e-mail policies, and how to write individual work plans, program reports, and project studies. A staff member with an international NGO said that her expatriate managers asked her to attend several of these workshops, even some conducted outside of Sudan: "They paid for me to attend these workshops [abroad]. That [gave me] motivation and encouragement."[11] Another activist summed up her experience with an international NGO by focusing on the training she received to comply with bureaucratic procedures and rules, which bolsters future job applications: "When the project finished, I left. [But] I got experience [for my later position at the United Nations.]."[12]

Human Resource Management. Efforts to formalize and standardize human behavior shape and constrain power and those subjected to that power. With limited state involvement, international aid groups import a standard form of bureaucratic legalism rooted in the formalization of dispute-resolution and claim-making practices, centralized in human resources departments. The concept of human resources as a managerial-level profession was introduced in South Sudan with the arrival of aid groups and, through it, civil society activists have come to understand their legal order mediated by the demands of managers overseeing staff policies. The focus of these managerial efforts is on educating local staff to be knowledgeable participants in this system.

Human resources managers in international aid organizations also designate spaces and processes for employees from different backgrounds to discuss and resolve disputes related to the war or reconstruction efforts. One Sudanese human resources manager with an international NGO said, "Some

[South Sudanese] staff feel the Arabs [of northern Sudan] are behind their tragedy. I am the human resources manager. I put them in a [conference] room to . . . speak [and] let it out. It's about rebuilding relationships. We are all Sudanese."[13] For civil society actors, the dispute resolution process becomes formalized in the workplace and outside of courts—materializing in conference rooms and under the procedures designed by human resources professionals.

Codes of Conduct and Employment Handbooks. As a result of employment with aid agencies, South Sudanese staff members tend to reflect and internalize a new rights consciousness and an appreciation of the benefits of operating in a rules-based environment. Speaking of the many regulations in her international NGO, one former Sudanese staff member said, "There [were] a lot of 'codes of conduct' [including] a bad behavior *qanoon* [law], procurement [rules], not abusing [one's] office, no looking at personal websites at work. You have to sign these codes."[14] Sudanese women I met in international NGOs spoke of coherent sexual harassment policies and detailed health-coverage policies, often nonexistent in local NGOs. Others spoke of how international aid groups adhere to progressive maternity leave, sick leave, annual leave, and severance regulations. National staff referred to these rules as the "law" in their staff handbooks, available in English and Arabic.

Writing Reports and Keeping Receipts. The juridical order within NGOs involves the transnational transmission of legalistic practices associated with accountability, a process aid groups label "capacity building." National staff must create reports, which serve as legal memorials to display legitimacy and satisfy donors. These transnational legal practices become the means through which South Sudanese earn donor trust domestically. On the importance of documentation, a Sudanese NGO director said, "We need receipts, so it will not raise suspicion [among donors]."[15] An expatriate manager at an international NGO in Juba told me that her organization terminated a grant to a South Sudanese NGO that was unable to "demonstrate accountability."[16] When I asked how NGOs demonstrate accountability, she replied, "Receipts and reporting. We need to see original receipts."[17] Staff at South Sudanese NGOs told me, however, that this insistence on receipts presents a practical challenge. "Few of the shop owners here understand," explained one worker. "They say, 'Why don't you trust me?' But donors won't listen to you that you're insulting the shop owner if you ask for a receipt."[18] Assimilating to these mundane juridical requirements—including using receipts to document expenditures—helps to entrench this new juridical order in postconflict settings.

"Internal Control Systems." Expatriate managers at international NGOs agreed that their aid agencies aim to fund South Sudanese NGOs that adopt the juridical processes imported by international NGOs and UN agencies. These include "internal control systems . . . time sheets, vehicle logs, [and] accounting policies and procedures."[19] A program manager said foreign donors required her national NGO to complete complicated Excel spreadsheets tracking workplace activities and project "deliverables."[20] "In the West, you have been trained [to] like writing. You like [written] reports," said one South Sudanese activist. "But we . . . like giving verbal accounts, verbal reports. This is our difference."[21] Even to submit a funding application, an organization must demonstrate its acceptance of the legal and archival logics of foreign aid groups and form a relationship with the military-dominated government—the organization needs an accounting department, a government registration certificate, a constitution, and a bank account (which itself requires documents, including government registration certificates). Another activist echoed the need to showcase an organization's internal legal culture in order to submit a funding proposal, saying simply, "They want us to have bureaucracies."[22]

Transferring Documentation Practices to South Sudanese Employees and NGOs. Over time, even South Sudanese employees of international aid groups have come to expect domestic NGOs' conformity to foreign aid groups' juridical and regulatory practices. A local employee with an international NGO shared with me her strong feeling that NGOs should develop internal "systems," including financial and documentation protocols "based on the one we have here. . . . to prevent corruption and maintain transparency."[23] She continued, "If I went to administer a local NGO, I would teach them how to put policies into place, how to be more organized, how to have a system."[24] The UN "has stringent and rigid procurement processes," a UN legal officer told me, so the expectation is that its aid recipients will adopt similarly strict policies and regulations.[25] One national NGO employee noted how her organization had changed markedly after the arrival of a particularly sophisticated director previously employed by an international NGO: "There is a lot of paperwork, new procedures, and details. Now you have to make requests in writing. In the past . . . they didn't have forms. . . . Now, there [are] just more details."[26] These procedures govern employment relationships and activities, including signing out vehicles, tracking mileage, keeping logs, signing contracts, and recording requests. Employees copy the executive director on every e-mail message sent outside the organization to convey a chain of accountability.[27]

With so much emphasis placed on learning and adhering to technical and hierarchical managerial norms and practices, procedures themselves become internalized as a form of legal consciousness, one that is divorced from the substantive rights consciousness that humanitarian and development efforts are designed to impart. When a Sudanese woman, who had been employed by an international NGO prior to its expulsion from Sudan, found new work with a South Sudanese NGO, she brought with her a number of training programs and policies that followed the international aid agency model. She introduced written rules to request materials, forms for procurement of goods or services, stationery, professional e-mail addresses, scopes of work and terms of reference, regular performance reviews, new policies on sexual harassment, and training sessions on the appropriate use of technology. She made the organization's reporting structure more vertical, so that each program had an assistant who reported to a manager, who then reported to the executive director. This hierarchy became the sovereign structure within which new legal norms were created and enforced. All of these changes contributed to a new culture of legality within the NGO. Similarly, human resources managers in international NGOs demand that staff of national NGOs assimilate to the internal juridical processes of foreign groups, through unplanned office visits and required attendance at workshops.

Constitutions. To meet donor demands, a constitution-writing industry has emerged in South Sudan, as foreign consultants rush in to help national NGOs draft organizational constitutions and policies, register with the government, design organizational structures, and develop accountability systems. Many impoverished South Sudanese volunteers and employees, eager to portray themselves as in line with international aid group standards, hire consultants (typically from Kenya or Uganda) to draft organizational constitutions in English, the operating language of international aid groups in South Sudan.

Constructing Legal "Experience." Employees of sophisticated South Sudanese NGOs able to compete for UN or donor-country funds alongside international

NGOs strategically adopt these foreign juridical systems and speak admiringly of the expatriates who have worked outside of South Sudan. "They bring experience," said one director. "That's really important for capacity building."[28] In the process, South Sudanese knowledge is sidelined as the transmitted technical legal practices of foreign organizations gain prominence.

Legal Assimilation. The juridical character of the rules and processes governing employment in aid groups enhances their legitimacy for those who seek to realize their humanitarian impulses and allows those rules to be imposed and reproduced at local levels, precisely because the state is developing. Local activists trained to act in accordance with new rules then replicate these legalistic modes of behavior found in foreign aid agencies, either through a process of required assimilation (top-down coercive measures tied to contracts, salaries, or program funding) or aspirational assimilation (a bottom-up desire to mimic the internal management processes of international NGO operations). The boundary between these two forms of legal assimilation is a blurred one, as local NGOs and employees define their activities in relation to available funding from the international community. In this way, the meaning of the law and people's perceptions of themselves as activists or employees are defined by aid agencies and not necessarily produced through the substantive human rights work they perform. The legalistic relations between local staff and NGOs and their human resources managers or expatriate bosses mediate their broader human rights and humanitarian work. People may still view themselves as activists, but their work is compartmentalized within and subservient to transnational legal structures.

The Impact of Workplace "Law"

The transnational juridical environment within aid agencies governs the behavior of aid agency staff, influences the work of local activists, defines relationships between funders and the funded, and greatly affects local understandings of the law. Activists once branded as outlaws during wartime become junior aid agency employees required to follow rules and regulations designed by expatriate management staff.[29] In these ways, civil society becomes entrenched in and subservient to the administrative regulations and processes of international aid organizations. The following

section discusses the impacts of these legal norms and management processes for (1) South Sudanese employees of foreign aid groups and (2) South
Sudanese NGOs.

Legal Assimilation Among Local Employees of
Foreign Aid Groups

South Sudanese employees of foreign aid groups learn to document their activities in a specialized manner that compartmentalizes and quantifies
achievements in legal learning (i.e., documentation of the number of persons
who attended a women's rights training program) rather than a manner that
supports analytical inquiry (i.e., the actual content of the program or the
challenges that participants faced in engaging with the material). Reports that
focus on technical and numerical goals ultimately depersonalize the relationship between locals and international staff, replacing people's experiences
with quantifiable indicators more relevant to expatriate managers than local
subordinates (Davis, Kingsbury, and Merry 2012). South Sudanese staff share
context-specific information with international NGOs and provide access to
local communities that aid groups would not otherwise be able to reach. But
juridical forms and transnational regulatory practices allow foreign managers to digest and utilize this information in ways that serve the aid group's
funded mission, rather than in ways that respect the details of the situation
or local significance.

South Sudanese employees of UN agencies recounted that, while they
wanted to learn about the substance of international human rights law, their
training was largely procedural, or, as they put it, "just for administration,
routine, [and] how to write minutes."[30] While this training prepares local employees to climb a transnational job hierarchy atop which sit lucrative posts
with UN agencies overseas, it also reinforces subservience to and acceptance
of this hierarchy in which local staff are subordinate to expatriate managers.
South Sudanese staff underscored that among the most important skills to
acquire are technical ones related to policies and procedures, including how
to document work and complete forms. Aid groups then measure local capacity on these technical and regulatory grounds.[31]

South Sudanese employees recognize that their participation in international NGOs legitimizes workplace structures and policies that can also dis-
empower them. According to one activist, "There are these SMTs [senior

management teams]. They make decisions on behalf of nationals. They just send copies [of their decisions] to nationals. . . . And you have to sign them." He continued that "these . . . internal policies . . . often do not favor the nationals."[32]

Another said the senior management teams ask national staff to "review the policies, but . . . you're not involved in making any of these policies."[33] Top-down in structure and reporting procedures, international aid organizations often leave national staff without the ability to shape the rules that will govern their daily behavior and, ultimately, define their national future. South Sudanese employees come to internalize a perception of themselves as subordinate to foreign managers and incapable of leadership under an everyday legal order that they do not participate in shaping. For instance, while one of the most senior Sudanese staff I met had been employed by an international NGO for more than twenty years, he lamented his inability to be the organization's country director because of the extensive technical rules and reporting procedures associated with the position. The job was, in his words, "too sophisticated."[34]

From the perspective of local staff working with aid organizations in post-conflict settings, expatriate managers become a kind of unelected lawmaking body—framing how civil society actors experience legal rules and closely regulating how they conduct activities. Particularly in light of weak justice institutions overseeing NGO activity, locals saw expatriate managers trained in foreign legal systems as their supervising "legal" authorities whose rules demanded obedience. The hierarchical structure of a bureaucratic organization is designed to create this "interest in obedience" (Weber 1978: 212) and cultivate a "belief in [the organization's] legitimacy" (213). The impersonal commands of these managers enforce a new kind of legalistic domination of civil society through technical rules. The relevant considerations to empower civil society become "functional, financial, and managerial," rather than alternative concerns about building human rights in the Global South (Commission on Global Governance 1999).

The internal culture of aid organizations promotes a culture of transnational bureaucratic legalism that often does not translate into actual domestic rights for employees, even within NGOs whose outward mission is to promote human rights. While some workplace policies (i.e., sexual harassment) exist, rights mobilization was rare among the activists I met and was at times actively curtailed by agency management or colleagues. One Sudanese employee sought to improve the working conditions of national staff, but she faced substantial opposition from expatriate managers who feared "they would lose their jobs if [I] educated the national staff [about] fighting for their rights."[35] Her concern was the lack of safe transportation, particularly for female Sudanese employees forced to live in inexpensive and higher-risk areas, further from the office neighborhood where foreign aid workers live and rents are unaffordable.

Transnational forms of bureaucratic legalism focused on technical proficiency, when imposed in a conflict setting like South Sudan, often disable employees from changing or utilizing the organizational structure. One Sudanese civil society activist told me that when he was laid off by an international NGO, he was given two months' severance, short of Sudanese labor law's requirement of three months' severance. When I asked whether he filed a grievance, he quickly replied that he did not want to "pull rope" because he was grateful for the work experience the foreign-based organization had given him and was hoping his training there would help him obtain another "good job."[36] With weak government oversight of international aid groups and the transferability of technical and rules-based skills, some individuals are willing to forgo legal rights for themselves or others in exchange for career advancement. In a sense, rights have become "managerialized" by serving the interests of managers rather than their staff (Edelman, Fuller, and Mara-Drita 2001). By offering vital material resources to those who reinforce the status quo and refrain from change advocacy, the transnational transmission of bureaucracy subjugates local actors.

The professional workplace environment becomes a site for the diffusion of knowledge about the procedural norms and bureaucratic rules governing office environments. Knowledge is documented, archived, and "legalized" through computer software and spreadsheets. As Sudanese staff ascend an employment hierarchy from local organizations to international ones (Sudanese I met more than tripled their salaries doing so), they must also internalize the relative importance of computer-based legal memory creation over on-the-ground rights-related engagement.

Legal Assimilation Among South Sudanese NGOs

Adherence to the juridical forms and practices of international aid organizations provides material benefits to national staff, including stable employment, good salaries, job security, and training opportunities. But it also subjugates national staff to a disadvantageous bureaucratic hierarchy rooted in the transfer of Western legal principles, undermines their autonomy, and limits their rights-based consciousness. International agencies also export this legalistic model to national NGOs, pressuring them to adopt a similar model as a condition of funding and access to resources. This forced replication—the process of making Sudanese NGOs' internal structures match those of international NGOs—is ostensibly a form of capacity building. At root it involves mimicry of international aid groups' measures of standardization, formalization, and proceduralism to ensure accountability to rules, such as drafting contracts, terms of reference, and other forms of documentation.

Like South Sudanese employees of international NGOs, those employed by national NGOs are impacted by their engagement with transnational legal regimes. In order to receive international aid, national NGOs must adopt and adhere to international NGOs' external and internal legal schemes based on reporting, writing, and documentation. The rules come from norms associated with legal compliance, accountability, and anticorruption. Workers must also assimilate to the goals of legal awareness sought by expatriate managers for South Sudanese survivors of war. One activist with a local NGO told me that all of his organization's activities "are basically geared by the funding. The funding decides whether we work on poverty, environment, women's rights, [or] peacebuilding."[37] Local NGOs often apply for grants to fund law-related programs that do not fit their mandates. I met with a sports-related organization, for instance, that was doing rights-based civic education. "Sometimes you're not even mandated to do something from your organization's constitution," the program director told me, "but you do it anyway, because of the money."[38]

When I asked employees of a local NGO about the impact of adapting to donor requirements, no one mentioned the organization's overall mission or efficacy. I was told the new legalistic rules would help the organization compete with international NGOs for funding and set "a good example for how things should be done."[39] The procedural focus had supplanted the substantive one. Similarly, international aid groups demarcate the appropriate range of activities national NGOs may undertake. As a project coordinator told me, "[International aid groups] limit our chances to develop. . . . They see us [Sudanese NGOs] as a necessary evil. . . . This is why they hold onto the entire process and leave you limping about."[40]

A foreign aid worker in South Sudan echoed these comments and abruptly said during one interview, "We're just stuffing local NGOs down this chute to make them become just like international NGOs."[41] To do so, interviewees told me of intense competition among national NGOs to replicate the internal legal processes and regulations of international aid groups. The most successful mimics are the ones most likely to receive donor funding and the prestige that comes with it. Civil society groups "imagine that just the white person brings money," said one activist. "So even if you have money in your [Sudanese] NGO, people don't believe it."[42]

The importance of mimicking legal rules creates a new politics of parroting, whereby local groups use legalistic discourse they think foreign funding agencies want to hear. Staff members admit that "using the language that donors are expecting to hear is really challenging."[43] For this reason, some national NGOs find and pay foreign "experts" to write their project proposals (as they do their constitutions) on their behalf, paying USD 1,000 or more per proposal in the hopes that it will bring long-term revenue and stability.[44] The ghostwriters serve as legal translators, putting Sudanese-generated ideas in a form that local activists hope foreign organizations can accept.

When I asked a Sudanese NGO director whether lawyers play a role in implementing workplace policies, she echoed others I met by saying that the legal profession is absent from the process. "Lawyers don't do these things. . . . They don't know about these things concerning websites and policies."[45] International aid organizations bring opportunity in the form of financial assistance, but they demand subjugation to their own legal culture in return. Remarkably, Sudanese staff members I met referred to the workplace and funding policies issued by international aid agencies as their *qanoon* (law). While not South Sudan state law, international aid groups' internal policies are meant to build civil society and, ultimately, the state by compelling obedience to modern management and human resources systems. These groups follow a strikingly similar model to the one employed by the British colonial administration in Sudan many decades earlier, which required local groups to reproduce foreign modes of governance by creating and enforcing a juridical order (Sharkey 2003).

Sudanese employees of national NGOs whom I met were aware of the need to assimilate to the policies and procedures of their funders. One activist put it simply: "Local NGOs are like beggars to the internationals."[46] A national

NGO director confided, "Our organization would not exist if it were not for [international funding]."[47] These actors said the receipt of foreign aid was necessary for them to find work. "The beggar has no other option. If [international aid organizations] say no, then there is no money."[48] Expatriate workers with international NGOs were also aware of national NGOs' reliance on their aid dollars: "[Our national-NGO] partners become dependent on any source of funding they can find, and there are not a whole lot of opportunities for them to diversify."[49]

As the discourses and activities within national NGOs become more infused with transnational juridical concepts, practices, and techniques and focused on internal management and monitoring systems, they obtain more foreign funding. As one expatriate aid worker put it, "We need to help local NGOs play the game or else they will not get any funding to play it."[50] As local groups become better funded, they contract more work out to smaller NGOs or community-based organizations, which end up fulfilling the substantive mission. The result is an increasingly stratified domestic civil society. "Capacity" no longer refers to an organization's ability to do public outreach around the principles of human rights, but rather to its ability to obtain funds and create documentation and files. "If you declare yourself international, it means you no longer implement [programs]," said a national NGO staff member. "Let's say [our NGO] gets big funds. We will find local people to implement [the project]."[51]

Office spaces themselves seem to undergo a metamorphosis as national NGOs transition to more legalistic and bureaucratic models. The walls of a national NGO office had been covered with motivational posters, prints, and photos from activities in displaced-persons encampments when I spent time there in 2007. Three years later, after the organization had received an influx of donor aid and moved to a larger building, the motivational posters had been replaced with cork boards covered with phone directories, lists of tasks and deadlines, and, in one case, a photocopy of a set of cartoon-like faces portraying various workplace "moods." The feel was considerably more removed from the populations with whom the NGO employees were actually working. As NGOs create and enforce new rules governing workplace activities and tasks, the rules come to dominate every aspect of workplace life.

Expatriate employees with international NGOs and UN agencies say replicating legalistic infrastructures is necessary in order for national NGOs to be able to implement projects according to their design. Certainly, humanitarian impulses lie behind the export of this new bureaucratic legalism, much as it also animates the actions of many Sudanese staff members. Concerns of fraud, misallocation, theft, and other violations of law back home compel donors to transmit and adopt policies that ensure aid dollars are transparently and efficiently allocated to those who need it most. However imperfect or potentially detrimental, the juridical red tape is part of the process. In one national NGO, each programmatic unit must write a monthly report to the executive director in order to provide assurance that projects are on track. Others require spreadsheets that detail the "activity, name, proposed budget, workshop done, and number attended."[52] One program manager asks all of her "implementing partners" to provide documentation of their activities, including their workshops and the attendee counts. "I copy them. So, there's a file. Then when anyone comes, I can tell them [the number of] lectures [and] attendees."[53]

Resistance and Hierarchy

National NGOs can become sites not only for the transmission and reproduction of foreign legal practices and techniques, but also sites of resistance. Some national NGO staff members do not aspire to join the ranks of the large international groups that fund them. "There are two versions: either your own interests or the international organizations' interests," said one Sudanese activist. "It's your gut feeling."[54] For them, resistance to new juridical techniques may be masked by a sense of defeatism or passive acceptance of the power that international NGOs and UN agencies wield in civil society. But others see their work, often volunteer-based or with national NGOs not funded by foreign aid groups, as a form of resistance to those groups. "To work with a local NGO, you need inspiration," said one activist. "Even though there is no money . . . I prefer [it]. I know that one day, one time, whatever the situation, without finances, I can still help to turn life around for people down there."[55] Another employee agreed, "I want to make change. If I go to the UN, I'm not going to make any change. If I go to an international NGO, I won't be able to change the system they have there. But here in national NGOs, I can do it. I can make changes."[56]

A refusal to submit to certain juridical requirements of international agencies is another form of resistance, although managers often misinterpret this resistance as a lack of capacity. National NGO staff members, for example, will ask expatriate colleagues in international NGOs to ghostwrite proposals, progress reports, or other required forms of documentation on their behalf in order to avoid participating in the system. International aid workers acquiesce because they are reliant on national NGOs to implement projects. One expatriate aid worker in an international NGO said, "It's implied that I will be the one to produce the proposal [for funding] and submit on [the national NGO's] behalf."[57] Other Sudanese NGOs resist by not applying for funding at all. One local activist said, "Every week you have to write something . . . go to a workshop, a lot of things. You have to go. You have no time for your work [in the community]. So [we] . . . decided [not] to apply for funds. There's too much reporting."[58] Legalistic requirements impact daily work life, but resistance still occurs in the spaces set up and managed by expatriate-imported rules.

A tension exists in aid work between promoting domestic rights and serving the transnational aid agency bureaucracy. Rather than focusing on rights mobilization, many directors of national NGOs say they spend their time implementing projects favored by funders and trying to cover the salaries of a few employees. Their positions are precarious enough that they do not mobilize to demand fuller rights. Employment is difficult to obtain and typically temporary, so many feel fortunate to be in a paid position at all. They also see their employment as a step toward contracts with UN agencies or international NGOs (what some Sudanese people refer to as "big NGOs"[59]).

In a few cases, national staff members develop a rights consciousness and advocate for their interests successfully to senior managers, but they do so in a way that reifies the structure that subjugates them. For instance, one employee wanted two of the five senior management positions in his organization to be reserved for women. "The issue I brought forward was that we are talking about . . . [the] promotion of women's rights. I said, look, there should be a [senior management] position created for a woman."[60] He drafted a petition, which many staff members signed, and ultimately the policy changed.

More often, however, managers dismiss or ignore rights-based activism by national staff members. Local employees who confronted or resisted the decisions and actions taken by their North American or European line managers did not seek to oust international groups from the country; rather, they sought to infuse in these groups a sense that bureaucratic structures and transnational practices can coexist with employee rights. A national staff member in one international NGO said that employee concerns had to follow a specific process to be heard "usually . . . up from the staff association to the management." She continued that the process, while formalized, silenced staff complaints: "Sometimes management says it's beyond their capacity [or] they have to consult with HQ [headquarters] and so on. They leave it there, that way [the issue] will die."[61] Even as organizations teach human rights to the South Sudanese poor, they tend to discourage or quash rights-based resistance to office conditions.

Social Impacts of Aid Groups' Juridical Practices

The benefits to the South Sudanese who participate in and obey the transnational juridical systems of international aid organizations are real—higher salaries, job security, and the opportunity to realize humanitarian impulses. However, these benefits do come with social costs. For instance, competition for jobs, salaries, and seniority can overshadow the substantive legal work of international aid groups and civil society actors.[62] Activists denounced their colleagues who undertook this work because of "the availability of" international funds.[63] Reflecting on the common attraction to higher salaries, one activist said that her colleagues are "always looking for greener pastures."[64] Many civil society actors find themselves jumping between positions in different aid organizations, obtaining jobs by touting technical-training certificates. "Legal" training then becomes a proxy for one's potential in international groups. "After the training, you are left alone. [But] then you find out that [other] guys [from the training] are moving one by one to work with international NGOs," reinforcing an employment hierarchy built on adherence to bureaucratic legal techniques and practices.[65]

As Sudanese personnel climb the aid agency ladder, they have less direct contact with the impoverished Sudanese whom they purportedly serve. Interviewees commented to me that working with national NGOs means exposure to "rural areas, violations of human rights, [and] how people suffer."[66] At international NGOs, national staff members are expected to remain in the office and educate expatriate staff based on local knowledge. Nationals move from fieldwork in neighborhoods with the poor to sitting in offices with their computers. They construct a new legal archive through the technologies of documentation—reports, e-mail messages, forms, handbooks, constitutions, and contracts—few of which existed in South Sudan during the civil war.

Transitioning national staff from on-the-ground activism to internal organizational management is portrayed as a form of grassroots development of
civil society.

Conclusion

How does the turn to bureaucratic and legalistic modes of behavior recon-
figure civil society after war? Following what had been Africa's longest civil
war, aid agencies converged on South Sudan to build public acceptance of
human rights and the rule of law, bringing with them a common set of routinized and bureaucratic management practices, rules, and processes. Local
civil society actors who sought stable employment learned to conform to these
rules and new political grammars under the threat of sanction by management staff. Their conformity to managerial directives is important because
it occurred alongside the South Sudanese state's construction of a legal infrastructure.

Sudanese staff learned about and signed employment contracts and terms
of reference, obtained employee policy handbooks, wrote reports documenting their priorities and accomplishments, and used new accounting systems.
These novel and transnational knowledge practices became the repetitive and
formalistic processes constituting an everyday legal culture that pervaded local employees' new postwar livelihoods. Understanding aid agencies as
makers of legal culture experienced by local activists expands the range of
governance settings in which law becomes the ultimate source of coercive
power, particularly as the shadow of state officialdom lurks behind the techniques and processes imparted by foreign managers to their local subjects.

Aid agencies in South Sudan introduced a new discursive grammar of law
and politics into the lives of war survivors. They exported mundane workplace rules—documentation protocols, formalized procedures, and professionalized practices—into a nation torn apart by warfare, and then reframed
them into the power of law over employee behavior. Ultimately, the interactions associated with this "juridification" of workplace life manufacture cultures of discipline (Silverstein 2009). Employees learn to be part of a new
technological framework in which legal discourse and transnationalism
flourish, through the forms they are required to sign, files and records they
are required to produce and maintain, and workplace rules they are required
to follow. This bureaucratic legalism ultimately matters more for the creation

of local knowledge than the content of human rights found in the missions of the organizations where these locals work. Power is no doubt at work, but it is a specific type of power rooted in the transnational expansion of legalized concepts and techniques.

What does this case of transnational bureaucratic legalism in South Sudan reveal about the nature of law in conflict and postconflict settings and for sociolegal research more generally? First, this study reveals the importance of decentering local interactions with the state as the basis of understanding the lived experience of the law. The experience of war does not necessarily mean civil society is without legal norms. That is, nonstate actors are transmitters of legal techniques and practices, and it is necessary to look beyond the state to access the spaces where law, including Western law promoting accountability, reconfigures social relations in the Global South. Second, elites construct legal order for their purposes, often at the expense of those who might challenge elites' authority or decisions. By obeying new workplace regulations, individuals may accrue discursive and material resources. Third, consistent with findings from sociolegal studies, while institutional rules certainly can sustain hierarchies, these same legal codes may also be subversive when war survivors use them as part of a broader strategy of rights mobilization or resistance in and out of the workplace (Chua 2014; Massoud 2018; McCann 1994).

Some scholars may question whether the legalistic order established by aid agencies results in a net good or net harm for local aid activists. That is, even if some hierarchies are created, at least workers have salaries, learn to participate in a legal order, and gain access to international funding for humanitarian projects. While other work documents the myriad ways that aid agencies operate in postconflict settings, here I illuminate empirically the impacts of local adherence to transnational organizational practices. Even as employees fight for the human rights of South Sudan's hundreds of thousands of displaced persons, many are paradoxically prevented from making rights claims against their own employers.

The data in this chapter support the argument that transnational workplace rules transmitted to conflict settings impact the career mobility of ordinary people and their experience of the law. Three areas of continued research would expand on this study: First, investigating organizational behavior in other settings in the Global South would continue to build comparative law and society scholarship on (1) the extent to which law's endogeneity operates outside the United States, (2) whether transnational bureaucratic forms in aid agencies ultimately lead to domestic claim making in courts or legislatures, and (3) the extent to which private workplace regulations translate into actual state laws. Second, scholars able to gather internal documents, employment contracts, protocols, and policy frameworks—where safe for the researcher and his or her subjects—would supplement the data in this chapter to build richer ethnographies of local and international NGOs. (While these documents are not necessary to support this chapter's argument on the impacts of legal culture on civil society, my informants were clear that sharing internal documentation with me would risk their jobs.) Finally, while it is certainly true that aid groups are promoting democratic rights in postconflict settings, further research is needed to document whether the legalistic and regulatory style they import displaces their outward mandate to become an imprinted legacy on local society and a new "informal empire" based on imparted knowledge practices (see, e.g., Knop 2011; Riles 2001).

In her historical study of files, Cornelia Vismann (2008: 1) asks, "Faced with Babylonian stacks of files, the question arises whether there can ever be a legal culture devoid of files. How are we to conceive of a state *off the record*? How is the law to function without record-keeping devices?" The transnational practice of documentation and filing embodies not only state legalism but also organizational legalism—a mode of workplace practice rooted in bureaucratic practices and technical skills common to Western organizations. Managerial practices produce an everyday culture of legalism that is highly standardized, professionalized, and rooted in the interests of the founding organization. While a bureaucratic administrative staff generates the "purest" type of legal authority (Weber 1978: 220), it is unclear whether this new legalism in South Sudan filters through civil society to the marginalized and displaced masses, and to what effect. While career mobility is clearly a benefit, the ascension of NGO staff members reifies stratification between upwardly mobile civil society activists and the poor whom they claim to serve. These issues remain enduring areas for future research in conflict settings in and beyond South Sudan.

Transnational cultures of law thrive in conflict and postconflict settings, in new governments, new courts, and new aid agencies, and in the mixture of international law with national and local frames of reference. In South Sudan, the transmission of professionalizing techniques has created new forms of sovereignty largely outside of government purview, through repeated and regularized interactions between local employees and their expatriate managers, and between local organizations and the international groups that fund them. The discursive and symbolic power of the legal process is revealed through the supervision and training of local staff, through the rules they find in their workplace handbooks, and through their acts of resistance to those managerial rules. In these ways, aid agencies importing bureaucratic and legalistic modes of behavior are sites of political struggle in conflict settings, where survivors of war must confront and experience the regulatory circuitries of law's power.

Notes

Note to epigraph: All names have been changed to preserve confidentiality. This chapter uses "Sudanese" and "South Sudanese" interchangeably, as did those interviewed in South Sudan prior to its 2011 secession from Sudan.

1. This chapter is a modified version of Massoud (2015). The author thanks *Law & Society Review* for reuse permission and Carol Greenhouse and the anonymous reviewers for helpful feedback. Research and writing were supported by grants from the University of California, Santa Cruz; the Andrew Mellon Foundation; the John Simon Guggenheim Memorial Foundation; and the Carnegie Corporation of New York. Views expressed in this chapter are the author's responsibility. This chapter would not have been possible without the kindness of many respondents in South Sudan and Sudan.

2. Classic studies of judicial review in the United States (Bickel 1962; Casper 1976; Dahl 1957; Rosenberg 2008) have spurred comparative research on courts in East Asia (Ginsburg 2003), Europe (Cichowski 2007), sub-Saharan Africa (Ellet 2013), and Latin America (Helmke and Rios-Figueroa 2011; see also Woods and Hilbink 2009). Comparative law and society scholars have similarly called attention to the functions of courts in authoritarian, developing, or newly democratizing states (Cheesman 2015, 2011; Ghias 2010; Ginsburg and Moustafa 2008; Hurst 2018; Massoud 2013; Moustafa 2007; Rajah 2012; Stern 2013).

3. Seventeen of these twenty-three women were South Sudanese working for international or national NGOs or UN agencies; the remaining six were expatriate staff in international NGOs. Twelve of the eighteen men interviewed were South Sudanese.

4. Interview with Omera, United Nations official, Juba, South Sudan, June 2010.

5. According to an umbrella group that coordinates the activities of international NGOs in South Sudan, when the civil war ended in 2005, its coalition included 47 international NGOs. By 2010, that number had jumped to 167. (I do not name the group so as to protect the confidentiality of sources.)

6. Interview with Yonah, Sudanese NGO director, Juba, South Sudan, June 2010.

7. Interview with Baseema, NGO employee, Khartoum, Sudan, June 2010.

8. Interview with Honora, Sudanese aid worker, Juba, South Sudan, June 2010.

9. Interview with Baseema.

10. Interview with Gabriel, human rights program manager, Juba, South Sudan, June 2010.

11. Interview with Philippa, Sudanese aid worker, Juba, South Sudan, June 2010.

12. Interview with Destiny, Sudanese staff member with the UN, Juba, South Sudan, June 2010.

13. Repeat interview with Samira, human resources manager with an international NGO, Khartoum, Sudan, June 2010.

14. Interview with Ranya, NGO director, Khartoum, Sudan, June 2010.

15. Interview with Luca, Sudanese program manager in an international NGO, Juba, South Sudan, June 2010.

16. Interview with Eileen, foreign aid worker, Juba, South Sudan, June 2010.

17. Ibid.

18. Interview with Millie, Sudanese NGO finance manager, Juba, South Sudan, June 2010.

19. Interview with Joel, foreign aid worker, Juba, South Sudan, June 2010.

20. Interview with Ghania, NGO program officer, Khartoum, Sudan, June 2010.

21. Interview with Michael, NGO program director, Khartoum, Sudan, June 2010.

22. Interview with Paul, Sudanese NGO program director, Juba, South Sudan, June 2010.

23. Repeat interview with Samira, human resources manager with an international NGO, Khartoum, Sudan, June 2010.

24. Ibid.

25. Interview with Joseph, foreign aid worker with the United Nations, Juba, South Sudan, June 2010.

26. Interview with Ghania.

27. Ibid.

28. Interview with Ranya.

29. The end of the war and arrival of aid groups moderated and channeled activists' protestation into increasingly bureaucratized legal practices, including documenting routine office work, writing grant proposals, and attending staff meetings. One activist explained the transition: "Some of us [would] speak out" against government activities during the war and face arrest and imprisonment, but "now we write projects" to secure funding for approved NGO activities. Interview with Zechariah, civil society activist and church official, Juba, South Sudan, June 2010.

30. Interview with Judith, local staff member with the United Nations, Juba, South Sudan, June 2010.

31. Ibid.; interview with Gabriel.

32. Interview with Luca.

33. Interview with Patricia, Sudanese staff member with an international NGO, Juba, South Sudan, June 2010.

34. Interview with Michael. In some aid organizations, however, national staff may be prevented from advancing to senior positions to keep them insulated from potential political troubles the organization may generate with a host government.

35. Interview with Patricia.

36. Interview with Luca.

37. Interview with Taha, NGO director, Khartoum North, Sudan, November 2006.

38. Interview with Dominic, Sudanese youth activist and NGO program manager, Juba, South Sudan, June 2010.

39. Interview with Michael.

40. Interview with Rosie, Sudanese NGO project coordinator, Juba, South Sudan, June 2010.

41. Interview with Eva, foreign aid worker, Juba, South Sudan, June 2010.

42. Interview with Dominic.

43. Interview with Eileen.

44. Interview with Maximus, Sudanese NGO director, Juba, South Sudan, June 2010.

45. Interview with Ranya.

46. Interview with Dominic.

47. Interview with Paul.

48. Repeat interview with Isiah, Sudanese NGO volunteer director, Juba, South Sudan, June 2010.

49. Interview with Joel.

50. Interview with Eva.

51. Interview with Dominic.

52. Interview with Ghania.

53. Interview with Maysa, NGO program coordinator, Khartoum, Sudan, June 2010.

54. Interview with Paul.

55. Ibid.

56. Interview with Ranya.

57. Interview with Eileen.

58. Interview with Figaro, NGO director, Khartoum, Sudan, June 2010.

59. Repeat interview with Isiah.

60. Interview with Gabriel.

61. Interview with Philippa.

62. A former schoolteacher, for instance, told me that she joined a UN field office because the salary offered to UN secretaries was substantially higher than what was offered to local schoolteachers. Interview with Judith. While some Sudanese workers say that national NGOs are "much better than international NGOs because . . . [of] direct contact with beneficiaries," they also say that their time with national NGOs is a step toward better employment. "We know that this is our opportunity to learn and gain experience, to be powerful enough to go to another organization." Interview with Ghania.

63. Interview with Ilham, lawyer, Juba, South Sudan, April 2007. Poverty in South Sudan also, in her words, "made it difficult for people who had a genuine interest to offer their contribution without international funds."

64. Interview with Nawel, Sudanese aid worker, Juba, South Sudan, June 2010.

65. Interview with Maximus.

66. Repeat interview with Samira.

References

Asad, Talal. 2004. "Where Are the Margins of the State?" In *Anthropology in the Margins of the State*, eds. Veena Das and Deborah Poole, 279–288. Santa Fe, NM: School of American Research Press.

Autesserre, Séverine. 2010. *The Trouble with the Congo: Local Violence and the Failure of International Peacebuilding.* Cambridge: Cambridge University Press.

Bickel, Alexander M. 1962. *The Least Dangerous Branch: The Supreme Court at the Bar of Politics.* Indianapolis: Bobbs-Merrill.

Bernal, Victoria, and Inderpal Grewal. 2014. "The NGO Form: Feminist Struggles, States, and Neoliberalism." In *Theorizing NGOs: States, Feminisms, and Neoliberalism,* eds. Victoria Bernal and Inderpal Grewal, 1–18. Durham, NC: Duke University Press.

Bumiller, Kristin. 1987. "Victims in the Shadow of the Law: A Critique of the Model of Legal Protection." *Signs* 12 (3): 421–439.

Carothers, Thomas, ed. 2006. *Promoting the Rule of Law Abroad: In Search of Knowledge.* New York: Carnegie Endowment for International Peace.

Casper, Jonathan D. 1976. "The Supreme Court and National Policy Making." *American Political Science Review* 70 (1): 50–63.

Cheesman, Nick. 2011. "How an Authoritarian Regime in Burma Used Special Courts to Defeat Judicial Independence." *Law & Society Review* 45 (4): 801–830.

Cheesman, Nick. 2015. *Opposing the Rule of Law: How Myanmar's Courts Make Law and Order.* Cambridge: Cambridge University Press.

Chua, Lynette. 2014. "Rights Mobilization and the Campaign to Decriminalize Homosexuality in Singapore." *Asian Journal of Law and Society* 1 (1): 205–228.

Cichowski, Rachel A. 2007. *The European Court and Civil Society: Litigation, Mobilization and Governance.* Cambridge: Cambridge University Press.

Commission on Global Governance. 1999. *The Millennium Year and the Reform Process: A Contribution from the Commission on Global Governance.* London: Commission on Global Governance.

Dahl, Robert A. 1957. "Decision-Making in a Democracy: The Supreme Court as a National Policy-Maker." *Journal of Public Law* 6:279–295.

Davis, Kevin E., Benedict Kingsbury, and Sally Engle Merry. 2012. "Indicators as a Technology of Global Governance." *Law & Society Review* 46 (1): 71–104.

Deng, Francis M. 1995. *War of Visions: Conflict of Identities in the Sudan.* New York: Brookings Institution Press.

Deng, Francis M. 2011. "Customary Law in the Cross Fire of Sudan's War of Identities." In *Customary Justice and the Rule of Law in War-Torn Societies,* ed. Deborah Isser, 285–324. Washington, DC: US Institute of Peace Press.

Edelman, Lauren B. 1992. "Legal Ambiguity and Symbolic Structures: Organizational Mediation of Civil Rights Law." *American Journal of Sociology* 97 (6): 1531–1576.

Edelman, Lauren B., Sally Riggs Fuller, and Iona Mara-Drita. 2001. "Diversity Rhetoric and the Managerialization of Law." *American Journal of Sociology* 106 (6): 1589–1641.

Edelman, Lauren B., Linda H. Krieger, Scott R. Eliason, Catherine R. Albiston, and Virginia Mellema. 2011. "When Organizations Rule: Judicial Deference to Institutionalized Employment Structures." *American Journal of Sociology* 117 (3): 888–954.

Edelman, Lauren B., and Mark C. Suchman. 1997. "The Legal Environments of Organizations." *Annual Review of Sociology* 23:479–515.

Edelman, Lauren B., Christopher Uggen, and Howard S. Erlanger. 1999. "The Endogeneity of Legal Regulation: Grievance Procedures as Rational Myth." *American Journal of Sociology* 105 (2): 406–454.

Ellet, Rachel. 2013. *Pathways to Judicial Power in Transitional States: Perspectives from African Courts.* New York: Routledge.

Englund, Harri. 2006. *Prisoners of Freedom: Human Rights and the African Poor.* Berkeley: University of California Press.

Falk, Richard. 2009. *Achieving Human Rights.* New York: Routledge.

Felstiner, William L. F., Richard L. Abel, and Austin Sarat. 1980. "The Emergence and Transformation of Disputes: Naming, Blaming, Claiming . . . ." *Law & Society Review* 15 (3/4): 631–654.

Galanter, Marc. 1974. "Why the 'Haves' Come out Ahead: Speculations on the Limits of Legal Change." *Law & Society Review* 9 (1): 95–160.

George, Alexander L., and Andrew Bennett. 2005. *Case Studies and Theory Development in the Social Sciences.* Cambridge, MA: MIT Press.

Ghias, Shoaib A. 2010. "Miscarriage of Chief Justice: Judicial Power and the Legal Complex in Pakistan under Musharraf." *Law & Social Inquiry* 35 (4): 985–1022.

Ginsburg, Tom. 2003. *Judicial Review in New Democracies: Constitutional Courts in East Asia.* Cambridge: Cambridge University Press.

Ginsburg, Tom, and Tamir Moustafa. 2008. *Rule by Law: The Politics of Courts in Authoritarian Regimes.* Cambridge: Cambridge University Press.

Goodale, Mark, and Sally Engle Merry, eds. 2007. *The Practice of Human Rights: Tracking Law Between the Global and the Local.* Cambridge: Cambridge University Press.

Hagan, John, Gabrielle Ferrales, and Guillermina Jasso. 2008. "How Law Rules: Torture, Terror, and the Normative Judgments of Iraqi Judges." *Law & Society Review* 42 (3): 605–644.

Heckman, James J., Robert L. Nelson, and Lee Cabatingan. 2010. *Global Perspectives on the Rule of Law.* New York: Routledge.

Heller, Thomas C., and Erik G. Jensen, eds. 2003. *Beyond Common Knowledge: Empirical Approaches to the Rule of Law.* Stanford, CA: Stanford University Press.

Helmke, Gretchen, and Julio Rios-Figueroa, eds. 2011. *Courts in Latin America.* Cambridge: Cambridge University Press.

Hurst, William. 2018. *Ruling Before the Law: The Politics of Legal Regimes in China and Indonesia.* Cambridge: Cambridge University Press.

IDLO. 2011. "IDLO Helps College of Law of the University of Juba Finalize New Curriculum after Relocation from Khartoum." International Development Law Organization. On file with author.

Jalali, Rita. 2013. "Financing Empowerment? How Foreign Aid to Southern NGOs and Social Movements Undermines Grass-Roots Mobilization." *Sociology Compass* 7 (1): 55–73.

Johnson, Douglas H. 2003. *The Root Causes of Sudan's Civil Wars.* Bloomington: Indiana University Press.

Kamat, Sangeeta. 2004. "The Privatization of Public Interest: Theorizing NGO Discourse in a Neoliberal Era." *Review of International Political Economy* 11 (1): 155–176.

Kawar, Leila. 2014. "Commanding Legality: The Juridification of Immigration Policymaking in France." *Journal of Law and Courts* 2 (1): 93–116.

Keck, Margaret E., and Kathryn Sikkink. 1998. *Activists Beyond Borders*. Ithaca, NY: Cornell University Press.

Keith, Linda Camp. 2012. *Political Repression: Courts and the Law*. Philadelphia: University of Pennsylvania Press.

Kennedy, David. 2002. "The International Human Rights Movement: Part of the Problem?" *Harvard Human Rights Journal* 15:99–125.

Knop, Karen. 2011. "International Law and the Disaggregated Democratic State: Two Case Studies on Women's Human Rights and the United States." In *We, The People(s): Participation in Governance*, eds. Claire Charters and Dean R. Knight, 75–116. Wellington, New Zealand: Victoria University Press.

Leonardi, Cherry. 2013. *Dealing with Government in South Sudan: Histories of Chiefship, Community and the State*. London: James Curry.

Marshall, Anna-Maria. 2005. "Idle Rights: Employees' Rights Consciousness and the Construction of Sexual Harassment Policies." *Law & Society Review* 39 (1): 83–124.

Mason, Whit. 2011. *The Rule of Law in Afghanistan: Missing in Inaction*. Cambridge: Cambridge University Press.

Massoud, Mark Fathi. 2011. "Do Victims of War Need International Law? Human Rights Education Programs in Authoritarian Sudan." *Law & Society Review* 45 (1): 1–32.

Massoud, Mark Fathi. 2013. *Law's Fragile State: Colonial, Authoritarian, and Humanitarian Legacies in Sudan*. Cambridge: Cambridge University Press.

Massoud, Mark Fathi. 2014. "International Arbitration and Judicial Politics in Authoritarian States." *Law & Social Inquiry* 39 (1): 1–30.

Massoud, Mark Fathi. 2015. "Work Rules: How International NGOs Build Law in War-Torn Societies." *Law & Society Review* 49 (2): 333–364.

Massoud, Mark Fathi. 2016. "Field Research on Law in Conflict Zones and Authoritarian States." *Annual Review of Law and Social Science* 12:85–106.

Massoud, Mark Fathi. 2018. "Reflections on the Future of Global Legal Studies." *Indiana Journal of Global Legal Studies* 25 (2): 569–581.

McCann, Michael W. 1994. *Rights at Work: Pay Equity Reform and the Politics of Legal Mobilization*. Chicago: University of Chicago Press.

McClymont, Mary, and Stephen Golub. 2000. *Many Roads to Justice: The Law Related Work of Ford Foundation Grantees Around the World*. New York: Ford Foundation.

Merry, Sally Engle. 2006. *Human Rights and Gender Violence: Translating International Law into Local Justice*. Chicago: University of Chicago Press.

Meyer, John W., John Boli, George M. Thomas, and Francisco O. Ramirez. 1997. "World Society and the Nation-State." *American Journal of Sociology* 103 (1): 144–181.

Moustafa, Tamir. 2007. *The Struggle for Constitutional Power: Law, Politics, and Economic Development in Egypt*. Cambridge: Cambridge University Press.

Mutua, Makau. 2008. *Human Rights: A Political and Cultural Critique*. Philadelphia: University of Pennsylvania Press.

Poole, Deborah. 2004. "Between Threat and Guarantee: Justice and Community on the Margins of the Peruvian State." In *Anthropology in the Margins of the State*, eds. Veena Das and Deborah Poole, 35–66. Santa Fe, NM: School of American Research Press.

Rajagopal, Balakrishnan. 2003. *International Law from Below: Development, Social Movements, and Third World Resistance*. Cambridge: Cambridge University Press.

Rajah, Jothie. 2012. *Authoritarian Rule of Law: Legislation, Discourse, and Legitimacy in Singapore*. Cambridge: Cambridge University Press.

Riles, Annelise. 2001. *The Network Inside Out*. Ann Arbor: University of Michigan Press.

Rosenberg, Gerald N. 2008. *The Hollow Hope: Can Courts Bring About Social Change?* 2nd ed. Chicago: University of Chicago Press.

Schuller, Mark. 2012. *Killing with Kindness: Haiti, International Aid, and NGOs*. New Brunswick, NJ: Rutgers University Press.

Seawright, Jason, and John Gerring. 2008. "Case Selection Techniques in Case Study Research." *Political Research Quarterly* 61 (2): 294–308.

Sharkey, Heather. 2003. *Living with Colonialism: Nationalism and Culture in the Anglo-Egyptian Sudan*. Berkeley: University of California Press.

Sikkink, Kathryn. 2011. *The Justice Cascade: How Human Rights Prosecutions Are Changing World Politics*. New York: W. W. Norton.

Silverstein, Gordon. 2009. *Law's Allure: How Law Shapes, Constrains, Saves, and Kills Politics*. Cambridge: Cambridge University Press.

Stake, Robert E. 1995. *The Art of Case Study Research*. Thousand Oaks, CA: Sage.

Stern, Rachel. 2013. *Environmental Litigation in China: A Study in Political Ambivalence*. Cambridge: Cambridge University Press.

Suchman, Mark C., and Lauren B. Edelman. 2007. "Introduction: The Interplay of Law and Organizations." In *The Legal Lives of Private Organizations*, eds. Lauren B. Edelman and Marc C. Suchman. Aldershot, UK: Ashgate.

Talesh, Shauhin A. 2009. "The Privatization of Public Legal Rights: How Manufacturers Construct the Meaning of Consumer Law." *Law & Society Review* 43 (3): 527–562.

Thayer, Millie. 2010. *Making Transnational Feminism: Rural Women, NGO Activists, and Northern Donors in Brazil*. New York: Routledge.

Vismann, Cornelia. 2008. *Files: Law and Media Technology*. Trans. Geoffrey Wintrhop-Young. Stanford, CA: Stanford University Press.

Weber, Max. 1978. *Economy and Society*. Berkeley: University of California Press.

World Bank. 2019. "South Sudan." Accessed 9 July 2019. http://www.worldbank.org/en/country/southsudan.

Woods, Patricia J., and Lisa Hilbink. 2009. "Comparative Sources of Judicial Empowerment: Ideas and Interests." *Political Research Quarterly* 62 (4): 745–752.

Zwingel, Susanne. 2012. "How Do Norms Travel? Theorizing International Women's Rights in Transnational Perspective." *International Studies Quarterly* 56:115–129.

CHAPTER 7

Uncertain Sovereignties

Indigenous-State Relations in Colombia

Sandra Brunnegger

One day in the course of my fieldwork, I was sitting in a spacious judicial office on the upper floor of the building of the central Sala Administrativa del Consejo Superior de la Judicatura (Administrative Chamber of the Upper Judicial Council) in Bogotá. I was sitting on the couch next to members of both an international nongovernmental organization (NGO) and a regional Colombian NGO, the latter having invited me to this late-morning meeting. Across from us were two state employees from the Escuela Judicial Rodrigo Lara Bonilla (Rodrigo Lara Bonilla School for the Judiciary). The school forms part of Colombia's judicial framework, and serves as a training academy for Colombian judges and legal administrators. The meeting was cordial but formal, and we exchanged pleasantries as we sipped our *tinto* (black coffee). The conversation turned to a convening of state judges, prosecutors, and indigenous authorities scheduled to take place in the department of Tolima. The event, funded by the international NGO, was to facilitate an informal exchange between indigenous authorities (in particular, members of an indigenous tribunal) and representatives of the state on the relationship between indigenous and state legal systems. This kind of planned gathering was not unusual in Colombia. Since the recognition of indigenous legal systems in 1991, many such events have brought together state and indigenous authorities.[1]

During the meeting at this judicial office, the state functionary from the Rodrigo Lara Bonilla School for the Judiciary expressed a desire (or saw a need) to *formalizar las relaciones* (formalize relations) between the international NGO and the school. As conceived and planned by the international NGO, the school was not anticipated to be part of the convening. However, it quite quickly became clear that the state functionaries from the school expected to participate in the organization of the event. The school was implicitly talking about a *permiso* (authorization)—something required of judges and prosecutors taking part in an NGO-arranged event—that would have to come through the school. To the international and regional NGO members present, the state functionaries were conveying a message: Any future events they wanted to organize with judicial state officers would have to go through the school formally, as the school was part of the state's legal apparatus to train judges and legal administrators. After the meeting, the international NGO received a letter from the school formally confirming this position, and the judges and prosecutors who had been invited to the workshop by the international organization also received letters from the school instructing them not to attend. The convening went ahead anyway, led by the regional NGO under the auspices and funding of the international NGO. State judges were indeed absent, although one state prosecutor defied orders to attend. All indigenous authorities were present. Only a year earlier, this same international NGO had organized a similar event in cooperation directly *with* the Rodrigo Lara Bonilla School. The contrast with the preceding year was marked because this time the international NGO was working with a regional NGO, not with the school.

Taking this meeting as a starting point, my aim in this chapter is to unravel and map the different interests and agendas of parties enmeshed in the dynamics of indigenous-nonindigenous legal relations in Colombia, including state representatives and agencies, international funding agencies, indigenous community organizations, and their leaders. These positions and groups figure in a multiscalar, always contingent, and relational legal landscape in which indigenous and state legal systems relate in a variety of ways. This chapter's considerations radiate outward from the constitutional recognition of indigenous legal systems in Colombia. Specifically, my analysis considers the uncertainties that have unfolded from the constitutional recognition of indigenous legal systems on account of the sometimes contradictory, untidy, or uneven ways the state imagines "coordination" between indigenous and state legal systems.

The meetings and events, such as the one described above, that bring together state and indigenous authorities remain critical sites of the practice of state sovereignty. Sovereignty is itself a fragmentary, uncertain, performative, and ongoing project that by implication defines the reach of indigenous legal systems. In the context of this uncertain sovereignty, meetings between state and indigenous authorities represent interstices of sovereignty. In these terms, there are both old and new sites for state practices in which the reach of the indigenous legal system is at stake. This chapter construes sovereignty reflexively as a matter of relations through which actors traverse both the international aid obligations that fund such meetings and events and the national legal context that circumscribes sovereignty. In other words, sovereignty is performed as relational, especially insofar as the forms and outcomes of coordination between state and indigenous legal systems are uncertain.

To map Colombia's legal landscape, the chapter begins by examining some historical, social, political, and legal conjunctions in Latin America, in particular as these concerns relate to multiculturalism and Colombia's constitutional recognition of indigenous legal systems. It then explores how the politico-legal spaces enabled by the passage of the 1991 Constitution remain in a state of (legal) uncertainty. This legal uncertainty is precipitated by the unspecified conditions according to which the two legal systems—indigenous and state—relate to each other. Following a closer consideration of state-indigenous interactions, the chapter considers whether the Colombian state may be purposefully nurturing legal uncertainty in the wake of the constitutional recognition of indigenous legal systems. Is Colombia perpetuating a state of uncertainty to sustain its agenda and interests? Finally, through the example of the United States Agency for International Development (USAID), the chapter describes how international funding agencies and organizations fit into Colombia's management of its rules of law, and into practices of sovereignty and contestations of sovereignty and nation-building. This account aims to offer insights into how the Colombian state may be seen as acting under the sponsorship of international funding agencies.

Multiple Horizons

Since the 1980s, multiple historical, social, political, and legal horizons have shaped countries across Latin America. In particular, a swathe of neoliberal economic policies brought in through the 1980s and 1990s across the continent had long-term uneven effects on its politics, social life, and environment (Jordan 2016). (A wide literature, such as Escobar 2010; Fisher 2008;

and Goodale and Postero 2013, reflects on the social, political, and cultural implications of neoliberal economic reforms in restructuring Latin America countries.) One aspect of these modernization projects as conceived under the aegis of neoliberal economic policy was a deepening of decentralization in some countries. Often, decentralization has been pushed in the context of the evolving agendas of multilateral agencies, particularly the World Bank, the Inter-American Development Bank, and the International Monetary Fund, though in practice, it has been implemented in an asymmetrical, partial, and untidy fashion (Bossuyt 2013). These decentralization processes have often gone hand-in-hand with democratization projects.

Colombia is frequently portrayed as "one of the most decentralized countries in Latin America" (Rojas 2002: 136),[2] given the state's outsourcing or withdrawal of many of its services. The fiscal, legal, political, and administrative decentralization of Colombia's government flows from the state's 1991 Constitution. Along with constitutional and decentralization reforms in the 1990s, Latin American countries also witnessed an expansion in the adoption of multicultural programs of rights for indigenous peoples, which represented a new chapter in indigenous-state relations. In Colombia, the 1991 Constitution recognized many cultural rights of indigenous communities.[3] For instance, Article 246 recognizes the right of indigenous authorities to administer justice within their territorial ambit. The constitutional recognition of indigenous legal systems was, when framed differently, a form of decentralization of Colombian justice, as enshrined in Article 246 of the Colombian Constitution.

Article 246 highlights how the state scripted a partial representation of itself in the context of state-indigenous legal relations. By stating "indigenous authorities may exercise jurisdictional functions . . . in accordance with their own norms and procedures as long as they are not contrary to the Constitution and the laws of the Republic," the state circumscribes indigenous jurisdictional autonomy. This limiting of indigenous jurisdictional autonomy inscribes uncertainty in the operations of indigenous jurisdictional autonomy, even as political forces and constellations are established. More pointedly, in a disjunction between legal text and actual practice, a coordination mechanism—the so-called coordination law—stipulated in Article 246 has yet to be formulated, twenty-eight years after the passing of the Constitution. The proposed coordination mechanism was intended to specify terms by which indigenous legal systems would relate to those of the state. Instead, a degree of legal uncertainty prevails.[4]

We can narrow our formulation of uncertainty more precisely to the manner in which the state has sponsored not only a partial representation of itself but also contradictory, conflicting images of itself in the context of state-indigenous legal relations in connection with Article 246. While the article recognizes the application by indigenous communities of their own practices and requires the state to specify the relations between indigenous and state legal systems, the state seems to be without a coherent agenda with regard to its implementation through a coordination law. This could be attributable to a plethora of social or political reasons. For example, some lawmakers and policymakers might not see the coordination law as a political priority. Equally, some state actors could espouse cultivating uncertainty as a form of political management or containment. In other cases, some state actors may see the value of deferring a coordination law in order to rely on the existing decisions and emerging jurisprudence of the Constitutional Court. These reasons, obviously, do not exclude each other; and they are often shaped by disjunctive social, political, and legal imaginings.

In the absence of a coordination law, different kinds of spaces have opened up in which the relations between indigenous and state representatives have been refashioned, redefined, and reworked. In these indigenous-state interactions, images, or representations of, the state and of alternative sites of sovereignty emerge to engender a recently recognized "new" pluralized legal outlook. This legal pluralism must be held against a backgrounded conception of the state. In this backgrounded conception, the state is itself seen as a mutation of multifarious, ambiguous, intangible, and sometimes fictive formations, relations, and imaginations—a bricolage of institutional bodies, practices, and a plurality of agents, as many anthropologists attest (e.g., Das and Poole 2004; Sharma and Gupta 2009: 6; Thelen, Vetters, and von Benda-Beckmann 2014). In other words, there is no such thing as the (monolithic) state, a bounded entity.

As we shall see in a variety of ways in this chapter, the very discourse of conjoined legalities is problematic, given that there is no such thing as the state, just as there is no such thing as an indigenous legal system (as imagined by state authorities). That is why the state—and by extension sovereignty—cannot be imagined other than through its relations. In this sense, the question of uncertainty as formulated in this chapter is both practical and theoretical for multiple actors, including scholars.

It is worth noting the de facto role of coordination undertaken by Colombia's Constitutional Court, which has, through its *tutela* decisions, drawn many of the contours of indigenous jurisdiction and marked out relations between indigenous and state legal systems since 1991. A tutela is a writ for the protection of fundamental constitutional rights. The Constitutional Court, a product of the Constitution itself, has produced one of the richest bodies of jurisprudence—both criticized and lauded—relating to indigenous jurisdictional autonomy in Latin America. The existence of this flexible, extensive body of case law arguably accounts for why the state has not even attempted to draft coordination principles. Perhaps ironically, however, decisions made by the Constitutional Court—to at least some extent—feed into legal uncertainty because, by its very nature, a case-by-case decision-making body of jurisprudence constrains future knowability. This means that its revision of tutelas only takes effect *inter partes*, meaning only the actors involved in a particular claim are bound by the court's decision. However, it is important to note that while the inter partes effect is the court's usual practice, the Constitutional Court can decide to expand inter partes to the general effects of a ruling should it feel circumstances warrant it—something it does only infrequently (Cepeda-Espinosa 2004: 573, 575).

In the absence of a coordination law, spaces have opened since the adoption of the 1991 Constitution, creating room for various international funding agencies and organizations to push their own interests and agendas (as discussed below through the example of USAID). This allows me to pose the question in the Colombian context: Does the legal uncertainty with regard to indigenous-state relations compromise the state's assertion of sovereignty?

Practices of (Legal) Space

The question of indigenous-state relations relative to state sovereignty means we must understand how indigenous leaders occupy, or navigate, these uncertain spaces. Since 1991, indigenous leaders and their organizations, as intermediary figures and brokers between the state and their communities, have navigated the indeterminacy of the state's ambiguous presence, which might also be perceived as its absence. This refashioning takes place with respect to jurisdictional autonomy and in the relationship between indigenous and state legal systems. Jurisdictional autonomy is at stake because it has been the historical role of the state and state courts to administer justice to many indigenous communities in Colombia. With the 1991 Constitution and Article 246, many indigenous communities began to administer their own justice, breaking with a usual practice of these communities to refer internal disputes to state courts. Mostly since the beginning of 2000, indigenous leaders and organizations across Colombia began intensively to engage in legal experiments as many communities began re-imagining and refashioning their legal systems. This wave saw the establishment of indigenous tribunals and law schools, along with the creation of working groups to reflexively and discursively consider their own legal systems.[5] Space does not permit me here to expand on these legal experiments, such as the indigenous law school and tribunal. However, it is clear that these developments represented an initial response on the part of indigenous leaders and communities to the (legal) uncertainty that unfolded with 1991 Constitution and Article 246. The institutions set up were, by and large, particular to their localities to reflect the needs and circumstances of their communities.

At the same time, a few state authorities attributed, in some cases, a kind of uncertainty to specific indigenous authorities regarding the way they dealt with legal matters internally, deprovincializing the complexity of community life. After 1991, many communities took up the right to administer justice in their territorial ambit, with the response being a seeming increase in numbers of indigenous community members bringing cases to the state court in order to challenge their own authorities' decisions. State judges have received complaints from indigenous community members concerning indigenous authorities who, it is claimed, dealt with certain cases internally in an unsatisfactory manner or failed to address them altogether due to a wealth of reasons concomitant with the social and political life of a community, including reasons of internal politics.

Some state authorities seem to be uncertain as how to deal with indigenous legal systems. For example, individual state judges have expressed their frustration with the lack of education regarding Article 246, an activity that falls within the remit of the Rodrigo Lara Bonilla School for the Judiciary. At the meeting described in this chapter's opening, the school asserted its control over the "further education" of its judiciary. In the school's view, neither an international NGO that seemingly wants to "train" judges (especially without the authorization of the school) nor any other external institution should broker an exchange between indigenous and state authorities without the state's explicit permission. For many state judges, the Rodrigo Lara Bonilla School, however, has failed in this mission to "further educate."

From the very beginning of these debates, and over the course of the many coordination events and meetings, indigenous authorities have emphasized to state authorities that there are many indigenous legal systems. There is no single indigenous legal system since there are more than eighty different state-recognized indigenous communities. The emphasis on diversity in these debates has provoked more uncertainty for the state judges and prosecutors who have participated in these meetings; they have felt a need to grasp indigenous epistemology (their ways of knowing) and ontology (their ways of being), as these inform their legal systems. Those individual state authorities engage openly and voluntarily, often out of curiosity, in these mutual conversations and exchanges. But even now, some state authorities reject the right of indigenous authorities to administer justice. Given the ontological fragility at the heart of Colombia's legal pluralism, it is unsurprising that its epistemology of pluralism—how legal pluralism is to be known, disseminated, and practiced—reflects the fault lines and uncertainties of the state's sovereignty, a state that writes a constitution accompanied by unwritten provisions (i.e., the coordination law). In short, the lack of a coordination law affects most state judicial authorities as both epistemological and ontological matters, which conditions their assumptions regarding the nature and possible kinds of indigenous legal systems.

Within the ideology of international funding bodies and the state, though, the meetings seem to serve to make indigenous legal systems visible or legible (Scott 1998). Meetings are conducted in the search for the linchpins of indigenous legal systems, often in the form of a penal code as envisaged by many state authorities. This is the nexus of relations used by state agencies, although an epistemological challenge for state authorities lies in their attempt to map practices onto Western legal categories as imagined by state authorities. In this translation, what counts as law in reference to indigenous legal systems for state authorities? For state authorities, points of reference—the norms by which state and indigenous legal systems are related to each other—have to be specified and made commensurable. On this basis, state authorities tend to draw indigenous legal systems into the ambit of penal law. They often conduct meetings looking for essential and defining principles. The very premise of "coordination" presupposes for most state authorities *two* notionally coherent bodies of legal principle and practice.

Certainly, in these meetings, differences between legal systems as conceived systematically are drawn out, reinforced, and reinscribed, and seem to be a response to the pressure to produce revelatory representations of the functioning of both state and indigenous legal systems. State law is portrayed as a static, coherent, and unidimensional body, which effaces how it has, in fact, been assembled out of different and fluctuating customs and norms as well as international norms imported or transplanted from elsewhere. Meanwhile, indigenous legal systems are portrayed as fluid, oral, complex, and socially conditioned. When any of these interpretations are insisted upon, existing "mutually constitutive relations" (Merry 1992: 358) between indigenous and state legal systems are overlooked and instead differences are re-inscribed. The process works toward mutually *othering* legal systems as these legal systems are reimagined.

In the various "coordination" meetings and events between state representatives and indigenous leaders in which I have participated over the years as an ethnographer, it is clear participants quickly get to the core of debates over multiculturalism. For state authorities, they swiftly pose the ontological obstacles to legal pluralism. If a constitution brings law and nation into being through text (Buchanan and Pahuja 2004), then the very essence of sovereignty is simultaneously both scripted and—to a certain extent—unmade in Colombia by Article 246, in tandem with the unwritten coordination law.

In the face of this ontological obstacle, the question that repeatedly surfaces at these coordination meetings is on a visceral level: How should individual and collective rights claims be reconciled in this seemingly deep-rooted tension? This question cuts to the quick of cultural diversity as a theoretical concept, with the potential to challenge liberalism as figured in Western nation-building policies and imaginings. Can the recognition of difference through law be understood to reformulate the principle of a state, or of the craft of making a state, at a fundamental level? How does the future nation imagine itself? Is it premised on a fiction of a homogeneous sovereignty and built on the imagined nation, not on the state's actual fragmented and uneven practices? The question also raises the specter—misleading in any context—of an unambiguous, unevolving, and uniform sovereign state that determines and contains the place and reach of indigenous communities in the imaginary of the Colombian nation. One issue concerning the relationship between the state and indigenous legal systems turns not only on how the state represents itself but also on what kind of concept of sovereignty can be allowed to circulate in its name in indigenous-state interactions.

One maxim authored by state authorities over the course of meetings and associated events about indigenous legal systems is: First *fortalecimiento* (strengthening), then coordination. This maxim came into being in direct response to the many indigenous community members who continue to turn to state courts to challenge the decisions of their own indigenous authorities.

But what *fortalecimiento* might mean in practice has been left vague. And, to what end are indigenous legal systems being "strengthened"? Does this imagined linearity and sequentiality, as conceived by state authorities, leave space for any projections of a counternarrative? Does the strengthening only serve to make indigenous legal systems legible, or does it imagine an organization of difference? What are the cultural effects of this strengthening? Is the maxim a paradigm of "order in, through, and with difference" (Mall 2000: 15)?

What happens when incommensurability emerges as the essential principle in indigenous-nonindigenous encounters? As Povinelli asks about Australia: Is the direction of travel for indigenous legal systems to orient themselves "towards the nation's ideal image of itself" (Povinelli 1998: 580) and as *being worthy* of national recognition" (Povinelli 2002: 39)? In the context of the recognition of Aboriginal customary law, Povinelli lays bare the impossible demands placed on indigenous legal practices, which must both prove "evidence of the continuity of traditional beliefs and dispositions . . . as the condition of cultural recognition" (2002: 3) and follow "legal mandates on the form traditional culture must take" (2002: 55). A similar observation could be made of Colombia when state judges demand proof of "traditional" character of indigenous practices when deciding cases turning on indigenous jurisdictional autonomy. In Colombia, Article 246 from its outset enshrined a framework constraining indigenous legal systems and limiting the legal accommodation of difference by requiring indigenous legal systems to be congruent with state laws and the Constitution. More concretely, Povinelli notes that in Australia there is an obligation to "public reason and moral sense," and thus some "practices of 'customary law' are prohibited by common and statutory law and by a public sense of moral decency," vesting an idea of "the socially and culturally repugnant" and making norms of decency "the limits of recognition" for indigenous communities (2002: 17). These encounters would appear impeccably liberal in upholding conditions of asymmetric footings and uneven power relations, as liberal multiculturalism is seemingly enclosed in a dialectic of reason and repugnance.

Given that meetings and events with the Colombian state and indigenous authorities have engendered both new sites as well as continuing sites to fashion indigenous legal systems with the state legal system, the state's sequencing of "strengthening" and coordination takes on compound resonances. Povinelli draws on Slavoj Žižek (1994) when she says of indigenous legal systems in Australia, and their accommodation within state law:

"Multiculturalism is a deeply optimistic liberal engagement . . . [and] is generating 'utopian' narratives [that cannot but eventuate in] failed alternative histories" (Povinelli 2002: 25). For Povinelli, there is the danger that the "national telos" of inclusion—the optimism of multiculturalism—is both governed by law and proposed by the principles of legal pluralism, which potentially "seduce critical thinking away from an analysis of how social relations of power rely on a multicultural imaginary" (1998: 583).

While this suspicion of liberalism's undercurrents is important in making sense of social relations of power in Colombia, it would be a mistake to sift through meetings between state and indigenous authorities looking to unravel hidden (or not-so-hidden) scripts of the state's supposed purposes and dynamics. Such an approach might lead to overlooking how state and indigenous figures also participate in these relations. We would do better to explore generations of social relations because these provide sites for new social potential. This allows us to imagine new forms of relationality, and offers new ways of negotiating or translating meaning across cultural differences and perhaps forging a new cultural script of living together. As such, we should interrogate how hope, anxiety, and optimism, for example, have triggered and possessed agentive moments and opened spaces of new potentiality—however limited and momentary they may be—even when framed squarely or circumscribed within the terms of the state.

We may then ask (to pose the topic quickly) how social relations are generated when these meetings exhibit or invoke a certain kind of pragmatism. Against the backdrop of legal uncertainties, mechanisms for coordination relating to criminal justice have been created in informal, mostly localized, meetings between indigenous authorities and state prison authorities (such as prison governors, police officers, judges, and family commissioners). Colombian state prisons with indigenous inmates, through agreement, have accepted conditions set by indigenous authorities, and state medical officers have analyzed DNA for indigenous authorities, for example, in paternity cases in determining alimony claims. The indigenous tribunal in Tolima has started to work closely with state judges; consequently, the workload of state judges has fallen. One state judge told me that the number of complaints he received from indigenous members fell from a high of seven a day in the 1990s to only several a month in 2009.

In this instance, then, pragmatism and uncertainty have set the terms for each other's potentiality, even if the conditions are set within the frameworks of a decentralized, neoliberal, multicultural state. A better characterization would be to imagine the state as an amorphous ongoing project—even as we acknowledge there is no such thing as the state—working through different moments. The state, to be clear, is continuously forged, contested, and differently reimagined. In this continuously uneven and uncertain production, the notion of the state may be taken to rest on the incompleteness of its processes, including those that are intangible—or, to put this another way, on the revisability of the social relations that may constitute the "state form."

What roles do international funding agencies and organizations then play in extending this state discourse? Before exploring this more substantively with the example of USAID, the next section looks at the legal uncertainty—that is, the lacuna opened up by—the lack of a coordination law.

Crafting Uncertainty

What consolidations do uncertainties enable? What shapes (or motivates) legal uncertainty? And, what social anxieties does uncertainty foster?[6] Decentralized states are always theaters of ambiguity, rupture, and suspicion, but with the potential to turn into locations of experimental creativity that offer conditions of possibilities (see Comaroff and Comaroff 2006). Even with the possibilities of ruptures, flux appears to engender creative political responses that enact the potentials of new political spaces coming into being between the state and indigenous communities, as well as among and within indigenous communities. Therefore, within these new political spaces, possibilities have emerged for charting, and thus governing, beyond the ruptures, ambiguities, anxieties, suspicions, and paradoxes of the uncertain state. These issues seem especially pressing in regard to the coordination law. This coordination law, though—a possible means to end uncertainty, for better or worse—itself seems to be indefinitely postponed.

In one sense, the absence of a coordination law may be seen simply as a form of rupture. In another sense, it could be seen as a logic written into Colombia's structure of political relations. Jean and John Comaroff (2006: 5) make the point that "vastly lucrative returns . . . inhere in actively sustaining zones of ambiguity between the presence and absence of the law: returns made from controlling . . . from amassing value, that is, by exploiting the new aporias of jurisdiction opened up under neoliberal conditions."

Comaroff and Comaroff show connections in the interplay of neoliberal governmentality, law, disorder, and violence,[7] and the emphasis is valuable for the present discussion by taking the idea of the state's zones of ambiguity further. It would seem that the perpetuation of ambiguity is less about seizing control of newly opened political spaces and more about the perpetuation of ambiguity that appears to perpetuate a state of uncertainty so as to sustain the state's agenda and interests. In short, these uncertain times involve more than just myriad tensions over new realms of possibilities, new projects of political containment, or controlling opened-up political spaces.

Meetings between indigenous and state authorities over the coordination law started in the 2000s and continue today. International projects and funding pouring into Colombia—at the likely invitation of the Colombian state—stressed the need for coordination between indigenous authorities and state judges, prosecutors, and other officials. One may argue that, since 2000, the state has maintained zones of ambiguity through these workshops, events, and projects while tapping funding from USAID and other international agencies; or, as Comaroff and Comaroff put it, accessing "lucrative returns" (2006: 5). The uncertainty seems to be by design. The logic is inherent in the supposed "neoliberal multiculturalism" (Hale 2002). This logic of a so-called neoliberal multiculturalism is that multiculturalism colludes with neoliberal market reforms while conceding few rights to indigenous communities, which is consistent with impeding more radical or structural change (Hale 2002: 487; Lucero 2013: 24). This logic seems to be repeated in the logic of expedient uncertainty concerning indigenous-state legal relations. The sovereignty that would accrue to the state as a result of these relations would transpire as domination arising from the intervention in indigenous legal systems as made possible by the unequal power relations between them (McCreary 2014: 73).

The vignette regarding the Rodrigo Lara Bonilla School for the Judiciary in this chapter's opening clearly suggests that uncertainty may yield a strategic potential for the state. That is not to say that opportunities are not emerging for indigenous communities and their organizations—as seen in the possibility of their own law schools, tribunals, and other related projects receiving funding through international funding agencies—but that their room to maneuver to shape the scope of incoming international funding is squarely conditioned through the funding agencies' objectives. A question then emerges as to how the state acts under the sponsorship of international funding agencies. To put this another way, and returning to the initial question: Can Colombia assert its sovereignty through uncertainty? Uncertainty might be asserted, for example, by controlling the funding stream for projects related to decentralization; that is, a pretext for international fund-ing is to maintain uncertainty. Uncertainty can be perpetuated or managed through "outsourcing" when the administration of indigenous justice might be at stake. Outsourcing, in this sense, is like the event with the Ro-drigo Lara Bonilla School: Funding agencies are invited to sponsor coordi-nation events and projects. Uncertainty is the foundation on which actors set in motion specific forms of agency.

Bricolage of Relations

With the Rodrigo Lara Bonilla School for the Judiciary meeting described in this chapter's opening, it may be generative to see this episode in relation to the issue of funding, as discussed above. USAID and the European Union, among other government or international funding bodies, including inter-national NGOs, have sponsored similar kinds of projects and gatherings deal-ing with indigenous legal systems and their relationship with state legal systems. The Rodrigo Lara Bonilla School has carried out many, if not the majority, of these projects and events. One probable motivation for the school to want to accredit participants is to retain control of funding (or funding applications) for future projects and events in Colombia. This is clear from the supposed need of the international NGO, as mentioned at the beginning of the chapter, to formalize relations with the school, to meet the school's request.

It becomes important to ask: What is the role of international NGOs, the European Commission, the Inter-American Development Bank, and inter-national state agencies such as AECID (the Spanish Agency for International Development Cooperation; a Spanish government body) in sponsoring events pertaining to this coordination between indigenous and state legal systems? What role do they play in extending a multicultural, neoliberal, decentral-ized state discourse? Concerns with access to justice, the rule of law, and other comparable ideas fall within the state's purview while also being priorities for a number of international funding agencies, mostly USAID and those in the European Union. It is also clear that these funding agencies come with their own particular—that is, ideological—understandings of the rule of law (e.g., of its meaning, functions, benefits, elements, and limits) as well as of the tools and functions of justice, and the means to access justice. Differen-tiating between the ideologies of these agencies is beyond the scope of my chapter. My focus is specifically on USAID, as USAID has been particularly active in Colombia. The funding of these projects and gatherings dealing with indigenous legal systems and their relationship with state legal systems is part of a larger USAID funding strand concerned with access to justice, the rule of law, and other comparable ideas.

USAID's Access to Justice Program (AJP), for instance, is concerned with reinforcing Colombia's formal and informal justice sectors. Within this funding framework, USAID has contributed to the creation of Casas de Justicia (Houses of Justice), settings intended to offer access to alternative dispute resolution (ADR) and to direct users to various judicial authorities, such as judges, prosecutors, public defenders, and the police. The Colombian state inaugurated its Casa de Justicia project with USAID backing in 1995, promising marginalized and low-income individuals access to justice.[8] By 2013 there were eighty-one such houses in Colombia, staffed by lawyers, prosecutors, police inspectors, social workers, psychologists, and public defenders, often working with women's organizations or indigenous representatives (Cissé et al. 2014: 175). One House of Justice project sponsored a member of an indigenous tribunal in Tolima. The Houses of Justice offer free legal advice and conciliation and ADR services in cases of family disputes, *barrio* (neighborhood) conflicts, petty crimes, and so on. While people's access to justice can be enhanced through these facilities, Caroline Moser and Cathy McIlwaine (2000, 2004) make clear that the perception and reception of Houses of Justice varies from place to place. Some have been greeted by a "lack of trust" on the grounds that they serve the same purposes as (the often distrusted) state agencies, albeit in a different guise (2004: 78). This mixed response is also a reflection of the fact that some of the House of Justice staffers are public servants, like prosecutors, policemen, and public defenders.

International agencies and institutions that sponsor such projects also come with their own expectations. For the Houses of Justice program, for instance, these may entail offering marginalized sections of society access to the state, but with the effect that the state may recoup its legitimacy in these areas. This reassertion of state norms proceeds against a backdrop in which the sovereignty of the Colombian state is constantly challenged, not least on account of the political complexities of the armed conflict that has ravaged the country for over fifty years. Different armed groups, gangs, and narco-traffickers in effect vie with each other for control of whole areas, especially areas geographically remote from the center. These contested controls over space are also fostered by Colombia's challenging topography with few roads and poorly policed international borders (Marcella 2009: 13). In the face of these challenges, and in tandem with overseas funding bodies, Colombian state authorities have sought to create, in however limited a way, "legal and political systems [that are] more inclusive . . . and plural [or] participatory" (Van Cott 2000: 211). The 1991 Constitution, and the rights it awarded indigenous communities, are part of this broader state attempt to recoup state legitimacy and sovereignty in the face of armed conflict and narco-trafficking (Gow and Rappaport 2002; Jackson 2002).

Some Houses of Justice, as funded by USAID, are constructed in "consolidation areas," meaning land otherwise ceded in part by state agencies to armed groups (Cissé et al. 2014: 175). Many indigenous territories are also situated within these consolidated spaces as armed groups and gangs also occupy these territories. One USAID-funded program explicitly states its expectations in supplying funds on its website, noting that "in the Colombian consolidation regions . . . establishment of the rule of law contributes to building the legitimacy of the state" by "consolidat[ing] security and consolidat[ing a] state presence."[9] USAID, as do other international agencies, supports the Colombian state in its application of the rule of law and in a continuous project of asserting its sovereignty.[10] For these funding agencies, "without sovereignty, there [can be] no rule of law," even as this neglects the fact that sovereignty is sometimes a pretext to waive the rule of law (Koulish 2010: 24). Sovereignty both precedes and exceeds the rule of law (Agamben 1998).

This complexity relating to sovereignty may also explain why funding agencies have been at the forefront of underwriting coordination events, and indigenous justice projects, like the tribunal and law schools. Underwriting state legitimacy by strengthening the rule of law and legal pluralities appears to be a shared concern of the Colombian state and international funders.[11] These funding schemes often fall under the umbrella of "rule of law" programs of these agencies. Financial support, such as for indigenous law schools and tribunals, is than accompanied by the expectation of fostering decentralization, while at the same time seemingly bolstering the claim of the Colombian state to sovereignty. This double move sets the stage for international agencies like USAID, to the extent that, for them, legal pluralism would seem to underwrite or be subservient to the rule of law (Grenfell 2006: 305). Sovereignty, in the context of Colombia, then becomes conditioned on, and attenuated by, the project of establishing and maintaining a rule of law within an official plural legal landscape.

USAID has a broader and deeper mandate for its sponsorship of indigenous projects under the AJP (beyond sponsoring projects such as the indigenous tribunal in Tolima for the aim of fostering the rule of law): "[It will]
map those multicultural regions with notable indigenous populations ... and
facilitate inter-institutional dialogue to promote development of justice system policies to address indigenous justice considerations" (USAID 2011: 8).
The AJP proclaims that the significance of these projects "lies in the recognition of the need to enhance the training provided" to various government
and judicial authorities at different levels, as well as to indigenous authorities on various topics in order to steer "the process of mutual understanding, coordination and cooperation" between indigenous and state legal
systems (USAID 2012: 46). This funding stream also pays directly for meetings and events on coordination topics. Given that USAID's concern, according to their vision, is to map—or one may say "to render legible" (Scott
1998)—indigenous legal systems, this process of systematizing, producing,
and distributing materials (between international funders, state, and nonstate legal systems) acts as a dynamic of the events and meetings. At these
events and meetings, USAID recommendations and materials are distributed
to state judges and other state judicial officials but need to be approved by
state agencies before they are distributed in this manner. Through its power
to approve these USAID materials, the state negotiates control over some aspects of these engagements.

The vision, at least on USAID's part, is quite clear and clearly stated
because the supposition is that through this process of mapping indigenous
legal systems, USAID is furthering the incorporation of indigenous legal systems within a national rule of law: "Indigenous projects have likewise been
incorporated and have devoted substantial effort to *integrating and harmonizing indigenous justice with the majority justice system*" (USAID 2010: 39;
emphasis added). It is also palpable that in processes of coordination and efforts toward commensurability, the weight of cultural accommodation and
transformation rests with indigenous peoples. In other words, these apparently plural engagements once again uphold conditions of uneven power relations; indigenous peoples participate in legal pluralism on an asymmetrical
(and subordinate) basis.

State and nonstate practices, as fostered by international funding bodies
such as USAID, converge with the engagements of state and indigenous authorities in a series of processes that form the individual self-understanding
of many parties. All the same, the Colombian state liaises with international

agencies in ways highly mindful of its image and legitimacy in the eyes of the international community. This concern for image would sometimes seem premised on the legal fiction of a homogeneous sovereignty, built on an imagined nation, not on factual practices of sovereignty and the challenges it faces. Colombia seeks to assert state sovereignty in the context of an official plural legal landscape; as such, its processes of state sovereignty remain fragmentary, uncertain, performative, and ongoing. The power of the putatively sovereign state has been regularly and tangibly circumscribed through encounters with funding agencies who take on new powers of sovereignty in the name of the rule of law, therefore inserting themselves in the interstices of the indigenous and state relations (Bonilla 2017: 331; Dunn and Cons 2013: 92). International funding pouring into Colombia—at the likely invitation of the Colombian state—stresses the need for coordination between indigenous authorities and judicial state officials. This engenders an "often unstable footing of sovereign power" that effectively reconfigures the appearance and functioning of the state (such as in the education of judicial authorities, securing of funding, and so on) (Dunn and Cons 2013: 92). In theory, it is within the power of these international agencies to bear and bend sovereign power—and all power, by implication—to the dictates of legality and official requirements for a plural legal landscape (Stack 2010: 351). Funding agencies, it is clear, have a hand in the neoliberalization and decentralization of Colombian sovereignty. It is also clear that sovereignty here cannot be imagined other than through its uneven, unexpected, and fragmented relations and terrains. Against the backdrop of an officially pluralized legal setting, an array of relational, even fictively sovereign, bodies contest and interact with each other. Sovereignty depends and is contingent on a plethora of practices, rather than on a single practice or single rule, like the state itself (Chalfin 2010: 42).

Multiple Horizons

Let us now return to the opening vignette, as banal as the situation initially seemed. We were on the upper floor of a state judicial building in Bogotá sipping coffee, discussing a coordination event that would never take place in the relational form in which it was imagined in that civil moment. As events unfolded, state office holders would not participate. This vignette glosses over some of the messiness of legal and social realities. The state's assertion of authority in this seemingly banal moment conceals both insecurities and interests—such as the vested interest in getting access to international funding. The school also felt it was incumbent for its authority to perform the ceremony of sending its written letter. The inscribed authority of the letter took place *after* the meeting, as if the performativity of the NGO's request in the meeting would somehow create the conditions of possibility for the state's officers to participate by attending the meeting. The contradiction between the informality of the discussion over coffee and the authority of the letter forbidding state employees to attend highlights the international NGO's failure to understand that it was required to channel every proposal for dialogue—on the subject of coordination!—through the state. The meeting and the letter became platforms for the state to sustain a level of relational sovereignty vis-à-vis the NGOs. In a nutshell, the opening vignette displays sovereignty as relational, even as it displays the uncertainties of sovereignty in coordinating state and nonstate actors. Augmenting the uncertainties of the event, one prosecutor defied the order by attending in a personal capacity— itself a challenge to entrenched distinctions between state nonstate identities. As with similar meetings and encounters, different interests and agendas— from those of state representatives and agencies to international funding agencies and indigenous leaders—all form part of a multiscalar legal landscape. Despite competing politico-legal interests, or indeed *through* them, new forms of relations are emerging and being brokered in a dialectical process. These relations come into being, for instance, when a judge receives fewer tutelas from indigenous community members, when indigenous authorities send community members to state prisons, and when state officials revise US-AID recommendations on indigenous-state relations in the guidance they send out to state judicial authorities. For the most part, it seems the state is concerned to accommodate itself strategically to international funding agencies while periodically asserting its own control whenever possible.

Colombia's Constitution, as with any constitution, is emblematic in inaugurating state sovereignty while also scripting its absence, thus setting the stage for the legislative inertia with regard to formulating a coordination law. Without this law, for better or worse, many forms of uncertainty radiate outward from Article 246 of the 1991 Constitution. Uncertainty has led to alternative scripts and sponsored new initiatives (i.e., indigenous law schools and tribunals). Uncertainty, further, marks the very sites or settings for the possibility of new and alternative potential for change itself in the relationship between indigenous communities and the state and within communities themselves. For some state agencies, however, the uncertain spaces created by the Constitution call not only for management but also for active preservation. One immediately compelling way to grasp uncertainty as a concept is when the state dispels possible "threats" to its sovereignty by outsourcing, diffusing, and multiplying its forms of authority and by recognizing a plural legal landscape only on its own terms. It also bears emphasizing that, in these endeavors, the state often acts under the sponsorship of international funding agencies.

At the same time, these uncertainties are less an interruption and more an extension of the checkered history of interactions between indigenous and nonindigenous peoples in Colombia. These narratives and figurations are unfinished. However, marked with ambiguities, many possibilities remain open along multiple new horizons.

Notes

1. The context for this chapter involves a larger project on the Tribunal Superior Indígena del Tolima (Superior Indigenous Tribunal of Tolima). A forthcoming book will go into deeper detail. The tribunal was founded by the Consejo Regional Indígena del Tolima (CRIT; Regional Indigenous Council of Tolima). This chapter draws on extensive ethnographic fieldwork conducted on indigenous legal systems in Colombia. Over the course of my fieldwork, I attended numerous regional and national events and participated in projects dealing with coordination such as the Escuela de Derecho Propio Cristóbal Secué (Cristóbal Secué School of Own Laws), founded by both the Asociación de Cabildos Indígenas del Norte del Cauca (ACIN; Association of Indigenous Cabildos of Northern Cauca) and the Superior Indigenous Tribunal of Tolima.

2. The late 1990s was a critical historical juncture in Latin America that saw the emergence of a new paradigm, commonly referred to as postneoliberal, or the "turn to the left." Sarah Hunt (2016: 443) points out that the rollback of neoliberal decentralization happened in some countries, such as Venezuela, Bolivia, and Ecuador, but not in others, such as Colombia.

3. The coexistence of multiculturalism and neoliberalism has been strongly debated among scholars, who take a range of positions about multiculturalism being subsumed by the neoliberal modernity project. At one end is the position that multiculturalism colludes with neoliberal market reforms, conceding a few rights but impeding more radical or structural changes (Lucero 2013: 24). At the other end is the position that sees potential for flourishing development and argues that cultural rights are opened up through processes of multiculturalism and neoliberalism.

4. The enduring lacuna of any coordination mechanism is contrary to what exists in many other Latin American countries, many of which also recognized indigenous legal systems during the constitutional wave of the 1990s. Many countries have written and implemented laws to specify modes of the interrelationship between indigenous and state legal systems. The degree of legal uncertainty is so striking in Colombia because it is not a familiar feature of many other Latin American countries.

5. These institutions are scattered across Colombia, founded by local indigenous organizations and sponsored by international funding bodies. One such tribunal was founded in 2002 by the indigenous organization CRIT, which represents 117 Pijaos communities in Tolima.

6. Faye Ginsburg and Fred Myers (2006: 108), for instance, suggest that "while the recognition of indigenous representations has served the interests of the state in some ways, they make the state's efforts at cultural and political containment anxious and unstable." Could underwriting "zones of ambiguity" be an approach that the state pursues in the expectation of "higher returns" (Comaroff and Comaroff 2006)? Or perhaps anxieties—which might be the negative of "false optimism" (Povinelli 2002) as this pertains to relations between the indigenous and nonindigenous—might refer here to the matter of whose jurisdiction should be "master." ("False optimism" is a hope premised on the legal fiction of a homogeneous sovereignty. It is hope built on the imagined nation, not on the actual practices and contestations of sovereignty.) Or, rather than anxieties, could there be mutual suspicion as legal orders are reimagined?

7. Comaroff and Comaroff (2006) are making sense of the disorder and violence in the postcolonial word in that they examine the dialectical interplay between neoliberal ways of deregulation (or neoliberal politics that are connected to the outsourcing of coercive social and economic state functions) and forms of criminal violence. In their words, they look at a "troubled dialectic: a dialectic of law and dis/order, framed by neoliberal mechanisms of deregulation and new modes of mediating human transactions at once politico-economic and cultural, moral, and mortal" (5).

8. USAID has funded Casas de Justicia in other Latin American countries, including Bolivia, Honduras, and Argentina (OECD 2011: 29).

9. Checchi Consulting has executed programs for the Access to Justice Activity, another program strand of USAID. See https://checchiconsulting.com/projects/colombia-access-to-justice-activity (accessed 8 February 2018).

10. The image of a sovereign state—or, better, of a modern sovereign state—is central to the imagery and modes of justification of the "rule of law." Sovereign states are distinguished by their even, or theoretically even, application of the rule of law (Agrama 2012: 109). Sovereignty thus represents a project of modernization, one of whose pillars is the rule of law or extension of the state's sovereign power (109). Another way to see this is as the rule of law constituting a mark of a nation's modernity—and something required by international funding agencies in those terms.

11. See Checchi Consulting, "Promoting More Just and Democratic Societies," http://www.checchiconsulting.com/index.php?option=com_projects&country_id=2&Itemid=8 (accessed 8 February 2018).

References

Agamben, Giorgio. 1998. *Homo Sacer: Sovereign Power and Bare Life*. Trans. Daniel Heller-Roazen. Stanford, CA: Stanford University Press.

Agrama, Hussein Ali. 2012. *Questioning Secularism: Islam, Sovereignty, and the Rule of Law in Modern Egypt*. Chicago: University of Chicago Press.

Bossuyt, Jean. 2013. "Overview of the Decentralisation Process in Latin America: Main Achievements, Trends and Future Challenges." Discussion Paper No. 148. July. European Centre for Development Policy Management. Accessed 7 July 2018. https://ecdpm.org/wp -content/uploads/2013/10/DP-148-Overview-Decentralisation-Process-Latin-America -2013.pdf.

Brunnegger, Sandra. n.d. *States of Uncertainty: An Indigenous Tribunal in Colombia*. Unpublished manuscript.

Buchanan, Ruth, and Sundhya Pahuja. 2004. "Law, Nation and (Imagined) International Communities." *Law Text Culture* 8:137–166.

Cepeda-Espinosa, Manuel José. 2004. "Judicial Activism in a Violent Context: The Origin, Role, and Impact of the Colombian Constitutional Court." *Washington University Global Studies Law Review* 3 (2004): 529–700.

Chalfin, Brenda. 2010. *Neoliberal Frontiers: An Ethnography of Sovereignty in West Africa*. Chicago: University of Chicago Press.

Cissé, Hassane, et al., eds. 2014. *The World Bank Legal Review*. Vol. 5, *Fostering Development through Opportunity, Inclusion, and Equity*. Washington, DC: The World Bank. Accessed 8 February 2018. https://openknowledge.worldbank.org/bitstream/handle/10986/16240 /82558.pdf?sequence=1&isAllowed=y.

Comaroff, John L., and Jean Comaroff. 2006. "Law and Disorder in the Postcolony: An Introduction." In *Law and Disorder in the Postcolony*, eds. Jean Comaroff and John L. Comaroff, 1–56. Chicago: University of Chicago Press.

Das, Veena, and Deborah Poole, eds. 2004. *Anthropology in the Margins of the State*. Santa Fe, NM: School of American Research Press.

Dunn, Elizabeth Cullen, and Jason Cons. 2014. "Aleatory Sovereignty and the Rule of Sensitive Spaces." *Antipode* 46 (1): 92–109.

Escobar, Arturo. 2010. "Latin America at a Crossroads." *Cultural Studies* 24 (1): 1–65.

Fisher, Edward F., ed. 2008. *Indigenous Peoples, Civil Society, and the Neo-liberal State in Latin America*. New York: Berghan Books.

Ginsburg, Faye, and Fred Myers. 2006. "A History of Indigenous Futures: Accounting for Indigenous Art and Media." *Aboriginal History* 30: 95–110.

Goodale, Mark, and Nancy Postero, eds. 2013. *Neoliberalism Interrupted: Social Change and Contested Governance in Contemporary Latin America*. Stanford, CA: Stanford University Press.

Gow, David, and Rappaport, Joanne. 2002. "The Indigenous Public Voice: The Multiple Idioms of Modernity in Indigenous Cauca." In *Indigenous Movements, Self-Representation and the State in Latin America*, eds. Kay B. Warren and Jean E. Jackson, 47–80. Austin: University of Texas Press.

Grenfell, Laura. 2006. "Legal Pluralism and the Rule of Law in Timor Leste." *Leiden Journal of International Law* 19 (2): 305–337.

Gustafson, Bret. 2009. *New Languages of the State: Indigenous Resurgence and the Politics of Knowledge in Bolivia*. Durham: Duke University Press.

Hale, Charles R. 2002. "Does Multiculturalism Menace? Governance, Cultural Rights and the Politics of Identity in Guatemala." *Journal of Latin American Studies* 34 (3): 485–524.

Hansen, Thomas Blom, and Finn Stepputat. 2006. "Sovereignty Revisited." *Annual Review of Anthropology* 35: 295–315.

Hunt, Sarah. 2016. "Rethinking the Politics of the Shift Left in Latin America: Towards a Relational Approach." *Bulletin of Latin American Research* 35 (4): 437–445.

Jackson, Jean E. 2002. "Caught in the Cross Fire: Colombia's Indigenous Peoples During the 1990s." In *Identities in Conflict: Indigenous Peoples and Latin American States*, ed. David Maybury-Lewis, 107–134. Cambridge, MA: Harvard University Press.

Jordan, Robert. 2016. "Neoliberalism and Free Trade in Latin America." In *Oxford Research Encyclopedia of Latin American History*. Accessed 27 July 2018. https://oxfordre.com /latinamericanhistory/view/10.1093/acrefore/9780199366439.001.0001/acrefore -9780199366439-e-227.

Koulish, Robert. 2010. *Immigration and American Democracy: Subverting the Rule of Law*. New York: Routledge.

Lucero, Jose Antonio. 2013. "Ambivalent Multiculturalism: Perversity, Futility, and Jeopardy in Latin America." In *Latin America's Multicultural Movements: The Struggle Between Communitarism, Autonomy, and Human Rights*, eds. Todd Eisenstadt, Michael S. Danielson, Moises Jaime Bailon Corres, and Carlos Sorroza Polo, 18–39. Oxford: Oxford University Press.

Mall, Ram Adhar. 2000. *Intercultural Philosophy*. Lanham, MD: Rowman & Littlefield.

Marcella, Gabriel. 2009. "Democratic Governance and the Rule of Law: Lessons from Colombia." PKSOI Papers Series. Carlisle, PA: Strategic Studies Institute.

McCreary, Tyler. 2014. "The Burden of Sovereignty: Court Configurations of Indigenous and State Authority in Aboriginal Title Litigation in Canada." *North American Dialogue* 17 (2): 64–78.

Merry, Sally E. 1992. "Anthropology, Law, and Transnational Processes." *Annual Review of Anthropology* 21 (1): 357–377.

Moser, Caroline, and Cathy McIlwaine. 2000. *Urban Poor Perceptions of Violence and Exclusion in Colombia: Conflict Prevention and Post-Conflict Reconstruction*. Washington, DC: World Bank.

Moser, Caroline, and Cathy McIlwaine. 2004. *Encounters with Violence in Latin America*. London: Routledge.

OECD. 2011. *Preventing and Reducing Armed Violence in Urban Areas: Programming Note, Conflict and Fragility*. Paris: OECD Publishing. Accessed 15 April 2018. https://www.oecd .org/dac/conflict-fragility-resilience/docs/47942084.pdf.

Povinelli, Elizabeth A. 1998. "The State of Shame: Australian Multiculturalism and the Crisis of Indigenous Citizenship." *Critical Inquiry* 24 (2): 575–610.

Povinelli, Elizabeth A. 2002. *The Cunning of Recognition: Indigenous Alterities and the Making of Australian Multiculturalism*. Durham, NC: Duke University Press.

Rojas, Fernando. 2002. "The Demand for Governance and Quality of Government." In *Colombia—The Economic Foundation of Peace (English)*, eds. Marcelo M. Giugale, Olivier Lafourcade, and Connie Luff, 131–142. Washington, DC: The World Bank. Accessed 15 May 2018. http://documents.worldbank.org/curated/en/118891468746361610/Colombia -the-economic-foundation-of-peace.

Scott, James C. 1998. *Seeing Like a State: How Certain Schemes to Improve the Human Condition Have Failed*. New Haven, CT: Yale University Press.

Sharma, Aradhana, and Akhil Gupta, eds. 2006. *The Anthropology of the State: A Reader*. Oxford: Blackwell.

Stack, Trevor. 2010. "A Just Rule of Law." *Social Anthropology* 18 (3): 346–355.

Thelen, Tatjana, Larissa Vetters, and Keebet von Benda-Beckmann. 2014. "Stategraphy: Toward a Relational Anthropology of the State." *Social Analysis* 58 (3): 1–19.

USAID. 2010. *Assessment of USAID/Colombia's Justice Reform and Modernization Program*. Accessed 8 February 2018. http://pdf.usaid.gov/pdf_docs/pdacr349.pdf.

USAID. 2011. *Access to Justice Program*. Third Quarterly Report. Accessed 8 February 2018. http://pdf.usaid.gov/pdf_docs/pdacw447.pdf.

USAID. 2012. *Access to Justice Program*. Seventh Quarterly Report. Accessed 8 February 2018. http://pdf.usaid.gov/pdf_docs/PA00HN5S.pdf.

Van Cott, D. L. 2000. "A Political Analysis of Legal Pluralism in Bolivia and Colombia." *Journal of Latin American Studies* 32 (1): 207–234.

Žižek, Slavoj 1994. "Introduction: The Spectre of Ideology." In *Mapping Ideology*, ed. Slavoj Žižek, 1–33. London: Verso.

CHAPTER 8

Between Sovereignty and Transnationalism

The European Union as an Incomplete
"Transnational Legal Space"

Marie-Claire Foblets and Katayoun Alidadi

The European Union (EU) serves as an oft-quoted illustration of a large-scale experiment in transnationalization at a regional level, of a space that has steadily grown to encompass twenty-eight (but soon twenty-seven, once Brexit is realized) sovereign countries as Member States. Indeed, from a regional economic organization of six Western European countries (the "Inner Six"), it has—through growth, accession, and migration—come to be a major economic and sociopolitical entity that directly affects more than 508 million inhabitants. This chapter explores the EU as a unique institution that is both shaped by law and shapes law, which in turn affects the Member States and other regions of the world in far-reaching ways, as it grounds its competences on subsequent transfers of institutional sovereignty.

This chapter is intended to demonstrate, by means of a number of examples drawn for the most part from case law (thus, in a sense, case studies), how difficult it is to implement the idea of a truly transnational space and how vulnerable the process of sovereignty transfer in such a context remains (Stavrou 2016).

In historical terms, the first objective in creating a European Union in the 1950s was to establish a peaceful space for the free movement of goods and services, including providers and/or users of those services. To achieve this required a complex system of transfer of powers—executive, legislative, and judicial—from the national level to a higher, transnational one (referred to as the "community" level in the case of the European Union).[1]

Today, some sixty years after its creation, can we speak of a successful transnationalization? Though we cannot fail to take into account the astonishing degree of growth of the EU—both in terms of geography and in terms of competences—the answer is far from decided, with recent developments such as the Brexit vote bearing witness to the EU's fragile political capital, and depends to a large extent on what one takes as the evaluation criteria.

Transnationalization (or Europeanization): An Incomplete, Open-Ended Process

The inquiry we propose here starts from the preliminary observation that transnationalization—at the European Community level—remains a process to be completed. Robert Schuman had foreseen, in 1950, that "Europe will not be made all at once. Or according to a single plan. It will be built through concrete achievements" (Juncker 2017b: 4). What's more, it is hardly a congruous, ever-progressing process but one that succumbs to some ups and many downs, currently shaped by waves of nationalism, which in recent years in many Member States has brought to power right-wing-to-center parties and popularized their ideas. It is to be expected that incompleteness will remain the prime characteristic of transnationalization in Europe for some time to come (thus it can be called an "incomplete transnational (legal) space").

While the transnationalization movement has historically been toward "more Europe," a recent white paper by European Commission president Jean-Claude Juncker broke some ground by including, at least under his "ways forward," the transfer of some sovereignty *back* to the Member States (Juncker 2017b: 4).[2] Up to some years ago, such a position would have been unthinkable; it would have been interpreted as a countermovement, opposed to the initial goal of gradual transnationalization. Some commentators have argued, "What makes this moment different from earlier existential crises is that the direction of integration is more diffuse now than in the past" (Techau 2016). However, in his 2017 State of the Union address, President Juncker left no doubt as to the road the European Commission proposes to take: one that involves "more Europe" in many different directions (economic and monetary union, trade, military, and counterterrorism, to name a few) and not "less Europe" or a "multispeed Europe" (Juncker 2017a: 24).[3]

It is not surprising that the European Commission favors the scenario of the "ever closer union." This scenario is referred to as the "Verhofstadt-scenario" in European quarters, after the former Belgian prime minister and Member of the European Parliament (MEP) Guy Verhofstadt. If, as stated by Juncker, "Member States decide to share more power, resources and decision-making across the board" (ibid.), this would imply a further transfer of sovereignty from the Member States to Europe. Without such further transnationalization, the way to a federal union, complete with a European arm, is unlikely.

In practice, however, the transfer ("pooling" as the European Commission would have it) of sovereignty has been accompanied by tensions and difficulties that have increased over the years and continue to grow in complexity, not only with the accession of new Member States (their number has more than quadrupled since the establishment of the European Economic Community (EEC) in 1957, and the 2004 accession round brought in no less than ten new Member States at the same time) but also with the competition among nation-states and European Community institutions regarding their respective powers (FT View 2016).[4]

In addition, the question remains as to the incentives that are necessary to bring sovereign nations (the Member States) to transfer, in the context of globalization and a crisis of trust, part of the (exercise of) sovereignty to a pan-national institution such as the European Union. In the context of a shortage of political legitimation, it is an audacious and potentially harmful avenue to pursue.

Yet, in Juncker's white paper as well as in much of the European Commission's discourse, the incompleteness of the transnationalization project is presented as the very cause of the divergence of people's expectations and the possibility of delivery under EU law and policy. Under such a perspective, the solution is seen by some—and not the least the Commission itself—to be the further transfer (or "pooling"[5]) of sovereignty.[6]

To be sure, the prospects for "more Europe" have changed considerably compared to a short time ago. In Juncker's words, "We started to fix the roof. But we must complete the job now that the sun is shining and whilst it still is" (Juncker 2017a: 10). For instance, the election of pro-EU presidential candidate Emmanuel Macron in France (and the defeat of Marine Le Pen) in the 7 May 2017 French presidential election and the continued—German and

European—leadership of Angela Merkel have stabilized the political situation somewhat in Europe. In the Netherlands too, populists have, for now, failed to take over. No doubt, the election of Marine Le Pen to the French presidency would have spelled a particularly acute disaster for the European project (BBC 2017). Therefore, the popular support for Le Pen—who gained an estimated 11 million votes in the presidential election—should remain a vivid reminder of the resonance and acceptance of populist, anti-EU, and xenophobic political discourses.[7]

The European Transnational Space: Dynamics of an Incomplete Project Lead to Mismatched Expectations

In order to show the challenges that the European transnational space has brought about, we focus on four particular examples that illustrate amply the difficulties of creating and upholding coherent rules or practices without feasible solutions. While we could not possibly provide an exhaustive discussion of the chosen topics, the deliberately broad and "dispersed approach" we adopt aims to show that the ramifications of the incompleteness of the European transnationalization project play out in a wide variety of spheres, from migration to the internal market, and from family law to fundamental rights in the European Union.

First, we look at asylum law and "free" movement rights within the EU for so-called Third Country Nationals (TCNs), more particularly those with Long Term Resident (LTR) status. Both issues, but in particular asylum law, have in recent years become some of the most contested in EU law, resulting in seemingly irresolvable tensions between, on the one hand, immigration control (the external dimension of EU migration policy), and, on the other, human rights, as well as between national and EU competences. Particularly when it comes to the external dimension of EU migration policy, Member States so far have been unable to agree on basic principles or to maintain old understandings of solidarity and mutual trust. Instead, important differences between national asylum systems remain. The failure of the EU's external policies on asylum and immigration has been and remains a tangible testimony to the incompleteness and ineffectiveness of European responses to humanitarian crises.

The second example is the problem of internal transborder migration of long-term EU residents who do not (yet) hold the nationality of one of the

Member States (TCNs). Currently, EU law clearly distinguishes between the free movement of EU citizens and their close relatives and the (subordinate) free movement regime for TCNs. Yet, as we try to explain, the limits put on the free movement rights of TCNs unequivocally conflict with the EU's rejection of the existence of such internal borders. Here again, what is at play is the strong reluctance on the part of the Member States to give up sovereignty when it comes to setting standards for immigration from outside the EU into their countries.

Third, the same free movement rules have created certain painful consequences under private international law for citizens or residents with particular family connections. "Limping family-law relationships" occur where, for instance, a marriage is recognized in one Member State but would be considered against public policy and not recognized in another Member State.[8] Domestic and European case law bears out that this is a reality for a steadily increasing number of both EU citizens and TCNs, and that this results from divergence between national legislations on personal status. The disparate treatment of same-sex unions across the EU is just one of the underlying reasons for limping relationships.[9] Thus, for some Europeans, the EU falls short of expectations not only as it struggles with financial, economic, and social crises, but also on an everyday basis, within the realm of private (family) life. The difficulties surrounding the transnational nonrecognition of same-sex marriages in the EU has both legal and social significance and shows the inherent limitations that come from using economic legitimation and single-market-motivated harmonization of family law in Europe in a context where not just legal norms but social values within the Member States collide so clearly (Bradley 2003: 69).[10]

Finally, we address a topic that pungently shows the limits of transnationalization in Europe. This final illustration regards the unwillingness of supranational *courts* to give up (or transfer) sovereignty to other international/ supranational mechanisms. While the accession of the European Union to the European Convention on Human Rights (constituting an overlapping transnational order complete with an effective judicial decision-making mechanism in the European Court of Human Rights [ECtHR] in Strasbourg) was foreseen under Article 6.2 of the Lisbon Treaty (signed 2007, entered into effect 2009), the Court of Justice of the European Union (CJEU; Europe's highest court) has opposed the accession and places considerable barriers in the way of a smooth accession of the EU to the European Convention (see CJEU 2014). This clearly has important human rights ramifications, but in the context of this chapter it serves to show the highly protective stance of European institutions in regard to what they may consider their acquired competences, which in turn sheds light on the (limited) prospects for a Europe "doing less" scenario.

The EU's External Policies on Asylum and Immigration: An Enduring Imbalance Between Member State Autonomy and EU Convergence

"The Syrian refugees form the first stress test for the European Asylum system" (den Heijer, Rijpma, and Spijkerboer 2016) is an observation often heard these past years and that can hardly be contested since it puts a finger on what since 2015 can be referred to as the refugee "crisis," not the least given the dramatic absence of a Europe-wide response.

In 2015, more than one million people fled Afghanistan, Syria, and other Middle Eastern and African countries torn by war and arrived in the territories of Member States of the European Union. This migration presented, unexpectedly, enormous political, legal, and social challenges for Europe and its individual Member States (Spijkerboer 2013).

The arrival of migrants from "third countries"—the technical term for non-European States—was of course not unprecedented; immigration from outside the EU has grown steadily since the 1980s, with fluxes ever more frequently made up principally of refugees seeking admission on humanitarian grounds. What differentiates the 2015 crisis was its sheer magnitude. The need to provide the growing numbers of asylum seekers and new immigrants with basic services has been cause for consternation among political decision makers. The events of the 2015 refugee crisis have provided striking evidence that certain EU Member States, especially those on the external boundary of the EU, such as Greece and Hungary, do not hesitate to ignore what EU law expects them to do with regard to immigration control (the external dimension of EU migration policy), with these countries maintaining that these expectations are simply not realistic (Spijkerboer 2013; see also Rankin 2016).

What went wrong, and what are the inherent weaknesses of the Common European Asylum System? To respond more effectively to the massive influx of newcomers fleeing their countries and arriving in Europe, as from the early 1990s, EU Member States agreed to transfer to the European institutions several areas of competence that had hitherto been exercised at the national level. This notably included control of external borders, protection of candidates for refugee status, and return policies (Eisele 2014; Guild and Minderhoud 2016). This transfer of competence has been carried out gradually since the Maastricht Treaty of 1993, giving rise to the adoption of EU legislative instruments—in particular a series of directives—with a twofold purpose: to ensure that the principle of free movement of persons within the European Union is upheld, while at the same time exercising greater control over migratory flows, especially of persons who can lay no claim to that right, namely non-EU nationals and persons without the necessary residency permits allowing free movement (Groenendijk 2012a; Zaun 2017: 64). The experience of more than twenty years of migration policy (since 1993) shows, however, that the adoption of legislative instruments in itself is not sufficient: The mutual confidence among Member States that is necessary to implement this twofold European mandate successfully on the ground is still lacking.[11]

The reality on the ground provides a dramatic illustration of the fact that European migration policy did not properly prepare to handle extreme situations causing massive migration into Europe such as was the case in 2015. This migration has caused numerous legal and political problems, which are highly complex and at the same time extremely urgent. For example, there is an (unstable) March 2016 arrangement with Turkey (some have referred to this as "a deal with the devil" [Mohdin 2015]) to cut refugee flows.[12] Turkey threatened to scuttle the deal entirely if the EU did not grant visa-free access to its citizens by October 2016 (Rankin 2016b), but as of September 2017 this issue was still not resolved. In the meanwhile, smugglers are still getting through, and the Greek islands are dangerously overcrowded, though after the EU-Turkey deal the migration flows did slow down. Italy is overwhelmed with the influx of boat refugees from Libya and Niger and put a planned reform of its nationality laws on hold to see what the EU will do (Wesel 2017). The next major challenge ahead is a decision by the CJEU as to whether or not Turkey qualifies as a safe third country (Larkin 2017).

The paradox, however, is that some Member States prefer the situation to stay as it is—be it with disastrous consequences, not the least for the asylum seekers—rather than engage in a fundamental reconsideration of the common European asylum system (Kessler 2016). They fear that this would mean ever less autonomy at the national level and increasing integration at the EU level.

At the risk of simplifying the root causes of a complex issue, one could identify at least three basic weaknesses in the European asylum system: first, there is the Dublin system that distributes the responsibility for asylum seekers among EU Member States, but does so unevenly (Römer 2015) so that the burden falls on the shoulders of the countries that are entrusted with external border control. Countries like Italy and Greece, and more recently also Hungary, have to take responsibility for the vast majority of asylum seekers. Unless asylum seekers arrive on airplanes in other European countries, they can only reach the European continent via certain national (and at the same time external EU) borders. As a result of the fact that northern—and more recently also eastern—Member States are unwilling to share the burden, the system turns out to be very unfair, with blatant human rights violations in the way asylum seekers are being treated in southern Member States.[13] Southern Member States are profoundly unhappy with the situation, and feel overburdened.

Second, both the EU and the individual Member States consider it unproblematic that asylum can only be granted to people who succeed in entering Europe, and yet the official migration policy at the EU level as well as at the national levels is to scrupulously select who comes in. Various procedures are in place to discourage the many others who may be tempted, for instance, visa requirements, airlines and shipping companies checking identity documents before embarkation, transit countries being pressured to introduce visa requirements, and so on (Maes, Foblets, and De Bruycker 2011).

Third, even if there is European legislation to coordinate asylum laws, in practice, the chances of being recognized as a refugee can be substantially higher in one Member State compared to another.[14] Not only does that prove to be deeply unfair to asylum seekers, but it also encourages secondary movements: Migrants refuse to apply for asylum or comply with identification obligations in the Member State they first arrive in as required by the Dublin system in order to move on to another Member State where they expect to have a better chance of being accepted.

It is no secret that "these secondary movements have resulted in many applications being made in Member States which are not those of the first point of entry, a situation which has in turn led several Member States to reintroduce internal border controls to manage the influx" (European Commission 2016: 4). The factual situation today shows that, on the one hand, an increasing number of Member States are no longer prepared to abide by their international obligations and, on the other, many asylum seekers feel justified to disregard the Dublin system and do not hesitate to travel onward after they have entered the territory of the EU, instead of abiding by the expectation that they apply for asylum in the first European country of arrival. In sum, both the Member States and the asylum seekers are destabilizing, not to say ruining, the system. These serious shortcomings in the implementation of European asylum and migration policy, which the crisis since 2015 clearly exposed, need, of course, to be addressed.

The EU, however, depends on its Member States for sustainable migration management (see De Baere 2011). The EU migration and asylum system is grounded on the principles of mutual trust and solidarity among the Member States, and it is defenseless in the face of obstruction on the part of Member States, since the EU has no executive powers. At present, the system provides for cooperation, not for complete Europeanization; it is based on minimum harmonization and on sharing responsibility for examining asylum applications across the EU, including mutual recognition of individual decisions (that is, also of rejections of requests and transfer of applicants) (Römer 2015). Such a form of cooperation can only work if Member States are prepared to work together. The experience of recent years has shown a clear absence of political will on part of an ever-greater number of Member States to join forces in the spirit of a common vision.

A clear illustration of the absence of such willingness has been the action brought by Slovakia and Hungary before the CJEU against a provisional mechanism for the mandatory relocation of asylum seekers. In response to the refugee crisis and in order to help in particular Greece and Italy deal with the massive inflow of asylum seekers, the Council of the European Union adopted in September 2015 a decision that provides for the relocation of 120,000 persons in clear need of international protection from those two Members States to other EU Member States, over a period of two years.[15] In the proceedings before the court, Slovakia and Hungary (Poland intervened in support of the action) put forward inter alia that the Council Decision was neither a suitable response to the refugee crisis nor necessary for that purpose. In a much-anticipated ruling of 6 September 2017, the CJEU dismissed in their entirety the actions brought by the Slovakia and Hungary and found the redistribution measure to be necessary to respond to an emergency situation created by a sudden influx of asylum seekers (CJEU 2017, C-643/15, and C-647/15).[16]

What is the way forward? It is easy to say that the EU needs a more effective asylum system for the future that is both fair for European societies and their citizens as well as for TCNs and countries of origin and transit. But for this to work not only in the short run but also in the long term, there are not so many options. To address the shortcomings, the EU would need to receive a new mandate from the Member States, that is, to transfer relevant competencies from the national level to the EU level (the "doing much more together" referenced in Juncker's white paper) with a view to enable it to fundamentally reconsider its asylum policy with, among others, a single common asylum procedure, including a more harmonized assessment of the applications, as well as a strengthened operational role for the EU. In the current political climate, the Member States have no political will to follow such path, apart from perhaps countries like Germany that have attracted large numbers of asylum seekers and therefore see the point of changing the rules.

The Subordinate Free Movement Regime
for Third Country Nationals

Despite the problems with current European asylum policies, one can imagine that in the months and years to come—once the situation has more or less stabilized—hundreds of thousands of people of non-European origin will be able to make a new start within Europe. Their presence will effect significant changes in the demographic, social, and cultural profiles of their host countries. This prospect gives fresh relevance to the issue of newcomer integration (Barwig, Beichel-Benedetti, and Brinkmann 2016). What type of integration policy ought to be pursued (Groenendijk 2012b)? Any such policy, if it is to be sustainable, will have to facilitate a process of adaptation that necessarily requires the willingness of newcomers to become part of the social fabric as well as the support of the host (majority) society.

As noted, EU law distinguishes between the free movement of EU-citizens and the (subordinate) free movement regime for so-called TCNs, long-term residents of the EU who do not hold the nationality of one of the Member States. Among the legislative instruments developed at the EU level, one in particular addresses the situation of TCNs, namely Council Directive 2003/109/EC of 25 November 2003 concerning the status of TCNs who are long-term residents (LTRs).[17] Alluding to this chapter's title, we argue that this directive serves as a second illustration of the incompleteness of the European transnational legal space.

At the Tampere European Council (15 and 16 October 1999), the EU Member States emphasized the need to give equitable treatment to non-EU country nationals (TCNs) legally residing in the EU (Halleskov-Storgaard

2012). (The members of the European Council are the heads of state or government of the twenty-eight EU Member States, together with its president and the President of the European Commission.) In particular, it was argued that all non-EU country nationals who have been resident in a Member State for a given period of time should be granted a set of uniform rights that are as near as possible to those enjoyed by EU citizens (point 21 of the Tampere conclusions). With this aim, the 2003 Council Directive was designed to give full effect to Article 63(4) of the Treaty Establishing the European Community (EC Treaty, 10 November, 1997): *First*, it ensures that legally resident citizens of non-EU countries (TCNs) can obtain long-term resident (LTR) status in a Member State after five years of legal residence in that Member State. This status confers a right to equal treatment in that Member State, subject to some exceptions, and a degree of protection against expulsion. *Second*, it allows non-EU country nationals with LTR status to move to another Member State, but here again subject to some limitations. The directive was adopted in 2003. Member States had to apply it by January 2006.

After ten years of implementation, one cannot conclude that Council Directive 2003/109/EC has proven a clear success. In reality it has been a mixed bag of a few successes and, probably even more so, missed opportunities. On the side of the successes, one can see the directive as a positive step in resolving some of the problems related to integration of newcomers coming from outside the EU.

The peculiarity of the directive is that it gives a special status to legal residents who have resided on the territory of Member States longer than five years, which differentiates them from persons who have resided within the territory of the EU for a shorter period. Moreover, the scope of rights that come with the status of LTR is significantly wider than that of persons with temporary stays or even persons who obtain residence permits under the national legislation of Member States. This is because the directive brings LTRs within the scope of EU law, thus allowing them to move freely between Member States and giving them also the right to invoke its general principles— not the least the right to equal treatment in relation to EU citizens in many areas (Halleskov-Storgaard 2012; see also Morano-Foadi and Malena 2012; Sánchez 2009)—and to rely on the CJEU for their interpretation.

On the side of missed opportunities, the directive does not apply to the UK, Ireland, and Denmark. Moreover, as already mentioned above, the right to equal treatment in relation to EU citizens comes with some significant national derogations, restrictions, and exceptions that severely interfere with the initial goal of the directive. The directive does not prohibit Member States from restricting equal treatment with respect to employment and education (e.g., by requiring proof of appropriate language proficiency) when transposing the status into their domestic legal order. In the field of social assistance and protection, Member States may restrict equal treatment to core benefits.[18] TCNs with LTR status and their families enjoy the rights of free movement to other Member States, although the Family Reunification Directive 2003/86/ EC limits the access of family members of LTRs. It stipulates that an LTR "with reasonable prospects of obtaining the right of permanent residence" will enjoy the right to family reunification. Therefore, only if the LTR can prove that he or she has the prospect of obtaining permanent residence can he or she apply for family reunification.[19] There are other limitations on the free movement rights of LTRs, for instance, with regard to the right to reside in another Member State; residency must be connected to the exercise of some economic activity as an employed or self-employed person or to the pursuit of an education.

Directives set minimum standards and do not prevent Member States from issuing permanent residence permits on terms that are more favorable,[20] but in practice, generally speaking, Member States tend to refrain from adopting more generous provisions. Indeed, whereas at the EU level the LTR Directive was originally adopted with a view to open the possibility for Member States to ensure near equality of TCNs and EU-citizens regarding employment and residence rights throughout the EU (Halleskov-Storgaard 2012), in reality it is anything but easy to become a LTR of the EU.

Member States make use of the possibilities—provided for in the directive—to put severe limitations on the acquisition of that status as well as to the rights that come with it (Guild, Groenendijk, Carrera 2016). Many countries, for example, require TCNs to comply with integration conditions before becoming LTRs, and thus tests are applied. These tests are usually reserved for granting an individual citizenship of a state, not merely LTR status. Therefore, it can be argued that there is no major difference between persons who are considering applying for LTR status and those applying for citizenship of an individual EU Member State. As a consequence, the number of TCNs with LTR status has remained strikingly low,[21] not least because citizenship offers a much better prospect of protection, including equal treatment to EU citizens.

Several scholars have written about the outcomes of the LTR directive. The opinions diverge, as do understandings of the LTR status. Some see it as a temporary status on the way to full citizenship, others see it as a permanent subcitizenship status, or as a transnational membership form, yet lacking certain citizenship rights (Baubök 2007; Joppke 2009). Be that as it may, the introduction of the LTR status is to be understood as part of a wider supranational development of EU migration policy and, as a complement to it, the strengthening of the legal position of TCNs by acquiring more secure rights. Also, successive amendments to the LTR Directive have been adopted. One major amendment has been the expansion of the scope of the directive with a view to include two particular groups of TCNs, namely refugees and persons with subsidiary protection status.[22]

The expansion of the scope of the LTR Directive can illustrate the incompleteness of a truly transnational European space and the shortcomings it entails. *First*, this expansion would not have been possible without the passage of the Treaty of Lisbon on 1 December 2009 (De Baere 2011; see also Wouters, Verhey, and Kiiver 2009). The treaty provides that legislation on legal immigration must be adopted by a qualified majority vote (QMV) in the European Council and give joint legislative power to the European Parliament—this is known as the "ordinary legislative procedure" (formerly "co-decision"). This means that national vetoes have been abolished.

This, in turn, enabled the council to give its consent to the expansion—an expansion that previously had been deadlocked by several Member States—and then negotiate an agreement with the European Parliament that both institutions could accept. It was the first time that a directive on legal immigration was agreed upon by QMV and under the ordinary legislative procedure. But *second*, and all the more relevant for the illustration we wish to offer of the shortcomings of the European transnationalization process, the agreed text of the new directive is marked by the search for a compromise between the European Parliament (the EU's legislative power) and the European Council. It followed wholly informal contacts between the two institutional bodies, and, in the end, the European Parliament had to give up pressing for some of the amendments that it initially sought. Basically, the amendments aim at removing the exclusion of refugees and persons with subsidiary protection from the scope of the then existing LTR Directive, by setting out a special rule for obtaining LTR status: namely, only half of the time spent waiting for a decision on an application for refugee or subsidiary protection status (and then spent waiting to obtain a residence permit afterward) would count toward the five-year period of legal residence necessary to obtain LTR status, unless the individual waited more than eighteen months for a decision and residence permit, in which case the whole time period would count.[23]

Refugees and persons with subsidiary protection are also better protected than other TCNs: permitted restrictions on equal treatment of TCNs do not apply, to the extent that the Qualification Directive that specifically applies to refugees and persons with subsidiary protection sets higher standards (see, generally, Ball 2014). But for the remaining conditions and procedures that are provided for in the directive for obtaining LTR status, and for moving to another Member State, the directive has not been amended: the same rules apply to refugees and persons with subsidiary protection, as well as to other TCNs.

Comparing the agreed text of the (new) directive to the initial proposal, it follows that the legislative power of the European Parliament has been limited (due to the pressure coming from the European Council, that is, the representatives of the Member States) in this case to the single issue of calculating the waiting period to qualify as LTR, that is, whether to disregard up to half or even in some cases all of the time spent waiting for a decision on an application for international protection and then spent waiting to receive a residence permit after a positive decision. The European Council and the European Parliament reached a compromise on the issue. Although the information available is limited, everything indicates that, in practice, the expansion benefits a relatively small number of persons who receive international protection.

"Free Movement of Same-Sex Couples Across Internal Borders": European Social Policy Versus National Sovereignty over Marriage Rights

The free movement of workers—one of the pillars of the EU's internal market—has an important impact on family life.[24] Yet the full exercise of rights has not yet been fulfilled for various families, including European same-sex couples.

When it comes to the legal aspects of cross-border family life, much still depends on the content of national norms, notwithstanding wide harmonization of European private international law (PIL). PIL, or, in US parlance, Conflict of Laws, involves the rules that regulate issues of judicial jurisdiction, the applicable law in case of a legal dispute involving a foreign element, and the recognition and enforcement of decisions and judgments. The EU has from early on sought to extensively engage with PIL issues, first with intergovernmental instruments and later with regulations (Nott 2002).[25] However, considering the inadequacies of PIL in fully facilitating the single market (Lord Mance 2005), some have looked to the unification of substantive law, that is, a new European *ius commune* (Fiorini 2008). The harmonization of family law, however, misses a legal foundation in the EC Treaty and is an unlikely priority for Europe (with the focus being on trade, security, migration; see Boele-Woelki 2003). Thus, in the short to middle term, differing substantive laws will stay untouched by Europeanization.

For some citizens or residents, however, with particular/distinct family patterns, the free movement has been hampered by PIL rules and has created certain painful consequences: So-called limping family situations can result from the denial of recognition in the domestic legal order of one Member State of a legal relationship created, or recognized, in another Member State. The classic example here is a marriage or divorce registered in one country but considered against public policy and not recognized in another country.

One mechanism for coping with divergences between national legislations on personal status is "forum shopping," that is, seeking solutions in the legal order/system of a country that offers the best outcome, but this strategy has its limits. This is also true with regard to the issue of same-sex unions.[26] Considering there are various countries within the EU that recognize same-sex marriage today, a Romanian or Hungarian couple could relocate to, for example, Belgium or the Netherlands, making use of free movement rights. However, not every same-sex couple can easily relocate to a more friendly location (or would want to do this), as resources, employment prospects, family connections, and language are clearly obstacles. Moreover, this flies in the face of free movement, as the unequal treatment of same-sex couples in certain Member States is clearly a limitation of this right.

It can be stated from the outset that discrimination on the grounds of sexual orientation is prohibited across the EU. This is in contrast with the situation in the United States, which has a patchy landscape of protection in this regard. In the EU, Directive 2000/78 prohibits various kinds of discrimination on the basis of age, religion or belief, disability, and sexual orientation in the area of employment across the Union.[27] All Member States have implemented this directive at this point, which is seen as a key part of the economic integration process, and many have gone beyond the area of employment, for example, also prohibiting discrimination on those or other grounds in education, health, or public services. However, whether a country allows same-sex couples to marry is dependent on the individual Member States: It remains a (strictly) national competence, and there is no legal rule thus far that Member States should ensure mutual recognition of various legal partnerships or same-sex marriage.[28]

The Netherlands was famously the first country in the world to legalize same-sex marriage in 2001. In 2003, Belgium followed course,[29] followed by various other European countries. On 30 June 2017, the Bundestag approved a same-sex marriage bill, and Germany is set to become the latest European nation to legalize the practice. As of July 2017, eleven EU countries legally recognize and perform same-sex marriage (Belgium, Denmark, Finland, France, Ireland, Luxembourg, the Netherlands, Portugal, Spain, Sweden, and the United Kingdom).

Additionally, various European countries legally recognize some form of civil union.[30] Poland, Romania, Lithuania, Latvia, Bulgaria, and Slovakia do not recognize same-sex unions of any kind,[31] making an East-West division painfully obvious. Italy is a prominent exception among Western European countries, and its historical ties to the Roman Catholic Church are part of the explanation. Still, the recognition process was put in motion, triggered in part by decisions from the ECtHR (Povoledo 2016).

This legal landscape means that same-sex couples in Europe must consider their options carefully, not only with regard to legal differences but also social attitudes they are likely to encounter. The 2010 European Social Survey showed that public opinion in most Central and Eastern European countries was stacked against gay couples, with the Czech Republic being the only country with a majority of adults (65%) supporting gay marriage.[32] Still, even same-sex couples in the Netherlands face hostility, threats, and even violence when they dare "flaunting" their lifestyle in public,[33] so that acceptance is a matter of degrees rather than a black-and-white situation.

The debate on the recognition of same-sex marriages (and same-sex civil unions) has culminated in a request for opinion from the CJEU involving a Romanian American couple. The request for a preliminary ruling was made by the Romanian Constitutional Court (a first for the court, since Romania acceded to the EU in 2007) and lodged on 30 December 2016. Under this process, the highest national court of a Member State seeks clarification from the CJEU on issues of EU law and the compatibility of domestic law with EU law. In the case of *Coman and others*, the CJEU held in 2018 that while

Member States have the freedom whether or not to allow same-sex marriages in their territories, they cannot refuse a derived right of residence for a same-sex spouse (from a state that is not a Member State of the EU) when a lawful (same-sex) marriage was concluded in another EU Member State.[34]

The decision has had a significant reach and has impacted the recognition of same-sex marriages in the seventeen EU countries that currently do not fully recognize these marriages. Indeed, the CJEU can "dictate social policy" (O'Neill 2004) in this regard, as it can push the Member States in a socially progressive direction, but it also risks trampling national sovereignty in a highly sensitive area (without a solid foundation for its decisions, some would argue). (Conservative) religion, too, has been a relevant player, *in casu* rooting on the side of national sovereignty (*Romania Insider* 2016).

The facts were as follows. Adrian Coman is a Romanian LGBT activist in his mid-forties. In many ways, he is the idealized European, making use of the free borders to progress in his personal and professional life. Leaving Romania when he turned thirty, he studied, lived, and worked in Madrid, Brussels, and New York City, where he studied human rights and where—in Central Park—he met and fell in love with his later husband, Robert Claibourn Hamilton, an African American man raised in Texas. When Adrian's mother stood up on his behalf and testified before the Romanian Constitutional Court in October 2016, a reporter wrote that, "In a country where homosexuality is still a taboo, it may be that Camelia Coman is the first mother who publicly stands up for her gay son" (Mesesan 2016). Romania decriminalized homosexuality in 2000, but, as in other Eastern European countries, attitudes are substantially opposed to the "gay lifestyle." Moreover, Romania's 2011 Civil Code prohibits the recognition of same-sex marriages performed abroad (as well as civil partnerships concluded between heterosexual persons), which became a bone of contention.

In 2010 Coman was at a personal and professional juncture, still living in Brussels but unemployed. As he and Hamilton thought about their future, they considered the places to live: Belgium, the United States, or Romania. They decided to obtain a marriage certificate in Belgium, marrying there, and then two years later attempted to relocate to Romania. When their request for Hamilton's residency permit was denied—their marriage performed abroad would not be recognized by the Romanian authorities—they went to court, drawing on Coman's network of lawyers and connections. Coman told a reporter in Romania that "I knew this was unjust, it was illegal under EU law, and I knew the context to take action" (Mesesan 2016). The legal anchor provided by the right to free movement within the EU came into play (though Coman is a Romanian national so questions of "reverse discrimination" may be relevant). This shows the breadth of the tool of free movement, in that it can venture into social policies and facilitate the "dictating" of progressive values that not all Member States may be comfortable with (let alone explicitly consent to). While this constitutes for some a welcome tool to advance social justice issues that accompany economic rights, for others, this expansive view of free movement is a pretext to intrude into the national sovereignty sphere.

In 1998, before the Netherlands legalized same-sex marriage, the CJEU decided in *Grant v. South-West Trains* that European employers did not have to treat a same-sex partnership in the same way as a marriage or a stable heterosexual relationship outside of marriage.[35] However, the social and legal context has substantially changed since, and it is no longer true that most Member States do not treat "stable relationships between two persons of the same sex . . . as equivalent to marriages or stable relationships outside marriage between persons of opposite sex," as the court then remarked (see the discussion in O'Neill 2004: 203). Yet, what may have changed in "European viewpoint" may not be entirely true for certain regions or countries in the EU. Publicity given to the *Coman* case allowed Romanian campaigners to rally against gay marriage, collecting in May 2017 three million signatures on a petition to block same-sex unions in Romania. In their arguments, these anti–gay marriage advocates link marriage rights to national sovereignty, and thus position EU values as antithetical to national values.

When the CJEU considered the *Coman* case, and clarified the scope of fundamental family and residency rights for same-sex couples, it considered not only issues of EU law but also the inherent questions of national sovereignty and of national sensitivity and the potential for political and social backlash within the EU. Indeed, the "European Union, a body that began as an alliance aimed at strengthening member states' economies, but now holds greater social and cultural significance" (O'Neill 2004: 200).[36]

Competing Transnational Orders and Their Ramifications for Human Rights and Religious Equality in the Workplace

The European legal framework may seem complicated for onlookers, but in reality, the supranational level is even more heterogeneous, or "multilayered."[37] We have alluded to the role played by the ECtHR in the area of sexual minority rights above. The court operates within the Council of Europe framework rather than the European Union framework.

The Council of Europe is an international human rights organization with forty-seven Member States, including the twenty-eight European Member States but also countries like Russia and Turkey (the United States, Canada, Japan, and other countries have observer status). It is an organization with a wider geographical scope (covering an estimated 800 million people), but operates in parallel to the EU and seeks to realize the same commitments to democracy and human rights in post–World War II Europe. While the EU started out as an economic union, the Council of Europe has sought to build solidarity in Europe based on shared values and human rights. Though the two institutions have grown closer in objectives, their backgrounds are different. For instance, the legitimation of Directive 2000/78 lies in economic integration, free movement, and human rights considerations, in no particular order.[38] One can thus safely speak of overlapping transnational orders, complete with effective judicial decision-making mechanisms in the ECtHR in Strasbourg and the CJEU in Luxemburg.

After many years of discussions on how to bring the two frameworks closer and to fill some gaps in legal protection due to the incomplete overlap of legal frameworks (Raba 2015),[39] the accession of the EU to the European Convention on Human Rights was foreseen under Article 6.2 of the Lisbon Treaty and was negotiated for a number of years. It was a question of *how and under which conditions*, not whether, the EU would accede to the European Convention. This accession would imply that rulings of the CJEU could be "appealed" to the ECtHR in Strasbourg. In a rather unexpected move, the CJEU opposed the accession, considering that it violated the primacy of EU law.[40] The CJEU decision showed that European institutions are protective of what they consider their "acquired sovereignty" and are unwilling to subordinate to or give up sovereignty to other international mechanisms.

With the ratification of the Lisbon Treaty on 1 December 2009, the Charter of Fundamental Rights of the EU became a binding document with the same legal value as treaties,[41] and human rights in Europe became effectively a matter for two supranational courts, the (more established) ECtHR and the (newcomer) CJEU (Morano-Foadi and Vickers 2015). There may or may not be conflict between these respective jurisprudences, but, in any event, there is interaction, which, depending on the particular norm at hand, can involve competition, imitation, adaptation, or convergence. Elsewhere, we have considered this competition and questioned whether this leads to convergence in jurisprudence or rather divergence of human rights norms (Alidadi and Foblets 2016).

Perhaps the most important limitation for present purposes is the effect of Article 6(3) of the EU Charter. Article 6(3) makes clear that where the EU Charter rights correspond to those guaranteed by the ECtHR, the rights shall have the same meaning as under the European Convention, although EU law may provide "more extensive protection." Any extended protection may prove difficult to accomplish in fact, however, as ECtHR jurisprudence is part of the general principles of the EU. Thus, it is in the area where the texts of the European Convention and the EU Charter diverge that the CJEU may retain some of its supremacy of interpretation, including Article 9 of the EU Charter. The CJEU perhaps is a newcomer to the human rights jurisprudential field, but it has established and progressive equality jurisprudence to draw upon.

We now briefly address the ramifications of this reality for the protection of freedom of religion or belief and the right to freedom from religious discrimination in the workplace. This is an area where considerable jurisprudence, and literature, exists with regard to the ECtHR, but the first CJEU decisions are very recent (e.g., the *Achbita* and *Bougnaoui* decisions of 14 March 2017) (McCrea 2017).

Despite being routinely considered the most effective human rights court in the world,[42] the ECtHR's specific decisions (from asylum seekers' rights to family life, disability rights, and anticensorship and free speech) have been the subject of fierce critique. In the area of religion in public life, the too-wide margin of appreciation is said to have rendered many of the protections under Articles 9 and 14 of the European Convention empty shells (e.g., Pastor 2018). Accordingly, high hopes were expressed in anticipation of the first decisions of the CJEU interpreting the prohibition of religious freedom in employment (Loenen 2012).

It took almost seventeen years after the adoption of the prohibition of discrimination on the basis of religion or belief in EU law, under EU Directive 2000/78, before the CJEU would receive the opportunity to decide on the scope and extent of protection against religious discrimination in the workplace. And when it did, two similar cases—one from France, one from Belgium—came its way at once. On 14 March 2017, the CJEU issued two highly anticipated judgments in *Achbita v. G4S Secure Solutions NV* and *Bougnaoui v. Micropole SA*.[43]

The opinions were preceded by two well-argued but contradictory Advocate General advisory opinions; one (by Advocate General Kokott) favoring limited protection against religious discrimination in the workplace, and the other (by Advocate General Sharpston) for a more expansive interpretation of the antidiscrimination provisions. *Achbita* involved the (worrisome) development among Belgian private-sector companies, from bookstores to shoe stores, to adopt "neutrality policies." These policies, inscribed in the company regulations or elsewhere and often supported by labor union representatives, prohibit staff—sometimes limited to employees with customer contact—from exhibiting religious as well as ideological and political symbols or signs of affiliation. Employers thus communicate in advance to (candidate) employees that they cannot wear a headscarf or turban, or risk dismissal if they violate the rule (Alidadi 2017: esp. 130–135, 157–166). The question before the CJEU was if such policies were legitimate under EU Directive 2000/78, which prohibits direct discrimination and indirect discrimination (the equivalent of disparate impact discrimination in the United States) in the European workplace. Different Member States have divergent approaches when it comes to these policies; while the Netherlands and the UK consider them in violation of their antidiscrimination provisions, Belgian labor courts have taken a very different perspective (ibid.).

In *Achbita*, the CJEU held that the prohibition on employees wearing any visible signs of their political, philosophical, or religious beliefs in the workplace did not give rise to direct discrimination. It also held that such policies, though they may constitute indirect distinctions, can be justified under certain conditions (e.g., consistent and systematic application, limited to employees who come into contact with customers).

However, in *Bougnaoui*, the French case, the CJEU held that customer preferences cannot justify limitations on the wearing of religious symbols. The relation between the two opinions is not entirely clear, in particular since the neutrality policy in the *Achbita* case was also adopted in response to a request made by the company to which the plaintiff was outsourced to work as a receptionist (it is striking that the policy was not in force until the day *after* Ms. Achbita was dismissed; the employer had argued there was an "unwritten rule" in place and this assertion was apparently not contested in the CJEU proceedings). Even if various questions remain following the twin religious discrimination cases, it is clear that EU law does not provide more protection than under Strasbourg jurisprudence (and despite the rather limited prospects under that case law post-*Eweida*; Alidadi 2017[44]).

In her advisory opinion on the *Bougnaoui* case, Advocate General Sharpston pinpointed instances where EU law could and should provide more protection than Article 9 of the European Convention, in light of the provisions in EU Directive 2000/78: "In the context of direct discrimination, the protection given by EU law is stronger. Here, interference with a right granted under the ECHR may still always be justified on the ground that it pursues a legitimate aim and is proportionate. In contrast, under the EU legislation, however, derogations are permitted only in so far as the measure in question specifically provides for them."[45] The European Convention standards thus would constitute the floor of rights, not the ceiling. Advocate General Sharpston considers such difference in approach as "a wholly legitimate one" in light of Article 52(3) of the EU Charter.[46] The CJEU, however, adopted an approach that, while it diverges from its own equality jurisprudence, in a sense ties in closely with Strasbourg jurisprudence.

The fact that human rights is an issue for two supranational courts in Europe has thus not spurred a heightened spiral of protection, but rather a modest convergence of—or imitation in—jurisprudence, at least in the area of religious discrimination in the workplace. Tying the decisions to the broader political context, Lucy Vickers (2017: 254) argues that "the reason for the backwards step in terms of equality can best be understood in the context of a deeper reluctance on the part of the CJEU to address issues of State sovereignty which arise when considering the highly contentious question of the proper scope of protection for religion or belief in Europe. Its failure to address this deeper matter of the integration of standards across the EU can be seen as second backwards step on the part of the CJEU." It is thus in indirect and continuous ways that notions of union and national sovereignty enter into play in different legal developments. Even if the competency of the EU is not at stake, interpretation of norms, on a continuous basis, is molded so that decisions stay within acceptable confines. The casualties are diverse and, for now, include those European workers seeking protection against discriminatory employment demands under EU law.

Conclusion

The Brexit vote has intensified debates on the future of the sixty-year venture that is Europe. Indeed, "Britain's vote to leave on June 23rd [2016] was a grievous blow to a club that has only ever known expansion" (*The Economist*

2016). But the current crisis is multifaceted; if anything, Brexit is a symptom of the fragility of the EU project. In this sense, Europe will be able to survive Brexit, but the larger question is whether Brexit is a harbinger of things to come. With a number of EU-favorable elections in Western Europe, disaster seems to have been diverted for now.

As suggested, the various crises Europe has faced in recent years can be better understood with the incompleteness of the European project in mind. Incompleteness is perhaps the prime characteristic of *European* transnationalization, but it has wider implications as it shows the inherent limits of intentional transnational law. In this chapter, we have sought to provide four concrete illustrations to document the ramifications of the incompleteness of the European transnationalization project that continuously limits the effectiveness of EU laws and policies, particularly in trade and security.

One might say that frailty is an inherent risk that comes with such a novel endeavor (as in the old adage that Europe is forged in times of crisis) and with the efforts that have been the EU's modus operandi all along in undertaking an unprecedented harmonization exercise that over the years has expanded from the economic sphere to include also the political, legal, monetary, cultural, and social. The process of transnationalization that accompanied the Europeanization of different areas of law in Europe is currently under pressure, and the populist turn across many parts of Europe is challenging the transfer of sovereignty (or "pooling" of sovereignty, as some would have it)—classically seen as the supreme authority within a polity—from the nation-state to the European institutions, which are considered bureaucratic, nontransparent, and out of touch with the concerns of everyday Europeans.

Our conclusion is a nuanced one: It was foreseeable from the outset that to build a transnational space in Europe is far from easy and that it would come up against numerous obstacles along the way, be those legal, technical, political, or ideological in nature. Instead of concluding that the experiment has failed—a view that is (increasingly) heard—our position is that we need to draw lessons from the failures and accept the fact that these flaws are an integral part of the experience of transnationalization in Europe (and, no doubt, elsewhere). Europe should draw on its past when it is challenged today and in the future in its policies and its very being if it seeks to pursue a venture that remains worthwhile after sixty years of effort.

To be sure, trust in EU institutions remains low: "About a third of citizens trust the EU today, while about half of Europeans did so ten years ago"

(Juncker 2017b: 12). Still, EU leaders are hopeful if nothing else, utilizing the Brexit negotiations to show their unified voice. At the G20 Summit in Hamburg, Germany, in mid-July 2017, the EU was present with Jean-Claude Juncker and Donald Tusk, president of the EU Council, in visible roles, including when an impending trade deal with Japan was made public (Macdonald and Bartunek 2017). One of the crucial checkmarks for the success of the "global approach" was the May 2019 European Parliament elections, which revealed a striking ambivalence as both pro-EU centrist and environmental parties on the one hand, and Eurosceptic and right-wing populist parties on the other, took substantial seats away from centrist parties.

In politics dominated by nationalistic discourses and programs (a sign of our times, with the election of President Donald Trump a clear example), pan-national projects have become vulnerable. But part of the vulnerability (some may say "weakness") and continuous crisis of legitimacy of Europe has to do with the fact that Europe does not have a direct electorate and speaks to Europeans through the nation-states and national governments (which have their own dynamics, interests, and concerns). The core problems are thus structural, not merely conjunctural, though it is common knowledge that Europe is facing unprecedented levels of skepticism. In this sense, if the question is posed as, "At the end of all this madness, what is the EU going to look like?" the answer is aptly, "There will never be an end to all this madness" (Techau 2016).

The discussions surrounding the future of Europe will continue, fed by the continuous input of electoral cycles and sociopolitical developments. In *The Politics of Everyday Europe*, Kathleen McNamara (2016: 1) argues that the legitimacy of the EU rests on strategies that the modern nation-state has long used, ranging from Euro European citizenship, arts and culture, and foreign policy as "the symbols and practices of everyday life." She thus points to the social and cultural supportive structures for the EU's governance. Her work remains of crucial relevance in these tense times, indicating the relative failure of the transformations of cultural architecture that the EU has invested in and at the same time the need for improved social and cultural strategies to bolster credibility for the European project in a time of need. By supporting such shared ventures, Europe can build support, credibility, and relevance for itself. Yet there is a dilemma in times of crisis in that such ventures may further discredit the EU as frivolous and or obsolete. Whether shared values across the EU are real or fiction, we believe they play a significant role. Desertion of the value-drivenness of the EU, we would argue, would not help the fragility of the project but rather exacerbate it. Europe still has a moral voice in today's world and should use it when the need arises.

Notes

1. EU law is certainly transnational law as Gregory Shaffer (2010: 11) defines it: "law in which transnational actors, be they transnational institutions or transnational networks of public or private actors, play a role in constructing and diffusing legal norms."

2. The white paper describes five scenarios: (1) carrying on, (2) nothing but the single market, (3) those who want more do more, (4) doing less more efficiently, and (5) doing much more together (Juncker 2017b: 29).

3. While reactions varied, many proposals launched in Juncker's State of the Union were fiercely critiqued, for instance, the suggestion that "anti-European extremist" political parties should not receive EU funding.

4. It should be clear that the choice of terms for the delegation of powers between different political layers is not neutral. Be that as it may, when it comes to policies that are explicitly conferred to the EU or are shared competences, European institutions have the power to override national authorities.

5. "The EU is a unique project in which domestic priorities have been combined and *sovereignty voluntarily pooled to better serve national and collective interests*. It has not always been an easy journey, it has never been perfect, but it has shown its capacity to reform itself and has proven its value over time" (Juncker 2017: 26; emphasis added). On the concept of pooled sovereignty, see Peterson (1997), who argues that states choose to pool sovereignty so as to reduce the likelihood of gridlock in policy areas, but pooling creates the possibility that individual Member States can be outvoted.

6. The EU generally points to "a mismatch between expectations and the EU's capacity to meet them" (Juncker 2017b: 13). In essence, this is the incompleteness of the European project framed as an argument for further expansion.

7. Significantly, the "return to sovereignty" (the Brexit/Leave campaign mantra of "take back control") was supported not only by right-wing Le Pen but also by the leftist candidate Jean-Luc Mélenchon, who also planned a "Frexit" referendum.

8. "Limping family-law relationships" refer to situations where a person has validly acquired a status under one state's system that is not recognized as valid under another state's law, so that, for instance, a person may be considered married in one state but not in another. These relationships include limping marriages or registered partnerships, limping divorces, even "limping fatherhood." See Dethloff (2003: 44).

9. This is a topic that has drawn considerable attention in the last two decades in both Europe and the United States, where the 2015 Supreme Court landmark decision in *Obergefell v. Hodges* (576 US ___ [2015]) rendered the issue of interstate recognition moot. A similar development in Europe, with the EU mandating member states to accept same-sex marriages, is in the given state of affairs highly unlikely. In fact, the competence of national courts of the EU Member States is also restricted in this regard and legalization has been advanced via statutory rules. See Boele-Woelki (2008).

10. David Bradley (2003: 70) notes that "family law appears to lack even initial criteria for unification, comparable to commercial practice or efficiency for contract law . . . family law is commonly presented as reflecting deeply embedded differences between states themselves." Bradley, however, considers this an excessively "limited view" and argues that "tradition, ideology and culture do not, by themselves, present insurmountable obstacles to development of a European law."

11. Natasha Zaun (2017: 3) notes that "the EU has harmonized asylum systems in its member States and regulated the distribution of asylum-seekers only on paper." See also ter Steeg (2006) and Foblets (2009).

12. The EU-Turkey migration deal was signed at a special summit on November 29, 2015, and came into force in March 2016. Turkey was (initially) to receive €3 billion ($3.4 billion) in aid and negotiations on Turkey joining the EU (long stalled) were promised. See Mohdin (2015). Amnesty International and other human rights organizations have called for a suspension of the migration deal until an effective monitoring system scheme is set up. See Gogou (2017).

13. A European Court of Human Rights decision that played a key role in this regard is the *M.S.S. v. Belgium and Greece* case (no. 30696/09; 21 January 2011), in which an Afghan national who had entered the EU via Greece before arriving in Belgium where he applied for asylum complained that Belgium—by returning him to Greece in accordance with the Dublin regulation—had exposed him to the risk of degrading treatment, because of his detention conditions and his living conditions in Greece. The court held that there indeed had been a violation of the prohibition of degrading treatment (Art. 3 of the European Convention on Human Rights). For an overview of the case law of the ECtHR regarding the Dublin regulation, see ECtHR (2016). In a Grand Chamber Judgment of 21 December 2011, the Court of Justice of the European Union (CJEU, C-410/11) adopted a similar position, referring explicitly to the judgment in *M.S.S. v. Belgium and Greece* The situation in some Member States however, continues to be profoundly disquieting, see, for example, Dearden (2017); In the ECtHR case of 2017, *Ilias and Ahmed v. Hungary* (appl. no. 47287/15), finding a violation of Article 5 §§ 1 and 4 (right to *liberty and security* in the detention of two Bangladeshi migrants in the border zone between Hungary and Serbia).

14. While the Qualification Directive (Directive 2011/95/EU of the European Parliament and of the Council of 13 December 2011 on standards for the qualification of third-country nationals or stateless persons as beneficiaries of international protection, and for the content of the protection granted; PJ L 337, 20.12.2011, p. 9) sets out the standards for the recognition and protection to be offered at the EU level to persons eligible for subsidiary protection, in practice, recognition rates vary, sometimes widely, between Member States. For instance, for the period between January and September 2015 the recognition rates for asylum seekers from Afghanistan varied from almost 100 percent in Italy to 5.88 percent in Bulgaria (European Commission 2016: 5n14).

15. Council Decision (EU) 2015/1601 of 22 September establishing provisional measures in the area of international protection for the benefit of Italy and Greece, *Official Journal* 2015 L 248, 80.

16. *Slovak Republic and Hungary v. Council of the European Union*, CJEU 2017, C-643/15, and C-647/15, Judgment of the Court (Grand Chamber) of 6 September 2017 (joined cases).

17. Council Directive 2003/109/EC of 25 November 2003 concerning the status of third-country nationals who are long-term-residents, *Official Journal* L L016, 23/01/2004, 0044–0053. In principle, TCNs with LTR status should have access to paid and unpaid employment, equal working conditions, education and vocational training, recognition of qualification and study grants, welfare and social benefits, family allowances and sickness insurance, tax relief, and goods and services, as well as freedom of association and union membership, freedom to represent a union or association, and free access to the entire territory of the EU country in which they obtained the status.

18. This cannot be done for EU citizens who have obtained permanent residence right after five years of residence.

19. It is only after the family is reunited in the country where LTR status has been granted that an LTR has the right to freely move around within the territory of the EU together with his or her family members. An EU citizen, in contrast, has a right to reunite with his or her family members in any EU Member State.

20. Even if such residence permits do not confer the right to residence in the other Member States.

21. In 2009, the European Commission's report on the application of the directive found that an insignificant number of TCNs had become EU LTRs (Huddleston and Niessen 2011).

22. Council Directive 2011/51/EU of the European Parliament and the Council of 11 May 2011 amending Council Directive 2003/109/EC to extend its scope to beneficiaries of international protection, *Official Journal* L 132, 19/5/2011, 1–4.

23. The amendments also set out special rules relating to indicating the status of the person applying for the residence permit, including cases where a refugee of subsidiary protection status had been transferred to a second Member State that the LTR was moving into.

24. We borrow the phrase "Free Movement of Same-Sex Couples Across Internal Borders" from Boele-Woelki (2008: 1949). The right of the free movement of workers derives from Article 45 of the Treaty on the Functioning of the European Union; Directive 2004/38/EC of the European Parliament and of the Council of 29 April 2004 on the right of citizens of the Union and their family members to move and reside freely within the territory of the Member States amending Regulation (EEC) No. 1612/68 and repealing Directives 64/221/EEC, 68/360/EEC, 72/194/EEC, 73/148/EEC, 75/34/EEC, 75/35/EEC, 90/364/EEC, 90/365/EEC and 93/96/EEC (*Official Journal* L 158, 30.4.2004, 77).

25. For example, Regulation (EU) No. 1215/2012 of the European Parliament and of the Council of 12 December 2012 on jurisdiction and the recognition and enforcement of judgments in civil and commercial matters (Brussels I Regulation); Regulation (EU) No. 1215/2012 of the European Parliament and of the Council of 12 December 2012 on jurisdiction and the recognition and enforcement of judgments in civil and commercial matters (Brussels II Regulation).

26. We concentrate on same-sex marriages, but the same discussion applies *mutatis mutandis* to registered partnerships in the EU.

27. Council Directive 2000/78/EC of 27 November 2000 establishing a general framework for equal treatment in employment and occupation, *Official Journal* L303/16.

28. The European Court of Human Rights, in *Schalk and Kopf v. Austria* (30141/04, 24 June 2010), accepted same-sex relationships as a form of "family life" but held that Member States were not obliged to legislate or legally recognize same-sex marriages under Article 12 ECtHR (which states that "Men and women of marriageable age have the right to marry and to found a family, according to the national laws governing the exercise of this right." Interestingly, the French version of the Convention states "l'homme et la femme ont le droit de se marier" [the man and the woman have the right to marry]). However, in *Vallianatos and Others v. Greece* (7 November 2013), the same court held that Greece had violated Article 14 (nondiscrimination) in conjunction with Article 8 (family life) ECtHR by enacting a law in 2008 that established civil unions but excluded same-sex couples from concluding such unions. Later Greece included same-sex couples under the law. The next step came in *Oliari and Others v. Italy* (21 July 2015), where the court, perhaps inspired by the recent *Obergefell v. Hodges* decision of the US Supreme Court, held that Italy had violated its duty under Article 8 ECtHR ("Right to respect for private and family life") by not providing any legal recognition to same-sex relationships (but reiterated there was no positive duty to legalize same-sex marriage).

29. "These two countries have begun a trend in family law that some had previously dismissed as an isolated incident in the Netherlands" (O'Neill 2004: 200).

30. For the most recent data, see Lipka and Masci (2017).

31. In a 2015 referendum, only 36.5 percent of Slovenians came out in favor of same-sex marriage (Noack 2015).

32. See "Data and Documentation by Round/Year," European Social Survey, accessed 21 July 2019, https://www.europeansocialsurvey.org/data/round-index.html.

33. For example, by walking hand in hand. See *The Guardian* (2017). A gay Dutch acquaintance of the authors living in Amsterdam notes that he avoids giving his spouse "big hugs and kisses" at Schiphol Airport but "suspends" their welcoming each other until they are home, and that they never hold hands in public, realizing that hostility against gays makes vigilance still necessary.

34. *Coman and Others*, Case C-673/16, 5 June 2018.

35. *Grant v. South-West Trains*, Case C-249/96, 1998 ECR I-621; see also Jones (2017).

36. Allison O'Neill (2004) predicted that the issue of same-sex marriage would come to the doors of the CJEU. Now, with the *Coman* case, it has.

37. See also Burchardt (2017), arguing for a norm-centered rather than system-centered strategy to understand the phenomenon of intertwinement in the transnational legal sphere.

38. This economic, market-driven background still gives shape to many interpretations (see O'Brien 2011).

39. Such a gap exists when an EU Member State violates the European Convention on Human Rights by implementing EU law.

40. Opinion 2/13 of the CJEU (Full Court) on 18 December 2014 on the Accession of the European Union to the ECtHR, [2014] ECLI 2454.

41. Unlike treaties, however, there are limitations to the charter's scope. For example, it is addressed to the EU and the Member States "only when they are implementing EU law." In addition, Article 6(1) states that the EU gains no new competences, nor does it extend the application of EU law.

42. The ECtHR has issued more than ten thousand judgments since it was set up in 1959 and has prompted numerous changes in legislation across the Council of Europe Member States. The court, together with the European Commission, is also routinely used as a scapegoat by nationalist, anti-EU leaders; see Henley (2013), who states, "Along with the European commission in Brussels, the Strasbourg-based ECHR could reasonably lay claim to being one of the most maligned institutions in Britain. . . . Conservative MPs have said it is high time for Britain to 'quit the jurisdiction' of a 'supranational quango.'" Unsurprisingly, the next frontier for Brexit campaigners is to withdraw from the European Convention and to scrap the Human Rights Act that makes the European Convention enforceable in Britain.

43. *Achbita and Centrum voor Gelijkheid van kansen en voor racismebestrijding v G4S Secure Solutions NV*, Case C-157/15, 14 March 2017; *Bougnaoui and Association de défense des droits de l'homme (ADDH) v. Micropole SA*, Case C-188/15, 14 March 2017.

44. See also *Nadia Eweida and others v. the UK*, [2013] ECtHR 37; *Ebrahimian v. France* (app. no. 64846/11) decision of 26 November 2015; and *S.A.S v. France* (app. no. 43835/11) decision of 1 July 2014.

45. Opinion of Advocate General Sharpston delivered on 13 July 2016, para. 63, accessed 22 July 2019, https://eur-lex.europa.eu/legal-content/EN/TXT/?uri=CELEX%3A62015CC0188. In contrast, Advocate General Kokott, in her opinion on the *Achbita* case, delivered on 31 May 2016, favored a very limited protection against discrimination on the specific basis of religion or belief under EU law.

46. Opinion of Advocate General Sharpston delivered on 13 July 2016, para. 64.

References

Alidadi, Katayoun. 2017. *Religion, Equality and Employment in Europe: The Case for Reasonable Accommodation*. Oxford: Hart /Bloomsbury.

Alidadi, Katayoun, and Marie-Claire Foblets. 2016. "European Supranational Courts and the Fundamental Right to Freedom of Religion or Belief: Convergence or Competition?" *Oxford Journal of Law & Religion* 5 (3): 532–540.

Ball, Richard. 2014. *The Legitimacy of the European Union Through Legal Rationality: Free Movement of Third Country Nationals*. London: Routledge.

Barwig, Klaus, Stephan Beichel-Benedetti, and Gisbert Brinkmann, eds. 2016. *Gerechtigkeit in der Migrationsgesellschaft* [Justice in the Migration Community]. Baden-Baden, Germany: Nomos.

Bauböck, Rainer. 2007. "Why European Citizenship? Normative Approaches to Supranational Union." *Theoretical Inquiries in Law* 8 (2): 452–488.

BBC. 2017. "Emmanuel Macron Defeats Le Pen to Become French President," 8 May 2017. http://www.bbc.com/news/world-europe-39839349.

Boele-Woelki, Katharina, ed. 2003. *Perspectives for the Unification and Harmonisation of Family Law in Europe*. Antwerp, Belgium: Intersentia.

Boele-Woelki, Katharina. 2008. "The Legal Recognition of Same-Sex Relationships Within the European Union." *Tulane Law Review* 82:1949–1981.

Bradley, David. 2003. "A Family Law in Europe?" In *Perspectives for the Unification and Harmonisation of Family Law in Europe*, ed. Katharina Boele-Woelki, 65–104. Antwerp, Belgium: Intersentia.

Burchardt, Dana. 2017. "Intertwinement of Legal Spaces in the Transnational Legal Sphere." *Leiden Journal of International Law* 30 (2): 305–326.

Dearden, L. 2017. "Hungarian Parliament Approves Law Allowing All Asylum Seekers to Be Detained." *The Independent*, 7 March 2017. https://www.independent.co.uk/news/world /europe/hungary-parliament-asylum-seekers-detain-law-approve-refugees -immigration-crisis-arrests-border-a7615486.html.

De Baere, Geert. 2011. "The Basics For EU External Relations Law: An Overview of the Post-Lisbon Constitutional Framework for Developing the External Dimensions of EU Asylum and Migration Policy." In *The International Dimension of EU Asylum and Migration Policy: Framing the Issues*, eds. Marleen Maes, Marie-Claire Foblets, and Philippe De Bruycker, 121–174. Brussels: Bruylant.

den Heijer, Maarten, Jorrit Rijpma, and Thomas Spijkerboer. 2016. *The Systemic Failure of the Common European Asylum System, as Exemplified by the EU-Turkey Deal*, 16 March. Accessed 4 September 2017. http://thomasspijkerboer.eu.

Dethloff, Nina. 2003. "Arguments for the Unification and Harmonization of Family Law in Europe." In *Perspectives for the Unification and Harmonisation of Family Law in Europe*, ed. Katharina Boele-Woelki, 35–64. Antwerp, Belgium: Intersentia.

The Economist. 2016. "The Future of the EU. Now What? Europe Vows Progress After Brexit, but Is Unsure Which Way to Go." 3 September 2016. https://www.economist.com/europe /2016/09/03/now-what.

Eisele, Katharina. 2014. *The External Dimension of the EU's Migration Policy: Different Legal Positions of Third-Country Nationals in the E.U.* Leiden, Netherlands: Brill Nijhoff.

European Commission. 2016. *Towards a Reform of the Common European Asylum System and Enhancing Legal Avenues to Europe*. Communication from the Commission to the European Parliament and the Council, No. 197. Brussels, 6 April.

European Court of Human Rights (ECtHR). 2016. *Factsheet—"Dublin Cases."* June. Accessed 22 July 2019. www.echr.coe.int/Documents/FS_Dublin_ENG.pdf.

Fiorini, Aude. 2008. "The Codification of Private International Law in Europe: Could the Community Learn from the Experience of Mixed Jurisdictions?" *Electronic Journal of Comparative Law* 12 (1): 1–16.

Foblets, Marie-Claire. 2009. "The Fragmented Development of EU Immigration and Integration Policy." In *European Constitutionalism Beyond Lisbon*, eds. Jan Wouters, Luc Verhey, and Phillip Kiiver, 81–109. Antwerp, Belgium: Intersentia.

FT View. 2016. "Pooled Sovereignty Has Advanced National Goals." *Financial Times*, 12 June 2016. https://www.ft.com/content/169fa2a2-2eee-11e6-a18d-a96ab29e3c95?mhq 5j=e2.

Gogou, Kondylia. 2017. "The EU-Turkey Deal: Europe's Year of Shame." Amnesty International News, 20 March. https://www.amnesty.org/en/latest/news/2017/03/the-eu-turkey-deal -europes-year-of-shame/.

Groenendijk, Kees. 2012a. "Integration of Immigrants in the EU: The Old or the New Way?" In *Which Integration Policies for Migrants? Interaction Between the EU and Its Member States*, eds. Yves Pascouau and Tineke Strik, 3–14. Nijmegen, Netherlands: Wolf Legal.

Groenendijk, Kees. 2012b. "Introduction: Migration and Law in Europe." In *The First Decade of EU Migration and Asylum Law*, eds. Elspeth Guild and Paul Minderhoud, 1–24. Leiden, Netherlands: Martinus Nijhoff.

The Guardian. 2017. "Dutch Men Walk Hand in Hand for Solidarity After Gay Couple Attacked." 5 April 2017. https://www.theguardian.com/world/2017/apr/06/dutch-men-hand-in-hand-solidarity-gay-couple-attacked.

Guild, Elspeth, Kees Groenendijk, and Sergio Carrera, eds. 2016. *Illiberal Liberal States: Immigration, Citizenship and Integration in the EU*. London: Routledge.

Guild, Elspeth, and Paul Minderhoud, eds. 2012. *The First Decade of EU Migration and Asylum Law*. Leiden, Netherlands: Martinus Nijhoff.

Halleskov-Storgaard, Louise. 2012. "The Long-Term-Residents Directive: A Fulfillment of the Tampere Objective of Near-Equality?" In *The First Decade of EU Migration and Asylum Law*, eds. Elspeth Guild and Paul Minderhoud, 299–328. Leiden, Netherlands: Martinus Nijhoff.

Henley, Jon. 2013. "Why Is the European Court of Human Rights Hated by the UK Right?" *The Guardian*, 22 December 2013.

Huddleston, Thomas, and Jan Niessen. 2011. *Migrant Integration Policy Index III*. Brussels: British Council and Migration Policy Group. Accessed 22 July 2019. http://www.mipex.eu/sites/default/files/downloads/migrant_integration_policy_index_mipexiii_2011.pdf.

Jones, Jackie. 2017. "Opening Marriage to Same-Sex Couples in the European Union." *Legal Dialogue*, 31 January. https://legal-dialogue.org/opening-marriage-sex-couples-european-union.

Joppke, Christian. 2009. "The Vulnerability of Non-Citizens." *Perspectives on Europe* 39 (2): 514–518.

Juncker, Jean-Claude. 2017a. "State of the Union 2017." European Commission, 13 September.

Juncker, Jean-Claude. 2017b. "White Paper on the Future of Europe: Reflections and Scenarios for the EU27 by 2025." European Commission, 1 March. Accessed 22 July 2019. https://ec.europa.eu/commission/sites/beta-political/files/white_paper_on_the_future_of_europe_en.pdf.

Kessler, Stefan. 2016. "Das Konsultativforum für Menschenrechte bei Frontex" [The Consultative Forum on Human Rights at Frontex]. In *Gerechtigkeit in der Migrationsgesellschaft* [Justice in the Migration Community], eds. Klaus Barwig, Stephan Beichel-Benedetti, and Gisbert Brinkmann, 249–257. Baden-Baden, Germany: Nomos.

Larkin, Kimberly. 2017. "Divergent Duties: Complementarity and Crisis in the CJEU's and ECtHR's Approaches to 'Safe Third Country' Legislation Within the EU-Turkey Refugee Deal." Stanford-Vienna European Union Law Working Paper, No. 18. Accessed 22 July 2019. https://law.stanford.edu/transatlantic-technology-law-forum/eu-law-working-paper-series/.

Lipka, Michael, and David Masci. 2017. *Where Europe Stands on Gay Marriage and Civil Unions*. Pew Research Center. 30 June. Accessed 25 July 2019. https://www.pewresearch.org/fact-tank/2017/06/30/where-europe-stands-on-gay-marriage-and-civil-unions/.

Loenen, Titia. 2012. "Accommodation of Religion and Sex Equality in the Workplace Under the EU Equality Directives: A Double Bind for the European Court of Justice." In *A Test of Faith? Religious Diversity and Accommodation in the European Workplace,* eds. Katayoun Alidadi, Marie-Claire Foblets, and Jogchum Vrielink, 103–120. Aldershot, UK: Ashgate.

Lord Mance. 2005. "The Future of Private International Law." *Journal of Private International Law* 1 (2): 185–195.

Macdonald, Alastair, and Robert-Jan Bartunek. 2017. "EU, Japan Seal Free Trade in Signal to Trump." Reuters, 6 July 2017. https://www.reuters.com/article/us-japan-eu-trade -idUSKBN19R17U.

Maes, Marleen, Marie-Claire Foblets, and Philippe De Bruycker, eds. 2011. *The International Dimension of EU Asylum and Migration Policy: Framing the Issues.* Brussels: Bruylant.

McCrea, Ronan. 2017. "Faith at Work: The CJEU's Headscarf Rulings." *EU Law Analysis,* 17 March. http://eulawanalysis.blogspot.com/2017/03/faith-at-work-cjeus-headscarf-rulings .html.

McNamara, Kathleen. 2016. *The Politics of Everyday Europe: Constructing Authority in the European Union.* Oxford: Oxford University Press.

Mesesan, Diana. 2016. "Love in the Time of Courts: Two Men Against the Romanian State." *Romania Insider,* 26 October 2016. https://www.romania-insider.com/love-time-courts -men-lawsuit-romanian-state.

Mohdin, Aamna. 2015. "A Deal with the Devil? A Damning Amnesty Report Claims Turkey Abused Refugees and Pressured Some to Return to War Zones." Quartz, 16 December., https://qz.com/575776/a-damning-amnesty-report-claims-turkey-abused-refugees-and -pressured-some-to-return-to-war-zones/.

Morano-Foadi, Sonia, and M. Malena, eds. 2012. *Integration of Third-Country Nationals in the European Union—The Equality Challenge.* Cheltenham, UK: Edward Elgar.

Morano-Foadi, Sonia, and Lucy Vickers, eds. 2015. *Fundamental Rights in the EU: A Matter for Two Courts.* Oxford: Hart.

Noack, Rick. 2015. "One of Eastern Europe's Most Liberal Countries Just Rejected Gay Marriage." *Washington Post,* 21 December 2015. https://www.washingtonpost.com/news /worldviews/wp/2015/12/21/one-of-eastern-europes-most-liberal-countries-just -rejected-gay-marriage/?utm_term=.d12529cf1fca.

Nott, Susan M. 2002. "For Better or Worse? The Europeanisation of the Conflict of Laws." *Liverpool Law Review* 24:3–17.

O'Brien, Charlotte. 2011. "Equality's False Summits: New Varieties of Disability Discrimination, 'Excessive' Equal Treatment and Economically Constricted Horizons." *European Law Review* 36 (1): 26–50.

O'Neill, Allison R. 2004. "Recognition of Same-Sex Marriage in the European Community: The European Court of Justice's Ability to Dictate Social Policy." *Cornell International Law Journal* 37 (1): 200–216.

Pastor, Eugenia Relaño. 2018. "The European Court of Human Rights: Fundamental Assumptions That Have a Chilling Effect on the Protection of Religious Diversity." In *Public Commissions on Cultural and Religious Diversity: National Narratives, Multiple Identities and Minorities*, eds. Katayoun Alidadi and Marie-Claire Foblets, 266–287. Abingdon, UK: Routledge.

Peterson, John. 1997. "The European Union: Pooled Sovereignty, Divided Accountability." *Political Studies* 45:559–578.

Povoledo, Elisabetta. 2016. "Italy Approves Same-Sex Civil Union." *New York Times*, 11 May 2016. https://www.nytimes.com/2016/05/12/world/europe/italy-gay-same-sex-unions.html.

Raba, Kristi. 2015. "Closing the Gaps in the Protection of Fundamental Rights in Europe: Accession of the EU to the ECHR." In *Fundamental Rights in the EU: A Matter for Two Courts*, eds. Sonia Morano-Foadi and Lucy Vickers, 21–46. Oxford: Hart.

Rankin, Jennifer. 2016a. "EU Unveils Plans to Reform Asylum Rules to Help Frontline Members." *The Guardian*, 6 April 2016. https://www.theguardian.com/world/2016/apr/06/eu-unveils-plans-reform-asylum-rules-refugee-migrant.

Rankin, Jennifer. 2016b. "Turkey Fails to Meet Criteria for Visa-free EU Travel." *The Guardian*, 15 June 2016. https://www.theguardian.com/world/2016/jun/15/turkey-misses-deadline-visa-free-travel-eu-ambassador-withdraw.

Romania Insider. 2016. "Constitutional Court Asks EU Court of Justice for Opinion in Gay Couple vs. Romania Case." 30 November 2016. https://www.romania-insider.com/constitutional-court-asks-eu-court-justice-opinion-gay-couple-vs-romania-case.

Römer, Lutz. 2015. *Europäisierter und internationalisierter Verwaltungsrechtsschutz gegen Überstellungen nach der Dublin III-Verordnung* [Europeanized and internationalized administrative protection against transfers under the Dublin III Regulation]. Baden-Baden, Germany: Nomos.

Sánchez, S. Iglesias. 2009. "Free Movement of Third Country Nationals in the European Union? Main Features, Deficiencies and Challenges of the New Mobility Rights in the Area of Freedom, Security and Justice." *European Law Journal* 15 (6): 791–805.

Shaffer, Gregory. 2010. "Transnational Legal Process and State Change: Opportunities and Constraints." *Legal Studies Research Paper* No. 10-28. Minneapolis: University of Minnesota Law School.

Spijkerboer, Thomas. 2013. "Are European States Accountable for Border Deaths?" In *The Ashgate Research Companion to Migration Law, Theory and Policy*, ed. Satvinder S. Juss, 61–76. Farnham, UK: Ashgate.

Stavrou, Protesilaos. 2016. "Is the European Union Sovereign?" Protesilaos Stavrou (personal website), 20 November. Accessed 22 July 2019. https://protesilaos.com/eu-sovereignty.

Techau, Jan. 2016. "Four Predictions on the Future of Europe." Carnegie Europe, 12 January. http://carnegieeurope.eu/strategiceurope/?fa=62445.

ter Steeg, Marcus. 2006. *Das Einwanderungskonzept der EU—Zwischen politischen Anspruch, faktischen Regelungsbedürfnissen und den primärrechtlichen Grenzen in Titel IV des EG-Vertrages* [The EU's immigration concept—Between political claim, regulatory needs, and the primary law borders in Title IV of the EC Treaty]. Baden-Baden, Germany: Nomos.

Vickers, Lucy. 2017. "Achbita and Bougnaoui: One Step Forward and Two Steps Back for Religious Diversity in the Workplace." *European Labour Law Journal* 8 (3): 232–257.

Wesel, Barbara. 2017. "EU Countries Decline to Help Italy with Mediterranean Refugee Crisis." DW, 6 July 6. www.dw.com/en/eu-countries-decline-to-help-with-mediterranean-refugee-crisis/a-39585373.

Wouters, Jan, Luc Verhey, and Phillip Kiiver, eds. 2009. *European Constitutionalism Beyond Lisbon*. Antwerp, Belgium: Intersentia.

Zaun, Natasha. 2017. *EU Migration Policies: The Power of Strong Regulating States*. Houndmills, UK: Palgrave Macmillan.

CHAPTER 9

The Emergence of Digital Communities

Generating Trust, Managing Conflicts, and Regulating Globality . . . Digitality

Teresa Rodríguez-de-las-Heras Ballell

"Time" and "Space" Coordinates in the Law

Time and space have traditionally defined how states outline the confines of their sovereignty to produce, enact, and enforce their laws and regulations. Time and space constraints indeed help states determine their positions in the international scene. Therefore, the increasing globalization of economies and societies has challenged the space-based distribution of regulatory powers in an international context. Transnationality has required the articulation of new legal formulae, structures, methods, and strategies beyond state institutions, practices, and instruments. Legal harmonizing initiatives, promoted and hosted by international and multinational organizations, have tried to respond to an increasingly globalized society. But, despite some successful outcomes, they still represent a multinational approach to globality. Today, the extraordinary development of digital technologies has transformed globality into a new, more challenging version of transnationality: digitality, where the mere essence of transnationality dissolves in the no-border immensity of the digital world, where time and space limits dilute.

The development of digital technology is fascinating in its potential to change the temporal and spatial dimensions of social life (McLuhan 1964;

Myrowitz 1985). Digital technology has facilitated the emergence of a new world: the digital world. Today, our society can live in two worlds—one where spatial limits exist, another where they do not. The digital world has no spatial limits. As a result of a still unfinished process of digital migration, people can live today "in" the digital world (Rodríguez de las Heras Pérez 2004). With the release from spatial limits, the significance of time, too, changes. "Where" and "when" must be redefined to explain things that happen "in" the digital space. More precisely, digital technology creates its own "spaces" for social interaction and business activities. Contrary to common belief, the digital world is not an enormous open space hosting a single universal community. Rather, it is a "space of spaces" and a "community of communities." The digital world is today populated by digital communities. Interestingly, digital life represents a "return to communities," but communities are no longer associated with a certain and common "place." Digital life is then a return but also a new trajectory—to "no-place communities." As far as time, such no-place communities create their own memories—the external memories of the Internet. We are indeed creating a collective, inexhaustible, complete, and maybe, eternal, social memory.[1] Time is retained in memory— memory being the essence of digital time. In short, it is fair to say that the digital revolution has transformed our perception of time and our ways of being present (Strate 1999).

With regard to law, the answers to questions as to who regulates, and how, depend on how time and space are perceived and managed. Time-space patterns in this sense articulate regulation. When states became the principal regulatory actors, the identity of territory and population delimited the sphere of their sovereignty. Transnationality challenges the logic of domestic law and sovereignty conceived in those terms, as it disturbs the legal discourse by inserting a different spatial factor (see the chapters by Basaran and Valverde, in this volume). Legal solutions and structures have had to be devised to manage the complex relationships between national powers and transnational situations. Likewise, new regulatory actors, intended to represent a global, or at least multinational, community, were set up. Harmonization initiatives and unifying processes are attempts to respond to the needs of a globalized economy. However, national powers remain relevant actors; in fact, transnationality fundamentally assumes a nation-based system.

The protocols to negotiate and produce harmonizing instruments by the leading international organizations inevitably incorporate the factor of nation-states in practices, procedures, and structures. Even those formulating agencies that proudly count on technical working groups and rely on academics, experts, and specialized staff for the elaboration of draft texts, need to include intergovernmental participation in the process. The presence of states is undeniable even when it is invisible. Language, legal traditions, and culture filter negotiations, stances, and final solutions in international deliberations. Languages and legal cultures constitute to a certain extent disguised national powers. The use of official languages in each organization to conduct negotiations infuses a particular distribution of power among participating actors and represents a landscape of legal cultures in the selection of terms and concepts, the preference for certain legal solutions, or the determination of the style. Despite the most laudable efforts to create a real pluralism, it is not a genuine global conversation, it is a dialogue among legal cultures (the dominant ones? the most widespread ones?). Harmonization initiatives are commendable attempts to level the international orography and draw a common horizon for a global landscape. But they are still a multinational response to globality.

Today, the emergence of the digital world dilutes the sense of *nationality* and, hence, in its own terms, renders the concept of *transnationality* literally senseless. The digital era requires new actors, new processes, and new legal solutions to understand and regulate *digitality*. Digitality represents a disruptive conception of time-space patterns from the standpoint of the discourse of nations and transnationalism. It is infused by a genuine concept of globality, but requires a deep reconsideration of actors, processes, and structures. It is in this context that digital communities come to the fore.

This chapter explores the fascinating emergence of digital communities as lawmakers in the digital space. Digital communities represent a socially formulated organizational model that provides a practical bottom-to-top response to a legal problem on a trust-generating basis. The inability of legislative mechanisms to manage globality has been skillfully counteracted by the ability of a community-based social structure to internally regulate a complex scheme of relationships. Against such a backdrop, on the one hand, I ask whether digital communities succeed in replacing legislative actions in the managing of globality or are they simply complementing them or signaling areas to regulate and interests to protect for a subsequent regulatory action that formalizes or qualifies the self-regulation initiatives. On the other hand, I critically analyze how regulation is proposed, developed, and adopted within digital communities. My purpose is to verify whether self-regulatory initiatives are actually democratizing or merely reproducing existing power schemes.

Digital communities definitively uncouple culture from location and citizenship from sovereignty. Individuals enjoy free membership in communities of like-minded people they decide to join. Digital communities seem to embody an idyllic society where individuals freely choose the communities they wish to belong to, that they feel they belong to. Location no longer determines belonging to a society, subjugation to a state power, immersion in a particular cultural environment. Everything is based on free choice. Nonetheless, this utopian reading of digital communities is only partial, and, therefore, it is not fully accurate. On the one hand, digital communities have admission policies, and are free to deal or not to deal. They are not necessarily inclusive, egalitarian, or guided by fairness standards. On the other hand, digital communities are not always built as a large-scale projection of a collective identity. Their scale may depend more on the growing effect of the centripetal force of networks than on a real affinity among free users willing to set up a social utopia. Therefore, it is critical to understand how common will is formed in digital communities, how trust and reputation are generated, how law is created and how it is applied.

The chapter is structured as follows. The next section briefly describes the context by outlining the regulatory responses, first, to transnationality, and subsequently, given the unsuitability of traditional transnationality-managing solutions to emerging digital situations, to the challenges of globality, which are indeed the challenges of digitality. The regulatory needs of the digital world have not only led to the formulation of new rules and the implementation of new structures, but, particularly, to the emergence of new law-making actors: digital communities. Following that discussion, a further section is entirely devoted to understanding these digital communities from a legal perspective: participants, relations, organizational schemes, and the strategies they use to play their role in the law-making process. In the analysis of these digital communities that operate within electronic platforms, it is argued that they seek to emulate legal systems by replicating, on a contractual basis, regulatory powers, supervision schemes (penalty policies, reputational systems), and dispute resolution mechanisms. In the pursuit of setting up a "private legal system," digital communities perform varied roles in relation to domestic (or supranational) legislation. The observation of the market reveals three main functions of digital communities' rules: replacing, complementing, and signaling. The last section explains the three roles and summarizes my argument.

The Context: From Transnationality to Globality . . . to Digitality

The consolidation of the digital world has shaken the foundations of regulatory architecture. To understand this process and contextualize the emergence of digital communities as lawmakers (discussed below), I offer a brief overview of the various solutions formulated to manage transnationality to date.

Managing Transnationality

The explosion of world trade has long since proven the inadequacy of domestic rules, driving the transnational factor into the legal system. Law has dealt with transnationality in three main ways, progressively configured to handle transnationality: the conflict-of-law approach, the uniform-law approach, and self-regulation.

The conflict-of-law method provides a domestically oriented solution to govern transnational situations with domestic rules. By identifying relevant connecting factors, conflict-of-laws rules aim to distribute and allocate transnational situations among domestic jurisdictions. Effectively, a conflict-of-law approach questions neither national sovereignty nor the leading role of states in lawmaking. On the contrary, it perpetuates the nation-based fragmentation of the international regulatory panorama (see Brewster, this volume).

A conflict-of-law approach succeeds in providing a solution that is operative, workable, and self-contained. Nonetheless, conflict-of-law rules operate ex post, do not provide material solutions, and lead to the fiction of governing transnational conflicts with domestic rules. As a matter of fact, a conflict-of-law approach simply applies the logic of domestic legal systems to transnational contexts (Juenger 1995: 497; Schmitthoff 1968: 540–543). It reflects, in practice, a "nationalization" of transnational conflicts (see Shaffer and Gao, this volume). Hence, a conflict-of-law approach may lead to uncertain results as the applicable conflict rules, and therefore the subsequently referred substantive rules, depend on which court finally decides; therefore, rulings may differ (Lando 1984; Wengler 1990). The unpredictability of applicable law may become even more so due to the increasing trend to opt for flexible conflict-of-law rules prioritizing the criterion of proximity (closest links), which may supersede predetermined connecting factors. Likewise, conflict-of-law logic faces the problem that national legislation may lack specific rules suitable for international transactions or concepts involved in transnational disputes rooted in other jurisdictions (Goldstajn 1990). Therefore, the conflict-of law approach has had to be supplemented, and ameliorated, by the harmonization method.

At both the international and regional levels, formulating agencies (intergovernmental organizations, international organizations, regional integration organizations) have been founded and entrusted with the task of elaborating harmonizing instruments under a variety of forms and with diverse scope and legal effects (treaties and conventions, model laws, principles, legislative guides, uniform customs and practices) (for example, see Foblets and Alidadi, this volume). Fueled by delicate processes based on either consensus or majority rule, triggered by either political discussions or technical analysis, international and regional regulatory organizations produce a varied range of solutions to deal with the needs of an increasingly globalized society.

Unlike the conflict-of-law method, the harmonization method produces uniform law, provides material rules, and attains to the management of transnational conflicts with genuinely international rules (Mistelis 2001) that are intended to be "legal system-indifferent" (Grosheide 1994). Certainly, the production of uniform law has created a particular fabric of diplomatic relationships among states, resulting from a peculiar concept of international consensus, flowing through complex negotiation processes, and revealing a set of compromises, agreements, imbalances, and power disequilibria (Estrella Faria 2009). Uniform law is the product of a new order, rescales political and social relations, and, indeed, to a certain extent, detaches lawmaking from national powers.

Although the harmonization method represents a step forward in the ability to manage transnationality, the underlying process has not been free of criticism (e.g., it is a new form of legal imperialism; it is insensitive to legal traditions; and it represents an impoverishment of legal solutions, disregard of cultural identities, primacy of political compromises, imperfect multilingualism) (see Dimaggio and Powell 1983; MacDonald 2009; McCormack 2011).

In addition to the above-referred methods, market players have strongly and widely relied on self-regulation to manage their conflicts in transnational situations, aiming to fill gaps in the law, and protect their interests more efficiently. From *lex mercatoria* (Giardina 1993; Lagarde 1982) to modern codes of conduct, international players have developed their "private legal frameworks" by exercising their private autonomy with extensive and multipurpose use of contracts/agreements as a mechanism to manage their private interests. As a matter of fact, the common practice of drafting detailed and highly complete contracts is an attempt to reduce the need to refer to default applicable legislation (Gessner 1994) and seeks to produce a self-contained and self-sufficient contractual framework. In that regard, standard terms contracts play a remarkable role in the harmonization of international trade law (Schmitthoff 1968).

Hence, contracts represent the most extensive and efficient legal tool to reduce uncertainties in transnational situations and manage parties' interests and, also, to advance the progressive settlement of an increasingly uniform common playing field.

Facing Digitality

As the realities of trade have challenged the law to handle transnationality in new ways, the penetration of digital technology in social relations and economic transactions has entailed the emergence of a new globality. The advent and expansion of digital technology has led to the most fascinating and unique phenomenon in the history of humankind: Today, as noted at the outset, we live in two worlds. We should not overlook the extraordinary fact that we are the creators of this new emerging digital world. A fruitful combination of electronic means of communication and digital media drives the emergence of the digital space. Consequently, digital activities are not in essence "transnational" but authentically "global," or if preferred, "anational." Domestic schemes and national (or regional) borders no longer hold any relevance in the digital space.

Accurately, digital activities "take place in" the digital space. Possible connections to territorial factors may be irrelevant, confusing, or mostly artificial (i.e., nationality, location of parties, situation of technological systems, stream of commerce). As a consequence, globality, or maybe more precisely digitality, cannot be rightly managed by conflict-of-law rules. By contrast, the uniform-law approach does actually offer more suitable solutions to global situations, and, hence, it might be prepared to provide an optimal response to the challenges of digitality. Nevertheless, the harmonizing process is slow, complex, and, in most cases, partial. Reality moves rapidly forward. Not surprisingly, private players have quickly reacted to combat legislative paralysis, once again with self-regulation techniques.

Contracts play a crucial role in managing private interests. But digital technology adds an additional dimension to self-regulation schemes: the formation of digital communities. Far from the initial perception that the digital space was an open, standard, flat space, its evolution in recent years proves that value is created within and in relation to platforms, as closed environments subject to prior registration or admission. The digital space is then increasingly populated by digital communities (electronic markets, social networks, P2P systems, business communities, sharing-economy platforms). The digital space is today a "community of communities," a "market of markets," a "space of spaces" (Rodríguez de las Heras Ballell 2014b).

Digital communities have become pivotal actors in the making of law for the digital space. With a fascinating and flexible contract-based structure, digital communities seem to aspire to become, or at least to emulate, private legal systems and to replace national communities, which are no longer representative of people in the digital world. As further explained below, digital communities articulate internal processes and structures emulating regulatory power, supervision systems, sanctioning procedures, and dispute resolution methods. Digital communities produce global (anational, purely digital) law to govern "digital situations." Thus, digital communities smooth over uncertainties arising from legal divergences, inadequate conflict-of-law rules, and lack of uniform solution with a self-regulated legal framework.

The expansion of digital communities triggers a fascinating reflection on the relationship between culture, territory, and community. The digital space definitively delinks social scenarios from any territorial element. Location is not relevant any longer. Is culture still associated with community, even if it is a "no-place" community? Likewise, digital communities deactivate the role of the state in the formation and the legitimacy of a legal system. Is a no-state legal system still a legal system? Can we envision a future society with no-state citizens? Do digital communities create real citizens? Do they stoke feelings and sentiments of digital citizenship?

The New Actor: Digital Communities in a Platform Economy

Digital communities emerge, "live," and "grow up" on electronic platforms. The term *digital community* captures the social base of these new actors in the digital society, whereas the reference to *electronic platforms* describes the structural dimension supporting their creation and functioning. Digital communities are the social response to the transformation of the digital economy into a platform economy.

The Digital Economy as a Platform Economy

The digital economy is actually today a platform economy. Electronic platforms are the dominant organizational model (Malone 1987; Malone, Yates, and Benjamin 1987) for economic activities, social networking, and emerging businesses in today's digital society. Interestingly, the emergence and increasing popularity of disruptive models, such as a sharing-based economy, crowdfunding, or fintech variants, have not only been made possible but are also greatly stimulated by platform-based organizational solutions.[2] Platforms have also transformed social, political, public, and educational contexts, by offering participative and collaborative environments, creating new opportunities, facilitating the creation of communities, mobilizing resources and capital, and promoting innovation.

The prominent position held by electronic platforms in the digital economy is based on their ability to reduce uncertainties, create a trustworthy environment, and generate value by combining a technological and structural solution (they are closed electronic platforms) and a complex legal and organizational strategy (they are contract-based architectures).[3] Platform-based models offer a flexible organizational solution to overcome problems that derive from the specific nature of digital technologies: high uncertainty, low-confidence relationships, information asymmetries, substantial transactions costs (e.g., searching, negotiating, monitoring compliance, solving disputes), and parties' identification problems. Likewise, platform models provide a regulatory solution suitable for digital relations, disconnected from national factors.

The scaling-up presence of platforms in the digital economy and their growing market power has unveiled a visible disruptive effect in several sectors. Social, economic, and legal disruptions are perceptible, or certainly expected to explode soon. Their social and economic disrupting potential is clearly observed in the transformation of social relationships, market structures, and economic paradigms induced by platform-based emerging models (i.e., sharing-driven business models, fintech variants, crowdfunding). Along with these noticeable social and economic disruptions, the platform model is also proving to be legally disruptive. Platform operators' self-regulation power, the critical role they are likely to play (Kannan et al. 2000) in prevention and civil enforcement, and the trust-generating capacity of platforms in a digital society have started to strongly attract the interest of regulators and supervisors.

In such a disruptive context, a subtle, but irrefutable, emergence of digital communities as new regulatory actors is also perceptible, along with a progressive shift of certain roles from public bodies to private ones. The trend of considering entrusting electronic intermediaries (electronic platforms) with "first-line" civil prevention and enforcement illustrates such a displacement of power. Given the material and technical incapacity of states to prevent and control infringements and offenses in the digital world, regulators and supervisors are inclined to rely on the collaboration and support of electronic intermediaries and platforms as more efficient, proximate, and flexible actors for prevention and enforcement.

Unpacking Electronic Platforms: Elements and Relationships

An electronic platform is a multilateral, interactive, centralized technological infrastructure managed by a platform operator and self-regulated by its associated community. Self-regulation within a digital community is contract based. Contracts are powerful and flexible tools for generating trust, anticipating conflicts, providing working solutions, and managing interests. Hence, a private legal system for the community of users is appropriately built on a contract-based structure.

Platforms are run by operators whose main business activity is precisely to create, manage, regulate, and supervise (under the conditions and to the extent that the obligations laid down in the membership agreements state, as further explained below) a digital environment that enables users, depending on the type of platform, to interact, negotiate, conclude and perform transactions, or carry out other activities within and in relation to the relevant community. Therefore, the existence of a platform is based on the activities of an operator and a community of users. The identification of these two personal dimensions is crucial to framing a concept adequately distinct from other service-providing business models.

For the purposes of depicting a legal paradigm of platforms, it is essential to understand which relationships are established between the operator and the users and how this plurality of actors interacts. To that end, two relational dimensions have to be explained: a vertical dimension and a horizontal one. Under the vertical dimension, the operator and each user enter into an agreement (the membership agreement). This agreement sets out the rights and obligations of the parties: the operator (as service provider, regulator, supervisor) and the user as a member of the platform (registered user). By virtue of the vertical agreement, the operator defines, delimits the extent, and sets out the conditions regulating its role as a service provider (e.g., supplying comparison services, recommender systems, rating facilities, payment services, insurance, aggregating activities), as a (contractual) regulator (adopting rules for the platform), as a supervisor (monitoring users' activity and applying the Infringement and Penalty Policy), and/or even as a mediator or dispute resolution facilitator. Such a contractual framework shapes the platform business model, articulates governance standards, and deploys a business strategy. Hence, as further explained below, platforms may, to better deploy the business strategy, decide to decentralize the involvement of users in regulation activities, facilitate user-driven reputation systems, implement decentralized supervision mechanisms (report systems, take-down systems, complaint mechanisms), or opt for user-led models in any of the dimensions of the platform. Inevitably, we wonder whether this bundle of vertical agreements shapes a new form of social contract.

Under the horizontal dimension, users interact with each other to exchange information (digital content, reviews, opinion, ratings), negotiate, provide services, or conclude transactions of any nature within the platform and in accordance with internal policies (codes of conduct, rule books, market rules, negotiation policy, community rules). Users commit to abide by these internal policies, anytime they are in force, as per the membership agreement. Interaction among users within the platform is a conspicuous distinctive feature distinguishing platforms from other third-party service-provision schemes. The voluntary acceptance of the binding character of community rules reopens the classical conceptualization of the legitimacy and the enforceability of the law by conviction or by deterrence.

The two-tiered architecture of platforms reveals that, as a general rule, platform operators and platform users carry out different activities. In fact, the operator is engaged in managing and operating the platform and providing the services due as per the membership agreement, whereas platform users may carry out a variety of activities either for business purposes or for personal, family, or household ones, depending on the platform variant involved. Thus, in a social network, the operator provides a venue for users to interact socially and exchange information; in an electronic marketplace, the operator manages (and usually regulates, monitors, and supervises) an environment enabling users to negotiate and conclude transactions; or, finally, in an equity crowdfunding platform, the operator facilitates the publication of projects and crowdfunding campaigns and provides a marketlike environment for fundraising. In all these hypotheticals, the operator is not undertaking the activity that users are expected to carry out. Accordingly, any regulatory action affecting platforms ought to take into account as a general rule this initial and presumed division of activities: the operator is always engaged in a commercial activity, whereas users' activities can, depending on the characteristics of the platform, be for commercial purposes or noncommercial ones.[4]

In sum, platforms are two-tiered, multiparty models. On one tier, the platform operator manages the platform. On the other, the community of users exchanges messages integral to their relationship as a community. A platform-oriented understanding should acknowledge and duly deal with the complexity of the structure, the plurality of users, the sense of community, and the relevant roles of the operator in regulating, supervising, enforcing, and generating trust within the platform.

The Platform Operator

Electronic platforms are self-regulated communities managed by a platform operator. Some functions can be designed and implemented to operate on a decentralized basis, as further explained below; however, platforms are essentially centralized structures. The role of the platform operator is crucial to creating and maintaining a predictable, reliable, and trustworthy playing field. The scope and the extent of operator's functions are determined in each case by the membership agreement. When joining the platform, every user enters into an agreement with the operator. This is the membership agreement that operates as a kind of "social contract" intended to build a community. Subsequently, registered users negotiate and enter into contracts and social interactions among themselves according to the relevant internal policies (platform rules) that serve as the "legal system" for the community.

Rarely, the operator is an individual (sole trader), that is, a natural person. More frequently, the operator adopts any of the organizational forms, available in the jurisdiction where it is located, to run a business (these include corporations, incorporate joint-ventures, private companies, but also associations, cooperatives, or partnerships). Interestingly, those organizational forms entailing a distinct and separate legal personality are preferred. Accordingly, commercial companies and corporations are the most common operators.

Be that as it may, platform users can participate as members or managers of the operator. There is no legal objection to such participation, although concerns as to the neutrality of the operator and its ability to perform its functions on an independent basis may arise. As a matter of fact, should some (or all) users become members of the operator (partners or shareholders), the neutrality of its decisions as a regulator or as a supervisor in relation to the same users may be questioned and its attractiveness in the market may be reduced accordingly. Therefore, the structure of the operator has to be very carefully considered in the assessment of the impartiality of the community's powers, the perception of "fairness" of rules and decisions, the "voluntariness" of the compliance, and, therefore, the effectiveness of community law; and even, finally, the "democratic aspirations" of the digital community. Just as states are concerned about the perceptions and realities of their democratic institutions, digital communities, free from the ties of democracy, need to inspire trust and predictability.

The Role of Platform Operator: Service Provider, Regulator, Supervisor

In managing the platform, the operator provides added-value services, adopts rules, monitors compliance, and applies penalties in the case of a breach of internal rules by users. In sum, the operator acts as a service provider, a (contractual) regulator, and a (contractual) supervisor. The provision of services (payment management, insurance, inspection, rating, marketing) has a visible commercial impact, increasing the appeal of the offer in the market, fostering loyalty of users, and providing additional financial support. More fundamentally, the tasks involved in regulation and supervision are key for the creation and preservation of trust and the consolidation of an authentic social community. Such tasks include the following:

Provision of Services. Beyond basic services supporting the electronic trading infrastructure (*software*, security measures, information exchange) that any platform requires, the operator may enhance the commercial appeal of the platform by providing a range of various added-value services: payment services, rating, insurance, search and comparison, reputation system, certification, inspection, or logistic services. The provision of added-value services tends to increase users' loyalty (raising switching costs), impede full substitutability with competing offers, and favor integration (Bakos and Brynjolfsson 1997). Likewise, from a more social perspective, these services may be considered "public-service" equivalents carried out by the operator to reinforce the "sense of community."

Adoption of Platform Rules (Rule Book). Electronic platforms are self-regulated environments. As per the membership agreement, the operator is entitled to adopt rules in the form of eligibility requirements to access the platform, codes of conduct, negotiation standards, model contracts, performance conditions, and infringement and penalties policies. Community models significantly differ in the structure of the regulatory scheme. Whereas more community-oriented platforms tend to articulate participative regulation models and user-driven penalty policies, business-oriented platforms normally opt for centralized regulation and supervision models likely to generate a trustworthy and predictable context for transactions.

By accepting the membership agreement, each user makes the commitment to abide by in-force community rules and internal policies. Accordingly, when the user fails to act in accordance with community rules and policies, the operator is entitled to claim default remedies.

Yet, infringement and penalties policies must be carefully drafted to reflect penalties in terms of contractual remedies in case of nonperformance, such as exclusion from the platform as termination of the contract or a clause establishing a fine as a penalty.

Supervision and Monitoring: Infringement and Penalties Policy. As per the membership agreement, the operator is entitled (by right) but not obliged to monitor and supervise compliance with the relevant rules and policies by users, and to take reasonable measures accordingly. In practice, the supervision model is frequently based on a decentralized report system where users give notice to the operator when infringements are committed by other users (e.g., complaint-handling mechanisms, report systems, and notice and takedown systems). Users feel themselves part of a community where rights are acknowledged and protected.

Such a contractual infrastructure designs the liability regime and indeed allocates duties and liabilities between operators and platforms' members (Rodríguez de las Heras Ballell 2016). Since the liability exemption regime is based on a lack of knowledge and lack of control, it can be argued that operators manage to preserve their position by the right (but not by the obligation) to monitor and supervise so as to enhance confidence without exposing themselves to liability risks. Conversely, if the existence of internal monitoring systems increases the operator's risk exposure,[5] insofar as they prove the capacity to control and prevent illegal activities and content, platform operators would be reluctant to implement monitoring mechanisms as they would create a presumption of control.

The Users: Building a Community

The broad term of *users* describes all registered members of the platform irrespective of the specific positions (buyer/seller, lessor/lessee, licensor/licensee, investor/promoter, driver/passenger, writer/reader, prosumer) they may hold in the subsequent transactions to be concluded or the relations or interactions of any nature entered into within the platform.

From a legal viewpoint, every user is the counterpart of the platform operator in the membership agreement and, at the same time, a prospective contracting party in future market transactions in relation to other users. From a technical perspective, on registration, users are entitled to access the platform and enjoy the services in accordance with the respective user profile. In practice, by logging in with an activation key (password, username, electronic signature), the user is enabled to exercise rights and enjoy services in accordance with the contractual framework (membership agreement and service-provision agreements). User account keys serve as contract-based electronic signatures for the purposes of any action carried out within the electronic platform. It is commonplace that the platform operator acts to that end as a certification agency, issuing the keys; monitoring their use; and managing cancellation, expiration, and any further circumstances likely to affect the validity of the contractual electronic signature. Nevertheless, the issuance and the monitoring of the electronic signature can also be entrusted to a third certification agency. In the latter case, the function of controlling user access is, at least partially, outsourced.

On admission, registered users join the business community, strongly linked by their common compliance with platform policies (internal protocols, rule books, codes of conduct, market rules). It may be questioned whether the mere sharing of common rules, sometimes purely technical and operational, creates a real sense of membership and a genuine community. Even more, it might be posed whether digital communities are able to produce a differential culture.

Law-Making Process in the Digital Communities

In exercising the role of regulator, the platform operator adopts rules of varied nature to govern access, use of services, negotiation, conclusion and performance of transactions, community life, and the exchange of information within the platform (e.g., internal policies, rule books, codes of conduct) (Ramberg 2002). As per the membership agreement, users are to abide by the platform (community) rules anytime they are in force.

The most widely adopted model is the centralized regulatory one. Under such a model, the operator is empowered by users (as per the membership agreement) to freely adopt, modify, or amend rules to be in force on the platform, and the "contractual legitimacy" of the operator as a regulator is assumed. More exceptionally, however, users' involvement in the regulatory process may also be encouraged. To create a sense of community, a more participatory model might be designed. Users would be informed, consulted, or even called to vote in reform projects, amendments, or the enactment of new policies, in a move parallel to greater political participation in national jurisdictions.

Joining a Digital Community: Our Digital Presence

As the number of digital communities proliferates, we can see more and more clearly how important membership in certain communities is becoming for the full development of a digital life. Membership in digital communities is also becoming essential for the effective exercise of individual and social rights, including access to education, freedom of expression, access to information, sense of belonging, visibility of minorities, availability of cultural content, access to public services, citizenship, identity building. Digital presence is today not only an opportunity to build and expand one's identity but a necessity for personal development, social integration, and cultural and educational growth.

Despite the relevant social meanings of membership, the registration process for joining a digital community or an electronic platform, in general, is indeed a contract-formation process. Thus, acceptance or refusal to admit the applicant has to be interpreted within the rationale of contract formation. I here describe the registration process and translate the successive stages in the language of contract formation.

A standard membership/registration process in theory follows the following stages.

First, the operator, by posting its previously drafted and predisposed standard terms, invites potential users (individuals, entities, undertakings) wishing to join the electronic platform to make an offer. As a general rule, membership conditions are not negotiated but simply accepted or refused by the applicant on a take-it-or-leave-it basis. Membership is therefore an adhesion contract,[6] with standard terms.[7] Even in highly sophisticated B2B electronic platforms, applicants are unable to negotiate membership terms. The rationale behind this is always the same. The ultimate aim is to establish a level playing field on which members can interact, compete, and cooperate. Since the alternative of concluding a multilateral agreement among all members would be absolutely impracticable, a centralized structure is the feasible solution. A bundle of bilateral agreements is entered into between the platform operator and every member according to which the playing field is leveled, members commit to comply with common rules in their relationships with other members, and the platform is thereby entitled to regulate, supervise, and punish violations. Standard terms manage to rationalize the complexity (Alfaro Águila-Real 1991; Pagador López 1999; Rakoff 1983; Roppo

1975: 25–80) of underlying transactions and envisaged relationships that may develop in the platform. A standard-term contract is the legal solution to solve that need.

Second, consequently, users willing to join the platform do make an offer to the platform operator proposing to become a member and adding all data, information, and even documentation required by the platform for the purposes of assessing compliance with eligibility rules. In this regard, it is worth noting here that in highly specialized markets, applicants' conditions are decisive factors in admission decisions, and the operator commits to verifying that the applicant is eligible. Not surprisingly, in such cases, membership agreements are concluded on an *intuitu personae* (by reason of its strictly personal nature) basis. At the final stage of the registering process, the operator adopts the decision to admit or refuse the applicant according to the eligibility rules and, in general, the rule book. In some sophisticated markets, several different kinds of user profiles may be available to the applicant. Each user profile entitles the admitted applicant to access or use a set of predefined services. Therefore, the platform operator's decision can be an acceptance, a plain refusal, or a conditional admission, proposing to confer on the applicant a "lower" profile than the one requested.

The platform operator, when adopting the decision to admit or refuse the applicant's offer, is arguably exercising its right to choose its trading partners (members, users, market players) and freely establish the conditions under which it is willing to deal. Conversely, it might be argued that the platform operator's freedom to deal has some limits. Economic reasons based on market structure and competition conditions or legal arguments banning abuse of rights and any violation of fundamental rights set restrictions on the freedom to deal.

Insofar as the digital realm is turning into a "market of markets" and a "community of communities," belonging to a market or a community represents a vital decision for economic activities, social interaction, and personal development. From that perspective, limits on right of admission and refusal to deal merit consideration.

Since digital communities encompass electronic markets, social networks, P2P systems, and a variety of platforms, regardless of their purposes, different perspectives have to be adopted to tackle the problem of limits on refusing to deal. Whereas refusal to deal in electronic markets and trading systems may lead to anticompetitive situations, admission practices in social networks would more likely arouse constitutional concerns.

At the very outset, the development of digital communities was linked to B2B electronic markets. Hence, their expansion and penetration into the real economy initially drew the attention of competition authorities. The proliferation of e-markets, along with the centripetal force of network effects and the lock-in effect of switching costs, soon aroused antitrust concerns (Alese 2001; Bell and Adkinson 2000; Bloch and Perlman 2000; Blumenthal 2000; Doda 2001; Rodríguez de las Heras Ballell 2003; Sculley and Woods 2001; Vollebregt 2000). The establishment of an electronic market for a specific industry may represent a collusion practice, or an agreement among undertakings or be treated as a concentration.[8] As far as admission conditions are concerned, exclusive commitments and noncompete agreements, on the one hand, and exclusionary practices, on the other, can lead to anticompetitive situations. In particular, the refusal of a market operator to admit certain applicants on an arbitrary basis or systematic exclusionary practices may entail a significant competitive disadvantage and even result in a total exclusion from the market.[9] Insofar as economic activity and business transactions are more and more frequently and extensively developed in the digital space, the risk of being "cyberspace handicapped" becomes more real. In certain sectors, due to intense network effects, leading electronic markets can be deemed "essential facilities" (Díez Estella 2003; Gerber 1988; Piraino 1999; Pratt, Sonda, and Racanelli 1997).

Today, there are other aspects of electronic platforms to consider besides their effect on competition in the "market of markets." Since not only economic activities and business exchanges depend on electronic platforms, but social interaction, access to culture, expression of ideas, entertainment, and education are dependent on belonging to digital communities, refusal to deal is likely to create new legal concerns other than those pertaining to competition rules.

I contend that a multiapproach analysis is needed. Digital technology has not only radically changed the economic scenario but also profoundly reshaped the social fabric. Despite the fact that I firmly believe that digital technology opens fascinating opportunities for freedom of expression, education, culture, entertainment, political participation, and, in general, social development, access to digital infrastructure is absolutely decisive for those purposes. A high concentration of e-markets, arbitrary refusal to allow membership in communities, or a manipulative use of filters and notice-and-takedown procedures would be detrimental to participation.

Not surprisingly, competition rules are not enough to deal with all those issues. Constitutional principles have to be applied to *inter privatos* relationships. Private autonomy does exist in jurisdictions subject to certain limits that prevent an abusive, unreasonable or antisocial use and exercise of rights:[10] law, good morals, and public policy. Public policy would entail the framing of private autonomy within the constitutional order and an indirect application of constitutional principles to *inter privatos* relationships. At the same time, the exercise of the right to deal and not to deal has to abide by general principles of good faith and bans on abuse of rights.

Should it be accepted that digital communities represent new "places" for the development of social life, access to these platforms is absolutely crucial for the shaping of a digital society, the exercise of individual rights, and the promotion of democratic structures, participative processes, and nondiscriminatory opportunities.

Analysis: The Role of Digital Communities in Law Making

The incursion of digital communities in the law-making process reveals that traditional regulatory actors and existing legislative structures fail to effectively respond to digital challenges. Digital communities rely on contractual tools to devise a complex, self-regulated "legal system" within an electronic platform and intended to operate therein, trying to minimize recourse to the inadequate nation-based model. To that end, digital communities should be expected to maximize their autonomy from national jurisdictions and build, to the maximum extent, a self-sufficient "private legal system." Despite that goal, platforms' regulatory power is framed and, as a matter of law, legally rooted in the private autonomy enshrined in legal systems. In that regard, the validity and the enforceability of digital communities' rules depends on applicable legislation—either supranational instruments, if they exist and where applicable, or domestic laws as applied in accordance to conflict-of-law rules.

Hence, domestic legislation and communities' rules enter into a relation of mutual dependence. Communities' rules increase the effectiveness of the law in terms of proximity and adaptability, whereas the validity of this private legal system depends on the legal acknowledgment of private autonomy exercised within legal limits. Within such a mutual-dependence context, an analysis of the operating platform models leads us to identify three main roles of digital communities' rules in the law-making process, which actually reveal three ways of interacting with traditional regulatory actors and legislative products: replacing, complementing, and signaling.

First, digital communities' rules may try to replace, to the maximum possible, applicable legislation and national courts. With that purpose, the platform operator develops a complex, contract-based internal system aimed to emulate, and ultimately substitute for, applicable legal systems. As previously explained, these private regulatory systems count on regulatory processes, supervision methods, infringement and penalty policies, and dispute resolution mechanisms. The need to refer to applicable legislation and recourse to traditional jurisdiction is minimized to the utmost extent possible. This model of replacement is, nevertheless, fully feasible only in a scenario of B2B commercial transactions and outside of regulated sectors. B2B platforms, in all their models (business communities, electronic marketplaces, supply-chain systems), make the most of private autonomy potential, within the limits of binding law. To that extent, these platform-based models play a regulatory role aimed to replace traditional actors and regulatory structures in the law-making process for the digital world.

Second, digital communities try to complement applicable legal rules, where the private autonomy sphere is more limited. Platforms involving consumers (i.e., B2C markets) or running regulated activities illustrate such a complementing role. In these scenarios, communities' rules cannot replace applicable legislation to a large extent due to the binding character and the protecting nature of the rules. Therefore, digital communities adopt rules and policies aimed at supplementing applicable legislation with specific solutions that are well adapted and suitable for the community. The autonomy of the platform-based legal system is narrower, and the dependence on domestic (or supranational) legislation is unavoidably more intense.

Third, digital communities anticipate problems and solutions in emerging sectors, signaling to national regulators relevant issues to be tackled. Crowdfunding platforms or sharing-economy models illustrate the meaning of that signaling role. These disruptive models have irrupted in the market before any regulation has been adopted. Low or even nonexistent barriers to entry in digital markets facilitate the access to the market and give priority to self-regulation solutions. With their self-regulation strategy, these platforms have developed contractual frameworks to manage risks, reduce uncertainties, and protect interests. Their contractual solutions signal risks, conflicts, and interests to be safeguarded. Nevertheless, the imperative need to ensure the protection of general interests, to underpin the stability of the market, or to discourage unfair competition soon elicited public regulatory action on these emerging sectors. The expansive regulation on crowdfunding and the more erratic and uncertain regulatory actions on the sharing economy well illustrate this staggered process (European Commission 2016).[11] Digital communities face the challenges posed by emerging and unregulated activities with a self-regulation response. Consequently, national (or supranational) regulatory actors interpret the signal, recognize the risks, and learn which conflicts to tackle and how to deal with them. In that sense, communities' rules serve as "accrued regulatory experience" for public regulators.

The above-analyzed roles of digital communities in relation to law-making play out within the framework of private autonomy that is indeed recognized and enshrined by applicable legislation. But, the extraordinary expansion of digital communities and their proven ability to better manage digital conflicts seem to lead to a progressive surrender of public regulatory actors in the law-making terrain. There is a visible trend among regulators and supervisors toward relying more and more intensively and widely on platform operators to collaborate on prevention and civil enforcement as "firstline" actors. The question becomes unavoidable: Should platform operators be regulated, or does private autonomy suffice?

If the answer to that question is decided in favor of regulating platforms, three main policy alternatives should be considered.

First, a "continuist" approach from the perspective of the electronic commerce rules would make platform operators equal to intermediaries, with the consequent extension to the former of the liability regime of the latter. No general duty to monitor would be in any way imposed on platforms. Actual knowledge would still be the trigger for the platform to adopt adequate measures. In such a framework, the implementation of supervision mechanisms, report systems, complaint handling schemes, and other internal trust-generating techniques within the platform would be deemed as private systems to obtain actual knowledge.

Second, a "hybrid" approach would preserve the no-general-rule-to-monitor principle but could impose on platforms some duties to introduce adequate monitoring mechanisms and implement report and complaint-handling systems in accordance with predetermined governance standards.

Thus, although the operator would not be obliged to carry out a general obligation to monitor, it would take a preventive role by fulfilling governance decisions.

Third, a "disruptive" approach would lead to a departure from the path of the "safe harbor" scheme for intermediaries and direct the regulatory option toward the investing of platform operators with an active role in prevention and civil enforcement. Under this policy approach, prospective rules on platforms might impose on operators a duty to protect users in cases of actual and imminent threat and a duty to verify the authenticity or the truthfulness of the information provided by users, or, for instance, liability for providing misleading information, making mistakes, or even nonperformance of relevant services, under certain circumstances to be determined by the law.

Should platform operators be regulated, the specific policy approach adopted will be decisive for the development and sustainability of a digital society. So far, that is a digital society that seems to have decided to "return to communities."

The emergence of these digital communities and their extraordinary expansion seem to express a desire to escape from states that show weakness and the inability to face globality. Perhaps the success of digital communities reflects the failure of classical states. In this pessimistic reading of the role of states in our future, what form will democracy take? Is this escape in pursuit of democracy, or an escape from democracy itself? That question stirs a deeper reflection on the survival of democracy out of the parameters of the state. Is democracy necessarily linked to a state, or does it emerge from the community? It is not clear whether digital communities attract "citizens" in search of satisfying their democratic aspirations, which are presumably ignored by state powers. It seems to me that digital communities do not promise a democratic paradise in place of a supposedly failing state. Plurality and participation are not sufficient to ensure democracy. Democracy involves a political aspect that is not met simply by the freedom to choose, to deal or not to deal, in a market. Digital communities provide new scenarios to exercise rights that state sovereignty recognizes, protects, and enforces. The complementary theory seems preferable here. Digital communities should complement the law-making function of states and international organizations, perform their roles in rights protection and civil enforcement within the borders of state legal systems, and empower individuals to be good "citizens" in a globalized society.

Life can be now lived in different layers. That is the fascination that digital communities provoke. Our "space" to live is today wider, more varied, more different, and definitively released from place-time limits.

Notes

1. A fascinating debate has opened up, pitting the eternal persistence of "digital memory" against the right to be forgotten (see Mayer-Schönberger 2009; Pariser 2011; Rodríguez de las Heras Ballell 2009). The right to be forgotten has recently attracted great attention, partly because of several recent cases involving intermediary service providers (ISPs) that have reopened the need to seriously consider the interoperability of user privacy rules with the existing liability regime of electronic intermediaries. On 13 May 2014, the European Court of Justice issued a landmark ruling on the matter in *Google Spain SL Google Inc. v. Agencia Española de Protección de Datos (AEPD) and Mario Costeja González*, C-131/12, http://curia.europa.eu/juris /document/document_print.jsf?doclang=EN&docid=152065.

2. For a further analysis of the technological trigger as one of the three enablers of the current expansion of crowdfunding, see Rodríguez de las Heras Ballell (2013, 2014a).

3. For a thorough legal and business analysis of electronic platforms (e-marketplaces), see Rodríguez de las Heras Ballell (2006).

4. A collaborative economy challenges the classical conceptualization of trader and consumer (Smorto 2017: 13, 14, 18).

5. Or even if, as proposed, *de lege ferenda* a case should be made for a right or a duty of the platforms to monitor, Caroline Cauffman (2016: 240) states: "The 'passive' nature of the platform, which under the current system leads to the application of the hosting exemption, could as well be regarded as lax behavior justifying liability if things go wrong."

6. As it is traditionally recalled, the legal concept of *contrats d'adhésion* was formulated by R. Saleilles (1901), who defines them as those "dans lesquels il y a la prédominance exclusive d'une volonté, agissant comme volonté unilatérale, que dicte sa loi, à une collectivité indéterminée" (those where there is an exclusive predominance of one will, acting as a unilateral will, providing for its own rules, to be applicable to an undefined group). Such a definition based on procedural criteria, the act of adhesion, opened a famous dogmatic dispute among scholars about the most precise expression to describe the emerging phenomenon. In that regard, M. Georges Dereux (1910: 504) advocated instead for *contrat par adhésion*.

7. To meet the same needs of mass trade and production that standard terms were called to satisfy from the outset (Berlioz 1976).

8. The creation of *Covisint* in the car industry and *Volbroker (Deutsche Bank/UBS/Goldman Sachs/Citibank/JP Morgan/Natwest)* in the financial markets was analyzed as an agreement between undertakings under EU competition rules. In Europe, among others, the following cases were controlled as mergers under concentration regulations: *MyAircraft.com* COMP/M.1969 *UTC/Honeywell/i2/MyAircraft.com*, 4 August 2000, IP/00/912 in the aerospace industry; *Chemplorer* COMP/M.2096 *BAYER/Deutsche Telekom/Infraserv/JV*, 6 October 2000, IP/00/1131 in the chemical industry; *Cofunds* COMP/M.2075 *NEWHOUSE/Jupiter/SCUDDER/ M&G/JV*, 1 September 2000, IP/00/971, in the financial sector; *ec4ec* COMP/M.2172 *Babcock*

Borsig/MG Technologies/SAP Markets/JV, 7 November 2000, IP/00/1266; *Governet* COMP/M.2138, *SAP/Siemens/JV*, 2 October 2000, IP/00/1102; *Supralift* COMP/M.2398 *Linde/ Jungheinrich/JV*, 25 April 2001, IP/01/611; *Date AS* created by *Telenor Bedrift AS, Den Norske Bank ASA, ErgoGroup As* and *Accenture Technologies Venture BV*, IP/01/638.

9. The famous case of *Covisint*, under the scrutiny of antitrust authorities in the United States, Germany, and the EU, was finally authorized on the grounds that the market was proclaimed open to all sector players (IP/01/1155). Similarly, many competition concerns aroused by the market *Volbroker.com* were triggered by the initial declaration of the founders to refuse access to some competitors.

10. Legal systems define "abuse of rights" as an exercise of the right that crosses normal limits. Depending on legal traditions, normal exercise is defined as "reasonable," "social" or "nonabusive" exercise (Martín Bernal 1982: 66–95).

11. See the Austrian Federal Act on alternative means of financing (Alternative Financing Act-*Alternativfinanzierungsgesetz, AltFG*)—Obligations for issuing bodies as well as operators of Internet platforms ("crowdfunding") regarding the financing of terrorism (sec. 4, para. 5; and sec. 5 para. 1 [2]), *Federal Law Gazette*, vol. 1, no. 114/2015; French *Décret n° 2014-1053 du 16 septembre 2014 relatif au financement participatif*, JORF no. 0215 du 17 septembre 2014, page 15228, texte no. 11; German Small Investor Protection Act, *Kleinanlegerschutzgesetz, Budesgesetzbakatt Teil I*, 2015, no. 28, vom 09.07.2015; Italian Regolamento sulla raccolta di capitali di rischio da parte di start-up innovative tramite portali on-line, Delibera no. 18592, 26 June 2013, *Gazzetta Ufficiale* no. 162, 12 July 2013; Portugese Lei no. 102/2015 de 24 de agosto, *Regime jurídico do financiamento colaborativo, Diário da República*, 1 série, no. 164, 24 Auguts 2015; Spanish Business Finance Promotion Act, no. 5, 2015, *Ley 5/2015 de Fomento de la Financiación Empresarial*, in the *Official Bulletin* (BOE) 101, 28 April 2015 (LFFE 2015); United States Capital Raising Online While Deterring Fraud and Unethical Non-Disclosure Act of 2012, Pub. L. 112-106, Title III, 126 Stat. 318 (US Crowdfunding Act).

References

Alese, F. A. 2001. "B2B Exchanges and EC Competition Law: 2B or not 2B?" *European Competition Law Review* 22 (8): 325–330.

Alfaro Águila-Real, Jesús. 1991. *Las condiciones generales de la contratación* [Standard contract terms]. Madrid: Civitas.

Bakos, Yannis, and Brynjolfsson, Erik. 1997. "Organizational Partnerships and the Virtual Corporation." In *Information Technology and Industrial Competitiveness: How Information Technology Shapes Competition*, 1–17. London: Kluwer Academic.

Bell, Robert B., and William F. Adkinson Jr. 2000. "Antitrust Issues Raised by B2B Exchanges." *Antitrust* 15 (1): 18–24.

Berlioz, George. 1976. *Le contrat d'adhésion* [Contract of adhesion]. 2nd ed. Paris: LGDJ.

Bloch, R. E., and S. P. Perlman. 2000. "Analysis of Antitrust Issues Raised by B2B Exchanges: Practical Guidelines and Insights from the FTC B2B Workshop." *Antitrust Report* (September): 15–31.

Blumenthal, William. 2000. "B2B Internet Exchanges: The Antitrust Basics." *Antitrust Report* (May): 34–55.

Cauffman, Caroline. 2016. "The Commission's European Agenda for the Collaborative Economy—(Too) Platform and Service Provider Friendly?" *European Journal of Consumer and Market Law* 5 (6): 235–243.

Dereux, M. Georges. 1910. "De la nature juridique des contrats d'adhésion" [On the legal nature of contracts of adhesion]. *Revue Trimestrielle de Droit Civile* 9:503–541.

Díez Estella, Fernando. 2003. "La doctrina del abuso en los mercados conexos: del '*monopoly leveraging*' à las '*essential facilities*'" [The doctrine of abuse of related markets: From "monopoly leveraging" to "essential facilities"]. *RDM (Revista de Derecho Mercantil)* 248:555–604.

Dimaggio, Paul J., and Walter W. Powell 1983. "The Iron Cage Revisited: Institutional Isomorphism and Collective Rationality in Organizational Fields." *American Sociological Review* 48 (2): 147–160.

Doda, Daniel. 2001. "Antitrust Concerns in the B2B Marketplace: Are the 'Bricks and Mortar' Solid or a 'Virtual Haze'?" *William Mitchell Law Review* 27 (3): 1733–1759.

Estrella Faria, José Angelo. 2009. "Future Directions of Legal Harmonisation and Law Reform: Stormy Seas or Prosperous Voyage?" *Uniform Law Review* 14:5–34.

European Commission. 2016. "Communication from the Commission to the European Parliament, the Council, the European Economic and Social Committee and the Committee of the Regions: A European Agenda for the Collaborative Economy." Brussels, 2.6.2016 COM(2016) 356 final, SWD(2016) 184 final. https://ec.europa.eu/transparency/regdoc/rep/1/2016/EN/1-2016-356-EN-F1-1.PDF.

Gerber, D. J. 1988. "Rethinking the Monopolist's Duty to Deal: A Legal and Economic Critique of the Doctrine of 'Essential Facilities.'" *Virginia Law Review* 74:1069–1113.

Gessner, Volkmar. 1994. "Global Legal Interaction and Legal Cultures." *Ratio Iuris* 7:132–145.

Giardina, Andrea. 1993. "La Lex Mercatoria et la sécurité du commerce et des investissements internationaux" [Lex Mercatoria and legal certainty of international trade and investments]. In *Hommage à F. Rigaux*, 223–234. Brussels: Bruylant.

Goldstajn, Aleksandar. 1990. "Reflections on the Structure of the Modern Law of International Trade." In *International Contracts and Conflicts of Laws (A Collection of Essays)*, ed. Petar Sarcevic, 14–35. London, Boston: Graham and Trotman, Martinus Nijhoff.

Grosheide, F. W. 1994. "Legal Borrowing and Drafting International Commercial Contracts." In *Comparability and Evaluation: Essays on Comparative Law, Private International Law, and International Commercial Arbitration, in Honour of Dimitra Kokkini-Iatridou*, ed. Katharina Boele-Woelki, 69–83. The Hague: Kluwer.

Juenger, Friedrich K. 1995. "American Conflicts Scholarship and the New Law Merchant." *Vanderbilt Journal of Transnational Law* 28:487–501.

Kannan, P., P. K. Kannan, Ai-Mei Chang, and Andrew B. Whiston. 2000. "The Internet Information Market: The Emerging Role of Intermediaries." In *Handbook on Electronic Commerce*, ed. Michael Shaw, 569–590. Heidelberg, Germany: Springer.

Lagarde, Paul. 1982. "Approche critique de la lex mercatoria" [A critical approach to lex mercatoria]. In *Etudes offertes à B. Goldman*, 125–150. Paris: Litec.

Lando, Ole. 1984. "The Conflict of Laws of Contracts: General Principles." *Recueil des Cours* 189 (6): 227–447.

MacDonald, Roderick A. 2009. "Three Metaphors of Norm Migration in International Context." *Brooklyn Journal of International Law* 34 (3): 603–653.

Malone, Thomas W. 1987. "Modelling Coordination in Organizations and Markets." *Management Science* 33 (10): 1317–1332.

Malone, Thomas W., Yates, Jo A., and Benjamin, R. I. 1987. "Electronic Markets and Electronic Hierarchies." *Communications of the ACM* 30 (6): 484–497.

Martín Bernal, José Manuel. 1982. *El abuso del Derecho. (Exposición, descripción y valoración del mismo)* [The abuse of law. (Explanation, description, and assessment)]. Madrid: Montecorvo.

Mayer-Schönberger, Viktor. 2009. *Delete: The Virtue of Forgetting in the Digital Age.* Princeton, NJ: Princeton University Press.

McCormack, Gerard. 2011. *Secured Credit and the Harmonisation of Law: The UNCITRAL Experience.* Cheltenham, UK: Edward Elgar.

McLuhan, Marshall. 1964. *Understanding Media: The Extensions of Man.* New York: McGraw-Hill.

Mistelis, Loukas. 2001. "Is Harmonisation a Necessary Evil? The Future of Harmonisation and New Sources of International Trade Law." In *Foundations and Perspectives of International Trade Law*, eds. Ian F. Flechtner, Loukas Mistelis, and Marise Cremona, 3–27. London: Sweet & Maxwell.

Myrowitz, Joshua. 1985. *No Sense of Place: The Impact of Electronic Media on Social Behavior.* Oxford: Oxford University Press.

Pagador López, Javier. 1999. *Condiciones generales y cláusulas contractuales predispuestas: La ley de condiciones generales de la contratación* [Standard terms and non-negotiated contractual conditions: Standard terms act]. Madrid: Marcial Pons.

Pariser, Eli. 2011. *The Filter Bubble: How the New Personalized Web Is Changing What We Read and How We Think.* New York: Penguin.

Piraino, Thomas, Jr. 1999. "An Antitrust Remedy for Monopoly Leveraging by Electronic Networks." *Northwestern University Law Review* 93:1–63.

Pratt, W. H., James D. Sonda, and Mark A. Racanelli. 1997. "Refusals to Deal in the Context of Network Joint Ventures." *Business Lawyer* 52:531–558.

Rakoff, Todd D. 1983. "Contracts of Adhesion: An Essay in Reconstruction." *Harvard Law Review* 96: 1173–1284.

Ramberg, Christina. 2002. *Internet Marketplaces: The Law of Auctions and Exchanges On-line.* Oxford: Oxford University Press.

Rodríguez de las Heras Ballell, Teresa. 2003. "E-Marketplaces: La competencia entre mercados." *Gaceta Jurídica de la Unión Europea y de la Competencia* 228:53–64.

Rodríguez de las Heras Ballell, Teresa. 2006. *El régimen jurídico de los Mercados Electrónicos Cerrados (e-marketplaces)* [Legal regime of electronic marketplaces]. Madrid: Marcial Pons.

Rodríguez de las Heras Ballell, Teresa. 2009. "Legal Framework for Personalization-Based Business Models." In *Personalization of Interactive Multimedia Services: A Research and Development Perspective*, ed. Pazos-Arias, 3–24. New York: NOVA.

Rodríguez de las Heras Ballell, Teresa. 2013. "Modelos jurídicos para el *Crowdfunding*. Nuevas formas de financiación colectiva de proyectos" [Legal models for *Crowdfunding*. New methods to collectively finance projects]. *La Ley*, 28 May 2013, 1–4.

Rodríguez de las Heras Ballell, Teresa. 2014a. "El Crowdfunding como mecanismo alternativo de financiación de proyectos" [Crowdfunding as an alternative finance method for projects]. *Revista de Derecho Empresarial (REDEM)* 1:121–140.

Rodríguez de las Heras Ballell, Teresa. 2014b. "Refusal to Deal, Abuse of Rights and Competition Law in Electronic Markets and Digital Communities." *European Review of Private Law* 22 (5): 685–702.

Rodríguez de las Heras Ballell, Teresa. 2016. "La responsabilidad de las plataformas: Alcance, límites y estrategias" [Plataform liability: Scope, limits, and strategies]. In *Crowdfunding: Aspectos Legales* [Crowdfunding: Legal aspects], eds. Luis Cazorla and Enrique Moreno, 369–393. Cizur Menor, Spain: Aranzadi.

Rodríguez de las Heras Pérez, Antonio. 2004. "La migración digital" [Digital migration]. *TELOS: Cuadernos de comunicación, tecnología y sociedad* 61:4–6.

Roppo, Enzo. 1975. *Contratti Standard*. Milan: Giuffré.

Saleilles, R. 1901. *De la Déclaration de volonté. Contribution a l'étude de l'acte juridique dans le code civil allemand (art. 116–114)* [On the declaration of consent. Contribution to the study of legal act in the German Code]. Paris: F. Pichon Sucesseurs.

Schmitthoff, Clive M. 1968. "The Unification or Harmonisation of Law by Means of Standard Contracts and General Conditions." *International and Comparative Law Quarterly* 17 (3): 551–570.

Sculley, Arthur B., and Williams W. Woods. 2001. *B2B Exchanges: The Killer Application in the Business-to-Business Internet Revolution*. New York: Harper Business.

Smorto, Guido. 2017. *Critical Assessment of European Agenda for the Collaborative Economy*. IP/A/IMCO/2016-10, February. European Parliament, Committee on the Internal Market and Consumer Protection. Accessed 12 July 2019. http://www.europarl.europa.eu /studies.

Strate, Lance. 1999. "The Varieties of Cyberspace: Problems in Definition and Delimitation." *Western Journal of Communication* 63 (3): 382–412.

Vollebregt, Erik. 2000. "E-Hubs, Syndication and Competition Concerns." *ECLR* 21 (10): 437–443.

Wengler, W. 1990. "L'évolution moderne du droit international privé et la prévisibilité du droit applicable" [The modern evolution of private international law and the predictability of applicable legislation]. *Revue critique de droit international privé* 79:657–674.

CHAPTER 10

Landscapes of Actually Existing Liberalism

Some Thoughts on the Historical Dialectic of Liberty and Philanthropy

Mariana Valverde

This collection's exploration of some conceptual and empirical roots of current-day political and legal norms, myths, and emotions seeks to understand and diagnose transnational phenomena that press against and sometimes breach the boundaries of liberal democracy, particularly "populism," but other phenomena as well. In undertaking such explorations, this volume's initial refusal to hobble critical political-legal analysis by artificially separating the "domestic" from the "transnational" scale (see the Introduction) is a particularly fruitful methodological move. I am only one of many scholars who have recently experimented with multiscalar thinking, rejecting zero-sum views of jurisdiction and power in favor of concrete and dynamic analyses of how different forms of power-knowledge flow and ebb, accumulate, and change (see, e.g., Valverde 2015).

I contribute to this collective project by placing today's eruptions of illiberal political views not in the context of previous antiliberal traditions (fascism, communism, religion-based regimes) but rather in the context of the European/Western liberal mainstream. I do so without directly engaging with the history of liberal philosophy, as people such as John A. Hall (1987) and Charles Taylor (1989) do. Rather, adopting a loosely Foucaultian genealogical frame, I complicate the accepted abstract notion of "the" liberal subject by examining some of the unpredictable games of power and knowledge that make up "actually existing" liberalisms in specific contexts. In this matter

I am greatly inspired by the historical research on English practices of liberal governance carried out by Patrick Joyce in two books, one on actual liberalism at the urban scale and another covering the scale of the (British) state (Joyce 2003, 2013; see also Gunn and Vernon 2011).

In my account, as in these pioneering studies, nineteenth-century Britain figures prominently. However, my chapter is meant not as British intellectual history, but rather as a genealogy of certain liberal practices that flourished in Britain and its empire but were not confined to those spaces (or times). While I fully endorse Uday Mehta's (1999) influential claim that the liberalism of that time and place was thoroughly, not incidentally, imperialist, I also believe, and I do not think Mehta would disagree, that in the case of rationalities that were widely disseminated, my conclusions should be at least partially relevant elsewhere.

I approach the question of liberalism by focusing on a game of knowledge/power that has been noted by social and cultural historians but has not received attention from theorists: the historically shifting, somewhat but not completely dialectical relationships between liberty and philanthropy. And at the outset it must be noted that I use the term *philanthropy* not as it is used today, meaning charitable donations by the superwealthy, but in its nineteenth-century meaning. Contrary to the stereotype of the busybody lady charity visitor, nineteenth-century philanthropy was in fact a set of practices and mentalities of rule that sought to use modern organizational forms to address "social" issues at home and abroad. In the mid- and late nineteenth century, organized philanthropy's ambitious goal was to displace and replace older, religiously motivated, or purely customary local practices of charity with more rational, often data-driven efforts to provide efficient help in a way that would not undermine the wage labor imperative but rather supplement it, on a long-term basis. In this sense philanthropy complemented liberal political economy—and arguably undermined the potential for a socialist revolution in the UK and France.

The ambitious scientific goal of putting the relief of poverty on an organized and scientific basis was not rigorously pursued by all philanthropists, it must be recognized, or perhaps even by most of them. The Charity Organization Society, in Britain the leading advocate of rational calculation and efficiency in poverty relief, was widely ridiculed at the time for its lack of humanity. It is likely that most active members of most late-nineteenth-century British philanthropies were not rational calculators of the most efficient way of giving out help but were rather moved by a mixed bag of motives, from Christian charity through protofeminism to protosocialism. But nevertheless, analytically one can distinguish organized philanthropy from old-style charity, and it is the philanthropic tradition that has had, historically, a very close, if bumpy, relationship with liberalism's practices and ideals.

Historians have given us a wealth of knowledge about the governance of poverty and "misery" in the nineteenth century (especially in France, the UK, and the United States) and have explored, usually in case studies, the complex and constantly shifting relationship between projects designed to promote liberty and projects of a more or less clearly philanthropic or humanitarian bent. One recent addition to this vast literature, too vast to be referenced here, is Padraig Scanlan's detailed analysis of British West Africa just after the abolition of the slave trade in the British Empire. Scanlan shows that "antislavery," at the turn of the nineteenth century, was a very fuzzy ideal compatible with a wide array of economic and political practices, including many that depended on slave labor being performed just offstage (Scanlan 2017). To that extent Scanlan helps to deconstruct the binary opposition of liberty versus slavery that dominated antislavery discourse and imagery.

Numerous studies of nineteenth-century politics and culture similarly paint a complex picture of how the late-eighteenth-century ideals of liberty and equality fared over the course of the nineteenth century, and how people who we would call liberals (some of whom were Conservatives, such as British prime minister Benjamin Disraeli) tried to square those ideals with the emergence of seriously deprived urban and rural underclasses. Perhaps because most political and legal theorists do not read historical studies, the shifting relationship between liberty and philanthropy has not been considered theoretically significant.

To begin, then, *liberty*, like *democracy*, acquires effective meaning only in particular semiotic and sociocultural networks—that is, in relation to the converging or diverging political projects that situate *liberty* in concrete settings. As Martti Koskenniemi (2005) has eruditely shown, "pure" liberalism is—or would be, if it existed—an ethically empty, formalistic project. To counter the perpetual risk of ethical emptiness, many self-proclaimed liberal theorists have tried to provide some substantive ethical content for liberty claims. Today, multiculturalism is often deployed, in Europe as well as North America, to give liberalism some political and ethical content (Canadian thinkers Will Kymlicka and Charles Taylor being notable authors here). A different, historically very popular strategy to provide some ethical content for the otherwise empty project of personal autonomy has been for liberty seekers to take on a divided agenda, one that promotes liberty for people "like us," for fellow citizens, while demonstrating a strong benevolent interest in those Others who may or may not be suitable for liberty, but who are experiencing suffering that ought to be corrected. From the antislavery movement to today's gender-and-development NGOs, alleviating the suffering of Others has been important not only in the macrogovernance of inequality and poverty but also as an important, arguably constitutive technique of the Western liberal self (on techniques used to fabricate the liberal self, see, among others, Osborne 2011; Rose 1999; Valverde 1996a).

Liberty for "us" at home, as proclaimed in the mid-nineteenth century not only by John Stuart Mill but by the growing educated, often anticlerical, European liberal middle classes, risks falling into sheer selfishness. Some embraced that selfishness (e.g., Herbert Spencer), but many other "thought leaders" filled the ethical vacuum of "pure" liberalism with a profound concern for rescuing the unfortunate. Some did so by giving away money but also, and more importantly, by personally participating in the rescue of unfortunate Others, be they children working in coal mines in England or Africans being sold into slavery. (British prime minister Gladstone's forays into London slums to "rescue" fallen women is a notable case in point.) Despite this historical complementarity, an opposing dynamic, a persistent tension between liberty and philanthropy, has also been constitutive of liberal culture and the larger liberal ethos.

Rescuing Others, especially voiceless others, might be an important exercise of the rescuer's own liberty, insofar as it is a choice (and not a necessity, as paying taxes is). But philanthropic discourse and action also had (and still has) the effect of structurally reinforcing the passivity and subordinate status of the objects of philanthropy, whatever one's intentions might be. Didier Fassin (2012) has influentially argued that, regardless of the motivations or political views of individuals, organized humanitarianism (today's philanthropy) is necessarily implicated in structural inequalities. As Fassin shows with a variety of examples from both domestic French and transnational settings, major structural inequalities have to exist before one type of person/group/country can be interpellated as an aid giver, while another group (AIDS orphans in Africa; refugee claimants in Europe) is interpellated only as suffering victims. International aid, humanitarian armed intervention, and domestic and transnational philanthropy all presuppose structural inequalities, Fassin convincingly argues, and the actual work of "helping" Others can be said to reinforce that initial diagram of inequality. Humanitarian reason, Fassin concludes, is very different from the revolutionary ideals of equality and fraternity/solidarity, even if many of the people working in humanitarian organizations are sincerely attached to those equality ideals.

Putting Fassin's argument about the inequality inherent in humanitarian governance in conversation with literatures on populism and the crisis of liberalism today, we see that in the United States and the UK (and in other European countries), we are witnessing a curious and I believe unprecedented reversal of the subject-object, actor–acted upon binary of nineteenth-century liberalism. Today, white privileged leaders in the richest and best-armed nations on Earth are busy portraying their own people not as liberty-wielding citizens but as victims of collective historic injustices (see Brown 1995). The peoples of powerful states are construed by populist leaders (mainly of the Right, but occasionally also of the Left) as needing not more or a different kind of liberty, but rather a twenty-first-century Moses to come down from the mountain and deliver them from their collective suffering. That Brexit promoters portray the EU as having turned England into a "vassal" state, and Britons into the very slaves they once claimed to free, contrary to the lyrics of "Rule Britannia," is not an accident. Philanthropy has been turned inward, as it were.

The current reversal of the traditional split between liberal subjects and philanthropic objects—the endpoint of the genealogy I wish to trace here— is clearly visible in an important contemporary text, Donald Trump's inaugural address. Breaking with the "Morning in America" tradition of inaugural optimistic patriotism, most of Trump's time was devoted to painting an extremely dark picture of his country—one surely influenced by Steve Bannon's paranoid nationalism, but which also drew heavily on the Dickensian imagery that has since the days of Frederick Engels been a staple of left-wing critiques of capitalist market failures.

> For too long, a small group in our nation's capital has reaped the rewards of government, while the people have borne the cost. . . . The forgotten men and women in our country will be forgotten no longer. . . . Mothers and children [are] trapped in poverty in our inner cities; rusted-out factories [are] scattered like tombstones across the landscape. We've made other countries rich while the wealth, strength and confidence of our country has [sic] disappeared over the horizon.[1]

Trump's "darkest America" rhetoric (for an analysis of the predecessor, "Darkest England," see Valverde 1996b) performs a complete reversal of the traditional relationship between the civilized subjects of liberty and the Othered objects of philanthropy. White, nonelite male Americans, referenced in the "rusted-out factories" image, are portrayed not as active citizens of a republic, but as long-suffering victims who passively await deliverance. Their sad condition is said to have been brought about not by financial capitalism but by "a small group in our nation's capital," who, for unexplained reasons, have decided to sell the country to foreigners behind the people's back (with the anti-Semitic flavor of the anti-global-elite claim being perhaps unintended but certainly helpful to Trump, in the current US white nationalist context.)

African Americans, traditional American objects of both right-wing and left-wing philanthropy, make a cameo appearance as objects of the new philanthropic gaze—but only as "mothers and children," a phrase that to men of Trump's background connotes inherent helplessness. Adult African American males, for their part, are only visible in a brief invocation of "drugs" elsewhere in the speech. The implication is thus that African American males will continue to rot in prison, leaving it to Trump to save "inner-city," that is, African American, "mothers and children."

Invocations of historic injustice have long been the staple of those seeking liberty, from the Boston Tea Party and the French Revolution's attack on aristocratic privilege onward. In a different, more objectifying manner, vivid images of unjust suffering have also been the staple of those who offer philanthropic remedies. But in Trump's inaugural, "compassionate conservatism," the Republican word for philanthropy, is wholly absent. Also notable by its absence is the Tocquevillian spirit of self-help and civic republicanism that has historically overlapped a great deal with the American philanthropic tradition.

So pity replaces civic republicanism. But the pity evoked in the audience through "darkest America" imagery does not function as the premise for a philanthropic conclusion. The pity turns out to be self-pity. And since pity, unlike justice or, for that matter, liberty, doesn't connote much political agency, the only solution is a Moses-style savior: "I will fight for you with every breath in my body—and I will never, ever let you down. America will start winning again, winning like never before." The winning trope is at odds with biblical rhetoric, of course; but all leaders have their distinctive way of combining old tropes, and Trump's contribution to political rhetoric may be the unusual juxtaposition of hypermasculine, competitive, warlike boxing-ring imagery ("my nuclear button is bigger than his") with biblical tropes of collective deliverance. We see the uneasiness of the juxtaposition in the passage below. The conclusion of the speech begins with prophetic discourse ("a new decree to be heard in every city"), but then, very suddenly, the speech ends not with the redemption of the world but with the boxing-ring slogan "America first":

> We assembled here today are issuing a new decree to be heard in every city, in every foreign capital, and in every hall of power.
> From this day forward, a new vision will govern our land. From this moment on, it's going to be America First.

Contrary to the inaugural genre, the future does not play much of a role in the speech: the very dark vision of the rusted-out factories currently scattered like tombstones across the American landscape remains the only visually powerful image in the speech. And the landscape is to be magically transformed not by a new democratic process or even a new government but only through an individual, one who, in the best monarchical tradition of "the king's two bodies," is the body politic itself, not its temporary representative.

The British Conservative Party's discourse during the 2016 Brexit referendum and the June 2017 election campaign featured the same historic inversion of the philanthropic gaze. Britain, but especially England (since Scotland did not want to leave the EU), was frequently portrayed as a "vassal state," a hapless victim of evil Brussels bureaucrats. And the Conservative campaigns that constructed the main problem as one of Britain in general and England in particular having sunk from imperial power to lowly colony also featured an unusual personalization of the "rescue" operation supposed to deliver the (passive) people from their foreigner-caused ills. Against all parliamentary tradition, Theresa May, who had not even been elected prime minister, did not hesitate to paint the Conservative campaign bus with her own name in outsized letters, rather than with the party's election slogan. And as every political satirist pointed out, she responded to every media question by robotically repeating that Britain needed "strong, stable leadership," rather than providing any vision or indeed any content.

This personalization of the work of rescuing the oppressed from collective suffering is at odds with many American and British political and cultural traditions; the vast networks of nineteenth-century philanthropy, as we shall shortly see, differentiated themselves from charity precisely through formal organization, bureaucratic rules, structures of accountability, and clear policies. Committees and boards, newsletters and international conferences, large meetings of elected delegates run with parliamentary rules—those were the techniques of organized philanthropy, from international antislave trafficking campaigns to the transnational women's temperance movement.

Breaking both with the representative, individual-liberty affirming logic of democratic elections and with the bureaucratic but accountable forms of organized philanthropy, Trump's speech makes it clear that the people's power is to be operationalized only in the one act of sending Trump to the White House. There is no mention of popular participation in decision-making; and significantly, the Congress elected on the same day as Trump is wholly erased. The claim is that a single man can pull America from the pit of despair, Napoleon-like, and "make America great"—by virtue of his own prior greatness, one presumes, since no mechanisms of the US Constitution or democracy more generally are actually mentioned. Of course getting into the details of democratic elections would have been awkward, since the popular vote elected Hillary Clinton and not Trump as president; but the sacred doctrine of the separation of powers would have been a safe topic, since the Congress elected in 2016 was majority Republican.

Uncovering the substantive and rhetorical continuities linking Trump (and similar postliberal strongmen) with the fascists and populists of the 1930s, as many people are doing today, is of course important. However, we can shed new light on today's "right-wing populism" and other challenges to liberalism's heritage by seeing how elements that have long been mainstays or at least frequent companions of liberalism have been not so much rejected as rescaled to the point of inversion—in the case of Trump's inaugural and much Brexit discourse—by turning the philanthropic gaze away from the "wretched of the Earth" and inward, towards "us and people like us."

Interlude: There Is No Such Thing as a Free Liberal Subject

Taking the relationship between philanthropy and liberty as the main plot of this tale additionally helps to decenter an implicit assumption found in critical legal studies as well as among mainstream liberals, namely, that there is such a thing as "the" liberal subject. A brief consideration of this assumption and its consequences may be useful here, before we return to the substantive story of the game of philanthropy and liberty.

Left-wing critics of liberal legality have long pointed out that legal techniques and discourses associated with liberalism and Enlightenment tend to problematically posit a prelegal, more or less natural, isolated individual as the "subject" (in both senses of the word) of liberal legality. Highlighting the central role played by what political theorist C. B. McPherson ([1962] 1968) called "competitive individualism," seen as the natural state of humanity, has been fundamental to the rise of critical legal studies in all its forms. From classic Marxism, through the Critical Legal Studies authors of the 1970s and 1980s, to feminist relational legal theory—and, more recently, a range of work similarly critical of "the legal liberal subject" but drawing on postcolonial studies, queer theory, and more—"the liberal subject of law" has been critically analyzed at length (e.g., Brown and Halley 2002).

Reiterations of the Left critique of liberal legal subjectivity over the past few decades may have had the unintended effect of homogenizing and almost essentializing certain elements or versions of liberal legal subjectivity, obscuring important differences and even conflicts between the varied logics inherent in different practices associated with liberalism. Along with other historical sociologists, I argue that progressive sociolegal thought needs not better abstract definitions (of *liberty* or anything else) but rather concrete, nuanced, rich analyses of the rather different things that liberal legality has meant for subjectivity, in practice. Some of this work has been done for the history of the rational economic actor, the protagonist of economic liberalism, and work has also been done on the psychological and cultural dimensions of the "free" citizen of liberal democracies (Mary Poovey and Nikolas Rose being important authors in this regard). A full picture, however, remains to be finished.[2] Such a work would require a large transnational team of theorists, cultural historians, and legal scholars. In a short essay, one can only sketch the outlines of a not wholly coherent story featuring just a few of the many characters in the long-running and unfinished saga of liberal legality.[3]

Liberty and Philanthropy

One tradition that everyone would agree features centrally in any genealogy of existing liberalisms is that associated with *liberty*. Documenting the transnational genealogy of liberty would of course be a monumental task; but for present purposes I am selecting a few moments in the history of discursive and political moves that rely on invoking liberty, moments that can be used to shed light on the complex relationships between practices explicitly associated with liberty and the overlapping tradition of thought and action that I am calling *philanthropy/ humanitarianism*.[4]

After a short reflection on the invention of both liberty and philanthropy in the age of Voltaire, we focus on a key moment: the British Empire in the mid-Victorian period. Contrary to John Stuart Mill's view that missionaries and other philanthropists were puritanical conformists who threatened British liberty, we see that philanthropy had facets beyond puritanical repression, and played a key role in stabilizing market liberalism (see Dean 1991).

I then briefly discuss aspects of the urban philanthropy of the 1880s and 1890s (focusing on Britain). I show how the positive link between liberty and philanthropy that had been built in antislavery circles was weakened and destabilized late in the nineteenth century, as the denizens of the "urban jungle" at home came to be seen through the same highly objectifying lenses through which "darkest Africa" had come to be observed/imagined (Koven 2004; Valverde 1996b).

Skipping over many interesting historical conjunctures, including the very important optimistic postwar moment of decolonization and universal human rights, I then move back to the present, showing that current forms of regressive nationalism, instead of being compared to the fascism of the 1930s, might be understood by being placed in the historical context of the philanthropy-liberty relationship.

Inventing Liberty, Inventing Humanitarianism: Voltaire

In an important essay, cultural historian Thomas Laqueur (1989) argued that "the humanitarian narrative" is a genre that emerged in the mid- and late eighteenth century, not only in literary texts such as sentimental novels but also in non-fiction writings, especially in autopsies (or rather detailed accounts of autopsies) and in British parliamentary inquiries on children's labor in mines and factories. Suffering, more specifically unjust suffering, can be narrated as a tragedy, in which case it has a universal quality, like Greek or Shakespearean tragedies (this is my addition, not a point made by Laqueur). But unjust suffering can alternatively be narrated as a humanitarian tale. If the latter genre is chosen, then a great deal of detail is provided—details about suffering bodies, in particular, presented so as to provoke strong feelings in the bodies of the audience: "The humanitarian narrative relies on the personal body, not only as the locus of pain but also as the common bond between those who suffer and those who would help" (Laqueur 1989: 177; see also Fassin 2012: 83–106).

Details about bodily suffering inflicted on individuals would become the standard rhetorical trope of the antislavery movement; but many decades earlier, Voltaire used the same format to denounce the judicial torture of Jean Calas and launch an early strike in the battle to "humanize" the criminal justice system in Europe (Hunt 2004). Cesare Beccaria and other legal reformers picked up the baton later in the century to launch an all-Europe effort to "civilize" European law and justice, by inventing new state punishments that sought to replace bodily suffering with the deprivation of liberty and the micromanagement of the soul.

While Voltaire is mainly known as an early prophet of free speech, as Ingvild Hagen Kjorholt (2012) has shown, he also played a role in the proto-antislavery movement—"proto" in that the denunciation of slave owners' violence in his best-selling work *Candide* takes the form of criticism of Dutch slavery practices in Surinam, with no mention being made of French slavery in neighboring Haiti.

Voltaire provided many rhetorical resources for the philanthropic tradition—while also playing an equally important role in early "liberty" movements, particularly the then radical defense of free speech. How these two elements or drives interacted with one another cannot be fixed in a definite manner, since Voltaire was not a systematic philosopher but an engaged writer producing different texts for different purposes and audiences. But, if we look at Voltaire's successors, Enlightenment figures such as Diderot and Montesquieu (and Kant), we can say that the Enlightenment humanism that owed much to Voltaire contained not only faith in reason and a great desire for "liberty" (Hall 1987) but also a great passion for remedying suffering, especially suffering needlessly caused by human cruelty or ignorance. When Beccaria railed against the ignorance and barbarity that still marred European legal practices (recounting the details of horrific European physical punishments at length, in keeping with Laqueur's thesis), or when Kant drew a plan for a civic union of all nations on Earth, a union that would put an end to war and to the misery caused by militarism, in all these projects the cause of liberty was very closely intertwined with philanthropy—a philanthropy that, contrary to the older traditions of purely local charity, would take place both on the national stage and on the global scale. If liberty was born at two scales, the national and what was then called "universal" (as seen in the French 1789 Declaration of the rights of "man" as such, alongside the rights of citizens of France), so too philanthropy, unlike charity, was created simultaneously at the national and the global scales.

If liberty, as personal autonomy, is the destiny and the mission of humanity, as Kant and many others thought, so too "the humanitarian narrative" recounted by legal reformers and thinkers of the Enlightenment was also a global-scale project involving nothing less than leaving behind the stage of human evolution known as "barbarism"—the barbarism that Beccaria and Voltaire and Montesquieu showed was still thriving in the heart of late-eighteenth-century Europe. But the double liberty-humanness project could only be turned into law nationally, especially in constitutions and rights declarations. Transnational benevolence had few if any legal hooks; even the acknowledged horror of horrors, the transatlantic slave trade, could only be abolished, legally, in the British Empire.

It was only toward the end of the twentieth century that transnational "humanitarian intervention," backed by the quasilegal doctrine of the "responsibility to protect" and new notions about domestic courts claiming "universal jurisdiction," gave some reality to the universalizing reform ambitions of the Enlightenment—ambitions that waver between philanthropy and liberty and try to negate the tensions between the two projects.

John Stuart Mill: Liberty for Britain, Philanthropy for the Orient?

John Stuart Mill drastically rescaled liberty. Rejecting—without so much as an acknowledgment—the Kantian vision of a world league of nations built on the basis of a humanist universalist ethical fabric, Mill's political thought reduced the scope of "liberty" to the scale of the educated British adult.

Indeed, one of Mill's objections to Jeremy Bentham's version of utilitarianism was Bentham's universalism. Mill complained that Bentham's political plans "precluded from considering, except to a very limited extent, the laws of a country as an instrument of national culture" (Mill [1838] 1987: 164). Mill's famous invocation of "the harm principle" as an operationalization of liberty, in *On Liberty*, was by contrast very explicitly limited to his own "national culture" and perhaps similarly mature, civilized cultures:

It is, perhaps, hardly necessary to say that this doctrine [the harm principle] is meant to apply only to human beings in the maturity of their faculties. . . . Those who are still in a state to require being taken care of by others, must be protected against their actions as against external injury. For the same reasons, we may leave out of consideration those backward states of society in which the race itself may be considered in its nonage. . . . a [British] ruler full of the spirit of improvement is warranted in the use of any expedients that will attain an end, perhaps otherwise unattainable. Despotism is a legitimate mode of government in dealing with barbarians, provided the end be their improvement. (Mill [1859] 1975: 15–16)

On occasion Mill talks as if liberty were an end in itself for humanity as a whole, in keeping with the scalar thinking of the progressive Enlightenment; but reading the *On Liberty* essays as a whole, one sees that liberty for its own sake is in fact meant to be limited to a particular geographic/cultural space— Britain, or perhaps, at best, northern Europe. In the vast reaches of the British Empire, whose workings Mill knew intimately due to his thirty-five-year active participation in British rule in India, the true end of politics is not liberty but rather "improvement." And improvement, in the case of "backward" peoples, is likely to require external, imperial "despotism," as Mill [1861] (1975) argues at greater length in chapter 18 of *On Representative Government*.

Mill retains a very weak version of Enlightenment universalism, therefore, but his work, I would argue, sharply differentiates between a potential, far-off future of universal civilization and liberty (which is never described) and the urgent present-day need for cultivated, free Europeans to use despotism to rule Oriental cultures that have fallen into stagnation and conformity and thus cannot grow liberty on their own soil (see Mehta 1999).

The portrayal of Oriental decline as rooted in stagnation and a loss of the ability to innovate is closely connected to the passages in *On Liberty*, well known to criminal law scholars, where Mill waxes indignant about puritanical and moral-reform movements in Britain. In his view, philanthropists preaching temperance and imposing rigid Protestant morality intimidate or stifle those valiant English types who might otherwise become inventors, explorers, writers, and/or rulers of colonies. Unusually for the Victorian period, philanthropists are thus portrayed as enemies rather than companions of liberty. While the word *philanthropy* is not used, his denunciation of moralism would have had the effect, for his audience, of tarring all philanthropy with the same liberty-denying brush.

The figure of the free-born English man (or woman) actively defying convention and making their own moral decisions famously elaborated in Mill's liberty essays and reiterated in civil liberties and privacy law cases today is not at all independent from the spatiotemporality of imperial rule. Mill claims that the stifling of individual initiative and creativity that characterizes the nonstate social control that Victorian moralists wielded poses a major risk not only to the liberty of English men such as Mill himself but to the success of empire itself. It was brave, individualist men who built the British Empire, Mill states, and it is liberty-pursuing individuals who are now (in the 1860s) needed to ensure its continued success and dominance.

The specter of decline and imperial degeneration looms over the whole of *On Liberty* (though legal scholars generally ignore it, taking the harm principle out of its textual context). Missionaries are loudly denounced by Mill for their role in stifling liberty at home.[5] Philanthropy (reduced by Mill to a temperance-movement stereotype) unwittingly undermines empire by undercutting its subjective, domestic preconditions. Liberty is in part a good in itself; but it is also, perhaps most importantly, what educated English men need in order to innovatively and courageously explore and rule the empire. No doubt Mill would acknowledge that philanthropic endeavors to educate the "natives" of India and other colonies might be useful complements to empire, but only as long as the philanthropists did not curtail the independence of educated English men at home. If philanthropy has a role at all it is limited to the mission schools of the empire.

"Darkest England": The Remaking of British Philanthropy on the Domestic Scale

After the moral panic about urban industrial poverty that in the 1830s and 1840s led to the invention of public health medicine, child labor laws, and other social reforms including socialism, Britain went through a period of relative social and political peace. In the 1880s, however, a number of factors (economic and cultural) coincided to reignite middle- and upper-class fears about urban overcrowding, poor health, immorality, drunkenness, and loss of gender and family norms. As is well known, it was in these decades that a host of social reform movements were either invented or revived, from housing reform to labor laws. Organized philanthropy played a major role—alongside but more influentially than socialism—in the reforms that eventually led to Labour Party victories and the British welfare state.

That some of the most influential philanthropists, especially in the "university settlement" movement, were also important liberal thinkers is known (Koven 2004). But what I want to stress here is the way in which philanthropy at home, in the slums of London, acquired an oddly multiscalar character despite its very specific location—by being constantly analogized with imperial, specifically African, exploration. A key text was the Salvation Army's vivid and sensationalist tome *In Darkest England and the Way Out*, published in 1890, which drew very explicitly on the best-selling *In Darkest Africa*, by the explorer H. M. Stanley (Valverde 1996b).

Stanley was one of those imperial figures that, a couple of decades earlier, Mill feared were in decline. In his own account, he shows himself hacking his way through the tropical forest, not to Christianize the natives (barely described in a text that focuses more on vegetation than on humans) but rather to meet up, for no obvious reason, with the only other white man in central Africa, Dr. Livingstone. Stanley's focus on exploration and apparent lack of interest in philanthropy or any other social project did not deter his domestic Salvation Army plagiarists, however. The Salvation Army cleverly imported Stanley's vivid and widely disseminated imagery of rotting trees and dangerous swamps to spice up its accounts of urban vice and, indeed, to actually construct what came to be called "the slums."

While Stanley did not share Dr. Livingstone's missionary zeal, philanthropy nevertheless haunts his famous book in an unexpectedly secondhand way: His endless descriptions of the stifling African jungle draw very heavily on mid-Victorian Dickensian tropes of urban decay and degeneration. In a weirdly Freudian, much-repeated trope, Stanley deplores the fact that very tall, majestic, manly trees are falling down around him, to be engulfed by slimy swamps or invaded by nasty insect life. Elsewhere, trees that are not so majestic remind Stanley not of any British vegetation but of a group of British people probably more familiar from philanthropic writing than from his own experience, that is, the degenerate slum-dwellers of East London. Stanley writes that a particular stand of trees reminds him of "the human tide flowing into the city from London Bridge," "pale, overworked, dwarfed, stoop-shouldered" (quoted in Valverde 1996b: 503).

The intertextual movements visible here are dizzying. Stanley imports urban "slumming" tropes about overworked and degenerate British male workers into his account not of African cities (which he seems to have avoided) but of the African forest. For its part, the Salvation Army then used Stanley's exciting account of his explorations to spice up their first-hand descriptions of vice in British slums, descriptions that, absent the frisson of masculine imperial exploration, might not have appealed to the middle classes from which they sought financial support for their 'urban jungle' adventures. Strictly urban philanthropy, as practiced by the Salvation Army, could thus, through intertextuality, acquire an imperial aspect without losing its practical focus on British slums.

And what about liberty? Liberty was of little or no interest to either the Salvation Army or to Henry Stanley. As for the respectable, educated philanthropists of both sexes, who contributed heavily to the invention of sociology by means "slumming" (Heap 2009; Koven 2004), some of them, like T. H. Green, did think seriously about the relationship between liberty and poverty—but, perhaps because universal male suffrage had just been granted, and women's suffrage remained a minority interest, liberty did not figure very prominently in their vocabularies.

The torch of liberty, arguably, was most vigorously taken up at the end of the nineteenth century not by the explorers of either urban or African jungles but rather by small coteries of anarchists and socialists. They, however, profoundly resignified liberty by rescaling it at the level of "workers of the world." This rescaling implied, of course, a thorough rejection of Mill's vision of the educated British man or woman seeking liberty in the face of moral conformists; but it also broke in fundamental ways with Kantian universalism. The "human race" is indeed invoked in the refrain of the communist anthem, but the song makes it very clear that it is only the proletariat that will guide and free the human race.

At the end of the nineteenth century, then, the explosion of philanthropy (in missionary activity abroad as well as in urban reform at home) was but weakly linked to liberty, in sharp contrast to the situation in the late eighteenth century, when liberty and love of humanity to a large extent coincided, or at least were projects supported by the same kind of actor. There were some people in the late nineteenth century who tried to bring philanthropy and liberty together (in the UK, some of the Fabians and early democratic socialists); but overall, by the turn of the twentieth century, neither philanthropy nor socialism had much time for liberty.

Perhaps because of this historic break, liberty at the personal level could languish for a long while, being later in the twentieth century appropriated by liberal economics. Through economic theorist Friedrich von Hayek and others, liberty became linked not to the passion to relieve human suffering (as in Beccaria, Adam Smith, and the Scottish Enlightenment) but rather to the desire to be free from state control so as to maximize one's wealth and one's independence. The liberty of neoliberal economics would have been completely unrecognizable to the original apostles of liberty. For the humanists of the late eighteenth century, such as Beccaria, political liberty and economic freedom went hand in hand with strong "moral sentiments," with a passionate desire to relieve unjust suffering everywhere. The strong link between the desire for liberty and the passion for social reform was maintained and heightened, at the collective scale, in the national liberation struggles of the decolonization period; but personal liberty was detached from philanthropy in neoliberal economics.

The Uncertain Future of Liberty and Philanthropy

The vignettes in European intellectual and cultural history presented here, which have focused on changes in the relationship between liberty and philanthropy, might perhaps help to shed new light on the recent rise of white nationalist and related regressive discourses in the very places that gave birth both to liberty and to philanthropy.

As we saw in the initial discussion of Trump's inaugural speech, the claim that the most powerful nation on Earth has fallen into decadence through a combination of foreign machination and domestic feminized political correctness has its subjective correlate in Trump's constant complaints about being personally persecuted and maligned. But neither liberty nor philanthropy play much if any role in Trump's discourse of personal and national victimization.

The same unlikely rise of collective-victim political discourse is visible in Britain. Many UK political leaders appear willing to give up free trade with Europe (a liberal dream of British provenance if there ever was one) if that is the price to be paid for getting out from under the boot of the EU, imagined as a giant transnational bureaucracy that has destroyed the custom-based, purely national laws that are dear to the hearts of "free-born Englishmen" (Thompson 1966). Elsewhere in Europe, right-wing politicians instill nationalistic fear by noting that fertility among Muslim immigrants is higher than in the "native" population—as if today's Muslim immigrants were part of Suleiman the Magnificent's victorious army of centuries ago.

Collective victimism generally suggests that revenge is in order—not rational discussion among equal citizens (Brown 1995). The fact that leaders of many powerful countries in Europe now daily deploy a variety of narratives of collective victimhood is totally at odds with the liberty tradition: In the liberty tradition, citizenship equals independence and agency, not revenge for past real or imagined harms.

It is a sign of the times that we have to remind ourselves that the agency of the subjects of liberty was long imagined as generous. A century ago, reform-minded liberal Britons sought to break the chains of other people's slavery, showing through their humanitarianism that the liberal subject is not just an economically rational subject but is also an ethical subject. Many Britons today value and practice varieties of humanitarianism and posthumanitarian inclusionary politics, of course, as do many Americans; but those people, instead of being valued as moral leaders, are portrayed as "bleeding hearts" by the majoritarian right-wing forces that have come to claim liberty as theirs.

The rescaled liberty proclaimed by Mill, which features the civilized individual rather than humanity, and is suspicious of all organizations that would impose norms, has more resonance today than the original, generous, Enlightenment version. Edward Snowden has more than a few admirers in different political quarters, for example. But the constant repetition of the terms *security, risk,* and *emergency*—terms that Mill would barely have understood, despite his imperial fervor—has limited the scope and the strength of that liberty. Liberty is deployed by civil liberties lawyers, certainly, but more to restrain occasional egregious uses of state power than to mobilize peoples in favor of any overall positive vision of the future.

Meanwhile, the collective liberty claims of oppressed peoples, powerfully expressed in the post-1945 world by using the language of national liberation rather than individual liberty, have also lost much of their emotional and political appeal. The post-Yugoslavia and post-Arab Spring Euro-American disenchantment with national liberation projects has many roots, which obviously cannot be explored here, but we can say that today's cynicism about the progress of collective liberty abroad and the West's traditional responsibility to support it is matched by an equally deep level of skepticism about philanthropy. Foreign aid is no longer seen, in the United States and the UK especially, as a worthy object of state funding.

So if liberty is today at risk of being severed from humanitarianism and appropriated by right-wing libertarians, is the philanthropic tradition itself dead, other than the brave efforts made by civil society organizations such as Oxfam and Doctors Without Borders?

It would be foolish to try to diagnose the present in such general terms. But anyone familiar with the rhetorical strategies of classic nineteenth-century philanthropy, both in its earlier, Dickensian modalities and its later, more imperially inflected and sometimes paranoid versions, cannot but be struck by the way in which the philanthropic gaze is being directed inward, as it were, today. The paranoia seems on its surface quite bizarre; to give a personal anecdote, when right-wing white nationalists were chanting, in Charlottesville, "Jews shall not replace us," I could not help but remember that the one year I lived in Charlottesville I did not meet a single Jew. But self-pity seeps easily from one imaginary enemy to another, so it is not "the facts" that matter, it is the feeling of having been collectively victimized.

The sensationalist descriptions of suffering and injustice that in Voltaire's day gave rise to "the humanitarian narrative" (Laqueur 1989) are thus being revived and rescaled now for rather different, regressive nationalistic purposes. The primary objects of philanthropy now are neither pagans abroad nor slum-dwellers at home, but the very people who were once seen primarily as subjects of liberty. This reflexive reversal of the philanthropic gaze converges with the (domestic) legal reversal of constitutional or civil rights, whereby white men can claim to be the victims of racial and gender discrimination, in US courts especially.

If philanthropy, while alive and well in NGOs and community agencies, has simultaneously experienced a very odd turning inward of the European male gaze, in victimist nationalist discourse, what about the relationship between philanthropy and liberty?

On the political right, liberty is today usually counterposed to philanthropy/the welfare state; on the left, by contrast, freedom/human rights and a concern for relieving suffering through both voluntary efforts and by means of state laws go together. Neither side can claim to have the authoritative account—as has been shown, liberty and philanthropy were close siblings when they were invented but have diverged and converged on many occasions. It can be said that both liberty and philanthropy are capacious megasignifiers whose deep semantic and emotional resources can either reinforce each other or undermine each other; but both semantic-political-ethical traditions are important dimensions of the story of liberal modernity, and they have often been intertwined. That neither communist nor fascist regimes have had much if any time for either liberty or philanthropy underscores this point.

To conclude, then: If we want to understand not so much liberal political philosophy but rather actually existing liberal subjectivities and liberal practices, considering the sharp shifts in the relationship between liberty and philanthropy is instructive. Although liberty has always and still does have a close relationship with "equality," and whereas philanthropy can only exist in conditions of structural inequality (Fassin 2012), the two traditions, or the two "megasignifiers," if one prefers, can and do nevertheless actively support each other—in domestic social reform projects as among international NGOs. "Human rights," the key liberty project at the transnational scale today, was historically intertwined, in the post–World War II context, with humanitarian concerns for Jews, stateless people, and refugees, and these liberty-philanthropy connections are still deep today, in many quarters.

Whatever happens in the coming decades to the descendants and offshoots of eighteenth-century liberty and philanthropy, a more nuanced understanding of the complex genealogy of these two interrelated key projects of liberal modernity should be useful. This chapter is not such a genealogy, clearly, but it provides some signposts that may help future researchers to write a proper genealogy of the sometimes dialectical and sometimes undialectical relationship of liberty and philanthropy—and their offspring.

Notes

1. "The Inaugural Address," WhiteHouse.gov, 20 January 2017, accessed 11 July 2019, https://www.whitehouse.gov/briefings-statements/the-inaugural-address.

2. A major contribution toward this genealogy is Charles Taylor's old but still valuable *Sources of the Self* (1989). Taylor acknowledges the hugely important role played by what he calls "benevolence" in the formation of modern subjectivities, especially in the eighteenth century—and his account has informed mine. However, Taylor is tracing the history of philosophical notions, whether in "high" philosophy or in the broader public sphere, and so he does not distinguish between ideas about humans as naturally benevolent and the organized social practice that is philanthropy.

3. Many legal and cultural historians trace an almost unbroken line from Christianity and/or Greco-Roman philosophers all the way to the UN Declaration of Human Rights (Hunt [2007] is a notable example). This teleological bias has been challenged, but often by going to the other extreme and denying all path-dependence. An example of the latter move is Samuel Moyn's argument that today's international/humanitarian "human rights" have little to do with the "rights of man" of the late eighteenth century because the latter are national and the former, he claims, are international (Moyn 2010). This claim is conceptually as well as empirically problematic; few important legal-political notions are truly confined to one scale.

4. There are of course major differences between today's secular humanitarian NGOs and their nineteenth-century mainstream philanthropic ancestors, but there are also obvious

continuities, indicated among other things by the repeated use of phrases such as "modern slavery" and "human trafficking."

5. My argument here is very compatible with Koskenniemi's influential analysis of the fundamental dilemma of Mill-style liberty, namely that if liberty means that everyone is free to decide what counts as "flourishing," then liberty cannot be deployed as a principle to resolve social and political problems (Koskenniemi 2005: chap. 2).

References

Brown, Wendy. 1995. *States of Injury: Power and Freedom in Late Modernity.* Princeton, NJ: Princeton University Press.

Brown, Wendy, and Janet Halley. 2002. *Left Legalism, Left Critique.* Durham, NC: Duke University Press.

Dean, Mitchell. 1991. *The Constitution of Poverty: Toward a Genealogy of Liberal Governance.* London: Routledge.

Fassin, Didier. 2012. *Humanitarian Reason: A Moral History of the Present.* Trans. Rachel Gomme. Berkeley: University of California Press.

Gunn, Simon, and James Vernon, eds. 2011. *The Peculiarities of Liberal Modernity in Imperial Britain.* Berkeley: University of California Press.

Hall, John A. 1987. *Liberalism.* London: Paladin.

Heap, Chad. 2009. *Slumming: Sexual and Racial Encounters in American Nightlife 1885–1940.* Chicago: University of Chicago Press.

Hunt, Lynn. 2004. "The Eighteenth-Century Body and the Origins of Rights." *Diogenes* 203: 41–56.

Hunt, Lynn. 2007. *Inventing Human Rights: A History.* New York: W. W. Norton.

Joyce, Patrick. 2003. *The Rule of Freedom: Liberalism and the Modern City.* London: Verso.

Joyce, Patrick. 2013. *State of Freedom: A Social History of the British State Since 1800.* London: Verso.

Kjorholt, Ingvild Hagen. 2012. "Cosmopolitans, Slaves and the Global Market in Voltaire's *Candide.*" *Eighteenth Century Fiction* 25 (1): 61–84.

Koskenniemi, Martti. 2005. *From Apology to Utopia: The Structure of International Legal Argument.* Cambridge: Cambridge University Press.

Koven, Seth. 2004. *Slumming: Sexual and Social Politics in Victorian London.* Princeton, NJ: Princeton University Press.

Laqueur, Thomas. 1989. "Bodies, Details, and the Humanitarian Narrative." In *The New Cultural History,* ed. Lynn Hunt, 176–204. Berkeley: University of California Press.

McPherson, C. B. (1962) 1968. *The Political Theory of Possessive Individualism: From Hobbes to Locke.* Harmondsworth, UK: Penguin.

Mehta, Uday Singh. 1999. *Liberalism and Empire: A Study in Nineteenth-Century British Liberal Thought.* Chicago: University of Chicago Press.

Mill, John Stuart. (1838) 1987. *Utilitarianism and Other Essays.* Harmondsworth, UK: Penguin.

Mill, John Stuart. (1859) 1975. *On Liberty, in Three Essays.* Oxford: Oxford University Press.

Mill, John Stuart. (1861) 1975. *On Representative Government.* Oxford: Oxford University Press.

Moyn, Samuel. 2010. *The Last Utopia: Human Rights in History.* Cambridge: Cambridge University Press.

Osborne, Thomas. 2011. "Was There a Liberal Historicism?" In *The Peculiarities of Liberal Modernity in Imperial Britain*, eds. Simon Gunn and James Vernon, 91–101. Berkeley: University of California Press.

Rose, Nikolas. 1999. *Powers of Freedom: Reframing Political Thought.* Cambridge: Cambridge University Press.

Scanlan, Padraig. 2017. *Freedom's Debtors: British Antislavery in the Age of Revolution.* New Haven, CT: Yale University Press.

Taylor, Charles. 1989. *Sources of the Self: The Making of Modern Identity.* Cambridge, MA: Harvard University Press.

Thompson, E. P. 1966. "The Free-Born Englishman." In *The Making of the English Working Class*, 77–101. New York: Vintage.

Valverde, Mariana. 1996a. "'Despotism' and the Ethical Liberal Subject." *Economy and Society* 25 (3): 201–217.

Valverde, Mariana. 1996b. "The Dialectic of the Familiar and the Unfamiliar: 'The Jungle' in Early Slum Travel Writing." *Sociology* 30 (3): 493–509.

Valverde, Mariana. 2015. *Chronotopes of Law: Scale, Jurisdiction and Governance.* London: Routledge.

CONTRIBUTORS

Katayoun Alidadi Assistant professor of legal studies at Bryant University in Smithfield, Rhode Island, and a research partner at the Max Planck Institute for Social Anthropology in Halle, Germany.

Tugba Basaran Deputy director and senior researcher at the Centre for the Study of Global Human Movement at the University of Cambridge.

Rachel Brewster Professor of law and codirector of the Center for International and Comparative Law at Duke University Law School.

Sandra Brunnegger Official fellow in law and anthropology and lecturer at St Edmund's College, Cambridge.

Christina L. Davis Professor of government at Harvard University and Susan S. and Kenneth L. Wallach Professor at the Radcliffe Institute.

Sara Dezalay Senior lecturer in the Department of Politics and International Relations in the School of Law and Politics at Cardiff University.

Marie-Claire Foblets Director of the Department of Law and Anthropology at the Max Planck Institute for Social Anthropology in Halle/Saale, Germany, and professor of law at the Catholic University of Leuven, Belgium.

Henry Gao Associate professor of law at Singapore Management University and Dongfang Scholar Chair Professor at Shanghai University of International Business and Economics.

Carol J. Greenhouse Arthur W. Marks '19 Professor of Anthropology emeritus and former chair of the Anthropology Department at Princeton University.

David Leheny Professor in the Graduate School of Asia-Pacific Studies at Waseda University, Tokyo, Japan.

Mark Fathi Massoud   Associate professor of politics and director of legal studies at the University of California, Santa Cruz.

Teresa Rodríguez-de-las-Heras Ballell   Associate professor of commercial law at University Carlos III, Madrid, and member of the Expert Group to the EU Observatory on the Online Platform Economy.

Gregory Shaffer   Chancellor's Professor of Law at the University of California, Irvine School of Law, and director of the Center on Globalization, Law, and Society (GLAS).

Mariana Valverde   Director and professor in the Centre for Criminology and Sociolegal Studies at the University of Toronto.

INDEX

"abuse of rights," defined, 274n10
academia, WTO studied in, 74–79
accession protocol, China and WTO, 66–67, 68, 69
Access to Justice Program (AJP, USAID), 206, 208
Achbita, Samira, 236
Achbita v. G4S Secure Solutions NV (CJEU case, 2017), 235–236, 244n45
Afghanistan, 221
Africa, 97–126, 292–293; mining in, 97–99, 100–102, 121, 123; "resource curse," 97, 99, 120, 123. *See also* international NGOs in South Sudan, bureaucratization of activism within; Paris, France, Africa Bar in
Africa Bar. *See* Paris, France, Africa Bar in
African Americans, liberalism and, 283
African Development Bank, 110
African Legal Support Facility (Abidjan), 110, 119, 124
Agboyibo, Yawovi, 105
Agboyibor, Pascal, 105–106, 117, 119–120, 124n4, 125n10
airports, waiting zones, 23, 24, 31–32
Alidadi, Katayoun, 16, 17, 18
AllBright (law firm), 82
alternative dispute resolution (ADR), 206
American Foreign Corrupt Practices Act (FCPA), 37
Amuur siblings, 23, 24, 29–30, 31–32
Amuur v. France (ECtHR, 1996), 23, 24, 29
anthropology and anthropologists: culture, concept of, 5, 7; legal studies and practice, 11, 12, 14, 196; liberalism and, 17; NGO studies, 161, 162; state practices and, 17, 27, 196

anticorruption law, 6; as economic issue, 37, 41, 45, 49–50; enforcement of, 37, 38, 39–41, 42, 53–57, 58, 59; fragmentation and, 49–53; as national security issue, 37, 39, 49–50. *See also* international trade law, anticorruption law and
antidumping law, 81–82, 83, 84, 91n45
Antidumping Law and Practice of China (Wu), 81
asylum law, 23, 24, 219, 221–225, 241nn13–14
Australia, 201

B2B electronic markets, 268, 270
Bank for Reconstruction and Development (World Bank), 42
Bannon, Steve, 282
Barbé, Marc, 104
Barnes, Julian, 150
Basaran, Tugba, 14, 17
BCTG et Associés (French corporate law firm), 104
Beccaria, Cesare, 288, 289, 294
Belgium, 230, 231, 232, 236, 241n13
Bentham, Jeremy, 289
Berne Convention (1886), 47
bilateral investment treaty (BIT) negotiations, 83
Bolloré, Vincent, 107
borders and boundaries: law's effect on shifting, 24, 25, 27, 33–34; refugee status and, 23, 29–30; territory, physical *vs.* legal, 24–28, 29, 30, 33–34. *See also* scalar classifications
Bougnaoui v. Micropole SA (CJEU case, 2017), 235–237
Bourdon, William, 103–105, 117, 124n4
Bourgi, Robert, 107–108
Bozizé, François, 108

Brazil, 48, 49, 57, 161

Brewster, Rachel, 6, 17

Brexit, 9, 217, 237–238, 244n42, 285

bribery: definition, under FCPA, 44; tax-deductible, 39, 51. *See also* anticorruption law

Bridges (ICTSD periodical), 78

Britain: Brexit and, 9, 217, 237–238, 244n42, 285; liberalism in, 279, 284, 285, 289, 290, 291, 294. *See also* United Kingdom (UK)

British Commonwealth, 42

British Conservative Party, 284

British Empire, 287

Brunnegger, Sandra, 6, 16

Bulgaria, 231

Bush, George W., 137, 142

Calas, John, 288

Canada, 54

Candide (Voltaire), 288

Casas de Justicia (Houses of Justice, Colombia), 206–207, 212n8

Central Committee of the Communist Party of China (CPC), 71

Chaplin, Robert, 148–149

charged processes, of nationalization and denationalization, 13

charity, 279–280. *See also* liberty and philanthropy, liberalism and

Charity Organization Society (Britain), 279

Charter of Fundamental Rights of the EU, 234, 243n41

Chen An, 77

Chihaya (Japanese MSDF ship), 147

China, 53, 57, 67, 97; GATT and, 66, 89n3

China (Shanghai) Pilot Free Trade Zone (SPFTZ), 74, 90n20

China, WTO membership of, 6, 64–92; academic legal study, 74–79; accession protocol, 66–67, 68, 69; challenges in joining, 66–71; Chinese citizens' attitudes about, 73–74, 87–88, 90n6; Chinese companies' and trade associations' engagements with trade law, 84–87; domestic legal capacity and policy development, 65, 68–70, 70–74; EU and, 67, 70, 82, 89; global market economy integration, goal of, 65, 67, 68; industry associations and, 85–87; private law firms' involvement, 79–84, 91n33, 91n48;

research methods for study, 65–66; trade bar development, 80–82; trade barriers prior to, 84–85; United States and, 67, 69, 70, 74, 82, 89, 92n56. *See also* Ministry of Commerce, China (MOFCOM); World Trade Organization (WTO), dispute resolution, China and

China–Auto Parts case (WTO dispute, 2006), 70

China Law Society, 77

China–Rare Earths (WTO case), 88, 91n33

China–Raw Materials (WTO case), 88

China Society for World Trade Organization Studies (MOFCOM), 77

China Youth Daily (newspaper), 80

Chinese Society of International Economic Law (CSIEL), 77

Chirac, Jacques, 107

civic republicanism, 283

civil union law, 231. *See also* same-sex marriage

CJEU. *See* Court of Justice of the European Union (CJEU)

Cleary Gottlieb Steen & Hamilton (US corporate law firm), 118

Clifford Chance Europe LLP (UK corporate law firm), 118

Clinton, Bill, 140

Clinton, Hillary, 285

Clinton administration, 52

Coast Guard, US and Japan, compared, 149–150

Cohen, Richard, 137

Cold War, 115–116

collective-victim political discourse, 282, 284, 294–295, 296

Colombia, indigenous-state relations in, 6, 192–212; ambiguity, deliberate perpetuation of, 203–205, 212n6; Constitutional Court's *tutela* decisions, 196–197, 210; coordination law, absence of, 195, 196–197, 199–200, 203–205, 210; decentralization and, 195, 203; funding organizations and, 192, 193, 194, 197, 199–200, 203–210, 211; indigenous leaders in, 197–202; indigenous legal systems, constitutional recognition of (Article 246), 193–194, 195–198, 201, 210, 246; indigenous legal systems, plurality of, 199; informal pragmatism surrounding, 202–203;

maxim of strengthening, then coordination, 200–202; roles and goals of organizations, 205–209; "rule of law" programs, 207, 212n10; state sovereignty and, 194, 196, 197, 204, 207, 209, 212n10; USAID and, 194, 197, 205–208

colonialism, 99, 110–111, 122–123, 280; decolonization, 115–117; neocolonialism, 98, 125n11

Coman, Adrian, 232–233

Coman, Camelia, 232

Coman and others (CJEU case, 2018), 231–233, 243n36

Comaroff, Jean, 203–204, 212n7

Comaroff, John, 203–204, 212n7

Comité Catholique contre la Faim (CCFD), 117

Common European Asylum System, 221

"compassionate conservatism," 283

"competitive individualism," 286

conflict and postconflict settings. *See* international NGOs in South Sudan, bureaucratization of activism within

conflict-of-law regulatory approach, 269; to digitality, 257; to transnationality, 254–255

Conflict of Laws, 229

conflict resolution. *See* dispute resolution

"CONNEX Initiative," 110, 119, 124

contracts, digitality and, 257, 262, 264–265, 267, 270, 271; *contrats d'adhésion* concept, 273n6; self-regulation, 259. *See also* digital communities, legislation and regulation of and within

Cooper, Frederick, 123

coordination law, Colombia, 195, 196–197, 199–200, 203–205, 210

corporate crimes, criminalization of, 103–104

corporate legal globalization, in Africa. *See* Paris, France, Africa Bar in

Corporate Social Responsibility Committee (American Bar Association), 109

corporations, legal status of, 54

corruption. *See* anticorruption law; international trade law, anticorruption law and

Coudert Brothers (US corporate law firm), 112, 131

Council Directive 2003/109/EC (LTR Directive), 225–229

Council of Europe (human rights organization), 234

Court of Justice of the European Union (CJEU), 220, 222, 224; asylum law and, 241n13; *Coman* case, 231–233, 243n36; free movement for TCNs and, 226; human rights cases and, 234–237; same-sex marriage and, 231–232, 233, 243n36. *See also* European Court of Human Rights (ECtHR); European Union (EU)

criminal prosecution. *See* dispute resolution; international trade law, anticorruption law and

cultural collectivity, 5–6

culture, 7–9, 10–11, 16; concept defined, 5, 7; digital communities and, 253, 257

Czech Republic, 231

"darkest America" rhetoric, 282–283

decentralization, 195, 203

decolonization, 115–117

De Gaulle, Charles, 116

Deltour, Antoine, 103

Democratic Republic of Congo, 121

democratization projects, 195

Den Hideo, 137–138, 140, 141

Denmark, 226

Department of Justice (US), 40

Department of Treaty and Law (DTL) (China MOFCOM), 72, 78, 81, 82–83. *See also* Ministry of Commerce, China (MOFCOM)

Department of WTO Affairs (China), 71–72

Diderot, Denis, 288

digital communities, legislation and regulation of and within, 250–274; B2B electronic markets, 268, 270; conflict-of-law rules, 257; dispute resolution and, 253, 257, 260, 270, 271; domestic legislation and, 253–254, 269–270; globality and, 250, 252–253, 256–257; harmonization initiatives in, 251–252, 255–256, 257; law-making processes, 252, 257–258, 265, 269–273; regulatory responses, 253, 256–258, 265, 269–273; self-regulation, 252–254, 256, 257, 259, 261, 263, 269, 270–271; time and space variables changed by, 250–254, 257–258, 273n1; transnationality and, 250, 251,

digital communities (continued)
252, 253–256; uniform-law rules, 254,
255, 257. *See also* contracts, digitality and;
electronic platforms
discrimination law, 230–231, 233, 236–237;
nondiscrimination principles of GATT,
42–43; nondiscrimination rules of WTO,
42–43, 53. *See also* same-sex marriage
dispute resolution, 45–47, 106, 229, 255, 256;
ADR, 206; Africa Bar and, 116, 117, 119,
124n4; in Colombia, 198, 206; within
digital communities, 253, 257, 260, 270,
271; GATT and, 51, 52; humanitarian aid
in South Sudan and, 166–172; ITO and,
42; in Japan, 133–136; OECD and, 55;
transnational legal ordering and, 64.
See also conflict-of-law regulatory
approach; World Trade Organization
(WTO), dispute resolution, China and
"Dispute Resolution in Contemporary
Japan" (Kawashima), 133–134
disruptive economic models, 258, 259,
270, 272
domestic legislation: China and WTO,
policy development and, 65, 68–70,
70–74; digital communities and, 253–254,
269–270; EU Member States and, 216
domestic political organizing: humanitarian
intervention weakens, 161; transnationality regulation and, 254. *See also* European
Union Member States
Dominic (youth activist and NGO program
manager), 157
Dossou-Aworet, Samuel, 107, 108–109
DTL (Department of Treaty and Law)
(China MOFCOM), 72, 78, 81, 82–83
Dublin system for asylum seekers, 223–224,
241n13
Duncan Allen & Mitchell (US corporate law
firm), 111

economics, anticorruption law as issue of,
37, 41, 45, 49–50
Economy and Society (Weber), 157
ECtHR. *See* European Court of Human
Rights (ECtHR)
Edelman, Lauren B., 162
"effective sovereignty," 27
Ehime Maru (Japanese fisheries training
boat) incident, 131–154; apologies after,

137, 151, 152; closure and, 150–151;
description of events, 141–143; Japanese
demands following, 137, 140–141;
jurisdiction questions, 132–133, 132–133;
language of accountability/generosity,
150; media coverage of, 136; Mori and,
136, 136, 154n3, 154n3; national culture
and, 131–132, 134, 137–139, 149; victims'
bodies, recovering, 136, 137, 139–141,
144–149, 153. *See also* Japan; United
States and Japan; Waddle, Scott
elastic scales, 31–32. *See also* scalar
classifications
electronic platforms, 257, 258–272;
disruptive models, 258, 259, 270. *See also*
digital communities, legislation and
regulation of and within
electronic platforms, operators, 259–268,
270–272; admissions oversight by, 266,
267, 268; penalty oversight by, 260,
263–264; roles of, 259–260, 261–264;
user-operator relationship, 260–261,
262, 263–264, 266–267
electronic platforms, users, 253, 259–267,
272; interactions with other, 260–261,
264–265; membership agreements for,
260–261, 262, 263–264, 266–267
Engels, Frederick, 282
England. *See* Britain
Escuela Judicial Rodrigo Lara Bonilla
(Rodrigo Lara Bonilla School for the
Judiciary), 192–193, 198, 204–205
ethnography, 14–15
European Commission, 217–218
European Community, 42; GATT and, 49,
52, 60n4; transnationalization as open
process, 217–219; TRIPS Agreement and,
48–49
European Convention, 220, 244n42
European Convention on Human Rights,
220, 234, 243n39
European Council, 228–229
European Council (Tampere, 1999),
225–226
European Court of Human Rights (ECtHR),
33, 220, 233–237, 241n13; *Amuur v.
France*, 23, 24, 29; number of cases
brought to, 244n42; same-sex marriage
law and, 231, 243n28. *See also* Court of
Justice of the European Union (CJEU)

European Parliament, 228–229, 239, 241n14, 242n25

European Union (EU), 216–240; antidumping law and, 82; asylum law, 219, 221–225, 241n13; China in WTO and, 67, 70, 82, 89; Common European Asylum System, 221; discrimination law, sexual orientation grounds, 230–231, 233; EU-Turkey migration deal, 241n12; family law and, 220, 227, 229–233, 240n8; free movement rights, for TCNs with LTR status, 219–222, 225–229, 242n17, 242nn19–21, 242n23; free movement rights, same-sex marriage and, 220, 229–233, 242n24; goals in creating, 216–217, 234; growth of, 216; human rights and, 219, 223, 233–237; immigration control in, 219, 220, 221–225, 228, 241n12; migration influx of 2015, 221–222; pooled sovereignty, 218, 238, 240n5; public opinion of, 238–239; religious equality in the workplace and, 233–237; "return to sovereignty" movement, 240n7; transnationalization as open process, 217–221, 240n6; WTO creation, 66

European Union Member States: asylum law, 219; autonomy imbalance, 221–225; domestic laws shaped by EU, 216; EU immigration laws ignored by, 221–223; "Inner Six," 216; nationalism in, 217, 284; same-sex marriage law and, 230–231; social values, 220; sovereignty transfers, 217–218, 220–221, 222, 234, 238, 240n2, 240n5. See also individual countries

Eversheds LLP (UK corporate law firm), 114

Extractive Industries Transparency Initiative, 109

Fair Trade Bureau (China MOFCOM), 71–72

Falciani, Hervé, 103

family law, 227, 229–233, 241n10, 242n19; limping, 220, 230, 240n8

Family Reunification Directive 2003/86/EC, 227

Fargo, Thomas, 143, 144

Fassin, Didier, 281–282

FCPA (Foreign Corrupt Practices Act). See Foreign Corrupt Practices Act (FCPA)

Feldman, Eric, 133–134

feminism, 161

Flaubert's Parrot (Barnes), 150

Foblets, Marie-Claire, 16, 17, 18

Foley, Thomas, 137, 139–140

Forbes Afrique (magazine), 105

Foreign Corrupt Practices Act (FCPA) (US, 1977), 44, 50, 59nn1–2, 109; enforcement after passage of, 39–41, 58, 60n6. See also international trade law, anticorruption law and

forum shopping, 47, 230

fragmentation, in international legal obligations, 13, 27–28, 33, 38, 45–53, 194; in anticorruption law, 49–53; conflict-of-law approach and, 254; in international law, 45–49

Françafrique legacy, 107, 125n11

France: Amuur siblings and, 23, 24, 29–30, 31–32; asylum law in, 23, 24; discrimination law in, 236–237; elections in, 218–219; human rights and, 101, 103, 115, 116; relationship with former colonies, 110–111. See also European Union (EU); Paris, France, Africa Bar in

free movement rights, EU: marriage rights and, 220, 229–233, 242n24; for TCNs with LTR status, 219–222, 225–229, 242n17, 242nn19–21, 242n23

French Bolloré group, 107

French Office for the Protection of Refugees and Stateless Persons (OFPRA), 23

G20 Summit (2017), 239

Gao, Henry, 6, 16, 17

Gaopeng and Partners (law firm), 82

GATT 1995, 49

General Accounting Office (GAO), 50

General Agreement on Tariffs and Trade (GATT): China as founding member, 66, 89n3; dispute resolution and, 51, 52; European Community and, 49, 52, 60n4; GATT 1995, 49; nondiscrimination principles, 42–43; OECD and, 58; Uruguay Round of negotiations, 43, 48, 66; United States and, 42, 47, 49, 50–53; WTO and, 58, 72–73. See also international trade law, anticorruption law and; World Trade Organization (WTO)

Geneva Convention, 23

Germany, 56, 218–219, 231
Ghana, 123
Gibaud, Stéphanie, 103
Gide Loyerette (French law firm), 82
Ginsburg, Tom, 87
globalization, 3, 7, 13; populism and, 1, 5, 9–10, 14; scalar classifications and, 27–28; sovereignty transfers and, 218
globalization, corporate legal dynamics in Africa. *See* Paris, France, Africa Bar in
globalization, digital communities and. *See* digital communities, legislation and regulation of and within
Grant v. South-West Trans (CJEU case, 1998), 233
Great Britain. *See* Britain
Greece, 221, 222, 223, 241n13, 243n28
Green, T. H., 293

Habré, Hissène, 104
Hall, John A., 278
Hamilton, Robert Claibourn, 232
harmonization initiatives, 3, 251–252, 255–256, 257
harm principle doctrine, 289–291
Hayashi Hideki, 147–148, 149
Hayek, Friedrich von, 293–294
Herbert Smith Freehills (UK corporate law firm), 108, 113
Hobbes, Thomas, 29
horizontality, 16
Houphouët-Boigny, Félix, 125
Huawei, 85
Hughes, Howard, 145
humanitarian intervention, liberalism and, 281–282. *See also* international NGOs in South Sudan, bureaucratization of activism within
humanitarian narrative genre, 287–288, 289
human resource management, 168–169
human rights, 244n42, 297n3; CJEU cases on, 234–237; EU and, 219, 223; European Convention on Human Rights, 220, 234, 243n39; EU's transnational orders and, 233–237; France and, 101, 103, 115, 116; liberty and philanthropy and, 296, 297; scalar classifications and, 30, 33, 34. *See also* European Court of Human Rights (ECtHR)

human rights, NGOs and, 181–183; bureaucratic tasks overshadow substantive work in, 159, 167, 172–174, 178, 183; in France, 103; legal culture and, 160; mission of, 158, 165, 167, 172; rights claims prevented within NGOs, 181, 183
Hungary, 221, 223, 224, 230
Hylands Law Firm, 81

Ikeda Naoki, 151, 152
Ilias and Ahmed v. Hungary (ECtHR case, 2017), 241
immigration: EU and, 219, 220, 221–225, 228, 241n12; populism and, 10, 294
import relief law, 81
In Darkest Africa (Stanley), 292–293
In Darkest England and the Way Out (Salvation Army), 292, 293
India, 48, 49, 53, 57
Indicative List of WTO Panelists (China), 75, 78, 91n32
indigenous legal authority, in Australia, 201
indigenous legal authority, in Colombia. *See* Colombia, indigenous-state relations in
industry associations (China), 85–87
Institute of Global Trade and Investment (WTO Center), 74
intellectual property issues, 47–49, 60n5, 73
interlegality, 12–13
International Centre on Trade and Development (ICTSD), 78
International Chamber of Commerce, 115
International Economic Law (mandatory course in China), 75
International Federation for Human Rights (FIDH), 103, 104, 116
international investment law, 54
International Monetary Fund (IMF), 42
international NGOs, 6, 38, 192, 194
international NGOs in South Sudan, bureaucratization of activism within, 157–160, 162–187, 186n29; dispute resolution and, 166–172; employment opportunities for local South Sudanese, 165–166, 167–168, 175, 187n62; focus on documentation *vs.* rights consciousness, 167, 169–170, 171, 173, 184; goals of groups, 165–166; impact, social, 181–182; impact on local employees of foreign

groups, 173–175, 183; impact on national aid groups, 175–179; research methods for study, 162–164; resistance against, 179–181; subjugation of personnel through hierarchical structures, 167, 171, 173–175, 176, 179–181, 183; transmission of protocol to national groups, 158–159, 170–172, 175–179

international relations scholarship, 12, 14, 26, 39, 67

international trade law, anticorruption law and, 37–60; enforcement differences, 37, 38, 39–41, 42, 53–57, 58, 59; fragmentation in anticorruption law, 49–53; fragmentation in international law, 45–49; geographic scopes of, 53, 55; interstate bribery situations, 43–44; multilateral consensus for action, 58; mutual influence, 41–42; separate development of, 41–45. *See also* Foreign Corrupt Practices Act (FCPA); General Agreement on Tariffs and Trade (GATT); World Trade Organization (WTO)

international trade law, China and. *See* China, WTO membership of

International Trade Organization (ITO), 42

international zones, 23, 24, 31–32

Ireland, 226

Italy, 222, 223, 231, 243n28

Jackson, John, 81

Japan: China in WTO and, 70; dispute resolution and, 133–136; EU and, 239; family relationships in, 138; GATT and, 52; modernization *(kindaika)* in, 134; size of economy, 67. See also *Ehime Maru* (Japanese fisheries training boat) incident; United States and Japan

Jeantet, Fernand-Charles, 112, 115

Jeantet et Associés (French corporate law firm), 105, 106, 112

Jeune Afrique, 113

Jiang Zemin, 71, 73, 91n53

Jincheng, Tongda and Neal (JTN) (law firm), 82

Ji Wenhua, 88–89

Jones Day (US corporate law firm), 118, 119

Joyce, Patrick, 279

J. P. Morgan, 44

Juba, South Sudan, 158, 162–163

Juncker, Jean-Claude, 217–218, 239, 240n3

jurisdiction, 4, 13; *Ehime Maru* incident and, 132–133; OECD and, 57–58, 59; PIL and, 229–230

jurisdiction, Colombian indigenous autonomy. *See* Colombia, indigenous-state relations in

Kant, Immanuel, 288–289

Kantorowicz, Ernst, 102

Katzenstein, Peter, 9

Kawashima Takeyoshi, 133–134

Kennedy, John F., Jr., 139–140, 144–145, 150

Kenya, 23

King and Wood Mallesons (KWM, law firm), 82

Kishi Nobusuke, 132

Kjorholt, Ingvild Hagen, 288

Klemm, William, 150

Koizumi Chikashi, 141

Kokott, Juliane, 236, 244n45

Kōno Yohei, 140–141

Koskenniemi, Martti, 280, 298n5

Labour Party (Britain), 292

Laqueur, Thomas, 287

Latin America, 120–121, 211n4; neoliberal economic policies, effects on, 194–195, 211n2. *See also* Colombia, indigenous-state relations in

Latvia, 231

lawyers, in South Sudan, 164

lawyers' role in extractive African economies, 100–102, 107–108, 109–110, 121–122, 124n4

lawyers' role in negotiating sovereignty, 102–106; Agboyibor, 105–106; Bourdon, 103–105, 117, 124n4

legal pluralism, 6, 12–13

legal studies scholarship, 12, 74–79, 133–134, 183, 285–286

Leheny, David, 6

Lemaire, Philippe, 104

Lepaulle, Pierre, 112–113

Le Pen, Marine, 218–219, 240

liberalism, 17, 278–298; Brexit discourse and, 285; in Britain, 279, 284, 285, 289, 290, 291, 294; collective victimism and, 282, 284, 294–295, 296; "darkest

liberalism (continued)
American" rhetoric and, 282–283; "free liberal subject" and, 285–286; Mill and, 281, 287, 289–291, 295, 298n5; multiculturalism and, 280; "pure", 280, 281; Trump's inaugural address and, 282–285, 294; in United States, 282–285, 294, 295, 296; "us" and "Others" in, 281; Voltaire and, 287–289. *See also* liberty and philanthropy, liberalism and
liberal legal subjectivity, scholarship on, 285–286
liberal *vs.* illiberal rule, 30–31
liberty and philanthropy, liberalism and, 279–281, 282–283, 286–297; human rights and, 296, 297; inward philanthropic gaze, 282, 285, 296; liberty defined, 280; in mid-Victorian British Empire, 287, 289–294; Mill and, 281, 287, 289–291, 295, 298n5; neoliberal economics and, 294; philanthropy defined, 279; urban, British, 1880s and 1890s, 287, 291–294; Voltaire and, 287–289. *See also* liberalism
Libya, 222
Li Chengang, 81
Ligue des droits de l'homme et du citoyen (LDH), 116
Lisbon Treaty (2009), 234
Lithuania, 231
Livingstone, David, 292
Long Term Resident (LTR) status (EU), 219–222, 225–229, 242n17, 242nn19–21, 242n23

Maastricht Treaty (1993), 222
Macron, Emmanuel, 218
maps, 25, 26
Maritime Self-Defense Force (MSDF), 147, 153
marriage, same-sex, 220, 229–233, 240n9, 242n24, 243n28, 243n31, 243n36
Marsh, Bert, 148
May, Theresa, 284
Mazzarella, William, 5
McIlwaine, Cathy, 206
McKinsey report, 97
McNamara, Kathleen, 239
McPherson, C. B., 286
Mehta, Uday, 279
Merkel, Angela, 219

Michelin, 104
migration. *See* immigration
Mill, John Stuart, 281, 287, 289–291, 295, 298n5
mining, 97–99, 100–102, 120–121, 123
Ministry of Commerce, China (MOFCOM), 71–72, 73; China Society for World Trade Organization Studies, 77; consultation with law professors, 78; dispute resolution and, 81, 83, 87–89; DTL, 72, 78, 81, 82–83; Foreign Trade Barrier Investigation mechanism, 85; as MOFTEC, 69, 71, 81, 85–86; officials nominated to WTO Appellate Body, 79
Ministry of Education (China), 76
Ministry of Foreign Trade and Economic Cooperation, China (MOFTEC, later MOFCOM), 69, 71, 81, 85–86
Ministry of Justice (China), 80
Mitterrand, François, 116
Montesquieu, Baron de, 288, 289
Mori Yoshirō, 136, 154n3
Moser, Caroline, 206
Most Favored Nation (MFN) principles, 42–43, 53, 60n8
Mouffe, Chantal, 10
M.S.S. v. Belgium and Greece (European Court of Human Rights case, 2011), 241
multiculturalism, 202, 204, 211n3, 280

national culture, 1–4, 7–8, 10–11, 16, 289–290; *Ehime Maru* incident and, 131–132, 134, 137–139, 149. *See also* European Union Member States
nationalism, 1–3, 4, 6, 287; in EU member states, 217, 284; Trump's inaugural address and, 282–285, 294. *See also* populism
national NGOs, 179–181, 192. *See also* international NGOs in South Sudan, bureaucratization of activism within
national security (US), anticorruption law as issue of, 37, 39, 49–50
National Treatment principles, 42, 43, 53
Nawa Kiyotaka, 146
neocolonialism, 98, 125n11
neoliberal economic policy, 212n7, 294; Colombia and, 194–195, 204, 211n3; Latin America and, 194–195, 211n2; multiculturalism and, 204, 211n3

the Netherlands, 219, 230, 231, 236, 243n29, 243n33
Niger, 222
Nigeria, 123
nongovernmental organizations (NGOs). *See* international NGOs; national NGOs

Obergefell v. Hodges (US Supreme Court case, 2015), 240
On Liberty (Mill), 289–291
On Representative Government (Mill), 290
Operation Lifeline Sudan (humanitarian aid), 164–165
Organisation for Economic Co-operation and Development (OECD) Anti-Bribery Convention (1995), 39–41, 45, 52–53, 56; member states' jurisdictional grounds, 57–58, 59; monitoring reports used for dispute resolution, 55. *See also* international trade law, anticorruption law and
Orrick Herrington & Sutcliffe LLP (US law firm), 105
outlaw status, 30

Paris, France, 122; corporate bar structure in, 110–111, 114–115
Paris, France, Africa Bar in, 99–100; Agboyibor and, 105–106, 117, 119–120, 124n4, 125n10; Bourdon and, 103–105, 117, 124n4; Cold War politics and, 115–116; corruption cases, 107–108; dispute resolution and, 116, 117, 119, 124n4; entry into, 117; financialization and regulation, 108–110; Paris's imperial legacy and, 101, 115–116; research methods, 100–102, 124n4; social microcosm of, 100, 102–120; structuration and transformation of, 111–120
Paris Convention (1883), 47
Pearl Harbor attack, 139
philanthropy: defined, 279. *See also* liberty and philanthropy, liberalism and platforms. *See* electronic platforms
Poland, 231
political nationalism. *See* nationalism
political science and political scientists, 12, 14, 34, 162
Politics of Everyday Europe, The (McNamara), 239

pooled sovereignty, 218, 238, 240n5
populism, 1–2, 6–10, 278; in EU Member States, 219; globalization and, 1, 5, 9–10, 14; liberalism reversal in, 282; Trump's inaugural address and, 282–285, 294. *See also* liberalism; nationalism
poverty, 279–280, 291
Povinelli, Elizabeth A., 201–202
Powell, Colin, 137
private international law (PIL), 229–230
private legal frameworks, 253, 256; digitality and, 257, 259, 270
Project Azorian (1974), 145
Pu Ling-chen, 83

Qualification Directive (Directive 2011/95/EU), 229, 241n14
questions of liability, 6

race, liberalism and, 282–283
Reagan administration, 50
record keeping, 184
refugee status, 23, 29–30
regulatory responses: conflict-of-law approach, 254–255, 257, 269; to digitality challenges, 253, 256–258, 265, 269–273; to globality challenges, 253; self-regulation approach, 252–254, 256, 257, 259, 261, 263, 269, 270–271; to transnationality, 251, 253, 254–256; uniform-law approach, 254, 255–256, 257. *See also* digital communities, legislation and regulation of and within; electronic platforms, operators
religious discrimination, 244n45
religious equality in the workplace (EU), 233–237
Riles, Annelise, 9
Rocard, Michel, 107
Rockwater II (oil-drilling platform), 146
Rodrigo Lara Bonilla School for the Judiciary (Escuela Judicial Rodrigo Lara Bonilla), 192–193, 198, 204–205
Rodríguez-de-las-Heras Ballell, Teresa, 3, 16, 17, 18
Romania, 230, 231–233
Rome Statute for the International Criminal Court, 103
Ruggie, John G., 6
Russia, 234

Sakurai Tokutarō, 146
Sala Administrativa del Consejo Superior de
    la Judicatura (Administrative Chamber of
    the Upper Judicial Council), 192
Salvation Army, 292, 293
same-sex marriage, 220, 229–233, 240n9,
    242n24, 243n28, 243n31, 243n36
Sassen, Saskia, 13
scalar classifications, 23–35, 278; Amuur
    case and, 23, 24, 29–30, 31–32; avoiding
    symbolic traps in, 34–35; counter-scalar
    practices, 27–29; creating authority in,
    32–34; disruption of, 27–29; elastic scales,
    31–32; geography and borders and, 27, 28;
    globalization and, 27–28; human rights
    and, 30, 33, 34; law and, 27, 28, 29–30,
    34–35; legal landscapes elude, 23–24;
    maps, 25, 26; messy governing practices
    and, 24, 27; national, transnational, and
    international distinctions, 26–27;
    normative functions, 29–31; politics,
    divisions, and discriminations authorized
    by, 24, 25; state sovereignty, 25–27; statist
    vision, 26, 29. See also borders and
    boundaries
Scanlan, Padraig, 280
Scheppele, Kim, 15, 16
Schuman, Robert, 217
Scott, James, 34
Securities and Exchange Commission
    (SEC), 40
Seiron (magazine), 147
self-regulation, 252–254, 256, 257, 259, 261,
    263, 269, 270–271
sexual harassment policies, 161
sexual orientation, same-sex marriage and,
    220, 229–233, 240n9, 242n24, 243n28,
    243n31
Shaffer, Gregory, 6, 16, 17
Shanghai Institute of Foreign Trade
    (Shanghai University of International
    Business and Economics (SUIBE)), 78
Shanghai University of International
    Business and Economics (SUIBE), 78
Sharpston, Eleanor V. E., 237
Sherpa (NGO), 103
Shokun (magazine), 137
slave trade, 280; antislavery and, 287, 288,
    289, 295
Slovakia, 224, 231

Snowden, Edward, 103, 295
social memory, 251
sociolegal studies of law, 12, 157, 159, 183, 286
sociology and sociologists, 14, 27, 100, 161,
    286, 293
soft power, 157, 159, 167
Somalia, 23
Sousa Santos, Boaventura de, 12
South Sudan, history of humanitarian aid
    to, 164–166. See also international NGOs
    in South Sudan, bureaucratization of
    activism within
South Sudanese Bar, 158
sovereignty transfers, between EU and
    Member States, 217–218, 220–221, 222,
    234, 238, 240n2, 240n5
Soviet Union, 8
Stanley, Henry M., 292–293
State Council (China), 71, 90n10
state sovereignty, 8; Colombia and, 194, 196,
    197, 204, 207, 209, 212n10; scalar
    classifications and, 25, 33
statist vision, 26
Status of Forces Agreement (SOFA, US),
    132, 133, 135
Stephenson Harwood (UK law firm), 104
Sudan, South Sudan's secession from, 158
Sun Wanzhong, 77
Sun Zhenyu, 77
Supreme Court, U.S., 240
Supreme People's Court (China), 76, 90n25
Syria, 23, 221

Tanabe, George, 145–146
tariff negotiations, 51
Taylor, Charles, 278, 297n2
Terata Masumi, 151–152, 153
Terata Yūsuke, 146
territory, physical vs. legal, 24–28, 29, 30,
    33–34
Third Country Nationals (TCNs, EU), free
    movement law and, 219–222, 225–229,
    242n17, 242nn19–21, 242n23
time and space constraints, 250–254, 273n1.
    See also digital communities, legislation
    and regulation of and within
Togo, 105
trade. See China, WTO membership of;
    General Agreement on Tariffs and Trade
    (GATT); international trade law,

anticorruption law and; World Trade Organization (WTO)
trade associations, China and WTO and, 84–87
Trade-Related Aspects of Intellectual Property Rights (TRIPS) Agreement, 48–49
transnational bureaucratic legalism, 183
transnationalism, defined, 9
transnationality, regulatory responses to, 251, 253, 254–256
transnational law, defined, 11–15, 240n1
transnational legal ordering, 12, 73, 84, 87; defined, 64–65
Transparency International (NGO), 56, 110
Traoré, Moussa, 108
treaties, fragmentation in international law and, 45–49, 47. See also fragmentation, in international legal obligations
Treaty Establishing the European Community (EC Treaty), 226
Treaty of Lisbon (2009), 228
Trump, Donald J., 9, 10, 74, 239; inaugural address, 282–285, 294
Trump administration, 74
Tsinghua University, 77
Turkey, 222, 234, 241n12
Tusk, Donald, 239
tutela decisions (Colombia's Constitutional Court), 196–197, 210

Uniform Code of Military Justice, 143
uniform-law regulatory approach: to digitality, 257; to transnationality, 254, 255–256
United Kingdom (UK): anticorruption law enforcement in, 56; Brexit and, 9, 217, 237–238, 244n42, 285; Council Directive 2003 and, 226; discrimination law in, 236; liberalism reversal in, 282. See also Britain
United Nations (UN), 42, 47–48, 163, 166
United Nations Convention Against Corruption (UNCAC), 45, 55
United States: antidumping law and, 82; China in WTO and, 67, 69, 70, 74, 82, 89, 92n56; Chinese law professors trained in, 77; discrimination law, sexual orientation grounds, 230; family relationships in, 138; FCPA enforcement in, 58, 59; GATT and, 42, 47, 49, 50–53; intellectual

property rights and, 73; ITO and, 42; liberalism in, 282–285, 294, 295, 296; same-sex marriage legalized in, 232, 240n9; TRIPS Agreement and, 48–49; unilateral trade measures, 58, 74; WTO creation, 66; WTO noncompliance, 54
United States, anticorruption law and. See international trade law, anticorruption law and
United States Agency for International Development (USAID), 194, 197, 205–208, 212n8
United States and Japan, 6; individualist vs. family-centered culture, 138–139; schoolgirl rape case (1995), 132–133, 136–137. See also Ehime Maru (Japanese fisheries training boat) incident
universalism, 289, 290
UN Mission in South Sudan (UNMISS), 166
Uruguay Round of negotiations (GATT), 43, 48, 66
US Congress, anticorruption law and, 49–50
US Navy, 131–132; Distinguished Visitors Program, 131, 135, 141–142, 144, 148
USS Arizona, 139
USS Greeneville, 131, 141, 142–143
USS Missouri, 142
US–Steel Safeguard (WTO case, 2002), 82
utilitarianism, 289

Valverde, Mariana, 12–13, 14, 17
Vergès, Jacques, 108
Verhofstadt, Guy, 218
verticality, 16
Vickers, Lucy, 237
Vietnam War, missing US service members after, 139, 145
Vismann, Cornelia, 184
Vogl, Frank, 51–52
Voltaire, 287–289

Waddle, Scott, 131; administrative vs. military criminal punishment for, 135, 143–144; career prior to Ehime incident, 141; Japanese protesters call for indictment of, 133, 137, 151, 152–153; meets with Terata, 151–152; personality of, 141, 142; testimony of, 154n9. See also Ehime Maru (Japanese fisheries training boat) incident

Wade, Abdoulaye, 108
waiting zones, 23, 24, 31–32
Walker, Rob, 34–35
war-torn societies. *See* international NGOs
  in South Sudan, bureaucratization of
  activism within
Washington Post, 137
Watergate scandal, 39, 49
Watson, Farley and Williams (UK law firm),
  105
Weber, Max, 157
West Africa, 280
women, sexual harassment policies and,
  161
workplace sovereignty, 159, 167
World Intellectual Property Organization
  (WIPO), 47–48
World Trade Organization (WTO), 6, 48,
  60n4, 60n7; academic study of WTO law,
  74–79; creation of, 66; GATT and, 58,
  72–73; legal framework, 67–68; nondiscrimination rules, 42–43, 53; OECD and,
  58; private and public actors and, 54;
  TRIPS Agreement in, 49. *See also* China,
  WTO membership of; General Agreement on Tariffs and Trade (GATT);
  international trade law, anticorruption
  law and
World Trade Organization (WTO), dispute
  resolution, China and, 65, 67–68, 70–71,
  72; claims settlement *vs.* litigation, 70, 79,

81, 82; MOFCOM and, 81, 83, 87–89;
  private associations and, 84, 86; SUIBE
  and, 78. *See also* China, WTO member-
  ship of
WTO. *See* China, WTO membership of;
  World Trade Organization (WTO)
WTO Centers (China training centers),
  73, 74
WTO Chairs Programme, 77–78
WTO Law Research Society (China), 77
WTO Ministerial Conference (Doha, 2001),
  68
Wu, Mark, 87
Wuhan University, 77
Wu Xiaochen, 81

Xiamen University, 77

Yamashita Keisuke, 137
Yang Guohua, 81, 83
Yao Meizhen, 77
Yeltsin, Boris, 145
Yūsuke Masumi, 146

Zaïre, 111–112
Zhang Yuejiao, 79
Zhang Yuqing, 91n32
Zhao Hong, 79
Zhong Lun (law firm), 82, 83
Zhu Rongji, 73
Žižek, Slavoj, 201–202

ACKNOWLEDGMENTS

The conference that generated the original versions of most of the chapters of this book was funded by the Princeton Institute for International and Regional Studies (PIIRS) and cosponsored by the Department of Anthropology and the Law and Public Affairs Program at Princeton University. PIIRS's generosity extended to support for this volume. We are grateful to Peter Agree for his editorial and collegial engagement. Our thanks, too, to Robert Lockhart and Lily Palladino, and to Brian Ostrander and his production team, as well as to the indexing collective at Twin Oaks. As conference co-organizers together with Kim Scheppele, we are grateful to everyone involved in bringing us together with this interdisciplinary and international group of scholars. Kim was an equal partner in the planning of the conference, and we owe her a debt of thanks. The volume has been shaped by the generous intellectual contributions of conference participants over the course of our days together, including some whose work does not appear here: discussants John Comaroff, Lauren Coyle Rosen, and Laavanya Kathiravalu; and presenters Alwyn Lim, Tonya Putnam, and Keren Yarhi-Milo. Our thanks to all.